P9-AOF-511

Sail and Power

A Manual of Seamanship for the United States Naval Academy

Sail and Power

THIRD EDITION

by Richard Henderson
with Bartlett S. Dunbar and William E. Brooks III

NAVAL INSTITUTE PRESS · ANNAPOLIS, MARYLAND

Copyright © 1967, 1973, 1979
by the United States Naval Institute, Annapolis, Maryland

All rights reserved. No part of this book may be
reproduced without written permission from the publisher.

Library of Congress Catalog Card Number: 78-62059
ISBN: 0-87021-578-7

Designed by Daniel Kunkel

Printed in the United States of America

In memory of

Captain Alexander G. B. Grosvenor, U.S. Navy

who, in such a short time, contributed so much
to the Naval Academy sailing program

Contents

Preface

The primary purpose of this book is to instruct the U.S. Naval Academy midshipmen in the essentials of small-boat handling and seamanship under sail and power. The book is intended as well to serve as a text for Navy-wide training. In addition, *Sail and Power* has proven a useful source of instruction for the general public, because sailing and boat handling are dealt with in general terms, and most of the boats discussed (with the exception of the Naval Academy's Yard patrol craft) are highly representative of types commonly used by civilian yachtsmen.

In the first and second edition of *Sail and Power,* Bartlett S. Dunbar wrote the powerboat portion of the book, but this section has now been changed extensively and reorganized. In addition, the entire book has been updated and expanded with the inclusion of the following new material: basic sailing hydrodynamics; recent theory on rigging and sails; a new class of Lasers and tips for Laser sailors; new winches; recent spinnaker theory; instrumentation; boat management in heavy weather offshore; gasoline auxiliary engines; offshore equipment lists; additional marlinspike seamanship; hull stability; a new section on outboards and inboard/outboard drive boats; new reefing techniques. There is also a new chapter on the rules of the road, a new chapter on the general fundamentals of powerboat handling, new Naval Academy power craft, the circumnavigation of Delmarva training cruise, and so forth. This third edition would not have been possible without the considerable help of William E. Brooks III, formerly an instructor in the Department of Seamanship and Navigation at the U.S. Naval Academy.

While some may argue that instruction in sail is not essential to the training of naval officers, there is no question that it is highly desirable. There is nothing like sailing to bring one into close contact with, and to develop a real love and respect for, the sea. In addition to improving and broadening skills in boat handling and seamanship, sailing helps build resourcefulness, general nautical knowledge, the ability to make quick decisions, team spirit, and the ability to give and take orders. Furthermore, sailing and racing under sail encourage an understanding and sensitivity towards the wind, tide, and waves, which are, after all, the seaman's environmental elements.

There was a time when yachtsmen wondered whether naval officers could really sail, but not so today. Great emphasis is now put on sailing at the U.S. Naval Academy, and its training program is recognized as one of the finest in the world. The effectiveness of this training has been demonstrated by many outstanding, seamanlike offshore passages by Naval Academy yachts and numerous victories in prestigious racing events. Especially noteworthy is the Navy's prowess in intercollegiate sailing—for example, winning the coveted McMillan and Kennedy trophies in 1977 and the North American Intercollegiate Championship in 1977 and 1978. *Sail and Power* is a basic text for Naval Academy training, and the authors are gratified for whatever help the book has been in introducing the midshipmen to the fundamentals of seamanship.

Many people have been helpful and encouraging to the authors in their preparation of this book. I am especially grateful to Captain Robert D. McWethy, U.S. Navy; Roger C. Taylor; Lieutenant Karl R. Witschonke, U.S. Navy; the late Captain Jacob J. Vandergrift, U.S. Navy; Lieutenant (junior grade) Stuart A. Finlay, U.S. Naval Reserve; Lieutenant Paul Dodson, U.S. Navy; Lieutenant Commander Bruce McLaughlin, U.S. Navy; Lieutenant W. G. Furnholm, U.S. Navy; Chief Warrant Officer M. Kerekesh, U.S. Navy; Gary Jobson, Graham Hall, and Captains Richard C. Ustick and the late Alexander G. B. Grosvenor, U.S. Navy. In addition, the authors wish to thank Contemporary Books, Incorporated for permission to use many drawings from the book *Hand, Reef, and Steer*, two diagrams from *The Racing-Cruiser*, and one from The Cruiser's Compendium.

Richard Henderson

Sail and Power

1. Terminology

A prime prerequisite to boat handling is the ability to use the correct nautical language. The language of the sailor is not an affectation, but a traditional and functional means of communication. Improper use of nautical terms by a sailor is not only lubberly, but it can result in dangerous misunderstandings.

Since the boating novice is apt to be confused by an initial overdose of nautical terms, this chapter will serve merely as an introduction to the subject. More terms will be introduced in subsequent chapters, and all are indexed at the end of the book. When a new term is first introduced in the text, it will be italicized and explained or defined, and because definitions will seldom be repeated, the reader should familiarize himself with each new term the first time it is used.

To begin with, boats are traditionally thought of as being feminine, and they are referred to as *she* or *her*. A boat's front is her *bow* or her *fore* part, and her back end is her *stern* or *after* part. When we move towards the bow we say we are going *forward*, but when moving towards the stern, we are going *aft*. When one object on a boat lies farther aft than another object, we say the first object is *abaft* the second. Facing forward, the left side of a boat is the *port* side, while the right is the *starboard* side. *Amidships* is the middle of a boat, halfway from side to side or from bow to stern. *Athwartships* means across a boat, as opposed to *fore and aft*, from bow to stern. The *thwarts* or seats in a rowboat run athwartships, but the *keel* or main structural member at the bottom runs fore and aft.

Figure 1-1 shows the system used for expressing *bearings* or directions in which objects are observed from a boat. If an object lies *on the port beam* it is said to be *abeam*, at right angles to the keel (on the port side in this case). Should the object lie halfway between *dead ahead* and abeam, it is *broad on the bow*, or if halfway between abeam and *dead astern*, *broad on the quarter*. As the diagram shows, the distance around the boat is divided into 32 *points*, 8 points from dead ahead to abeam, and 8 points more to dead astern, or a total of 16 points halfway around the boat. If a buoy or some other object bears be-

3

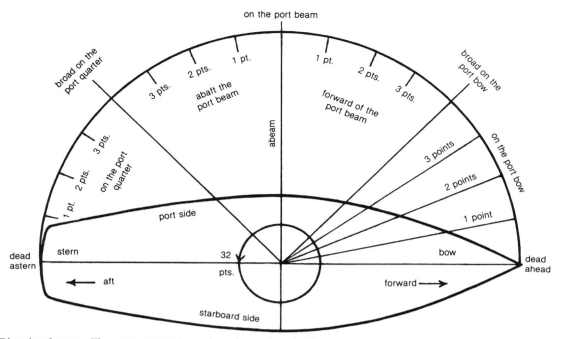

1-1. Directional terms. The same system is used on the starboard side.

tween dead ahead and broad on the bow, we say it bears one, two, or three points on the bow. If it bears between broad on the bow and on the beam, it is one, two, or three points forward of the beam. From abeam to broad on the quarter, the object bears one, two, or three points abaft the beam; while from broad on the quarter to dead astern, it bears one, two, or three points on the quarter. This is explained in the diagram.

Figure 1-2 deals with boat nomenclature. The boat illustrated is an old Naval Academy knockabout, a 26-foot *day sailer* (without any living accommodations and intended for short-range sailing), having a *ballasted* or weighted keel.

When we step on a boat we *board* her or *go aboard*. If we should drop or throw something over the side, we throw it *overboard*. Any part of the boat which extends beyond or is attached outside of the *hull*, the main body of the boat, is said to be *outboard*. If the object is inside the hull or near the boat's center it is said to be *inboard*.

When we board a knockabout we step on her *deck*, the flat surface at the top of her hull. Where the deck joins the *topsides* or upper sides of the hull, there is a low *toe rail* to prevent the *crew*, those who man the boat, from sliding overboard when the boat is *heeled*, tipped by the force of the wind when sailing. On small open boats (without decks), the extreme top of the sides is called the *gunwale* (pronounced gun'l). The large opening in the deck abaft the mast which accommodates the *helmsman,* who steers the boat, and the crew is called the *cockpit.* The fore-and-aft benches in the cockpit are called *seats.*

The knockabout is *sloop*-rigged—having one *mast* (vertical pole) supporting two sails, the *mainsail* and the *jib.* The mainsail's *foot* or bottom is secured to the *boom,* a horizontal pole hinged at its forward end to the mast with a fitting called the *gooseneck.* Poles used to spread sails are called *spars.* The sails are *hoisted* or pulled up the mast with *lines* (ropes) called *halyards.* They are pulled in or let out with lines called *sheets.* Halyards and sheets collectively are called *running rigging,* while the wire ropes which hold the mast upright and keep it straight are called *standing rigging.* Those wires which support the mast fore and aft are called *stays.* The *permanent backstay* is at the stern, and the *headstay* (outer stay) and *forestay* (inner stay) are at the bow. The wires which give lateral support are called *shrouds* and they attach at or near the rail to metal straps called *chainplates* and on the mast to metal straps called *tangs.*

The helmsman of a knockabout steers with a *tiller,* a wooden stick or handle which attaches to the *rudder,* a flat, underwater plate hinged to the *after* (back) end of the keel. The flat after part of the stern is called the *transom,* while the overhanging part of the stern below the transom is called the *counter.* Around the cockpit there is a low railing called the *coaming* which helps keep water from washing into the cockpit. The coamings on each side of the cockpit converge and meet just abaft the mast. Here they are raised slightly, and they are often referred to as *washboards* or *splashboards.* On the bow is a

1-2. Sailboat nomenclature.

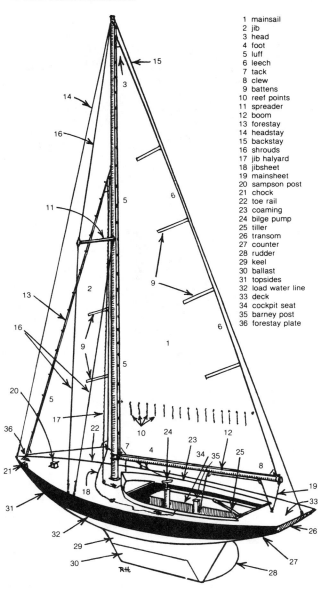

1 mainsail
2 jib
3 head
4 foot
5 luff
6 leech
7 tack
8 clew
9 battens
10 reef points
11 spreader
12 boom
13 forestay
14 headstay
15 backstay
16 shrouds
17 jib halyard
18 jibsheet
19 mainsheet
20 sampson post
21 chock
22 toe rail
23 coaming
24 bilge pump
25 tiller
26 transom
27 counter
28 rudder
29 keel
30 ballast
31 topsides
32 load water line
33 deck
34 cockpit seat
35 barney post
36 forestay plate

5

1-3. Hull construction.

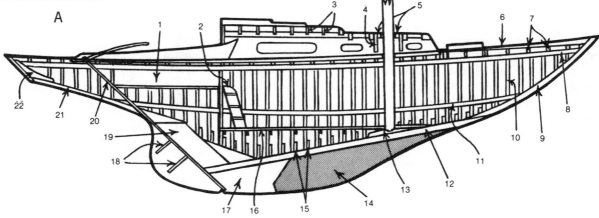

A

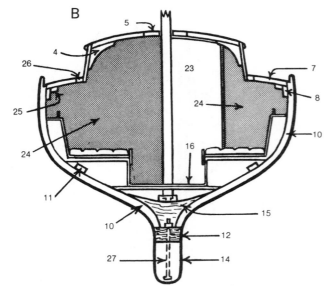

B

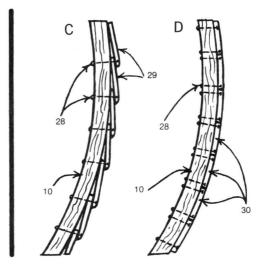

C   D

1 cockpit well	9 stem	17 false keel	25 deck shelf
2 companion ladder	10 rib or frame	18 rudder straps	26 carlin
3 cabin beams	11 bilge stringer	19 deadwood	27 keel bolt
4 hanging knee	12 keel	20 rudder stock	28 fastenings
5 mast partners	13 mast step	21 horn timber	29 clinker planks
6 rail	14 ballast keel	22 stern knee	or lap-strake
7 deck beams	15 floor timbers	23 doorway	30 carvel planking
8 clamp	16 cabin sole	24 bulkhead	

Sampson post or *deck cleat* to which a docking line, anchor line, or towline may be fastened. These lines are led through the bow *chocks* (shown in the diagram) to prevent the lines from *chafing,* or rubbing the rail.

At the bottom of the cockpit there are *floorboards* on which the crew stands. Floorboards are not to be confused with *floors* or *floor timbers,* which are constructional members bolted to, and running athwartships across the top of, the keel. These members often tie in with the *ribs* or *frames,* the framework pieces that rise from the keel upward, and to which the boat's planking is fastened. Below the floorboards is the *bilge,* the inside bottom of the boat which often contains, but should be kept clear of, bilge water. The place at which the bottom of a round-bottom boat curves upward to become its sides is called the *turn of the bilge.* On a V-bottom boat the bottom and sides join at a definite angle, and this is called the *chine.* Constructional parts for wooden hulls are shown in figure 1-3.

On *cruising boats,* those having cabins or roofed-over shelters with living accommoda-

1-4. Descriptive terms for the hull.

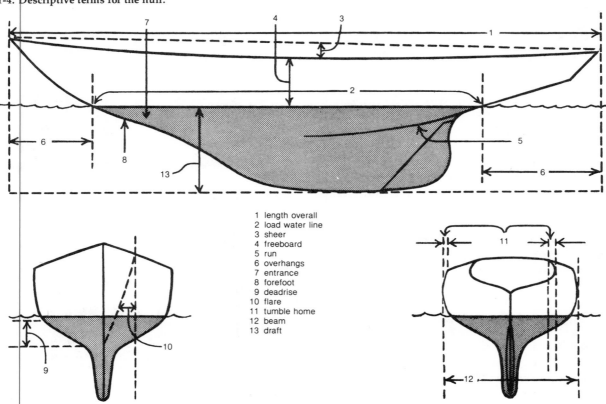

1 length overall
2 load water line
3 sheer
4 freeboard
5 run
6 overhangs
7 entrance
8 forefoot
9 deadrise
10 flare
11 tumble home
12 beam
13 draft

tions, the cabin floorboards are usually referred to as the *cabin sole*. *Bulkheads* are the athwartships walls with or without doorways. They divide a cabin for privacy, but their primary purpose is to stiffen and strengthen the hull. They are essential on fiberglass boats that customarily have few, if any, ribs. In the cabin there are *bunks* or *berths* (beds), the *galley* (kitchen), and *head* (toilet). The part of the cabin which sticks up above the deck is the *cabin trunk* or *deckhouse*. If the after end of the trunk is raised, it is often called the *doghouse*. If there is no cabin trunk, we say the boat is *flush-decked*. Holes or openings through the deck or cabin trunk which may be closed with covers are called *hatches*. The large hatchway through which we enter the cabin is called the *companionway*, and we climb down the *companion ladder*. We say we are going *below*, never downstairs. Small windows in the cabin which may be opened or closed are called *portholes*. Those that cannot be opened are called *port lights*.

Figure 1-4 shows thirteen frequently used terms which describe the shape or dimensions of a hull. The *load water line* (L.W.L.) is the line on which the boat floats. The hull is submerged below this line. *Tumble home* is the inward curving of the topsides, while *flare* is the outward slant of the topsides, usually at the bow. *Deadrise* is the vertical distance of the upward slant of a boat's bottom. If the bottom is flat, she has no deadrise. *Entrance* is the forward part of the immersed hull, while the *run* is the after part which sweeps upward towards the stern. *Forefoot* is the immersed part of the bow, between the load water line and the fore end of the keel. *Draft* is the distance measured vertically from the L.W.L. to the deepest part of the keel's bottom. We say that a knockabout, for instance, *draws* four feet.

8

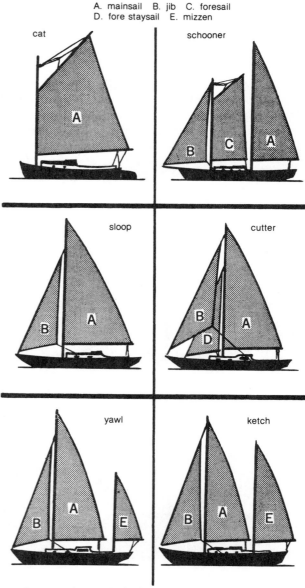

A. mainsail B. jib C. foresail
D. fore staysail E. mizzen

cat

schooner

sloop

cutter

yawl

ketch

1-5. Common fore-and-aft rigs.

Sheer is the horizontal curve from bow to stern along the rail. With *conventional sheer* the *freeboard*, height of the rail above the water, is lower amidships than at the bow or stern. Some boats, however, have a *straight sheer,* in which freeboard is constant, or a *reversed sheer,* where the freeboard is highest amidships. *Beam* is the maximum width of a boat. The rest of the terms in figure 1-4 should be self-explanatory.

Today's most common sailing *rigs* (the system or arrangement of masts and sails) for *yachts* (pleasure boats) are shown in figure 1-5. All these rigs are called *fore-and-aft* rigs as opposed to *square* rigs. The latter have sails, approximately square-shaped, that hang from *yards,* horizontal spars running athwartships which may be swung fore and aft to a limited extent only. Fore-and-aft sails may be pulled into a true fore and aft position and their forward edge is attached to a mast, stay, or semi-fixed location. All the sails shown in figure 1-5 are *Marconi* or *jib-headed* except the mainsail (pronounced mains'l) of the *cat boat* and the *foresail* (pronounced fors'l) of the *schooner.* The *heads* (top edges) of these sails are attached to a *gaff,* a spar that may be hoisted *aloft* (high off the deck), and thus these sails are said to be *gaff-headed.* The cat boat has her mast *stepped* (put in place) far forward, and she carries no jib (the foremost sail). Like the cat boat, *cutters* and *sloops* are single-masted, but they carry jibs. The cutter's mast is stepped much farther aft than the sloop's, and the cutter often carries a *forestaysail* (pronounced forstays'l) in addition to her jib. *Yawls, ketches,* and *schooners* each have two masts, although the schooner may have more than two. Yawls and ketches are quite similar, except that a ketch's *mizzen* (the aftermost sail) is much larger and farther forward than a yawl's, which is almost always abaft the helm or rudder post. Notice that the schooner's mainsail is the aftermost sail.

2. Elementary Seamanship

Seamanship is a very broad term used to cover a variety of subjects, including general boat-handling, steering and maneuvering, managing a vessel under adverse conditions, and *marlinspike seamanship*, or knots, splices, and general ropework. This chapter is merely an introduction to the subject; more advanced seamanship and other areas of the subject will be introduced in later chapters.

Small-boat safety. Every sailor should constantly be conscious of safety. Boating is a relatively safe activity, but hundreds of people drown every year as a result of careless seamanship. To begin with, every sailor should be able to swim well. He should be able to float with his clothes on for at least five minutes.

Personal gear should include a knife and boat shoes, the latter with soles especially designed to grip a slippery deck (see figure 2-1). A knife is not only extremely useful for numerous small jobs around a boat, but it might be needed to cut a line in an emergency. The sailor's knife usually has a locking *marlinspike*, which is handy for splicing and can be inserted into the eye of a shackle screw to tighten or loosen it (see figure 2-1).

Small open boats should carry Coast Guard-approved life preservers (at least one for each person on board), an anchor and anchor line, a large bailer or bucket for removing bilge water, and oars with oarlocks or a paddle. In addition, a small day sailer should have a *chart* (nautical map) of the local area, tools (at least a screwdriver and pliers), a horn or whistle, spare parts (shackles, pins, etc.), a small compass, extra line, waterproof tape, twine, lubricating oil, a sponge, and a flashlight.

Many small boats, particularly certain *dinghies* (small, open rowing or sailing boats, often used as tenders and carried aboard larger vessels), have little initial stability. Boarding one of these boats should be done with caution. To some extent, stability can be judged by looking at the hull form. A flat-bottomed skiff or a beamy dinghy with flotation tanks on either side should be fairly stable or *stiff*, as sailors often say, but a boat with a narrow bottom and slanting sides,

2-1. Boat shoes and knife.

the dory form, will tip quite easily, or be *tender*. Never board any kind of small boat by stepping on her gunwale, and never jump aboard. Keep your weight amidships as much as possible. Avoid standing up in a small boat, and don't overload her, especially when the water is rough.

Basic rowing. With the increasing use of the outboard motor for small boats, there seems to be a diminishing interest in the skill of rowing. Handling a boat with oars, however, is one of the basics of good seamanship, and no one can call himself an accomplished boatman until he has learned to row well. To acquire this skill, he must not only have instruction but regular practice.

The simple principle of the rowing stroke is shown in figure 2-2. In step A the oarsman, with arms extended in front of him and the oar handles held side by side, dips the oar blades into the water. In step B he pulls the oar handles towards his chest and leans backwards slightly. This action causes the blades to move aft, which naturally makes the boat move ahead. At the end of this stroke, the blades are lifted from the water and are then brought back to the position shown in step A.

Notice in step B that the blades enter the water almost vertically, but as they are pulled aft, they are twisted somewhat, which adds much to the power and effectiveness of the stroke. This is called *feathering* the oars. When the blades leave the water at the conclusion of step B, they should be almost flat or horizontal and remain in that position until just before they enter the water again.

A common mistake made by beginners is to raise the oars out of the water with the blades vertical, which usually results in the oarsman being splashed with spray, or to dip the blades in the water when they are flat or horizontal. This often results in the oarsman losing his balance and falling over backwards, since the blades will not *catch* or have any resistance against the water.

Another sure way of recognizing a beginner is to see him use the "paddlewheel stroke." This is when the oarsman lifts the blades up high in the air and then sinks them unnecessarily deep in the water so that the oar blades describe great circles like windmill sails. Actually, the blades should be sunk only deep enough to get a good bite in the water, and on a calm day they should be lifted only a few inches above the surface.

When carrying one or more passengers in a dinghy, see that the boat is properly *trimmed*, so that she is not excessively down by the bow or the stern. This sometimes involves moving the oarlocks to another thwart, but it makes a tremendous difference in the ease with which the boat may be rowed. A boat should generally be trimmed so that she is slightly lower at the stern than at the bow.

Turning a rowboat is accomplished by pulling harder on one oar than on the other. A quick turn can be made by dragging one oar or even reversing the stroke direction of one oar while the other is driving the boat ahead. Backing down is done by reversing the stroke direction of both oars. When landing alongside a vessel or pier, do not land bow first but turn the boat (into the wind if possible) so that you land side to side. *Unship* or take in the oar on the side that will face the vessel or pier in plenty of time. The other oar may be dragged with the blade held vertically to make the boat turn. When within several feet of landing, *unship your oarlock* which faces the side of the vessel or pier. Failure to do

blade vertical

begin to twist or feather blades for extra power

2-2. Rowing.

this has caused many gouges in the topsides of boats. Keep the outboard oar in use to hold the boat steady until all passengers have disembarked. Before leaving the boat, be sure oars and oarlocks are unshipped and stowed. Oars should be stowed flat normally with at least one end under a thwart. Be sure the oarlocks are lashed to the boat so that they won't be lost.

Rowing in the conventional manner requires that the oarsman face aft; thus, a final word of advice is that he should constantly turn his head around to look where he is going. To facilitate holding a straight course, try, if possible, to line up a near object aft with a distant object aft so that you have a range along which you can sight.

Capsizing and righting. Although capsizing can usually be avoided with proper care, all small dinghies and boats with *centerboards* (a fore-and-aft board or plate that can be lowered through a trunk or well on the centerline to increase the boat's lateral resistance, as in figure 3-7) are subject to turning over. Most boats capable of being capsized, and all small rowing or sailing boats at the U.S. Naval Academy, have built-in flotation to prevent sinking after a capsizing or swamping. The cardinal rule after turning over is to *stay with the boat.* Even if you are an excellent swimmer, hang onto your capsized boat and don't strike out for a "nearby" shore. Distances can be deceptive when you are in the water, wind and current are hard to predict, and you have a much better chance of being spotted when you are with your boat.

To recover from a capsizing, the overturned boat must be *righted* or turned upright, and then she can be bailed out. A small nonsailing dinghy will sometimes *turn turtle* or completely upside down. She can usually be righted easily, however, if you lean backwards, grip the bottom or keel with your fingers, and exert pressure downwards at the gunwale with your knees or feet. A sailboat is usually more difficult to right because the weight of her mast and wet sails must be lifted up out of the water. Most sailboats will lie on their side with the sails resting

on the water's surface, but some with extreme beam, excessive flotation, or metal masts which can fill with water may have a tendency to turn turtle. Try not to let any sailboat turn bottom side up, because in this position she is very difficult to right and is subject to damage. If the water is shoal, her mast may get stuck in the mud. To avoid turning turtle, stand on the centerboard immediately after capsizing. If another crew member is present, have him attach a float, a life preserver for instance, to the masthead. This float should be made fast to the halyard, in such a way that the float may be hauled down after the boat is righted and bailed out.

As soon as possible after capsizing, don life jackets. Some small boats carry Coast Guard-approved kapok cushions in lieu of life jackets. These cushions may be worn over the chest and stomach with one handle strap around the neck and the other around a leg so that the hands are left free. Don't put one of these cushions on your back as it will tend to float you face down. Although cushions are legally allowed as PFDs (personal flotation devices) on boats less than 16 feet in length, and they are even allowed as Type IV (throwable) PFDs on larger craft, they are inferior to life jackets, ring buoys, or other devices that are designed for no other purpose than to keep a person afloat, face up.

Not long after capsizing, equipment will begin to float out of the cockpit and start to drift away. Try to gather it up and lash it or otherwise secure it to the boat, but do not swim any great distance away from the boat in pursuit of a float-

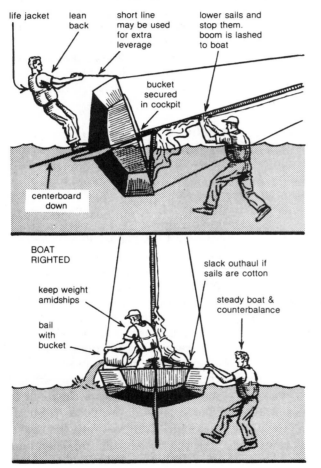

life jacket   lean
              back

short line
may be used
for extra
leverage

lower sails and
stop them.
boom is lashed
to boat

bucket
secured
in cockpit

centerboard
down

BOAT
RIGHTED

slack outhaul if
sails are cotton

keep weight
amidships

steady boat &
counterbalance

bail
with
bucket

2-3. Righting after capsizing. If float (life preserver, for example) is fastened to masthead to prevent boat from turning upside down, secure float to halyard so that it can be pulled down after boat is righted.

2-4. A buoyant boat capsized. The sailor has climbed onto the centerboard immediately to prevent the boat from turning turtle. Notice that he has put his weight fairly close to the boat's bottom to avoid bending or breaking the board. It will not be necessary to lower sail to right a boat this small.

ing object. The bailing bucket should be tied to the boat with a *lanyard* (short rope).

Figure 2-3 shows the procedure for righting a small sailboat. Lowering the sails will make the operation much easier. (With some very small modern sailboats having ample flotation, it is not necessary to lower the sails before righting. See section on Lasers in chapter 7.) The sails should be loosely *furled* and *stopped*, rolled or

bundled up and tied to the boom, and also the mainsheet should be pulled tight and cleated down to prevent the boom from falling off the deck. Lower the centerboard if it is not already down and climb up on it. Stand on the centerboard with your feet near the boat's bottom to prevent the board from breaking, and then lean backwards while holding on to the boat's rail or gunwale. With sails down, the boat should roll back upright. Since the waterfilled boat will have little stability, she may want to keep rolling beyond the vertical and capsize again in the opposite direction. Once she is upright, it is a matter of splashing, rocking, or bailing the water out of the cockpit with a crew member on each side for counterbalance. If the boat has ample flotation, the crew member on the windward or upwind side can climb aboard and bail much more effectively. If you are alone, you may be able to board the boat by climbing over her stern. Should a rescue craft come along, try to right your boat before accepting help, because a boat coming alongside a capsized sailboat can damage the rigging and get a floating line caught in her propeller. If the water is very cold, however, immediately board the rescue craft before your boat is righted. The rescue craft should never attempt to tow a capsized boat until she has been righted. More will be said on the subject of rescue from a motor boat in the chapter entitled "Boat Handling under Power."

Basic hull stability. To understand why some small sailboats will capsize and others will not, we must understand the relationship between the *center of buoyancy* (CB) and the *center of gravity* (CG). The center of buoyancy is the center of all forces keeping the boat afloat, in effect the geometrical center of the underwater volume of

15

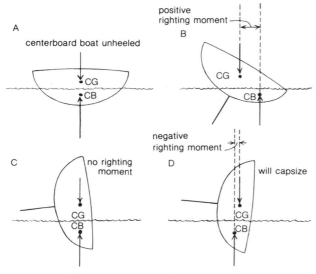

A
centerboard boat unheeled

B
positive righting moment

negative righting moment

C
no righting moment

D
will capsize

2-5. Center of buoyancy and center of gravity for a centerboard boat.

the hull. The center of gravity is the center of the boat's weight and all weights on board (including the crew). The positions of the CB and CG for typical centerboard boats and keel boats having ballasted (weighted) keels are shown in figures 2-5, 2-6, and 2-7. It can be seen in figure 2-5 that as the boat heels, the CB shifts to leeward to the center of the submerged hull. Since the CG acts downward and the CB acts upward, there is a force called a righting moment attempting to keep the boat upright.

It is important to understand the concept of a force moment, since it plays an important role in both stability and boat balance (to be discussed in chapter 6). A moment can be thought of as a rotating force acting on a lever arm some distance from the axis of rotation. The magnitude of the moment is found by multiplying the length of the arm by the force acting in a direc-

tion that is perpendicular to the arm. If you were using a lever to lift a 200-pound rock, for example, you could figure that more than 50 pounds of downward force would be needed at the end of a lever measuring four feet from the fulcrum (axis of rotation) to the lever's end in order to lift the rock. This same sort of rotating force occurs when a sailboat heels, as the forces acting through the CG and CB create the righting moment. The farther the two centers are apart, the greater the righting arm (corresponding to the lever arm) and therefore the greater the boat's stability.

All boats derive form stability from the shifting of the CB to leeward when heeling occurs, and the greater the boat's beam, the farther the shifting of the CB at moderate angles of heel. When a centerboard boat reaches a high angle of heel, however, the gap between the two centers becomes narrower. This reduces the arm length—as shown in figure 2-5—until the CG is directly over the CB, and any further heeling will result in a capsize. On the other hand, a keel boat develops a long righting arm, not only through her beam but through her deep ballast, which keeps the CG low.

Figures 2-6 and 2-7 show the approximate positions of the CB and CG of the Naval Academy knockabout and the 44-foot Luders yawl, two fairly typical keel boats. It may surprise some readers that the CG is above the CB; nevertheless, a normal keel boat's CG is considerably lower than that of an unballasted centerboarder. This feature—together with reasonably high freeboard—gives the keel boat a greater *range of stability,* meaning that it can heel much further than a centerboarder without capsizing.

Typical keel boats have about one-third to one-half of their *displacement* (total weight) con-

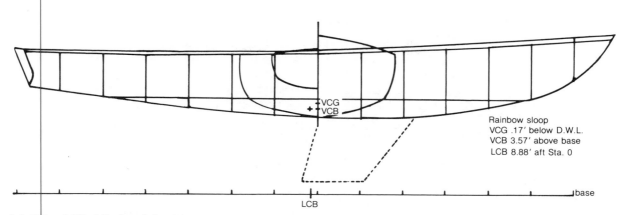

Rainbow sloop
VCG .17' below D.W.L.
VCB 3.57' above base
LCB 8.88' aft Sta. 0

LCB

base

2-6. CG and CB of the knockabout.

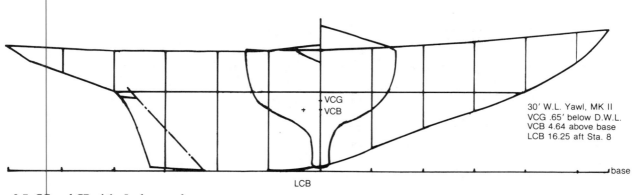

30' W.L. Yawl, MK II
VCG .65' below D.W.L.
VCB 4.64 above base
LCB 16.25 aft Sta. 8

VCG
VCB

LCB

base

2-7. CG and CB of the Luders yawl.

signed to keel ballast, and this will normally result in a CG that is positioned at or slightly below the load water line (contact line where the water meets the hull). This relatively low CG coupled with a proper hull form will give the yacht sufficient stability to right from almost any angle of heel.

Figure 2-8 is a graph showing the approximate curve of righting moments through vari-ous angles of heel for the Luders yawl. This curve indicates that at a heeling angle of 100 degrees the yawl still has a positive righting moment tending to rotate the yacht back to the upright position.

Basic marlinspike seamanship. Rope is almost constantly in use on all boats, particularly sail-boats, and so learning to knot and handle it is of

17

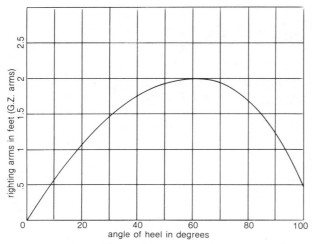

2-8. The approximate curve of righting moments through various angles of heel for the Luders yawl.

prime importance. Every sailor should know at least the basic knots shown in figure 2-10, and he should learn to make a *whipping* and an *eye splice* shown in figures 2-11 and 2-12. Of course he should also know how to cleat and to coil lines. These operations are shown in figures 2-8 and 2-9.

A variety of fibers are used for making rope: manila, hemp, linen, sisal, and coir, but presently the most popular rope fibers are the synthetics, nylon and Dacron. These are exceptionally strong, very resistant to chafe, and will not rot. Nylon is excellent for anchor or tow lines because it is quite elastic, but this characteristic makes it poor for most other uses. Dacron has very little stretch and therefore is very good for sheets and halyards.

In cleating a line it is customary to start off with a round turn on the cleat and then to follow this with criss-cross wraps, as shown in figure 2-9A. Finishing off with a hitch, as shown in

2-9B assures that the line will not jump off its cleat. This is a dangerous practice, however, if the line has to be released in a hurry, because it will often swell and jam when wet. Synthetic lines are not as likely to swell, but it is a good practice never to hitch a sheet unless a slippery hitch (figure 2-9C) is used.

The knots illustrated in figure 2-11 are self-explanatory. They are shown tied loosely for clarity but should be pulled tight. The square knot is used most often to tie reef points or *sail stops* (sail lashings usually of cloth). The hitches shown are most often used to secure a line to a post or part of the rigging. When it is necessary to prevent the knot from sliding, a rolling hitch

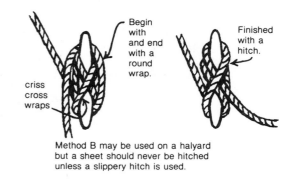

2-9. Belaying on a standard cleat.

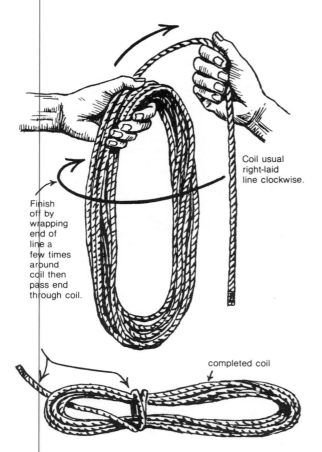

Coil usual right-laid line clockwise.

Finish off by wrapping end of line a few times around coil then pass end through coil.

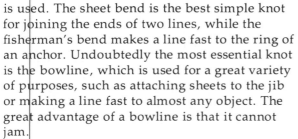

completed coil

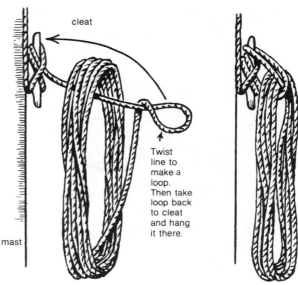

cleat

mast

Twist line to make a loop. Then take loop back to cleat and hang it there.

Hanging a coiled halyard

2-10. Coiling lines.

is used. The sheet bend is the best simple knot for joining the ends of two lines, while the fisherman's bend makes a line fast to the ring of an anchor. Undoubtedly the most essential knot is the bowline, which is used for a great variety of purposes, such as attaching sheets to the jib or making a line fast to almost any object. The great advantage of a bowline is that it cannot jam.

Whipping consists of wrapping the end of a line with twine to keep it from unraveling.

There are several ways to do this, but the one illustrated, called *needle whipping,* is probably the most permanent. It requires a heavy sailmaker's needle and twine. It consists of a series of round wrappings of the thread followed by diagonal weavings of the thread along the *lay* or twisting of the rope strands. This is explained in figure 2-12.

There are several kinds of splices but the *eye splice* illustrated (figure 2-13) is probably the most useful. The first series of tucks or interweavings of the strands (A, B, and C in the diagram) is the most difficult. Step C often gives the beginner the most trouble, but difficulty can be avoided if it is kept in mind that the strands are always tucked from right to left. In step C the entire splice is turned over, but strand C is still tucked from right to left. In making the tucks,

19

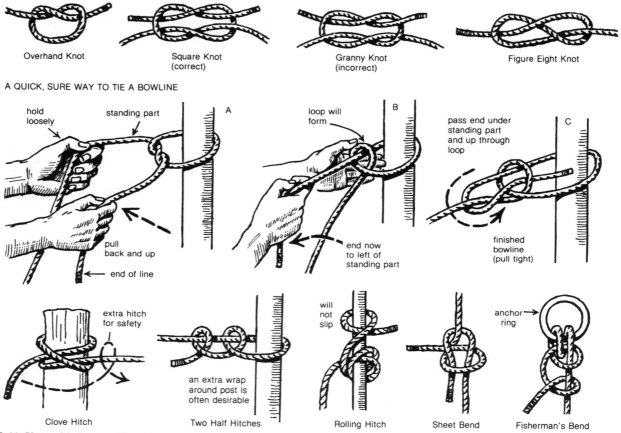

Overhand Knot

Square Knot (correct)

Granny Knot (incorrect)

Figure Eight Knot

A QUICK, SURE WAY TO TIE A BOWLINE

hold loosely

standing part

A

loop will form

B

pass end under standing part and up through loop

C

pull back and up

end of line

end now to left of standing part

finished bowline (pull tight)

extra hitch for safety

an extra wrap around post is often desirable

will not slip

anchor ring

Clove Hitch

Two Half Hitches

Rolling Hitch

Sheet Bend

Fisherman's Bend

2-11. Knots, hitches, and bends. (All knots are shown tied loosely for clarity, but they should be pulled tight.)

be sure that no two strand ends go through the same strand openings. A splice in a synthetic line should have at least four series of tucks. After the first series, it is a simple weaving operation where A, B, and C each go over their neighboring strand and under the following strand. Before turning in the last series of tucks, the splice should be tapered. This is done by cutting about half the fibers out of each strand prior to tucking them. After the last tuck, pull each strand end tight and cut it off flush with the rope. To give it a smooth, finished appearance, roll the splice under your foot. Ragged whiskers may be burnt off with a match.

In addition to the seaman's knife with its small spike (figure 2-1), there are several other basic tools used by sailors. The twine used for the whipping shown in figure 2-12 is commonly

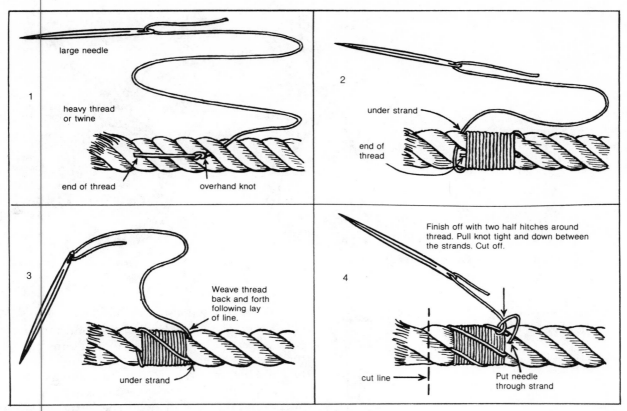

1

large needle

heavy thread
or twine

end of thread

overhand knot

2

under strand

end of
thread

3

Weave thread
back and forth
following lay
of line.

under strand

4

Finish off with two half hitches around
thread. Pull knot tight and down between
the strands. Cut off.

cut line →

Put needle
through strand

2-12. Whipping.

coated with beeswax (in stick or block form) to prevent drying and rot. The work with the large sail needle is made easier by using a *palm* (a thick leather band that fits around the hand and holds a sewing thimble next to the palm of the hand) which performs the same function as a seamstress's thimble. A large marlinspike made of tapered steel is used for opening the wire strands when splicing wire rope. Since the metal marlinspike may damage fiber line, a similar device called a *fid* is made of wood and is used

exclusively with fiber line. Both these tools are shown in figure 2-14. A special metal fid in the form of a long hollow tube is used in conjunction with a small metal pusher (figure 2-14) to splice braided synthetic lines made of nylon or Dacron. Splicing braided line is entirely different from splicing three-strand twisted line (figure 2-13). The technique for splicing braided line is adequately explained in an instruction booklet which accompanies each splicing kit.

While modern synthetic lines in some respects

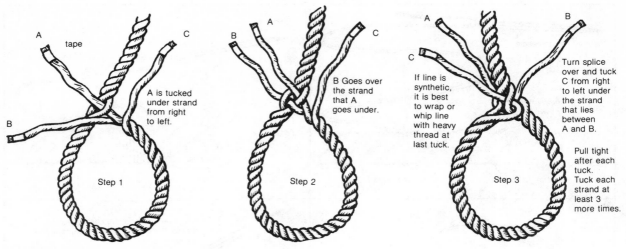

A · tape · C

A is tucked under strand from right to left.

B

Step 1

B · A · C

B Goes over the strand that A goes under.

Step 2

A · B

C · If line is synthetic, it is best to wrap or whip line with heavy thread at last tuck.

Turn splice over and tuck C from right to left under the strand that lies between A and B.

Pull tight after each tuck. Tuck each strand at least 3 more times.

Step 3

2-13. Eye splice for 3-strand twisted line. (The first series of tucks are illustrated.)

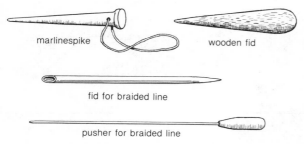

marlinespike · wooden fid

fid for braided line

pusher for braided line

2-14. Splicing aids.

make the work easier on board a sailboat, their increased strength does not ease the burden placed on the crew attempting to adjust the rigging or trim a large sail. A mechanical advantage is gained through the use of a number of different devices. A *turnbuckle* (see figure 6-14) is a simple opposing-screw arrangement which can provide tremendous power in adjusting standing rigging. Geared winches come in a

variety of sizes and also provide significant mechanical advantages when hoisting or trimming sails. A very common method of obtaining an increase in power is the use of a combination of line and blocks to form a *tackle* (pronounced tay-kle). Figure 2-15 shows two examples of tackles and the resulting theoretical mechanical advantage. We should also note that the direction of the applied force may be reversed through the use of a tackle.

It is important to handle and care for all lines properly. Not only will proper care make lines last longer, it will also give your boat a smart, seamanlike appearance. The following tips will help keep lines in excellent condition.

• Keep all lines clean. Wash dirt or sand out with clean, fresh water. Never use detergent on natural fiber lines. A very mild liquid soap can be safely used on synthetic lines. Always rinse thoroughly and allow line to dry before stowing.

22

• Coil lines neatly without kinks. A kink, especially under a load, can quickly weaken fiber line and it will ruin wire rope.

• Use chafing gear to prevent fraying. Never work a line over a sharp or rough surface.

• Use the right line for the job. Make sure that the blocks are the correct size for the line in use.

• When a line or wire rope becomes worn, do not hesitate to replace it. Never endanger a crew member or a piece of equipment by using line that is not capable of handling a strain.

In addition to various types of line, wire rope is commonly used on board sailboats for both standing and running rigging. Wire rope is described by the number of strands and the number of wires in each strand. A 7 × 19 wire rope has 7 strands with 19 wires in each strand. For a wire rope of the same diameter, a 7 × 19 rope is much more flexible than a 7 × 7 rope which has only 7 wires in each of its 7 strands.

Because of the heavy loads placed on wire rope, it is important to handle wire carefully and conduct frequent inspections for broken wires or signs of excessive strain.

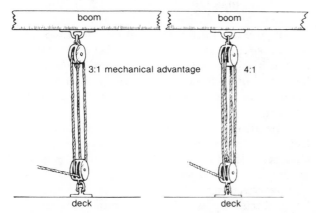

2-15. Tackles.

Anchoring. One of the basic skills required of a seaman is the ability to anchor a boat properly. Anchoring and handling *ground tackle* (anchors and related gear) is a lengthy subject, and only the rudiments will be touched on here.

Figure 2-16 shows anchor nomenclature and a group of the most commonly used, nonpermanent anchors. These are the ones that are put over temporarily and, when not in use, are pulled up and usually stowed on the forward deck. Permanent anchors, such as the mushroom type, are often left on the bottom for years and are used for offshore moorings. Of the anchors shown in figure 2-16, only the Navy anchor is unsuitable for a small boat. It has no stock so that it can be pulled into the hawse pipe of a large ship. In the smaller sizes, the Navy anchor doesn't have enough weight to dig in properly, and it can turn over on its side. The yachtsman's anchor is subject to fouling if the boat swings in a complete circle around her anchor so that the line wraps the exposed fluke (see figure 2-17). The Danforth anchor is a popular anchor in the Annapolis area, for it is especially effective in soft sand and sticky mud. One must be sure, however, that this anchor does not merely lie on the bottom, but that it digs in thoroughly by putting a strain on the line.

The holding power of an anchor depends on two principal factors aside from its design: its weight and the *scope,* or length of its *rode* (anchor line). The greater the anchor's weight and the longer the scope, the greater the holding power. As a general rule, the most effective length of scope is six or seven times the depth of water where the boat is anchored. A simple rule of thumb for weight is one-half pound per foot of overall length for a light anchor (one used only for temporary anchoring in fair weather—

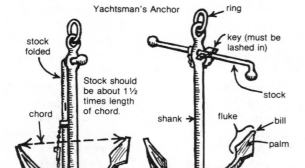

Yachtsman's Anchor

stock folded

chord

Stock should be about 1½ times length of chord.

ring

key (must be lashed in)

stock

shank

fluke

bill

palm

arm

crown

Wide palms for mud or soft sand bottoms. Sharp, narrow palms for hard sand, rock, weed, gravel, or shell.

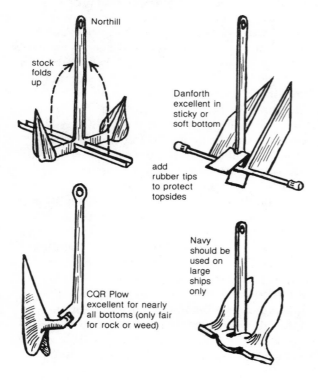

Northill

stock folds up

Danforth excellent in sticky or soft bottom

add rubber tips to protect topsides

CQR Plow excellent for nearly all bottoms (only fair for rock or weed)

Navy should be used on large ships only

2-16. Anchors.

sometimes called a "lunch hook"), and one pound per foot of overall length for a heavy anchor (one expected to hold for a considerable time in heavy weather). Of course, this rule depends on the type of anchor. Danforth and plow anchors generally need not be as heavy as the yachtsman's type.

When preparing to anchor, stand in the bow with the neatly coiled anchor rode shackled or tied with a fisherman's bend to the anchor ring (see figure 2-11). Then the boat is headed into the wind, and when she has stopped all forward motion, gently lower the anchor into the water making sure your feet are well clear of the coiled rode. Never throw it in, for it can easily foul its line. When the anchor's crown strikes bottom, let the boat drift backwards and *pay out* or *veer* (let out) scope gradually, keeping a slight tension on the line until the anchor flukes can bite into the bottom. Then *snub* the line, stop it from running out by taking a turn around the bow cleat. This should cause the flukes to dig in deeply and make the anchor hold effectively.

When raising or *weighing* the anchor, pull in on the line until it lies straight up and down. At this time, there is a minimum of scope and the anchor has little if any holding power. Then a hard tug up on the line will pull the anchor's *shank* (shaft) up and break the flukes out of the bottom.

If the anchor is difficult to break out, additional force may be applied to the line, once it is straight up and down, by taking a turn or two on the cleat and swaying on it. Taking a turn and swaying on the last few inches of line to bring it truly up and down is a most persuasive technique against a recalcitrant anchor. Or the anchor may be sailed out by heaving in to up-and-down, belaying, and setting a headsail and backing it to blow the bow off. With the anchor line straight up and down, any motion of the boat applies tremendous force to the line.

Sufficient scope is important for holding power because when the line makes a small angle to the bottom (when it is nearly parallel to the bottom), this causes the anchor to dig in. In many of today's crowded harbors, however, it is not always possible to let out all the scope one might desire. It is of the utmost importance to have *swinging room,* or room to clear other anchored boats no matter what direction the boats are swung in by the current or wind. Small boats should be anchored in shallow water so that they will need relatively little scope to achieve the aforementioned ideal scope to depth-of-water ratio (6 or 7 to 1). If large boats cannot veer sufficient scope due to crowded conditions,

their heavy anchor should be used. When veering scope be sure to take into consideration and allow for the rise or fall of the tide. After anchoring, take bearings on various stationary objects so that these may be checked later to see if the anchor is holding.

If the bottom is rocky, it is often wise to rig a *tripping* line, a line tied to the anchor's *crown* (see figure 2-18), so that the anchor can be broken out flukes first in the event it becomes jammed between two rocks. The free end of the trip line is often buoyed (attached to any floating object) and left overboard to float directly above the submerged anchor. Then if the anchor cannot be pulled up with its rode in the conventional manner, it can be done with the trip line.

Elementary steering. Small boats are usually equipped with tillers for steering while larger boats usually have steering wheels. A tiller usually turns the rudder directly, its length providing leverage, while a wheel often has a worm gear or is rigged in some other way to give the *helmsman* (steersman) a mechanical advantage. As a rule, tillers are quicker and more sensitive, while wheels are more powerful and require more movement to make the boat respond.

Figure 2-19 shows how the turning of the *helm* (wheel or tiller) affects the turning direction of the boat. A helmsman turns his wheel in the direction he wants his boat's bow to turn when moving ahead. This is similar to steering an automobile. But with a tiller the reverse is true. The helmsman pushes the tiller in the opposite direction from that in which he wants his bow to turn. When moving backwards the stern follows the direction in which the rudder is turned.

An important point the helmsman should al-

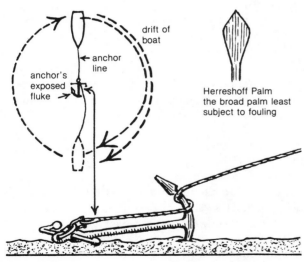

drift of boat

← anchor line

anchor's exposed fluke →

Herreshoff Palm the broad palm least subject to fouling

2-17. Fouled anchor.

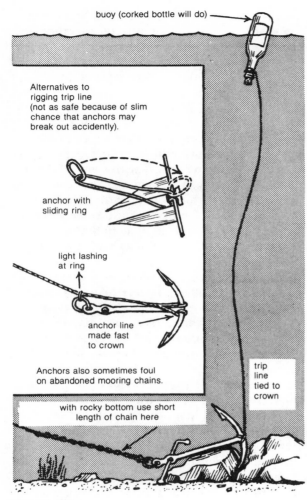

buoy (corked bottle will do)

Alternatives to rigging trip line (not as safe because of slim chance that anchors may break out accidently).

anchor with sliding ring

light lashing at ring

anchor line made fast to crown

Anchors also sometimes foul on abandoned mooring chains.

trip line tied to crown

with rocky bottom use short length of chain here

2-18. Trip line.

ways keep in mind is that the rudder is effective in turning the boat only so long as the boat is moving ahead or backwards. The more *way* she carries, or the faster she moves, the more effective is the rudder. Steering a boat under power

with single or twin screws and also the fine points of helmsmanship under sail will be discussed in subsequent chapters.

Shoal water. A good seaman always attempts to familiarize himself with the waters in which he sails. Knowledge of local topography, water depths, landmarks, the location of shoals, channels, and channel markers are readily obtained from government charts. Every boat above the size of a small dinghy should carry a chart of the area in which she sails.

A study of local charts will not only give proper orientation, but will prevent needless groundings. It is especially desirable to avoid running aground in a deep-keel boat. Centerboard boats usually can be freed quite easily by raising the board, provided care is taken to see that the boat is not blown farther onto the shoal, but keel boats are more difficult to get off. If a keel boat is driven hard aground it is usually a wise practice to lower all sails, so that the boat will not be driven farther aground. After the situation is studied and the exact shape of the shoal is obtained from the chart or from soundings taken around the boat or from a dinghy, then if the boat is headed in the right direction, sail may be hoisted and sheeted in to cause heeling and to drive her off.

There are several methods of freeing a boat. If she is small she might simply be poled off. If she has power she might be backed off or driven ahead after the vessel has been turned the right way. Placing all crew members on the bow often lifts the keel off the bottom. Of course, heeling the boat by sail, by putting the crew on one side, or putting a man on the end of the main boom and then swinging it out over the water help decrease the boat's draft. An effective

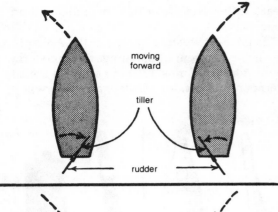

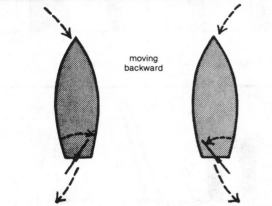

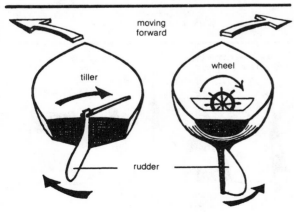

2-19. The helm.

method of freeing a vessel is by *kedging*. This means that an anchor is carried out some distance from the vessel by someone wading or going in a dinghy; then the anchor line is hauled on or winched in until the vessel is moved. If all these methods fail, it is necessary to wait until the next high tide or for a tow from a power boat. Remember that a power boat can damage a boat that is hard aground when trying to tow her off.

Shoals and channels are marked with *buoys* or channel markers. Figure 2-20 shows the principal types of unlighted, soundless, navigational aid buoys. It will be noted that they are painted solid or in combinations or red, black, and white. The age-old expression for understanding U.S. channel markers is *Red, Right, Returning*. This simply means that when returning to the harbor (from seaward), you leave a red marker on your right or starboard side. Of course, the reverse is true when leaving the harbor. The red is left to port. Figure 2-20 shows *mid-channel* and *junction* or *obstruction* buoys also. The former mark the middle of a channel and should be passed fairly close on either side. Junction or obstruction buoys can be passed on either side but should be given a wide berth. As shown in the illustration, the topmost band of color indicates the preferred channel.

Local weather. In the Annapolis area during the summer months, the most frequent wind direction is from the south or southwest. This area is frequently under the influence of the *Bermuda high*, a region of high barometric pressure near Bermuda whose winds rotate around the high in the clockwise direction. This brings warm,

27

moist, southerly winds up the Chesapeake Bay. Warm weather is often relieved by highs dropping down from Canada. These usually bring cool, dry, gusty northwest winds. Low-pressure cells with their cyclonic or counterclockwise rotation bring bad weather. These travel, as does the entire weather system in the middle latitudes, from west to east. When these lows pass to the north of Maryland, they cause only brief periods of stormy weather and these are usually accompanied by *veering* winds (changing clockwise) that bring clear northwesters. But when the low-pressure cells pass to the south of Maryland, the wind *backs* (changes counterclockwise) from south to northeast and often there is a lengthy period of stormy, rainy weather. This is known as the "northeaster," and it will often last for two or three days, perhaps longer.

Figure 2-21 shows storm warning signals which are displayed at most boating centers or weather stations and, of course, at the Naval Academy. These warnings should be heeded. Even if conditions look clear at the moment, it is likely that bad weather will soon arrive. Quite often boats are used when the small craft warning is up, but this should be done only with

2-20. U.S. Buoy system. Unlighted buoys without sound: In addition to the above federal markers, there are Intracoastal Waterway markers (along the Atlantic and Gulf coasts) and state markers within certain state areas (such as crowded inlets and lakes). However, these marker systems are generally compatible.

Intracoastal Waterway aids to navigation are distinguished by a special yellow border or other yellow mark. On this waterway, black markers are on the port and red markers on the starboard side of the channel entering from north and east and traversed to south and west respectively.

State "Regulatory Markers" use international orange geometric shapes with a white background on a sign or buoy.

great caution and never by a beginner sailing alone.

The greatest weather hazard in the Annapolis area is the frequent midsummer thunderstorm. These storms are most likely to occur in the late afternoon of a hot, humid day, and they will

Red Buoys
even numbering

Black Buoys
odd numbering

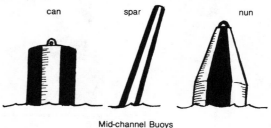

Mid-channel Buoys
black and white vertical stripes

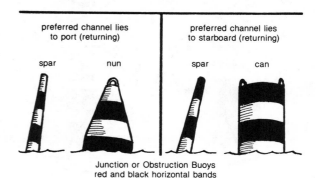

preferred channel lies
to port (returning)

preferred channel lies
to starboard (returning)

Junction or Obstruction Buoys
red and black horizontal bands

generally come from the west. Fortunately, they can usually be spotted a long way off because they have a very distinctive and awesome cloud formation, the *thunderhead* or *cumulonimbus*. This is illustrated in figure 2-22. Cumulus clouds, the white, puffy, "cotton wool" type of clouds, indicate fair weather, but look out when one of these clouds shows extreme vertical development. It could develop into a thunderhead. When a cumulus cloud has built up to such altitudes that its top fans out into ice crystals forming what looks like an anvil top, and when the cloud's bottom half begins to turn dark, it has turned into a full-fledged thunderhead, and you could well be in for a blow.

If you are far away from home base, take the sails down, and anchor in plenty of time. These storms can be severe, but usually they don't last.

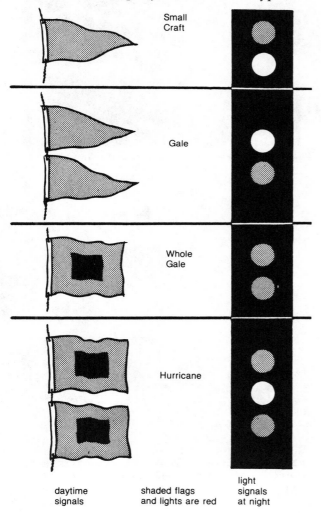

Small Craft

Gale

Whole Gale

Hurricane

daytime signals

shaded flags and lights are red

light signals at night

2-21. Storm warnings.

29

2-22. Cirrus clouds, "mares' tails" (over 25,000 ft.). If thick, often advanced forerunners (24 hours or more) ahead of a front.

2-23. Altostratus clouds (about 19,000 ft.). Gray sheet often warns of approaching warm front.

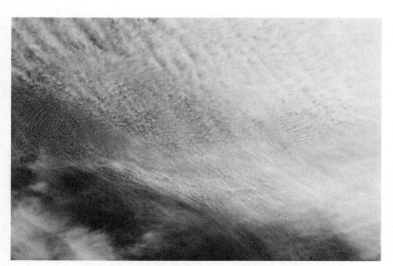

2-24. Cirrocumulus, "mackerel sky" (over 20,000 ft.). Can predict approach of warm front in unstable air.

2-25. Cirrostratus clouds. Whitish sheet (over 20,000 ft.) often causing halo around sun. Can warn of approaching warm front.

2-26. Altocumulus clouds (over 12,000 ft.). Like sheep. Can warn of cold front in unstable air.

2-27. Nimbostratus clouds (with fractostratus below). Dark rain cloud (about 3,000 ft.).

2-28. Stratus clouds (about 1,500 ft.). Gray sheet.

2-29. Stratocumulus clouds (with cumulus below). Globular rolls (about 8,000 ft.).

2-30. Cumulus clouds (over 4,000 ft.). Fair weather unless extreme towering up.

2-31. Cumulonimbus clouds. "Thunderhead" (thunderstorm cloud) can reach height of cirrus.

3. Theory of Sailing

This chapter describes the general fundamentals of sailing, such as the points of sailing, general sail positions, turning maneuvers, elementary aerodynamics and hydrodynamics. Practical details, specific procedures, and the fine points of steering will be discussed in chapter 5.

Points of sailing. A sailboat's directional heading with respect to the wind is called her *point of sailing*. There are five basic points of sailing: *running, broad reaching, beam reaching, close reaching,* and *beating*. These are illustrated in figure 3-1 along with the approximate sail positions for each point of sailing. When the wind is from dead astern to approximately two points on the quarter (see figure 1-1), the boat is running. When the wind comes from two points on the quarter to approximately one point abaft the beam, the boat is broad reaching. With the wind abeam the boat beam reaches. But with the wind ahead of a half point forward of the beam until the wind bears approximately three points forward of the beam, the boat close reaches. When the average boat sails with the wind

broad on her bow, she is beating. As the wind comes from farther ahead, the sails begin to flap or *luff,* and they become increasingly ineffectual until the boat is *head to wind* (headed directly into the wind) at which time they are totally ineffectual. A sail that is not luffing is said to be *full* (full of wind). The terms *luffing* or *full* can be applied to the boat herself, as well as to individual sails.

The sail positions shown in figure 3-1 are achieved by adjusting the sheets which pull the sails in towards the boat's centerline or allow them to swing out to a more athwartships position. When the sheets are pulled in, the sails are said to be *trimmed;* when the sheets are let out they are said to be *cracked, started, eased,* or *slacked,* to use the terms in increasing order. The word *trim* is also used to indicate whether or not a boat's sails are in exactly the right position for a given point of sailing, a vital factor for speed—as, for example, "Her sails are well trimmed," or "She is trimmed too flat."

In figure 3-1, the topmost boat is shown running. She is also said to be sailing *before the*

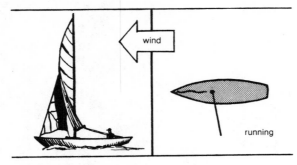

3-1. Points of sailing.

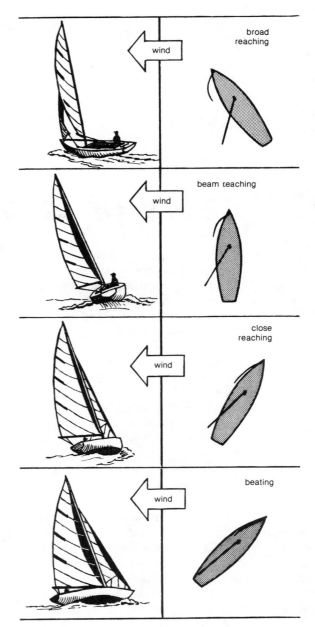

wind, off the wind (also applied to reaching), *sailing free* (with sheets eased), or sailing with *a fair wind.* The illustration shows her jib hanging limply because the wind is from nearly dead astern, and the mainsail is *blanketing* the jib or blocking off its wind. The jib might be made to *draw* (fill with wind) if it were *wung-out* or pushed out on the opposite side from the mainsail. The boat then would be said to be sailing *wing and wing.* (The term is usually applied to a schooner sailing with her foresail and mainsail on opposite sides.) Notice in the illustration that the *main boom* (mainsail's boom) is let out so that it is almost athwartships. When a boat is running with the wind nearly dead astern, her boom is let out as far as it will go without chafing against the aftermost shroud. As the boat is gradually turned towards the wind, her sheets are slowly trimmed until, when beam reaching, her jib and main boom are about halfway in, roughly 135° to the wind or 45° to the boat's centerline. When close reaching, the sheets are trimmed still closer, somewhere between the beam-reaching position and about 10° from the boat's centerline.

On various points of reaching, especially when beam reaching or sailing slightly farther

36

away from the wind, boats usually achieve their highest sailing speeds. Some lightweight boats having planing hulls and flattish bottoms will gain considerable speed by *planing* or lifting up on their bow waves and skimming over the top of the water rather than plowing through the water like a boat with a *displacement hull* (a deep, heavy hull). At most times when boats are traveling at their highest speeds, sails must be trimmed a little flatter than normal. This is due to the *apparent wind* which is explained in figure 3-2. Since the boat in the diagram is moving ahead at 4 *knots* (nautical miles per hour), she causes a 4-knot wind from directly ahead. The *true wind* or actual wind is 9 knots from slightly forward of the beam; thus the apparent wind is a resultant of these two forces (boat-speed wind and true wind), which in this case is blowing at 11 knots from broad on the bow. Sails should always be trimmed to the apparent wind. To put it very simply, the faster a boat travels (unless dead before the wind), the closer her sheets are trimmed. This becomes especially evident when the true wind is nearly on the beam.

When beating, a boat's sails are trimmed quite flat. Very generally speaking, this is to within about 10° or less of the boat's centerline. (Mainsails are sometimes trimmed to the centerline.) The average modern boat intended for day sailing or cruising-racing can be made to sail to within about 45° of the wind. Strictly cruising types will not sail quite this close, but some racers will sail closer than this. Progress directly to *windward* (upwind) is accomplished by making a series of *tacks* or zigzag courses towards the windward destination. On the zig course, the sails lie to one side of the boat, and on the zag course, they are swung by the wind to the boat's opposite side. With the sails on the port side

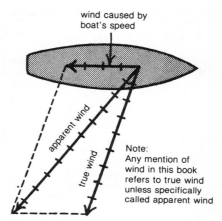

wind caused by boat's speed

Note:
Any mention of wind in this book refers to true wind unless specifically called apparent wind

If true wind is 9 knots and boat speed is 4 knots, then apparent wind is 11 knots.

3-2. Apparent wind. (Any mention of wind in this book refers to true wind unless specifically called apparent wind.)

and the wind blowing from the starboard side, the boat is said to be on the *starboard tack,* and she is on the *port tack* when the wind comes from the port side and the sails lie to starboard. Obviously, with an average boat that can *point* or head up to within 45° of the wind, the highest heading on the starboard tack will be at right angles to the highest heading on the port tack. Other terms for beating are *sailing close-hauled, sailing to windward, tacking, on the wind* or *hard on the wind,* and *by the wind. Full and by* means beating, with the emphasis on keeping the sails full rather than on heading as close to the wind as possible.

Turning maneuvers. There are two ways a boat can turn from one tack to the other. First, she may *luff* or *head up* into the wind and continue turning through the eye of the wind until her sails fill on the other tack. This is called *coming about* or *tacking.* Secondly, she may *bear off* or

37

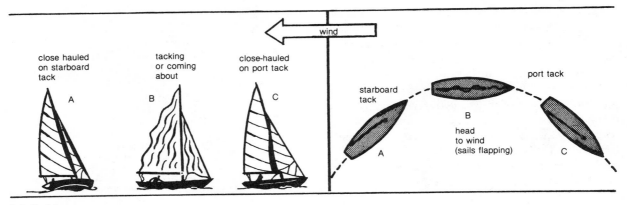

3-3. Tacking.

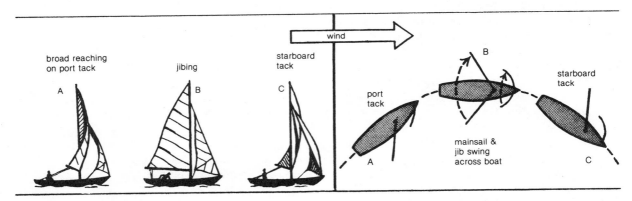

3-4. Jibing.

head away from the wind until the wind is dead astern and then continue turning until the wind suddenly swings her sails across to the boat's opposite side. This is called *jibing* or *wearing ship*. To put it simply, a tack is an upwind turn with the bow swinging across the wind, causing the sails to flap; but a jibe is a downwind turn with the stern crossing the wind and the sails suddenly filling on their opposite sides and swinging across the boat. These turns are illus-

trated in figures 3-3 and 3-4. Specific procedures involved in tacking and jibing will be discussed in chapter 5.

Prior to making the final tack when beating towards a windward destination, there arises the question of exactly when to tack in order to arrive at the mark in the quickest time without sailing any extra distance or having to make additional tacks. If the boat can be brought about at the proper moment so that she is pointed di-

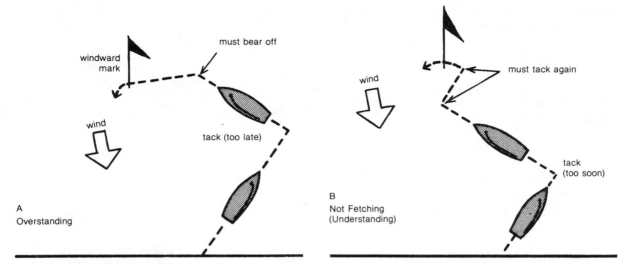

3-5. Fetching the windward mark.

rectly at the windward mark on her final tack, she is said to be *fetching* or *laying* the mark. This final approach tack which brings the close-hauled boat directly to the mark lies on an imaginary line called the *fetch line* or *lay line*. This is explained in figure 3-5. If the helmsman tacks his boat too soon, before reaching the fetch line, then he has *under-stood* the mark (he is heading *below* it) and must tack twice again. On the other hand, if he waits too long before tacking and sails beyond the fetch line, he has wasted time and distance. In this case he has *over-stood* the mark (he is heading too far *above* it). Assuming that the boat can sail to within 45° of the wind, then the proper time to tack is when the mark bears abeam or lies at right angles to the boat's centerline if there is no *current* (flow of water). The foregoing discussion has been concerned with only the final windward tack when approaching a mark. Planning windward

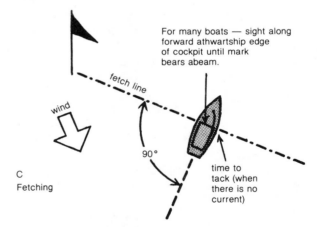

Fetch line (or lay line) — A boat pointed at and fetching a mark is on her fetch line. To take advantage of wind shifts, do not sail up to fetch line until fairly close to mark.

courses and the general strategy of beating will be discussed in chapter 10, "Basic Racing."

Aerodynamics of sailing. It is not difficult to understand how a boat sails before the wind. To quote an old saying of sailors "Even a haystack will sail downwind." But understanding how a boat can sail against the wind is not so easy. The force which drives a sailboat to windward is similar to the force which gives *lift* to an airplane's wing or, to be more exact, a glider's wing. The sail is actually an airfoil stood on end. The airfoil characteristic is achieved by building a fore-to-aft curve into the sail, which we call *draft* or *camber*. This curve is parabolic, having its greatest amount of curvature near the *luff* or forward edge of the sail, but the curvature flattens out or becomes straighter near the *leech*, the after edge of the sail. An explanation of how draft is built into a sail will be given in chapter 6.

When a boat reaches or beats to windward, the air flows around her sails from luff to leech or from front edge to back edge. As the wind meets the luff it splits to form an airflow to windward of the sail and another flow to *leeward* of the sail (on its downwind side). The molecules of air on the leeward side have the greater distance to travel around the sail, and they increase their speed as they race back to join the windward airflow molecules at the leech. As a result of this difference between windward and leeward flow speeds, the pressure is lowered on the sail's leeward side. This is in accordance with a principle of physics known as Bernoulli's principle, which tells us that in fluid motion wherever the velocity of flow is high, the pressure is low. When the pressure is lowered on a sail's leeward side, a suction pull is created which acts at right angles to the sail (see figure

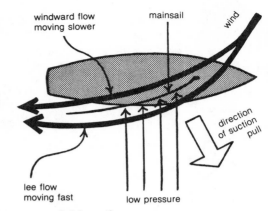

3-6. Leeward side suction.

3-6). If the boat is close-hauled, most of this suction pulls the boat to leeward and a small amount pulls her forward. All boats intended for windward sailing, however, are designed to resist making *leeway* or being blown sideways but to resist as little as possible being pulled forward; thus, for the most part, the suction pull can only draw the boat ahead.

Resistance to making leeway or *lateral resistance* is supplied by one of the means illustrated in figure 3-7. All Naval Academy boats are equipped with either keels, centerboards, or daggerboards which may be raised or lowered as shown in the diagram. Figure 3-8, which compares a child on a sliding board to a boat close reaching, perhaps gives the simplest explanation of how lateral resistance forces the boat ahead.

Up to this point we have been discussing the aerodynamic forces acting on a single sail, but the addition of another sail in close proximity to the first has a considerable influence on these forces. A correctly trimmed jib set just ahead of a mainsail creates a narrow space, often called a

40

slot, between the jib's leech and the mainsail's luff. Much of the airflow passing to leeward of the mainsail must first pass through this slot. The mainsail is, in some respects, made more efficient aerodynamically by the jib—partly because a proper slot helps eliminate a turbulent flow on the mainsail's leeward side due to the fact that when the wind first enters the slot it slows down, then accelerates as it is squeezed past the jib's leech. This is often referred to as a venturi effect (see figure 3-9). When sails are improperly adjusted and the slot is too narrow, however, the mainsail will be *backwinded* and detrimentally affected as shown in figure 3-10. Some quite recent investigations into sailing aerodynamics have given rise to the theory that the mainsail is not only affected beneficially for the most part by the jib, but more important, the jib is helped considerably by the mainsail. The latter alters the wind flow against the forward sail to allow higher pointing ability, and also more flow is diverted to the jib's leeward side to

3-7. Lateral resistance.

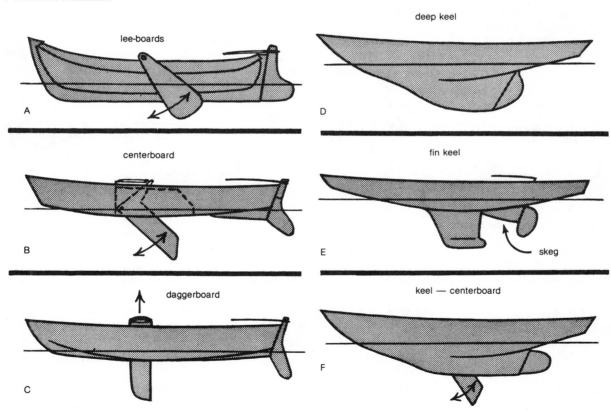

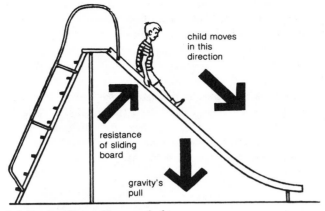

3-8. Forces when sailing upwind.

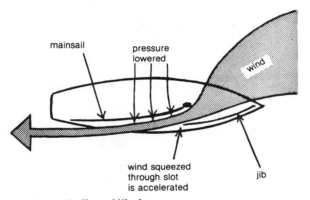

mainsail

pressure lowered

wind squeezed through slot is accelerated

jib

3-9. Venturi effect of jib slot.

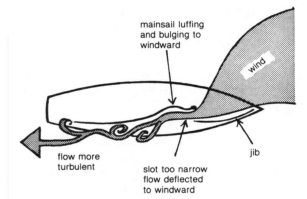

mainsail luffing and bulging to windward

flow more turbulent

slot too narrow flow deflected to windward

jib

3-10. Jib backwind.

increase the velocity and thus lower the pressure there.

The fine points of jib trimming will be discussed in chapter 6.

A simple demonstration of the venturi effect and Bernoulli's principle is shown in figure 3-11. Water (or any fluid) is forced through a large pipe which is pinched in at the middle. The flow speeds up as it passes through the constricted area. There are three pressure gauges, two at the

pipe's widest diameter and another in the pipe's constricted region. The diagram shows that when the flow accelerates due to the venturi effect it lowers the pressure in accordance with Bernoulli's principle. In this demonstration we can see that we are dealing with very real forces and not simply vague theories.

Sails alter the direction and velocity of the wind flow. They may do this in a beneficial way so as to give maximum drive to a boat, or they

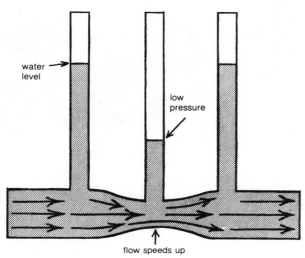

water level

low pressure

flow speeds up

3-11. Bernoulli's principle.

may do it in a harmful way so that they lose their drive or disturb the wind or other sails in close proximity. We have seen examples of disturbed air in the blanketed jib of figure 3-1 and the backwinded mainsail of figure 3-10. *Backwind* is the turbulent air which flows off a sail's leech and is deflected to windward. The blanket or *wind shadow* is the resulting turbulence and partial absence of air when the wind is blocked off or a *lee* is formed by a sail or other object. More will be said about disturbed air in chapter 10, "Basic Racing."

Sails can only reach maximum effectiveness when they have the proper shape, especially draft, and when they have the correct *angle of incidence* (angular position to the wind). Figure 3-12 shows two close-hauled boats sailing about 45° to the wind. On one boat, the mainsail is not trimmed close enough and its luff extends too far to leeward so that the wind blows directly on its lee side causing it to luff or flap. In this case, the sail is said to be *luffing*, and the forward compo-

nent of the suction pull is partially destroyed. The other boat in the diagram shows the other extreme; it is trimmed too flat. In this case, the sail is partially *stalled*. Instead of the leeward airflow being relatively smooth it becomes turbulent, and *eddies* or reverse currents are formed to leeward of the leech. The most effective angle of incidence lies somewhere between the stalling and luffing angles, and this depends, of course, on the heading of the boat and the trim of her sails. This will be discussed in chapters 5 and 6.

Hydrodynamics of sailing. While aerodynamic forces are acting against a boat's sails, similar hydrodynamic forces are working against her hull and appendages (keel or centerboard and rudder) under the water. The flow of water around a sailboat's submerged appendages is also comparable to the flow of air around an airplane's wings, and the *angle of attack* or incidence that the flow makes with the axis of a keel or centerboard creates lift as well as drag forces like those acting on a wing. The angle of attack, usually referred to as the leeway or *yaw angle* on

3-12. Luffing and stalling.

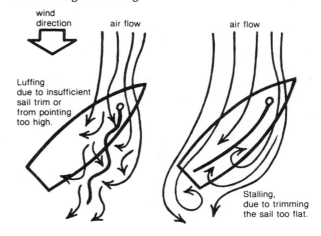

wind direction

air flow

air flow

Luffing due to insufficient sail trim or from pointing too high.

Stalling, due to trimming the sail too flat.

43

a sailboat, is a small one—normally four to seven degrees when she beats or reaches. Should the angle become much greater, leeway will be excessive, and the flow may become detached and turbulent. When this occurs the hydrofoil (underwater appendage) is partially stalled, at which time lift decreases and drag increases enormously. Figure 3-13 illustrates the lift-drag forces at work on a keel. Notice that lift acts at right angles to the water's force or flow, while drag, which is resistance to forward movement, acts parallel to the direction of the flow.

Fin keels or centerboards that have *high aspect ratios* (those that are deep but short in the fore-and-aft direction) have proven to be highly efficient, for they supply a maximum of lateral resistance at a minimum cost in resistance to headway (see figure 3-14). Such a deep, short appendage having a streamlined section has a high *lift-drag ratio,* because a long leading edge on a hydrofoil helps produce effective lift, while a short length reduces area and thus skin friction or *wetted-surface drag.* There is nothing new about high-aspect ratio appendages, but nowadays we are seeing a greater use of short fin keels on *racing-cruising sailboats* (those types

3-14. A PJ seen out of water. This Sparkman-Stephens design exemplifies the modern racing-cruiser with a short fin keel and separated rudder. The hull shape of this particular class has been influenced by the IOR handicap rule, which has encouraged narrow ends, great beam amidships, and a pronounced tumble home.

similar to the Luders yawls or other ocean racers).

Although there are advantages in short fin keels in terms of speed and efficiency, steering control is often adversely affected. When the keel is extremely short, steering may become overly sensitive, and the boat may be difficult to hold on a steady course. This difficulty can be alleviated, however, by separating the rudder from the after end of the keel and moving it aft as far as possible. There, the rudder can be attached to a *skeg* (a short appendage abaft the keel as shown in figure 3-7E, or it can be a freestanding *spade* rudder, which is held only by its rudder stock. This is the type used on the new Naval Academy knockabouts (see figure 7-1). A great advantage in a keel-separated rudder is that its location as far aft as possible permits the maximum distance from the boat's vertical turn-

3-13. Keel/water force.

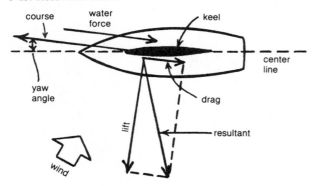

44

ing axis to the rudder's center of pressure. Such an arrangement gives the greatest possible arm length for steering leverage. A possible disadvantage in a separated rudder, however, is that the rudder cannot be used to give the keel camber to increase lift when beating to windward (more will be said about this when helm balance is discussed in chapter 6). Furthermore, spade rudders are subject to early stalling, and so they may require a slightly different steering technique. This will be discussed briefly in the section on knockabouts in chapter 7.

The two principal sources of underwater drag are from wetted-surface resistance and *wavemaking resistance*. The former source predominates at low to medium speeds, while the latter causes the most drag at high speeds. When a boat moves through the water, her bow pushes up a mound of water and other waves are formed farther aft. As boat speed increases, the length of these waves increase until the boat sits in the *trough* (hollow) between two waves with one *crest* (peak) at her bow and another crest at her stern. At this point, the boat has insufficient length to make longer waves, and so her speed theoretically is limited to the speed of a wave equal in length to her waterline. This is called *hull speed*, and it is equal to 1.34 times the square root of her waterline length. In actuality, it is possible for a boat to exceed her hull speed but only if she planes or lifts up and rides on the surface of the water as described earlier. Light-displacement dinghies such as the Lasers and 420s plane very easily in good breezes, but even relatively heavy-displacement ocean racers can plane to a very limited extent by *surfing* momentarily in strong winds with sizable following seas (figure 3-15).

Skin friction under water is caused not only

3-15. A Cal 28 in a blow. This William Lapworth design, like many other moderately light displacement cruisers, can partially plane or "surf" in following seas when there is sufficient wind. Notice her roller-reefed mainsail, which would be less wrinkled, perhaps, if the leech could have been pulled aft as the reef was being rolled in. In heavy weather especially, care must be taken not to let lines trail overboard that might foul the propeller should the engine be needed.

by surface area but also by the roughness and unevenness of a boat's bottom. If the boat is to be raced, every effort should be made to obtain a smooth, fair bottom. Underwater protuberances should be minimized with the use of flush through-hull fittings, whenever possible, and the bottom should be faired with filling compounds and thoroughly sanded before application of bottom paint. When antifouling bottom paint is used on boats left afloat, it is usually helpful to sand the final coat of paint with fine wet and dry sandpaper to remove the brush strokes. A very fine film of slime may not be harmful to speed, but weeds or barnacles on a boat's bottom can be disastrous. It is more important to obtain smoothness in the forward half of the hull than the after half, because forward, the water flow is mostly *laminar* or more closely attached to the hull surface.

4. Rules of the Road

On today's crowded waterways, it is important not only to know the various rules that govern boat traffic, but also to know which rules apply and where. Vessels making passages along the coast will very often have to comply with two sets of rules, the Inland Rules and the International Rules. The former rules apply to U.S. inland waters, while the latter apply on the high seas. The new boundary lines between inland and international waters are drawn closer inshore than the old lines, roughly parallel to the shoreline, and at the entrances to all major harbors, rivers, and bays.

Separate parts of the rules cover right-of-way situations for boats under sail and those under power. The first two sections of this chapter will discuss converging situations between sailboats, and the last section will discuss the converging of power boats. Incidentally, a sailboat using her engine for propulsion is considered a power boat. A sailboat has the right of way over a power boat except when overtaking it. Also, a sailboat must keep clear of vessels fishing with nets, lines, or trawls, and it is against the rules to interfere with a large ship in a narrow channel.

When a powerboat crosses a boundary line between inland and international waters, the basic steering and sailing rules do not change, but when a sailboat crosses the boundary line, her right of way with respect to other sailboats may change. Differences between the rules exist because the International Rules (72 COLREGS) have been modernized to take into account the greater upwind efficiency of contemporary sailboat rigs. On the other hand, Inland Rules have not been modernized, and are basically the same as they were in the days of square-riggers.

Inland steering and sailing rules for sailboats.
Figure 4-1 shows the various right-of-way situations for boats under sail. These are based on Article 17 of the Inland Rules. Notice that the close-hauled boat has the right of way over the one running free. This is a holdover from early times when square-riggers had great difficulties sailing to windward. Article 17 of the Steering and Sailing Rules reads as follows:

4-1. Right-of-way situations for boats under sail under the Inland Rules.

When two sailing vessels are approaching one another, so as to involve risk of collision, one of them shall keep out of the way of the other as follows, namely:

(a) A vessel which is running free shall keep out of the way of a vessel which is close-hauled.

(b) A vessel which is close-hauled on the port tack shall keep out of the way of a vessel which is close-hauled on the starboard tack.

(c) When both are running free, with the wind on different sides, the vessel which has the wind on the port side shall keep out of the way of the other.

(d) When both are running free, with the wind on the same side, the vessel which is to the windward shall keep out of the way of the vessel which is to the leeward.

(e) A vessel which has the wind aft shall keep out of the way of the other vessel.

A situation not covered under the preceding rules would arise if a sailboat overtakes another sailboat on the same tack and the same point of sailing when neither is to windward of the other. In this case, the overtaken boat is privileged (now called the stand-on vessel) and has the right of way. The overtaking boat is burdened (now called the give-way vessel) and must keep clear. In any converging situation the privileged, or stand-on, boat must hold her course until there is no longer any danger of collision. If a sailboat is equipped with an auxiliary engine, the only time she is considered a sailboat is when she is propelled by sail alone.

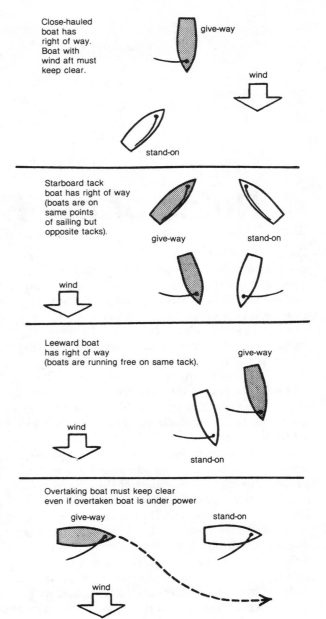

Close-hauled boat has right of way. Boat with wind aft must keep clear.

give-way

wind

stand-on

Starboard tack boat has right of way (boats are on same points of sailing but opposite tacks).

give-way

stand-on

wind

Leeward boat has right of way (boats are running free on same tack).

give-way

wind

stand-on

Overtaking boat must keep clear even if overtaken boat is under power

give-way

stand-on

wind

48

International steering and sailing rules for sailboats. As said earlier, vessels use the International Regulations on the high seas, and these rules for sailboats are basically similar to the USYRU racing rules explained in chapter 10.

Rule 12 (under Part B, Steering and Sailing Rules) of the International Rules reads:

(a) When two sailing vessels are approaching one another, so as to involve risk of collision, one of them shall keep out of the way of the other as follows:

(i) when each has the wind on a different side, the vessel which has the wind on the port side shall keep out of the way of the other;

(ii) when both have the wind on the same side, the vessel which is to windward shall keep out of the way of the vessel which is to leeward;

(iii) if a vessel with the wind on the port side sees a vessel to windward and cannot determine with certainty whether the other vessel has the wind on the port or on the starboard side, she shall keep out of the way of the other.

(b) For the purposes of this Rule the windward side shall be deemed to be the side opposite to that on which the mainsail is carried, or in the case of a square-rigged vessel, the side opposite to that on which the largest fore-and-aft sail is carried.

The main difference between Rule 12 of the International Rules and Article 17 of the Inland Rules is, of course, that Rule 12 gives no right of way to close-hauled boats over those running free. A boat's right of way is merely determined by which tack she is on or whether she is to windward or leeward of another boat.

4-2. On opposite tacks. NA 9 has the right of way, of course, since she is on the starboard tack, and she must hold a reasonably steady course so that the port tack yawl can take evasive action. There should be a crew member stationed at the mainsheet of the port tack boat in case the mainsail needs slacking to help the boat bear off. This is especially important in fresh winds.

Common sense and courtesy should be exercised at all times on the water. A sailboat skipper should never demand his right of way when converging with a large ship in constricted waters. In fact, International Rules and Inland Rules strictly forbid sailboats to hamper large power vessels in a narrow channel. Boats which are not racing should attempt to stay out of the way of boats which are racing, even though the former may have the right of way. Racing rules are quite different from the present Inland Rules of the Road and apply only to boats racing among themselves. Obviously, these rules don't apply to boats not racing. (Boats racing can usually be identified by a class flag attached to the permanent backstay and often a similar flag attached at the bow.)

Lights and shapes (International Rules). Sailboats over 23 feet long, and all powerboats, except those under 23 feet whose maximum speed does not exceed seven knots, are required to carry red, green, and white navigation or running lights when underway between sunset and dawn, in order that they may be seen by other vessels. These navigation lights include red and green side lights, a white stern light (also a yellow stern light if towing a vessel), and a forward mast light. A sailboat under 23 feet long only needs to show a flashlight or lantern under the International Rules, but if possible, she should display normal running lights. These rules also permit a powerboat under 23 feet with a maximum speed of seven knots or less to carry only a single all-around white light, but she should have additional side lights if possible. Running lights have definite sectors or arcs of visibility which are shown in figure 4-3. If there is any possibility that a boat will be taken offshore, she should be fitted with lights that meet the requirements of the International Rules, because these lights must be used on the high seas and they may be used on inland waters. Figure 4-4 shows International Rule lighting for motorboats and sailboats. When the engine is running on an auxiliary sailboat, the 20-point white light forward must be turned on, but when under sail alone, this light must be off.

Under International Rules, there is a lighting option that enables a sailing vessel under sail to carry (in addition to her normal side lights and 12-point stern light) a 32-point red light over a 32-point green light at the masthead, sufficiently separated so as to be clearly distinguished and visible for two miles. A further option for boats under 39.4 feet is the carrying of the stern light and side lights combined in a single multisector light at the masthead. This option has been added because normal side lights are often obscured by sails. The rule also says that a vessel may, if necessary in order to attract attention, in addition to the lights which she is required to carry, show a flare-up light. If you are on a sailboat, it is often wise to shine a flashlight on the sails when converging with another vessel at night.

If you are in shallow water and decide to anchor at night, you must turn off the running lights and display an anchor light. This is a white, 32-point light normally displayed on the forward part of the vessel.

A careful lookout should be kept at night, even in uncongested waters. When you spot another vessel, her approximate course can usually

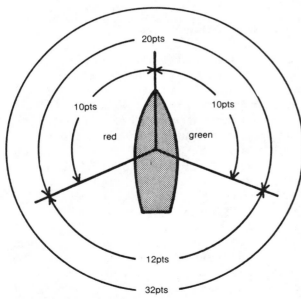

4-3. Arcs of visibility for running lights.

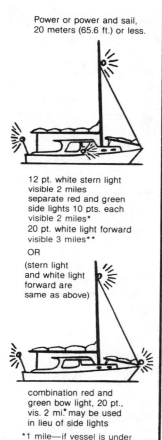

Power or power and sail,
20 meters (65.6 ft.) or less.

12 pt. white stern light
visible 2 miles
separate red and green
side lights 10 pts. each
visible 2 miles*
20 pt. white light forward
visible 3 miles**

OR

(stern light
and white light
forward are
same as above)

combination red and
green bow light, 20 pt.,
vis. 2 mi.* may be used
in lieu of side lights

*1 mile—if vessel is under
12 meters (39.4 ft.)

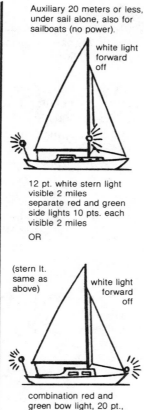

Auxiliary 20 meters or less,
under sail alone, also for
sailboats (no power).

white light
forward
off

12 pt. white stern light
visible 2 miles
separate red and green
side lights 10 pts. each
visible 2 miles

OR

(stern lt.
same as
above)

white light
forward
off

combination red and
green bow light, 20 pt.,
vis. 2 mi.* may be used
in lieu of side lights

**2 miles—if vessel is under
12 meters

4-4. Required lights for motorboats and auxiliary sailboats under International Rules. These are required on the high seas and may be shown on U.S. waters. A sailing vessel may also show optional red over green 32-pt. lights with 2-mile visibility* at or near the top of the mast. A sailing vessel under 39.4 feet has the option of carrying the stern light and side lights combined in a single multisector light at the masthead. If this is done, the above-mentioned red over green optional lights may not be used.

further accuracy by looking at her masthead and range lights which are white mast lights, one forward and one aft with the after light being higher than the forward one. If these lights are widely separated, the ship is not headed very close to you; if they are close together, the ship is headed toward you. When the masthead light and range light line up vertically, then obviously the ship is headed directly toward you.

When the lights of a distant vessel are spotted, the possibility of collision should be determined by taking bearings on her. If the bearing holds steady and the light becomes more and more distinct, then you are on a collision course. When the other vessel has the right of way, obviously you must change course. If you have the right of way, you hold your course, but make certain that the other boat sees you by shining a light on your sails or superstructure. In close passing situations, it is a good idea to be prepared to use a sound signal (one which cannot be mistaken for any other signal authorized in the rules), and to see that flares are readily available.

The International Rules also require that certain black shapes be hoisted during the day. For instance, a vessel proceeding under sail with her engine running shall exhibit forward where it can best be seen a conical shape, apex downwards. Also, an anchored vessel shall exhibit in the fore part a ball shape. Details of the Inland

be determined by looking at her lights. If the after white light can be seen, she is moving away from you. If her red and green lights show simultaneously, she is headed directly toward you. If only one red or green light can be seen, you are looking at her side or at her starboard or port bow as she approaches you at an angle. The course of a large ship can be determined with and International Rules can be found in appendixes A and B.

Steering and sailing rules for powerboats. When operating under power, whether or not sails are set, a sailboat must comply with those regulations governing motor vessels. She is no longer a sailboat. The applicable International Rules of the Road and Inland Rules of the Road are in appendixes B and A. Therefore, the explanation here will be brief.

In addition to knowing which boat has the right of way in meeting, overtaking, and crossing situations, the skipper of a boat under power must be familiar with the maneuvering whistle signals prescribed by International and Inland rules.

The diagrams in figure 4-5, A-F, illustrate the six basic situations encountered by vessels under power under Inland Rules, the rules that apply in Chesapeake Bay. The proper reaction to each situation should become instinctive to the skipper.

In figure 4-5A, both vessels are passing to port of each other, which is preferable in this situation. Each has signified her intent by one

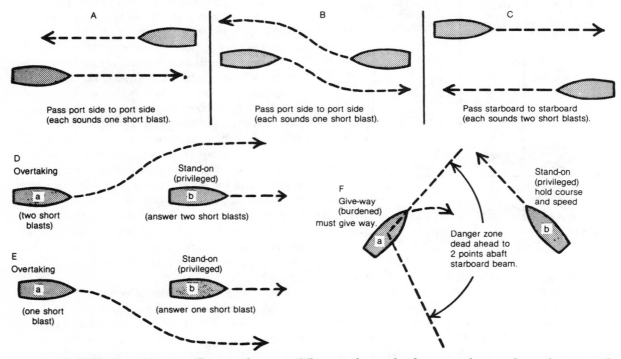

A

Pass port side to port side
(each sounds one short blast).

B

Pass port side to port side
(each sounds one short blast).

C

Pass starboard to starboard
(each sounds two short blasts).

D
Overtaking

(two short blasts)

Stand-on
(privileged)

(answer two short blasts)

E
Overtaking

(one short blast)

Stand-on
(privileged)

(answer one short blast)

F
Give-way
(burdened)
must give way.

a

b

Stand-on
(privileged)
hold course
and speed

Danger zone
dead ahead to
2 points abaft
starboard beam.

4-5. Inland Rules for motorboats or sailboats under power. When vessels meet head on or nearly so, each vessel passes on the port side of the other unless the courses of such vessels are so far to starboard of each other as not to be considered meeting head and head.

short blast of the whistle. Both are burdened, while neither is obliged to change course. At night the masthead light and red (port) side light would be visible to each.

In figure 4-5B, both vessels are headed directly toward each other. In this situation, the rule is that each shall turn to starboard and pass on the port side of the other. Each has signified her intent to do so by one short blast of the whistle. Both are burdened and both are obliged to alter course. At night, both side lights (red and green) and the masthead light would be visible to each before altering course, and the red side light and masthead light would remain visible after course alteration.

In figure 4-5C, the vessels are going to pass to starboard of each other. Each has signified this to be her intent by two short blasts of the whistle. Both are burdened, but neither has to alter course. At night, the masthead light and green (starboard) side light would be visible to each.

Figures 4-5D and 4-5E illustrate overtaking situations. (To be considered an overtaking, rather than a crossing, situation, the overtaking vessel must be at least two points or more abaft the beam of the overtaken vessel.) In both cases the overtaken vessel (b) is privileged and must maintain course and speed, while the overtaking vessel (a) is burdened and must alter course. In figure 4-5D, vessel (a) should signify intent to pass to port of vessel (b) by sounding two short blasts. If such a passage is clear, and acceptable to vessel (b), she should answer with two short blasts and the passing will be effected. In figure 4-5E, vessel (a) should signify intent to pass to starboard of vessel (b) by sounding one short blast. If the passage is clear and acceptable to vessel (b), she should answer with one short blast. If, in either case, the initially proposed passage is dangerous, vessel (b) should sound the Inland Rules danger signal of four or more short blasts. After the passage is clear, vessel (b) would sound the proper answering signal.

In the crossing situation diagrammed in figure 4-5F, two vessels are approaching each other at right angles or obliquely in such a manner that there is a risk of collision. Vessel (a), which holds the other to starboard, is burdened and should maneuver to keep clear either by altering course to starboard, slowing, or both. She may signify this to be her intent by sounding one short blast. Vessel (b), which holds the other to port, is the privileged vessel and is obliged to maintain course and speed. This intent should be signified by one short blast. Whistle signals are not mandatory, however, in the crossing situation under Inland Rules. At night, vessel (a) would see the masthead light and red (port) side light of vessel (b), while (b) would see the masthead light and green (starboard) side light of (a). In studying these situations, see Article 18 of the Inland Rules (appendix A).

For vessels under power, the Steering and Sailing Rules of the International Rules of the road are essentially similar to those of the Inland Rules. Rules 13, 14, and 15 of the International Rules (see appendix B) cover the overtaking, head-on, and crossing situations shown in figure 4-5. The terms "stand-on" and "give-way" correspond to the "privileged" and "burdened" terms used in the text above.

Although the Inland rules and the International Rules are similar in most respects, we have seen that there are certain differences in lighting and maneuvering rules for sailboats. It is therefore important that the crew of vessels proceeding offshore know the boundary lines between inland and international waters.

5. Helmsmanship and Maneuvering Under Sail

A thorough knowledge of the fine points of sailing can only be acquired after a great deal of practice and experience under sail. Before actually handling a boat, however, the beginner should study the basic principles of maneuvering, helmsmanship, and sail trim. With some preliminary reading, he will learn a great deal faster and avoid many pitfalls.

Wind direction. In chapter 2 we examined the simple rudiments of steering with a tiller or wheel. Obviously, this is a prime prerequisite of sailing. Another prerequisite is the determination of wind direction. Just as you can't control a boat's heading without knowing how her steering gear works, you can't properly trim her sails without knowing from what precise direction the wind is blowing.

Wind direction can be detected by carefully observing the water's surface. Small ripples move in the same direction as the wind; however, do not be misled by the movements of larger waves. Quite often the larger waves are controlled by a previous wind, and their move-ment doesn't indicate the direction of a new wind which has recently *shifted* or changed its direction. Watch the movement of the smallest ripples to determine the present wind.

Other signs of wind direction are flags flying; smoke from ships, chimneys, or cigarettes; and the heeling as well as the sail trim of other boats. If anchored by the bow, boats and ships will lie with their bows pointed directly into the wind unless their heading is controlled by a strong current. The most effective means of determining wind direction and observing momentary shifts is by using wind indicators, shown in figure 5-1. The *masthead fly* and *wind sock* illustrated are carried at the top of the mast where they are either permanently secured or are hoisted into position with a flag halyard when needed. *Telltales* are short pieces of yarn, thread, or ribbon tied to the shrouds about seven feet above the deck. They are easy to watch and respond instantly to even the lightest breeze. Remember, though, that wind indicators on a moving boat do not show the true wind, but only the apparent wind.

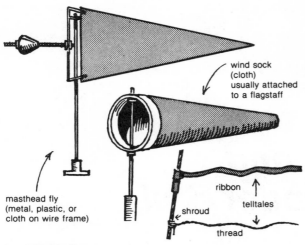

5-1. Wind indicators.

masthead fly (metal, plastic, or cloth on wire frame)

wind sock (cloth) usually attached to a flagstaff

ribbon

telltales

shroud

thread

Sight is not the only sense used to determine wind direction. Most experienced sailors develop a sensitivity to the feel of the wind. They can detect slight shifts and velocity changes by feeling the breeze on their cheeks, necks, arms, or hands. Of course, this is particularly valuable when sailing at night. More will be said of this in chapter 11.

Sailboat maneuvering at dock or anchorage. The fine points of sailing should be practiced in open water, where there is enough *sea room* (ample room for maneuvering) to hold a fairly long *board* (tack or leg to windward). But before reaching open water, a boat must be sailed from her dock or mooring, which nearly always involves tight maneuvering in crowded anchorages or other constricted areas. It is therefore very important to understand the basic principles of sailboat control. This involves *gaining way* (picking up speed), *killing way* (slowing down), turning, and holding a straight course.

Before getting *underway* (a vessel is considered underway when not anchored, made fast, or aground), a boat should be headed into the wind so that when her sails are hoisted, they will merely flap and not drive the boat ahead before she is ready to get underway. If she is at a mooring (permanent anchor), she is probably already lying head to wind, but if she is made fast to a dock or pier, she will probably have to be swung into the wind by *casting off* (releasing) her stern line. This is shown in figure 5-2. After the sails are hoisted and the boat is ready to leave, she is shoved straight back with the rudder *amidships* (held straight or on dead center). When she is well clear of the dock, the rudder is put over to the right or left to swing the bow in the opposite direction (since the boat has sternway), as illustrated in figure 5-2 (also see figure 2-18, The Helm). The sails will begin to draw, because the boat will turn so that the wind is

5-2. Leaving a dock.

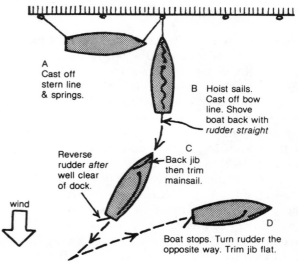

A Cast off stern line & springs.

B Hoist sails. Cast off bow line. Shove boat back with *rudder straight*

Reverse rudder *after* well clear of dock.

C Back jib then trim mainsail.

wind

D Boat stops. Turn rudder the opposite way. Trim jib flat.

broad on the bow. Putting the helm over too soon will result in the boat gaining headway too soon, which might cause her to strike the dock before she can be turned away from it. After the boat has stopped drifting backwards, the helm is turned the opposite way because the boat will begin to move ahead as her sails fill. Notice in the diagram that the jib is *backed* or pulled in by its windward sheet so that it is trimmed from the wrong side. This will cause the bow to fall off, away from the wind, very rapidly. When the boat has gained headway and if she is clear of the dock, the windward jibsheet is released and the jib is trimmed on the boat's leeward side.

The same procedure is followed when a boat leaves a permanent mooring. The mooring line is simply cast off and left afloat. Getting underway when anchored involves the same basic principles. Sail is hoisted while the boat is head to wind, the anchor is hauled in until the line lies straight up and down, then the anchor is broken out and hauled aboard, the jib is backed to make the bow fall off in the desired direction, and then the sheets are trimmed in on their proper side as the boat gains headway.

There are a few times when it might be advisable to hoist sail downwind instead of when head to wind; for instance, when the boat is in a very constricted docking area or if a strong current has swung the boat's stern into the wind when anchored or moored. In these cases it is best to drift with the wind or current or sail away under jib alone until the boat is clear of docks and obstructions, then head as close to the wind as possible before hoisting the mainsail.

Leaving the windward side of a dock under sail usually presents a problem. The boat must be moved so that she is headed into the wind while sails are hoisted. She might be moved by

warping (moving her with lines) or kedging with the anchor, or by paddling if the boat is small and the wind is light. No matter how she is moved, her bow should be fairly near the wind. If she cannot be brought directly head to wind, great care should be taken to see that her boom does not strike anything on the dock and the sheets do not catch on dock *pilings* (posts) or cleats.

Figure 5-3 shows the proper approach when landing at a dock under sail. Notice that in all five situations the boat is turned into the wind and held there with sails flapping until headway is lost. This maneuver is called *shooting*, and it is also used when anchoring, picking up a mooring, or landing alongside another boat. Helm control is very important when shooting for a dock or mooring. If the wheel or tiller is turned suddenly and to its full extent, the boat's *way* or momentum is partially killed because a rudder rapidly jammed to one side acts somewhat like a brake. If it is desired to make a long shoot, the helm is eased over slowly, and the boat carries a lot of way or coasts a long distance before coming to a stop. A boat's weight or displacement will have a great bearing on how much way she carries also. A heavy boat, such as a Luders yawl, will carry way for a very long distance compared to a light boat, such as a 420 dinghy or Laser. The exact distance a given boat will shoot under any given conditions will vary greatly and can only be determined by experience.

A boat's momentum also depends on conditions of wind and water. In a strong wind and rough water, a boat will carry less way. The strength and direction of the current must be noted, because naturally this will have a great effect on the boat's speed (not through the water but over the bottom).

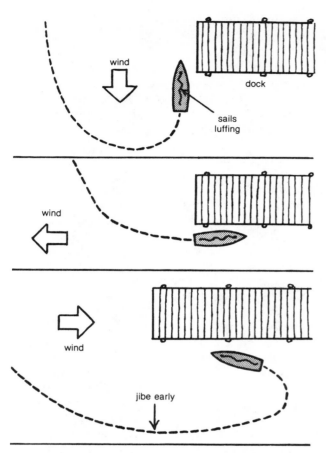

wind

dock

sails luffing

wind

wind

jibe early

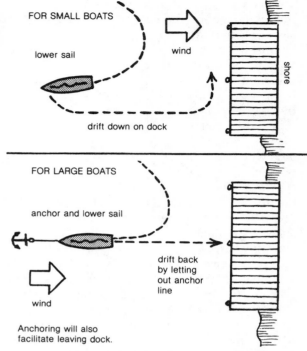

FOR SMALL BOATS

lower sail

wind

shore

drift down on dock

FOR LARGE BOATS

anchor and lower sail

drift back by letting out anchor line

wind

Anchoring will also facilitate leaving dock.

5-3. Approaching a dock under sail (in a weak current).

Since the latter part of a "shoot" will be at very slow speeds, any current will affect the maneuver out of all normal proportion. A boat with a favorable current under her seems to shoot forever. Many an otherwise well-planned maneuver has been spoiled because it was only when the boat slowed down in a shoot that a small but significant current announced its presence to a surprised skipper by taking over the situation. Even the best of sailors sometimes misjudge a boat's shooting speed and distance. When this happens, if the boat is carrying too much way, do not attempt to land at the dock or pick up the mooring, but bear off, sail away, and try the approach again. Notice in figure 5-3 that the shooting boats are never aimed directly at the dock, but they are landed almost parallel to the dock or in such a manner that they can easily be turned away from the dock at the last minute if they are carrying too much way. Occasionally it is necessary to make a direct, right-angle approach to the middle of the dock so that the landing must be made bow first. This can be very dangerous in a large, heavy boat, and it should be avoided if possible. If unavoidable, however, a very slow approach should be made. It is better to have the boat stop short than carry too much way. If she stops short without quite reaching the dock, a crewman stationed on the bow can often throw a line to someone standing on the dock. In a small, light boat a fast landing, with too much way, is not quite as serious, though it is certainly most unseamanlike. A crewman can sit on the foremost part of the bow facing forward with a leg on each side of the jibstay so that he can *fend* off (push off) with his feet just before the bow makes contact with the dock. Falling short and having to make another try is far preferable to risking damage to the boat and injury to the crew.

There is another basic method of slowing a boat down to land at a dock or pick up a mooring besides shooting into the wind. This is to slack the sheets while on some point of sailing between close-hauled and a beam reach. A close reach is the optimum heading. With sheets slacked and sails luffing on a close reach, no power is being applied to the boat, and she will lose headway. If more headway is desired during such a maneuver, the sheets need simply be trimmed back in. The amount they are trimmed back in will correspond to the amount of power applied to the boat. By alternately trimming in and slacking out the sheets to achieve the desired amount of luff, precise speed control can be attained, and the boat can be eased slowly up to a dock or mooring buoy.

The reason why a close reach is the optimum heading for this maneuver is that wind shifts can then be responded to merely by adjusting the trim of the sails, while maintaining the same heading. By contrast, if the boat were luffing along close-hauled, and the wind shifted more

ahead during the maneuver, the option of trimming in for more power would be lost, and the only way to gain headway would be to head off, which would take the boat away from the desired course to her dock or buoy. If, on the other hand, the boat were luffing along on a beam reach, and the wind shifted farther aft, then the option of continuing to luff the sails would be lost, and the only way to slow down would be to head up, again heading the boat away from her desired maneuvering course. Significant wind shifts are common in harbors, where this kind of maneuvering is likely to be done.

The following basic principles of sailboat maneuvering should always be kept in mind:

• For maximum *steerageway* or rudder control, keep way on the boat. Remember that the rudder is only effective when the boat is moving.

• Quick rudder action will slow a boat, but slow rudder movement will enable the boat to carry way for a long distance.

• Heading into the wind or releasing sheets so that the sails flap will stop headway.

• Sails should be hoisted or lowered when the boat is heading into the wind.

• When maneuvering a centerboard boat, see that the centerboard is all the way down, otherwise she will make leeway, especially at low speeds.

• When making a sharp turn, allow for some stern skid. During such a turn the bow turns in one direction and the stern skids somewhat the opposite way. This is important to bear in mind when landing alongside a dock or another boat. Stern skid is more apparent on flat-bottomed centerboarders.

• When headway is lost after unsuccessfully shooting for a dock or mooring, back the jib to make the bow fall off in the desired direction. If the boat has no jib, wait until she drifts backwards, and then reverse the rudder as explained in chapter 2 under "Elementary Steering."

• If the boat has too much way on when shooting for a mooring, she can be slowed by pushing her main boom forward so that it goes *aback* or fills from the wrong side.

• Maneuvering in constricted areas should be done under a *balanced* sail plan. This means that the boat should neither have too much sail forward nor too much aft, but a sail plan that will permit the easiest possible steering. Balance will be discussed in the next chapter.

• Remember that a boat tends to carry a lot of way when she is heavy and is moving fast against a light wind in smooth waters. On the other hand, a light boat moving slowly against a strong wind in rough waters carries very little way.

• Remember that even a small current is the biggest single factor affecting a boat's speed when getting underway or landing.

• The speed of a boat may be controlled precisely by putting her on a close reach and adjusting the sheets to luff the sails to produce the desired power.

Windward helmsmanship. The concern when sailing to windward is to sail the boat as close to the wind as possible but at her best possible speed on this point of sailing. If you sail her too close, her sails will begin to shake at the luffs, and you will feel her begin to slow down. On the other hand, if you bear off too far, the boat will pick up speed, but will not gain as much distance to windward as she could. Beating is always a delicate balancing of these two factors, *pointing* (heading as close as possible to the windward objective) and *footing* (sailing

through the water as fast as possible). When you sail too high so that you accentuate the gain to windward at a sacrifice of speed, you are said to *pinch*; when you sail too low, at a good speed but at a sacrifice to windward gain, you sail too *full*. Usually, under normal conditions, the best windward course lies somewhere between pinching and sailing too full. Making a boat do her best to windward is always an interesting challenge. Since the conditions of wind and sea that produce the challenge change continuously, the problem of getting to windward never loses its appeal. Even the most seasoned sailor must constantly solve it again.

Some winds are relatively steady, but most winds vary constantly in direction and velocity. A temporary increase in velocity over a limited area is known as a *puff*, and it appears as a dark patch of ripples darting across the water's surface. Most puffs allow a boat to point higher because they cause the apparent wind to blow from more off the beam. This is explained in figure 5-4. Some puffs are the radiating type, often called *catspaws*, which are also shown in the diagram. This type will force the helmsman to bear off when he first feels the puff, but then he is *let up* or allowed to point increasingly higher as he sails through the puff.

The wind nearly always fluctuates in direction as well as velocity. When the breeze blows from farther ahead (more from the bow) and forces the helmsman to bear off, this change in wind direction is called a *header*, but when it blows from farther aft (more on the beam) enabling the helmsman to point higher, it is called a *lift*. Fluctuations in direction can be detected immediately by watching the masthead wind indicator and particularly the telltales on the windward shrouds. When they swing more abeam the

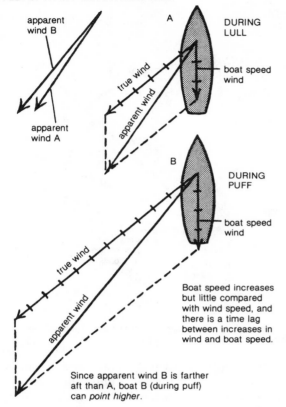

apparent
wind B

apparent
wind A

A

DURING
LULL

true wind

apparent wind

boat speed
wind

B

DURING
PUFF

true wind

apparent wind

boat speed
wind

Boat speed increases
but little compared
with wind speed, and
there is a time lag
between increases in
wind and boat speed.

Since apparent wind B is farther
aft than A, boat B (during puff)
can *point higher*.

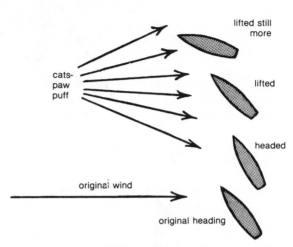

cats-
paw
puff

lifted still
more

lifted

headed

original wind

original heading

5-4. Wind puffs. A puff is a sudden increase in the wind's velocity, usually within a small area and of short duration.

helmsman should point up, but when they swing more ahead he must bear off. This is illustrated in figure 5-5.

The skilled, experienced helmsman uses all of his senses when sailing a boat to windward. In addition to watching the telltales, he watches the luffs of his sails. When they begin to flutter or luff in normal winds or sailing conditions, he is generally sailing too high and must bear off. The experienced helmsman also keeps a constant lookout for puffs on the water on his windward bow. When the water darkens with ripples from a puff, he is then ready to head up when the boat first feels its effect. He uses his sense of hearing when listening to the sound of the bow wave. A clearly audible bow wave indicates that the boat is moving at her best speed, while only a slight murmur of the wave suggests that perhaps the helmsman is pinching slightly or perhaps the sheets could be better trimmed for more speed. A good helmsman also uses his sense of balance as well as his vision to detect a change in the boat's angle of heel. When beating, a boat should heel to leeward at least slightly, but the heel should not be excessive. For the average boat, if the lee rail begins to *bury* (dip in the water), the boat is heeling too far. This can result in loss of speed and even a capsizing in a centerboard boat. Excessive heeling can be con-

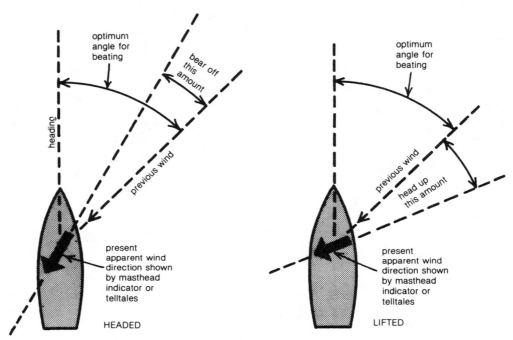

5-5. Use of wind indicators when beating. The optimum angle is the angle between apparent wind and the boat's most efficient heading when beating. The broad angle shown might be for a cruiser beating in choppy seas.

trolled in two ways, by heading up or pointing higher, or, as a last resort, by slacking the main sheet so that the mainsail begins to luff.

Another aid to helmsmanship is luff telltales. These are usually wool or acrylic yarns taped to the jib on both sides or threaded through the sail about ten inches abaft the luff at about a third of the luff's length up from the tack. The sail cloth is normally transparent enough to see the yarn on the leeward side as well as the windward side of the sail. One should try to sail so that the yarns are streaming directly aft rather than fluttering wildly or twirling around. If the windward yarn twirls, bear off, but if the leeward yarn twirls, head up a bit.

Perhaps the most important sense a skilled helmsman uses is the sense of feel or touch, often called the *tiller touch*—though, of course, it applies to steering with a wheel also. This is sailing "by the seat of the pants" or sensing when the boat is going to windward at maximum efficiency. Of course, this ability can be acquired only after a good deal of practice. The average, properly balanced boat will have a slight *weather helm* or tendency to turn into the wind in moderate breezes (this will be discussed in the next chapter). The weather helm will exert a light pull or pressure against the helmsman's hand. This pressure will increase as the wind freshens and heels the boat, or it will decrease when the wind slackens and causes a smaller angle of heel. In the former case, the helmsman should relax his pressure on the helm and let the boat point up until he senses that she is beginning to lose speed or until he sees her sails start to luff. When the helm pressure slackens, however, he should bear off slightly to see if the boat will pick up a little speed.

Watch luff yarns.

Watch sag of jibstay.

Watch and listen for shaking sails at luffs.

Watch telltales.

Watch and feel angle of heel.

Feel puffs on face.

Watch for puffs on water.

Listen for more or less sound from bow wave.

Feel balance of helm (weather or lee helm). In light airs use only two fingers on tiller of small boat.

5-6. Aids to helmsmanship through the senses.

Good helmsmanship to windward is really a matter of experimentation. The helmsman should alternately point up or prod the wind to see if she won't sail just a little higher without slowing down, and then, as soon as she shows signs of slowing down, bear off a little to see if she won't sail a little faster.

Figure 5-6 illustrates how the helmsman uses all his senses when beating to windward. Notice that the illustration shows a useful visual sign which has not been discussed, the sagging of the jibstay. Ordinarily the jibstay should be set up tight for best efficiency to windward, but it will always sag off to leeward slightly. When the boat is sailing full and by, the sag will be most pronounced, but when she is being pinched the stay will be almost straight. Thus, if there is considerable sag the helmsman should point up somewhat, but with little or no sag he should fall off a little. This aid to the helmsman should not be relied on in rough water because as the boat *pitches* (rocks fore and aft), the mast will move forward and aft somewhat, causing the jibstay to slacken and tighten accordingly.

When sailing into a *chop* (a short, steep sea) the helmsman should sail his boat full and by, because wave action tends to kill headway. The boat must be given enough power to drive through the waves. Also, in very light airs the boat should not be sailed extremely close to the wind. She should be kept footing to minimize leeway and to take advantage of a stronger apparent wind. In a moderate breeze, however, most boats can be sailed *fine,* or quite close to the wind. Rudder action in light airs should be slow and gentle, but in moderate breezes the helm of a small boat can be turned quite rapidly to respond to lifts and headers. With large, heavy boats a slower action must be used. Remember that excessive rudder angles have a braking effect.

In a strong or puffy breeze, the helmsman should be ready to release his mainsheet at a moment's notice. In a small, capsizable centerboarder, the mainsheet should be held in hand. If its pull is too great, a turn may be taken around a cleat as shown in figure 5-7. On larger boats jam cleats may be used (see figure 5-7). It is perfectly permissible to cleat the mainsheet on a large keel boat which will not capsize, but, as you will recall from chapter 2, it is a dangerous practice to hitch the mainsheet on a cleat, unless a slippery hitch is used. As previously mentioned, wind may be spilled from the sails by luffing up, and naturally this method of righting an excessively heeled boat should be used before the mainsheet is released so that distance can be gained to windward. Sheets should be slacked only as a last resort. Keeping a boat *on her feet* (as upright as possible) by luffing up sharply in the puffs is known as *feathering*. By using this technique, a skillful small-boat sailor can gain a much greater distance to windward than can a sailor who merely slacks his sheets to keep upright.

To summarize, here is a list of tips for the windward helmsman:

• Watch the water for puffs. Head up in them. In the radiating type, bear off when first entering the puff then head up.

• Watch the telltales for wind direction changes. Head up when they swing farther abeam, and bear off when they swing farther ahead.

• Watch the luffs of sails. When they begin to flap, the boat is usually being pinched. There are two exceptions to this. In a heavy breeze, the mainsail can be trimmed less flat than usual so

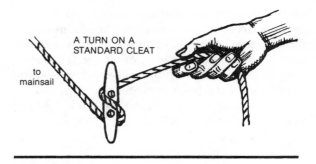

A TURN ON A STANDARD CLEAT

to mainsail

JAM CLEATS

narrow space under cleat

to mainsail

pull up to release

to mainsail

swivel block

only one turn on cleat is needed

cam action jam

5-7. **Cleating the mainsheet.**

that it carries a slight luff to prevent excessive heeling. Secondly, when carrying a large, overlapping jib, a certain amount of backwind can be expected, and this can cause the mainsail to luff slightly.

• Use your senses of hearing and balance, and use visual signs, such as jibstay sag, as aids to good helmsmanship.

• Develop a tiller touch by sensing when the boat is traveling her best through the feel of varying pressures on the helm.

• Constantly experiment to see if you can't sail your boat higher without reducing her speed.

• Be conscious of rudder action. Large boats

should be turned more slowly than small ones. In light airs turn the boat slowly, with a gentle touch. In moderate to heavy breezes, a quicker action should be used in responding to headers and lifts. In heavy breezes, feather up sharply to prevent heeling. Slacken sheets only as a last resort.

• Sail full and by in rough seas and light airs, but point high in smooth waters and moderate winds.

Tacking. The rudiments of tacking and the problem of when to tack to fetch a windward mark were discussed in chapter 3. Now we will deal with the specific procedures and helmsmanship involved in coming about.

Figure 5-8 shows a typical small centerboard sloop being tacked. Most Naval Academy boats do not have the kind of backstays illustrated. Those shown are called *running backstays* or *run-*

ners, and every time a boat is tacked the stays must be changed, with the windward one being set up *taut* (tight) and the leeward one being slacked off. Obviously, if the boat is not equipped with these stays, tacking her is a much simpler procedure. Navy yawls carry running backstays and set them up at certain times, and this will be discussed in chapter 8.

In any kind of boat that carries a crew, certain tacking commands should be given by the helmsman so that the crew can know what to expect and when to carry out their duties. The first command should be "Stand by to come about." This is especially important in a large boat, because it alerts the crew and gives them time to get to their proper stations. Details on tacking a large boat will be given in chapter 8. The next command is "Ready about," and this is promptly followed by "Hard a-lee," or "Helm's a-lee." The latter expressions are said when the

5-8. Tacking procedure.

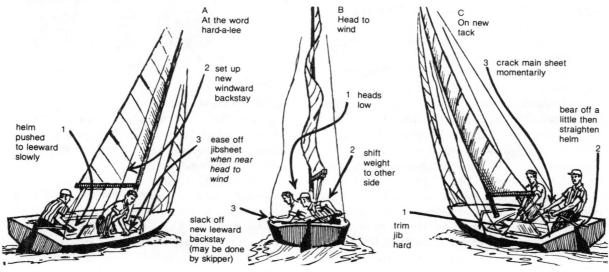

A
At the word
hard-a-lee

helm pushed to leeward slowly　1

2 set up new windward backstay

3 ease off jibsheet *when near head to wind*

3 slack off new leeward backstay (may be done by skipper)

B
Head to wind

1 heads low

2 shift weight to other side

C
On new tack

3 crack main sheet momentarily

bear off a little then straighten helm

2

1 trim jib hard

helm is actually moved. The tiller is pushed to leeward or a-lee (a wheel, of course, is turned to windward), and this naturally turns the bow into the wind. When the boat is head to wind, all crew members should keep their heads low and watch out for booms or flogging *fittings* (boat hardware) that could hit someone. Crew weight is usually shifted to the new windward side unless there is very light air. Notice that in Step 3 of figure 5-8A, the leeward jibsheet is not released until the boat is almost head to wind. It is a very common mistake to release the jibsheet too soon. This results in loss of boat speed and less distance gained to windward when making the turn.

After the boat turns through the eye of the wind, the jib should be trimmed in immediately for two reasons. First, it is easier to trim before it completely fills with wind, and secondly, the trimmed jib will help pull the bow around onto the new tack. After the tack has been completed, the boat will have lost some way, therefore the helmsman should bear off to slightly below his normal windward course in order to get her moving again. It often helps to *crack* or slightly slack the mainsheet until speed is regained. As the boat picks up speed, the helmsman can begin to head up and trim in the mainsail.

Immediately prior to tacking, the helmsman should see that his boat is moving at her best close-hauled speed, for if the boat is tacked without sufficient way, she is liable to get *in stays* or *in irons*. This means that so much way is lost when the boat is head to wind that she is unable to complete the tack. In such a predicament, the boat drifts helplessly backwards with her sails flapping. Figure 5-9 shows how to recover after being in stays. If the boat has a jib, the jib may be backed, and this usually is suffi-

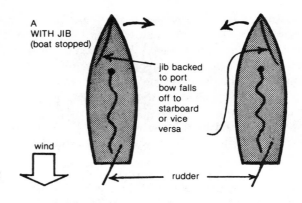

A
WITH JIB
(boat stopped)

jib backed
to port
bow falls
off to
starboard
or vice
versa

wind

rudder

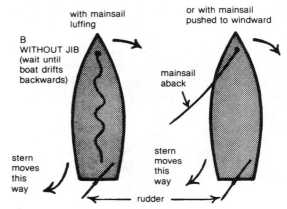

with mainsail
luffing

or with mainsail
pushed to windward

B
WITHOUT JIB
(wait until
boat drifts
backwards)

mainsail
aback

stern
moves
this
way

stern
moves
this
way

rudder

5-9. In stays.

cient to cause the bow to be blown off, away from the wind. In a cat-rigged boat, however, the helmsman must wait until the boat gains sufficient stern way so that the rudder may be used. The mainsail may be pushed to windward as shown in the illustration to accelerate the backward speed. Of course, the stern will follow the direction of the rudder when moving backward.

Proper rudder action is important to avoid getting in stays. If the rudder is jammed hard over, it will act as a brake and kill headway. On the other hand, if the rudder is turned too slowly, the boat may not have enough momentum to carry her through the resulting long, slow turn. As said before, have ample way on your boat before bringing her about. When tacking in a rough sea, wait for a relatively smooth spot before tacking, and be sure to trim the jib flat after passing through the eye of the wind.

Downwind helmsmanship. Getting the best performance from a boat that is broad reaching or running requires nearly as much skillful helmsmanship as getting the best windward performance. It might be said that sailing downwind requires rudder action which is almost directly opposite to that used when sailing to windward. The windward helmsman bears off in the lulls and heads up in the puffs, but the downwind helmsman bears off in the puffs and heads up in the lulls. This is illustrated in figure 5-10 which shows how a boat is properly worked to leeward. The boat in the diagram will surely reach the leeward mark before a boat which merely follows a straight course. The reason for this is that reaching is a faster point of sailing than running; thus, during a lull, the helmsman heads up from a running course to a broad reaching course in order to keep his boat moving despite the decrease in wind. During the puffs, he bears off to almost a dead run because he has sufficient power from the puff to retain his speed. Also, his boat will be less subject to speed-retarding heeling forces when the wind is from nearly dead astern. Furthermore, by heading far off during the puffs, the helmsman sails slightly below his course for the leeward destination and so compensates for the high heading he sailed during the previous lull.

Working to leeward is a constant weaving back and forth during the puffs and lulls to maintain boat speed. This principle applies when sailing slightly below a beam-reaching course, because as you approach a beam reach, the boat speed increases. In moderate to heavy winds when sailing higher than a beam reach, speed begins to decrease. In light airs, the best speed often occurs near the close-reaching point of sailing. Thus, it should be kept in mind that when sailing lower than a beam reach in moder-

5-10. Working to leeward.

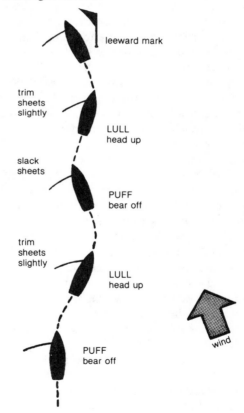

ate to heavy breezes or lower than a close reach in light airs, *the helmsman bears off in the puffs and heads up in the lulls.*

Sailing for longer than very brief periods with the wind from dead astern should be avoided if possible. As previously said, a dead run is a slow point of sailing; when the wind is dead astern, the after sails will have a blanketing effect on the forward sails causing a definite reduction in boat speed. To avoid this predicament, use the procedure called *tacking downwind.* It is illustrated in figure 5-11. Instead of running directly for the leeward mark, the boat shown in the illustration broad reaches towards the mark on one tack and then jibes over and broad reaches toward the mark on the other tack. Quite often the extra distance sailed to reach the mark is more than compensated for by the additional speed gained in broad reaching. It is easy to overdo this strategy, however, and to sail too high so that the extra speed does not make up for the extra distance sailed. Generally, a safe rule to follow is to sail as far off as possible and still keep the forward sails *drawing* or filled with wind. In puffy weather, of course, this strategy should be used with the previously mentioned "working to leeward" technique. Quite often, when tacking downwind, the boat can be headed (with her forward sails drawing well) closer to her desired course on one tack than on the other. In such a case, the helmsman should first take the tack which allows him to head closer to his destination. This will be discussed further in chapter 10, "Basic Racing."

Aside from the consideration of boat speed, there is another reason to avoid running with the wind flat aft or from dead astern. Since the wind is usually shifty or oscillating slightly in direction, a boat sailing dead before the wind is

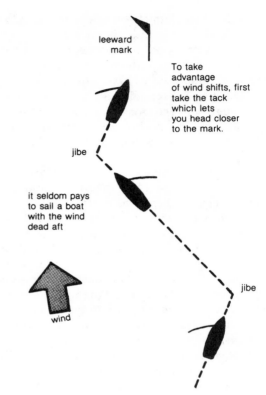

leeward mark

To take advantage of wind shifts, first take the tack which lets you head closer to the mark.

jibe

it seldom pays to sail a boat with the wind dead aft

wind

jibe

5-11. Tacking downwind.

subject to a shift from the "wrong side," or a shift which blows from the leeward side instead of the windward side. When this happens the boat is said to be *running by the lee.* To put it another way, when a boat, sailing with the wind dead aft, turns to leeward as though to jibe but does not jibe, she is sailing by the lee. Of course, she can only turn to leeward so far before she is forced to jibe, but from a dead run to the point where her sails go aback and force her to jibe, she is by the lee. This is a dangerous point of sailing, because there is always the possibility she might have an accidental or unintentional jibe. More will be said about this in the next section when we discuss the technique of jibing.

Jibing. It is very important to understand the principles involved in jibing, because if improperly executed, a jibe can be a somewhat dangerous maneuver. A heavy boom swinging suddenly and unexpectedly across the boat can strike a crew member, cause damage to the rigging, or cause a centerboard boat to capsize. A properly executed jibe, however, is a completely safe maneuver. It should be respected but never feared.

As previously stated, a jibe is a downwind turn from one tack to the other. When the sails cross from one side of the boat to the other, they do not flap as when tacking, but they fill from the lee side and swing over rapidly.

When it is blowing so hard that a jibe would be dangerous, an alternative method of getting the boat on the other tack is to bring her up close-hauled, tack, and then head off to the desired course.

Figure 5-12 shows the proper procedure for jibing a small sloop. As with tacking, certain commands should be given prior to jibing in order to alert the crew. The helmsman first calls out, "Stand by to jibe." At this warning, the crew get to their proper stations and prepare to duck their heads to avoid being struck by the boom. The helmsman then calls out, "Helm's to weather," as he begins to steer off dead before the wind. The sheets may have to be slacked to effect this maneuver, especially if the wind is blowing hard and the boat is reaching. Once dead before the wind, the helmsman shouts, "Centerline the main," and he or a crew member begins to haul the mainsail in by its sheet. It is important that the sheet is pulled in as far as it will come before the boat is turned onto the new tack. A crew member changes the jibsheets, casting off the cleated sheet and cleating the windward sheet which will be on the leeward side after the jibe has been completed. If the wind has much strength, avoid having both jibsheets cast off simultaneously, even for an instant, or the jib may blow out ahead and its flogging may quickly snarl the sheets. If the boat has running backstays, these must be changed so that the leeward stay on the new tack will be slack.

When the helmsman is ready to turn onto the new tack, he calls out, "Jibe-ho." This warns the crew that he is jibing at that moment. The crew duck their heads and shift their weight to the new windward side if the boat is a small one, while the helmsman steers slowly off to leeward until the main boom swings over. At this point the helmsman should straighten up his helm or steer almost dead before the wind until the mainsail is slacked off rapidly to where it should be for running. It is a common mistake, when it is blowing, to round up into the wind too quickly after jibing. This has led to the capsizing of many centerboarders. In a fresh breeze the mainsail must be slacked all the way off before rounding up. Unless this is done, the boat is exposing her beam to the wind with flattened sails which will cause extreme heeling, and furthermore she is heeled by the centrifugal force of her turn towards the wind. Immediately after jibing, most boats will have a natural tendency to turn into the wind. The helmsman must counteract this tendency by straightening his helm or even reversing it momentarily in order to hold his boat before the wind until the sheets are slacked.

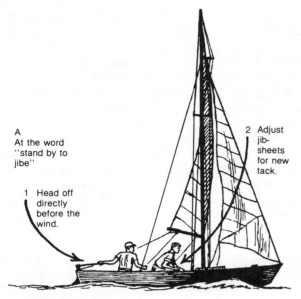

A
At the word "stand by to jibe"

1 Head off directly before the wind.

2 Adjust jibsheets for new tack.

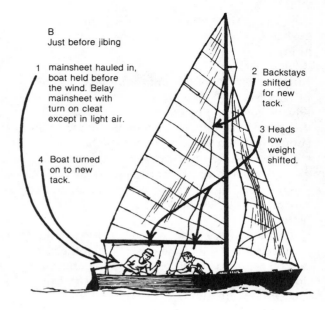

B
Just before jibing

1 mainsheet hauled in, boat held before the wind. Belay mainsheet with turn on cleat except in light air.

4 Boat turned on to new tack.

2 Backstays shifted for new tack.

3 Heads low weight shifted.

5-12. Jibing procedure.

When jibing in a fresh breeze, the mainsheet should have a turn around its cleat as illustrated in figure 5-7, because otherwise, the force of the boom crossing over the boat might cause the sheet to run through the hands of the one who is tending it. *Shortening sheet,* or pulling it all the way in, is particularly important when jibing in a strong wind. If the mainsheet is not shortened prior to jibing, the boom can swing up high in the air and result in what is called a *goosewing jibe.* This is illustrated in figure 5-13. Notice in the illustration that the lower half of the sail has jibed over while the upper half has not. The proper way to recover from this predicament is to jibe back onto the original tack. A goosewing jibe can always be avoided if the sheet is properly shortened or some other means, such as a *boom vang,* is used to hold the boom down when

jibing. The boom vang is a tackle or line attached to the boom for the specific purpose of holding it down. The boom vang will be dealt with further in the next chapter when we discuss sails and sail trim.

As previously said, an improperly executed jibe can result in a mishap. The most common mistakes which cause poorly executed jibes and the means of avoiding these mistakes are listed below:

• *The accidental or unexpected jibe.* This can result in personal injury or damage to the rigging from the boom flying across the boat.

To avoid accidental jibes, *do not sail excessively by the lee.* When sailing nearly dead before the wind, *watch the telltales* or masthead indicator for a wind shift which puts you by the lee. Also *watch the luff of the mainsail* for the first sign of

70

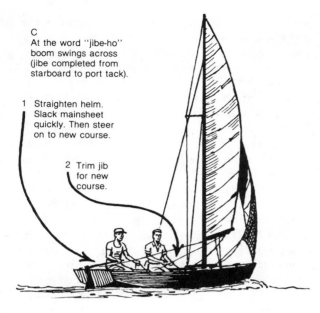

C
At the word "jibe-ho" boom swings across (jibe completed from starboard to port tack).

1 Straighten helm. Slack mainsheet quickly. Then steer on to new course.

2 Trim jib for new course.

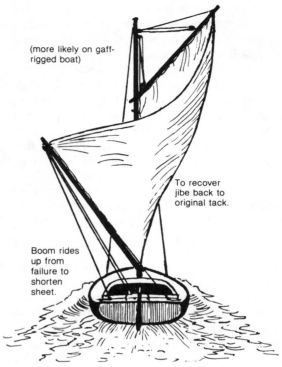

(more likely on gaff-rigged boat)

To recover jibe back to original tack.

Boom rides up from failure to shorten sheet.

5-13. Goosewing jibe. If rolling severely while running, a boat with low freeboard and a long boom might need her boom's end slightly lifted with the topping lift to prevent dipping the boom in the water. This may increase the tendency to goosewing.

its beginning to fill from the leeward side, and especially *watch the jib* because it will nearly always jibe before the mainsail. When the jib swings over, head up so that the wind comes more from the windward quarter. When running before a following sea which tends to make the boat *yaw* (turn from side to side) rig a jibing *preventer*. This is merely a line or lashing to hold the boom forward for the purpose of preventing an accidental jibe.

• *The goosewing jibe.* This can result in damage to the sail and rigging.

To avoid the goosewing jibe, shorten sheet. Be sure the mainsheet is pulled all the way in before the boom swings across. *Use the boom vang,* if your boat has one that fastens at or near the base of the mast (see figure 6-6). Set it up tight to prevent the boom from lifting. To recover

from a goosewing, jibe back to the original tack.

• *The broaching jibe.* When a running boat suddenly makes an involuntary turn towards the wind so that she lies beam to the wind, she is said to *broach to.* This turn can be caused by a yaw-producing sea rolling under her quarter while the bow is simultaneously buried in another sea. Most boats are particularly susceptible to broaching to immediately after jibing when they develop the aforementioned strong ten-

71

dency to turn into the wind. The dangers of a rapid turn towards the wind after jibing are that the boat will heel excessively due to the centrifugal force of the turn and the fact that the boat lies beam to the wind and waves, her most vulnerable position to heeling forces. Excessive heeling can cause the shipping of water, a capsizing, or the breaking of the main boom if it *trips* (if its end dips into the water).

To avoid broaching to, *reduce sail* when the seas are steep and the wind is heavy. Take in the aftermost sails first. *Move the crew aft.* Their weight will keep the stern down and keep the rudder submerged for better helm control. If the boat is a centerboarder, she will be running with the board nearly all the way up when the waves are not steep, because in this position, the board offers little resistance and allows the fastest hull speed. However, in rough water or when the boat develops a tendency to yaw or broach to, *lower the centerboard* slightly. This will help prevent broaching to. *Immediately after jibing, reverse the helm momentarily* in order to counteract the strong tendency most boats have to turn into the wind. *Slack off the mainsheet quickly after jibing. Be sure the mainsheet is clear* and does not foul. Keep the wind aft until the mainsheet is slacked. *Prevent heeling to leeward* by slacking the mainsail and moving the crew weight to windward. Heeling increases the tendency to turn into the wind. *Trim the jib in flat* when the boat shows a tendency to broach to. Flattening the jib will help hold the bow off before the wind.

Jibing in light airs usually presents no problems. Quite often the sheet tender can gather the mainsheet into a bunch and use a direct pull on the boom when he pulls it across the boat, rather than pulling on only a single line of the mainsheet tackle. In bunching the sheet, he obviously sacrifices power for speed, but this is perfectly permissible in light airs provided care is taken to see that the sheet does not foul. This same technique can be used in small dinghies in much heavier air if the boom vang is taut to hold the boom down.

6. Sails and Rigging

Classification of modern sails. Yacht sails are traditionally grouped into three general classifications: *working sails, storm sails*, and *light sails*. The first group includes mainsails, mizzens, and moderate-sized jibs or forestaysails of moderate weight cloth, which are carried most of the time for everyday, shorthanded sailing. The working sail most commonly mentioned is the *working jib*. Normally, this is a medium-sized jib that slightly overlaps the mast and is sometimes called a *lapper*, or else it is a nonoverlapping jib attached to a boom. Storm sails are small, heavy sails used in heavy weather. These include the *storm trysail*, a small triangular sail, usually not attached to the boom, which is set in place of the mainsail, and the *spitfire*, or small, heavy, storm jib. Light sails are large sails intended for light to medium winds when maximum speed is desired, and they are usually made of lighter weight cloth than that used for working sails. The most common light sails are *Genoa jibs, spinnakers, reaching jibs, drifters, spinnaker staysails*, and *mizzen staysails*, or *mizzen spinnakers*, which are actually balloon-like mizzen staysails. All but the last of these sails are illustrated in figure 6-1.

The well-known Swedish yachtsman, Sven Salén, is given credit for inventing the Genoa jib. It was first shown to the sailing world at a regatta in Genoa, hence its name. The Genoa, or *Jenny*, has a long foot which overlaps the mainsail. It is an effective sail for reaching and beating to windward because of its great area and the strong venturi it creates due to its overlap. It comes in various sizes and weights and is carried when racing in all breezes, except perhaps in the very lightest airs or in very strong winds.

The spinnaker is a balloon-like, triangular sail carried when the true wind is abaft the beam. Made from very light cloth, it is an essential sail for racing. The spinnaker can be tricky to handle, trim, and steer by; therefore, chapter 9 will be devoted entirely to it.

The drifter or *ghoster* is a lightweight jib for reaching in very light airs. It is cut high at the clew so that it will fill easily in the lightest airs and so that it can be sheeted to the main boom

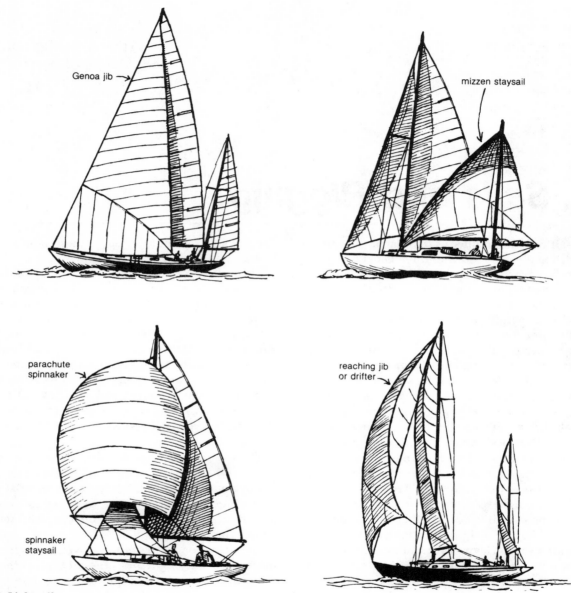

6-1. Light sails.

as shown in the illustration. The high clew also helps prevent excessive twist, a distortion of shape that will be discussed later in this chapter. The drifter is often cut fuller or with a deeper belly than a Genoa, and the drifter's leech or after edge is nearly straight, having little concave curvature as does a Genoa's leech.

The spinnaker staysail is a balloon-like fore-staysail of lightweight cloth which is set beneath the spinnaker as illustrated. In a good breeze, a well-designed spinnaker will rise or lift so that its foot or bottom edge is high above the deck. The spinnaker staysail, sometimes called the *cheater*, simply fills in the gap under the lifted spinnaker. In addition, there are tall, thin spinnaker staysails and Genoa jib-shaped staysails for specific points of sailing. These sails will be discussed at the end of this chapter and at the end of chapter 9.

The mizzen staysail is, of course, carried only by boats having mizzens—yawls or ketches. It is set forward of the mizzen and is sheeted to the mizzen boom. This sail will be discussed in chapter 8. The mizzen spinnaker is set identically, but its shape is that of a spinnaker.

Sail materials. Nearly all of today's sails are made from synthetic cloth. In almost all respects the synthetics are superior to cotton, the most commonly used natural fiber cloth for sails. Presently, the most suitable synthetic for most sails is Dacron (known as Terylene in England). This cloth is highly resistant to rot, mildew, and stretch. In addition, it is smooth, relatively non-porous, and it needs little, if any, breaking in, as is necessary with new sails made of cotton. A new cotton sail must be handled gently. At first, it must be used in light breezes only, and it must never be stretched extremely tight on its

mast or boom until it has been used for a considerable length of time. A new Dacron sail, however, can be stretched reasonably tight and can be carried in all but the strongest winds. It should set properly, have the correct shape, and almost fit its spars the first time it is used. In time, its luff and foot may grow slightly longer from being constantly stretched tight, but the lengthening will be very slight compared to that of a cotton sail.

The other most commonly used synthetic sail cloth is nylon. This has most of the major advantages of Dacron, except one. Nylon is not resistant to stretch. In fact, it is highly elastic, a characteristic which is very bad for all sails except certain downwind sails, such as the drifter and spinnaker. The big advantage in using nylon for these sails is that it is very strong and can be very light in weight, as light as one-half ounce per yard. Elasticity of sail cloth is detrimental to any sail that is carried to windward, especially in strong winds, because the sail stretches out of shape and loses its proper curvature. For balloon-like, downwind sails, however, this loss of shape is not really harmful, and the advantage of using lightweight cloth in light airs is more important.

Cut and draft of sails. Two typical modern sails, a jib and a mainsail, are shown in figure 6-2, along with their terminology and details of their fittings. The mainsail is *crosscut*, with its *cloths* (the narrow panels of material) running at right angles to the leech of the sail. This minimizes *bias stretch* (stretch which is diagonal to the direction of cloth weave) at the leech where it is particularly harmful. The jib shown in the illustration is *miter-cut* with the cloths at right angles to the leech and the foot, meeting at a diagonal

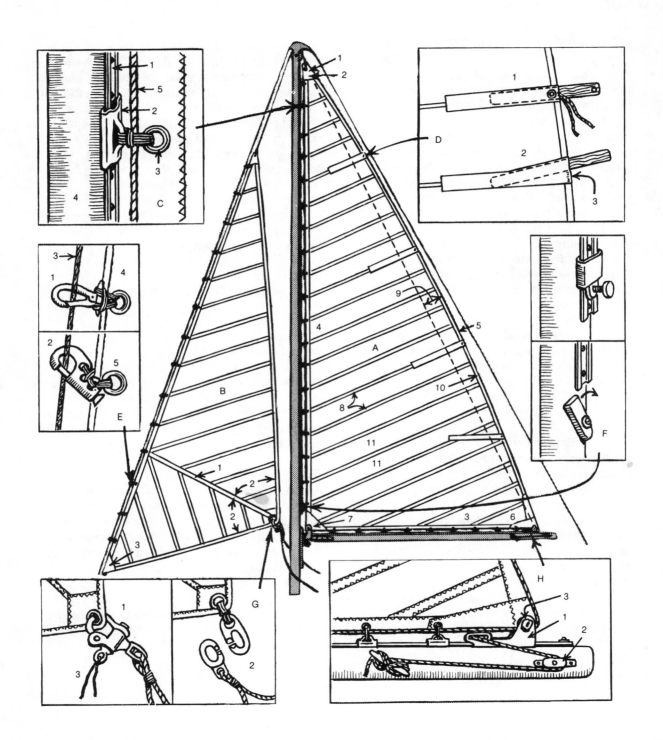

6-2. Working sails and related fittings.

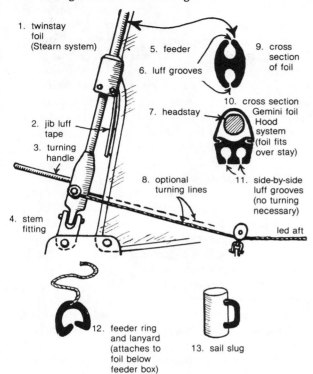

1. twinstay foil (Stearn system)
2. jib luff tape
3. turning handle
4. stem fitting
5. feeder
6. luff grooves
7. headstay
8. optional turning lines
9. cross section of foil
10. cross section Gemini foil Hood system (foil fits over stay)
11. side-by-side luff grooves (no turning necessary)

led aft

12. feeder ring and lanyard (attaches to foil below feeder box)
13. sail slug

A Marconi Cross-cut Mainsail
(1) head (2) headboard
(3) foot (4) luff (5) leech
(6) clew (7) tack (8) seams
(9) roach (10) tabling
(11) cloths

B Miter-cut Jib
(1) miter seam
(2) angle between foot and miter seam is equal to angle between leech and miter seam
(3) corner patch

C Sail Slide or Car
(1) track (2) slide (3) grommet
Small shackle may be used to secure slide to grommet.
(4) mast (5) bolt rope

D Battens and Batten Pockets
(1) conventional type with lanyards
(2) offset pocket sewn closed at (3)

E Jib Hanks (two types)
(1) snap hook (2) piston hank
(3) headstay or jibstay
(4) jib (5) grommet

F Slide Stops (two types)

to keep slides or cars from sliding off track when you wish to lower mainsail but not remove it from mast

G Jib Clew Shackles (two types)
(1) snap shackle
(2) Brummel or Inglefield hooks (hooks interlock when placed at right angles to each other)
(3) lashing cord (spring-loaded pin on snap shackle should be lashed in because it can open when jib flaps violently)

H Outhaul Fitting
(1) outhaul slide
(2) cheek block (3) clew pin

I Headfoils (grooved to accept jib's luff rope or occasionally sail slugs) used on some modern racer cruisers in order that sail can be changed without lowering the jib that is flying before its replacement is hoisted.

seam, called the *miter seam*, which bisects the angle at the *clew* (the sail's after corner).

Modern crosscut mainsails almost always have a *roach* or convex curve to the leech which adds to the sail's area. This requires that the leech be fitted with *battens* (strips of wood or plastic shown in figure 6-2) which hold out the leech, preventing it from curling inward. These battens fit into cloth pockets sewn to the leech. Two methods of securing battens in their pockets are shown in the illustration. There is another variation of the offset pocket which has the opening at the side of the pocket instead of above the pocket on the leech.

As previously mentioned, sails must be made with a luff-to-leech curvature called draft, or camber, in order that they function as efficient airfoils. Correct draft is perhaps the prime requirement of a high-performance sail. Draft is built into a sail by either or both of two principal methods. The usual method is to give the foot and luff a slightly convex round. When these edges are stretched along a straight mast, stay, or boom, curvature is thrown into the material abaft the luff and above the foot. The second method of building draft into a sail is to taper slightly the cloths of a crosscut sail at the luff and the leech. In other words, every cloth panel will be narrower at each end than it is near the middle. It seems that this latter method is being used more and more as improvements are made in the *stability* (resistance to loss of shape) of the newer sailcloths.

Figure 6-3 shows the draft curves of some typical sails. Good and bad cambers are shown for comparison. In general, a correct draft curve should have its points of maximum draft anywhere from one-third of the distance from the luff to the leech to almost halfway from luff to leech. The latter draft will work better in light airs and when sailing downwind. For upwind sailing, a draft curve should be flat in its after section. From the middle of the sail to the leech, the curve should gradually flatten until it is almost a straight line at the leech. For downwind sailing, the leech area should have a little more curvature. If a sail having excessive draft in the leech is trimmed in for beating, however, the lee-side suction pull in the after part of the sail will tend to pull the boat backwards because this suction force acts approximately at right angles to the surface of the sail.

The efficient upwind sail should not have excessive draft nor should the draft be too far forward, because when the boat is sailing close hauled, the wind will blow against the leeward side of the draft curve and cause the sail to luff prematurely. This is especially true for a mainsail, particularly if the jib overlaps the mainsail. A jib tends to deflect the leeward airflow towards the lee side of the mainsail. Draft curves should be considerable for light airs or in a rough sea, but less for a strong breeze that is not accompanied by a steep chop. In other words, it is usually desirable to have a flat sail for a breeze and a full sail for light airs or rough water. Unless a boat is equipped with two *suits* (sets) of working sails, one for light weather and another for heavy weather, her sails should be made for average conditions and with consideration for all points of sailing. For this kind of sail, draft should be average, with the maximum amount of draft (the distance, measured at right angles from a straight line running between luff and leech, to the deepest part of the curve) being about one-eighth of the sail's width (from luff to leech) at a height of slightly lower than halfway up the mast. This maximum draft's fore-and-aft location should lie forward of the halfway point between luff and leech but no farther forward than a third of the luff-to-leech distance abaft the luff (see A in figure 6-3).

Although draft is built into a sail, the curvature may be altered slightly by making certain adjustments. Of course, with only one suit of working sails for average conditions, the slight alterations in draft can be tremendously helpful in adapting the sail to varying wind conditions and different points of sailing. The principal draft-altering adjustments are: stretching or loosening the luff or foot of a sail, bending the mast, changing the angle of trim with the sheet, and the use of the boom vang. There are one or two special draft-changing devices, such as zippered or laced foot pockets which may be opened to increase draft or closed to decrease draft. When beating in a fresh breeze, a zipper may be difficult to close, so this should be done just before starting on the windward leg. Foot lacings usually are used in conjunction with a *Cunningham cringle* (small hole just above the tack), which is pulled down and lashed to the tack when it is desirable to flatten the draft and move it forward to the greatest possible extent.

The simplest and most often neglected draft alterations are the luff and foot adjustments. The foot is adjusted by tightening or slacking the *outhaul*, the line or device which pulls the clew out on the boom (see figure 6-3). Tightening the

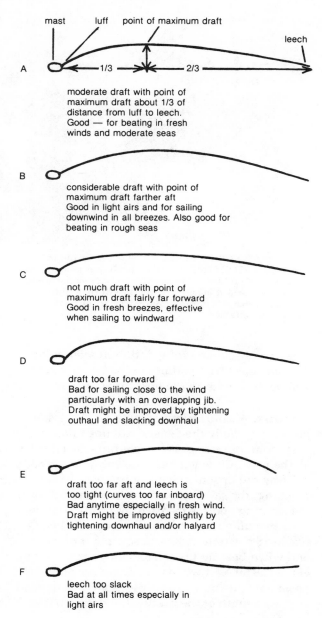

A **moderate draft with point of maximum draft about 1/3 of distance from luff to leech.** Good — for beating in fresh winds and moderate seas

B **considerable draft with point of maximum draft farther aft** Good in light airs and for sailing downwind in all breezes. Also good for beating in rough seas

C **not much draft with point of maximum draft fairly far forward** Good in fresh breezes, effective when sailing to windward

D **draft too far forward** Bad for sailing close to the wind particularly with an overlapping jib. Draft might be improved by tightening outhaul and slacking downhaul

E **draft too far aft and leech is too tight (curves too far inboard)** Bad anytime especially in fresh wind. Draft might be improved slightly by tightening downhaul and/or halyard

F **leech too slack** Bad at all times especially in light airs

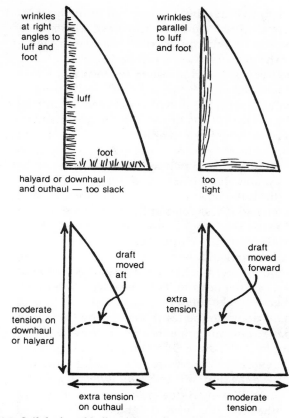

6-3. Sail draft and luff and foot adjustments.

outhaul stretches the sail's foot and in general flattens the sail, especially just above the foot. The outhaul is usually tightened in a breeze and when sailing to windward, but slacked in light airs and when sailing downwind.

The luff is adjusted by either the halyard or the *downhaul,* a line or tackle attached to the forward end of the boom which can pull it down. Of course this requires a sliding gooseneck (a gooseneck fitting which slides on a track) in order that the fore end of the boom can move up and down on the mast. The *tack* or forward corner of the sail is attached to the top of the gooseneck; so naturally when the gooseneck is pulled down, the tack will move down and stretch the sail's luff. Tightening the halyard with the downhaul cleated accomplishes the same thing as tightening the downhaul, except that the halyard adjustment has more effect on the upper part of the sail. A racing boat often has a black band painted around the top of her mast and also a black band near her gooseneck to limit the hoist and the amount the luff can be stretched. Class rules or handicap rules forbid that the *head* (top) of the sail be hoisted above the bottom of the upper black band and that the tack be pulled lower than the top of the lower band. Therefore, in such a case, it is customary to hoist the head to its highest legal limit and then to make luff adjustments with the downhaul down to the limit allowed by the lower band. Luff adjustments alter the fore-and-aft position of the draft. Stretching the luff tight will move the draft forward, and slacking the luff moves the draft aft. In heavy winds the draft is usually blown aft due to the stretch of the sail cloth; thus, it is wise to tighten the luff. In light airs, however, the luff should be quite slack especially when sailing downwind. It is a common mistake to overtighten the luff of a Dacron sail when the wind is light. In most breezes except heavy winds, the luff should be stretched just tight enough to smooth out the horizontal wrinkles along the luff. Heavy winds call for a very tight luff when beating, and this may require use of the Cunningham.

The other methods of altering sail draft will be discussed later in this chapter. Draft changes made with mast bend will be dealt with briefly

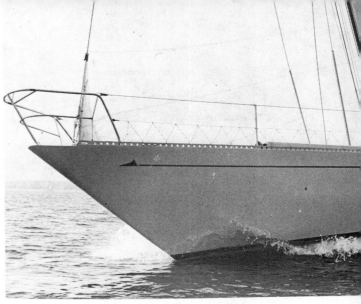

6-4. *Guerriere,* a 60-foot Morgan-designed sloop formerly owned by the U.S. Naval Academy. Notice the grooved luff foil in lieu of jib hanks. The network of lines on the lower lifelines are needed to help prevent the sail from blowing overboard when it is lowered, since there are no hanks to keep the luff attached.

when we discuss rigging, and draft alterations through sheet trim and use of the boom vang will be dealt with in the next three sections.

Sail trim. A sail is trimmed with its sheet. Let us review briefly the general sail positions for each point of sailing. When running, a sail is let all the way out; when beam reaching, it is about halfway out or somewhat closer; when broad reaching, the sail should lie somewhere between the running and beam-reaching positions; when close reaching, it should lie between the beam-reaching position and its closest point of trim; and when beating the sail should be trimmed in almost as far as it will come. These are only approximate positions. Exact positions will depend on the strength of the breeze, the design of the boat, the cut of her sails, the boat speed, and the size of the seas.

As said in chapter 3, sails are always trimmed to the apparent wind. The faster a boat travels, especially when she is beam reaching, the closer her sheets must be trimmed. When she is beating, the difference between the true and apparent wind will not be great in terms of direction, but there will be a great difference in velocity. On this point of sailing the boat speed is added to true wind which increases the apparent wind speed. When running, however, the boat speed wind is subtracted from the true wind to give a decreased apparent wind. There is no directional change in the apparent wind when a boat runs dead before the wind; therefore, in all breezes on this point of sailing the mainsail should be let out until the boom almost touches the after shroud. When trimming sails, always refer to the telltales or wind indicator, because these give the apparent wind direction.

The simplest way to obtain proper trim on a reach is to slack the sheets until the sail begins to luff, then pull the sheet in until the sail stops luffing. It is usually better to err on the side of trimming the sails too far out than too far in. A sail that is trimmed too far in will stall, as explained in chapter 3, and, in addition, will cause extra heeling. A sail that is trimmed too far out, although not correct, at least will be in such a position that the suction pull on the sail's leeward side has a more favorable angle with the boat's centerline to pull her ahead instead of sideways. It is usually advantageous to keep the sail *on edge*, so that it is just on the verge of luffing. This is when the sail is most effective. In order to do this while holding a straight course on a reach, the sheets must be tended constantly. Especially when racing, the sheets

should be *played* or adjusted for every wind shift and every puff or lull.

On the beat, sail trim is not changed as often as when reaching, because the helmsman changes his course more often to conform with changes of wind direction and velocity. When there are great variations in wind speed, however, sheets should be slacked slightly during the lulls and tightened during puffs. There are two exceptions to this rule. In heavy breezes when the boat is *overburdened* (carrying too much sail), the mainsail should be eased so that it carries a slight luff. The other exception is that when sailing into a rough sea which tends to slow the boat, sheets should be started, and as said in the last chapter, the helmsman should bear off slightly to keep the boat footing.

Sheet leads. When we consider sail trim, we must consider not only the in-and-out adjustment of the sheet, but also the location of its *lead*. A sheet lead is usually a *block* (pulley) on the deck or rail through which the sheet is led. Most leads are mounted in such a way that their location (fore and aft and/or athwartships) can be changed slightly to give the sheet the most favorable angle of trim for various sailing conditions. This altering of location is usually accomplished by attaching the block to a slide on a track, although sometimes a lead block slides on a low, athwartships metal bar called a *traveler* or *horse*.

Figure 6-6 shows correct and incorrect leads for working jibs. Notice that the fore-and-aft location should be at a point where neither the foot nor the leech is stretched excessively tight. A tight leech, caused by a lead which is too far forward, almost closes the upper venturi slot between the jib and the mainsail, thereby restrict-

6-5. The PJ-48 *Insurgente,* which became available to the Naval Academy in 1975 following confiscation by the U.S. Government for smuggling. The slot between the sails might be opened up a little more aloft if the jib lead were moved farther aft.

ing the air flow, and the leech deflects the flow into the lee side of the mainsail producing harmful backwind. A loose leech, on the other hand, opens the slot aloft too much so that the space between the jib's leech and the mainsail's luff is too wide, thereby harming the efficiency

of the venturi. A correct jib lead is placed so that neither the jib's leech nor the foot is stretched excessively tight when the sail is trimmed in flat. It is often very helpful to gauge the fore-and-aft lead position by its relationship to a projection of the jib's miter seam as shown in figure 6-6 when the miter seam bisects the clew angle. The correct lead position for most working jibs lies slightly forward of the point where the miter seam projection strikes the deck. When the sheet of the average close-hauled jib is properly led, the sail will first begin to luff along the general area just above the miter seam (see figure 6-6). If the jib's luff begins to shake below the miter seam, the lead is usually too far forward; if the luff shakes aloft near the sail's head, the lead is too far aft. When reaching, with the mainsail slacked off, it sometimes pays to move the jib lead slightly farther foreward than its normal position for beating. This is done to help prevent the upper part of the jib from twisting too much, which will cause the top of the sail to luff when the bottom is correctly trimmed.

In addition to the fore-and-aft sheet lead, we must consider the athwartships position, or how far inboard or outboard the lead is located. On many fast, narrow racing boats the jib lead should be placed about nine degrees out from the boat's centerline, but for the average daysailer with moderate beam, twelve degrees is a more realistic angle (see figure 6-6). Actually, this angular measurement should be used only as a guide. The exact athwartships point of trim should be determined by experimentation. It should be located as far inboard as possible without causing the jib to backwind the mainsail when the sails are trimmed in flat for beating.

The Genoa jib is most often led from an ad-

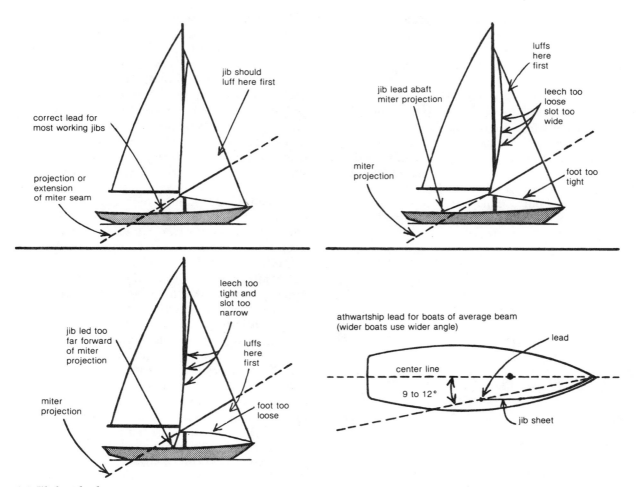

6-6. Jibsheet leads.

justable slide on a track which is mounted on or near the rail; thus, there usually is no athwartships adjustment but only a fore-and-aft choice for the lead position. This jib nearly always lies outside the shrouds; when the average Genoa is trimmed in flat for beating, its foot lies snugly against the shrouds while its upper leech lies an inch or so from the end of the *spreaders* (the struts which hold the shrouds away from the mast). Of course, the Genoa lead position will vary according to the size and shape of the particular jib, the position of the shrouds, the length of the spreaders, and the position of the lifelines around the boat. Some authorities say that the lead should be located slightly abaft the miter projection when the miter seam bisects the clew angle (see figure 6-7); however, some Genoas are more effective when the lead lies at the point where the projection strikes the rail or even slightly forward of this point. The after location is generally better in a fresh breeze in order to open up the slot aloft. As previously said, a little more backwind can be expected from a Genoa than from a working jib; therefore, with a Genoa, it is not usually harmful to carry a very slight shake in the lower luff of the mainsail, especially in a fresh breeze.

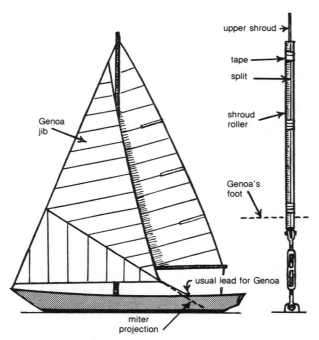

6-7. Genoa lead and shroud roller.

As with a working jib, when the Genoa's lead is too far forward, the leech becomes tight, and when the lead is too far aft the leech becomes loose. It is usually better to favor the loose leech, because the tight leech will cause excessive backwind. A leech that is too loose, however, will often develop an annoying flutter. Some authorities say that a leech flutter does no real harm; nevertheless, it should be minimized or stopped if possible. Sliding the lead forward slightly will help. If your Genoa has a *leech line* (a light adjustable line sewn into the leech), this can be tightened slightly to help eliminate the flutter, but take great care not to over-tighten the leech line as this can cause a tight, curling leech which can be harmful aerodynamically.

Quite often chafing problems arise from constant sailing with a Genoa. If the spreader ends touch the sail, it should have a *reinforcing patch* over the spot that is rubbed. This is especially true if the spreaders touch a sail seam, because the stitching will soon chafe through. Also the spreader ends should be wrapped with felt or some soft material. The Genoa foot will usually rub on the shrouds, therefore the outboard and forward shrouds should be equipped with *shroud rollers*. These are split tubes of wood or plastic which are taped closed on the shrouds in order that the tubes can turn or roll and minimize chafe to the jibs or sheets (see figure 6-7). Rollers will also speed up tacking because there is less friction when the jib wipes across the shrouds as the boat turns through the eye of the wind.

Mainsheet leads can only be adjusted athwartships because this sail is attached to a boom, and so there would be little point in having a fore-and-aft adjustment. When beating in light airs the mainsheet lead should be kept near, or

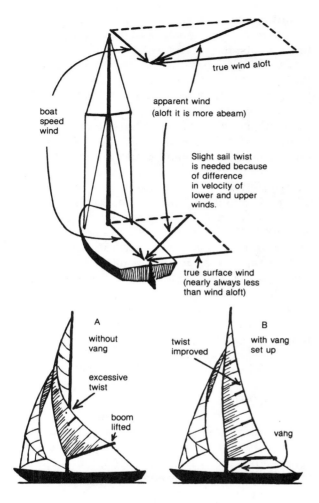

true wind aloft

apparent wind
(aloft it is more abeam)

boat
speed
wind

Slight sail twist
is needed because
of difference
in velocity of
lower and upper
winds.

true surface wind
(nearly always less
than wind aloft)

A
without
vang

excessive
twist

boom
lifted

twist
improved

B
with vang
set up

vang

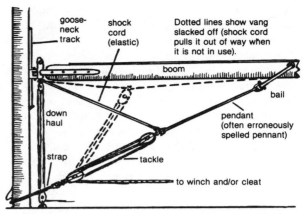

goose-
neck
track

shock
cord
(elastic)

Dotted lines show vang
slacked off (shock cord
pulls it out of way when
it is not in use).

boom

down
haul

bail

strap

tackle

pendant
(often erroneously
spelled pennant)

to winch and/or cleat

6-8. Boom vang. This type of vang requires a very strong gooseneck whose track should be bolted to the mast. Boats with light aluminum booms require more frequent use of the vang.

even slightly to windward of, the centerline of the boat. This will permit the boom to lift a little which will give the sail maximum draft. At the same time, of course, the sheet should be eased. When beating in a fresh breeze, the mainsheet lead should be moved farther to leeward where the sheet can pull the sail down as well as in. This will tend to flatten the sail and give it a more desirable draft for a good breeze. One word of caution, however; don't lead the mainsheet very far to leeward if carrying a Genoa, because this will tend to close the slot and increase jib backwind.

The boom vang. The boom vang, sometimes called the *kicking strap*, has been mentioned, and it is illustrated in figure 6-8. This is an important device for shaping and controlling the mainsail. Its fundamental purpose is to pull the boom down, preventing it from riding up when the sheet is eased. When the boom rides up or lifts, the leech curves or sags off and the sail becomes twisted causing the bottom area to be trimmed closer than the top area. This is shown in figure 6-8. With the vang set up, however, the leech becomes straighter and the head and foot of the sail lie almost in the same plane. The boom vang is most effective when reaching in a fresh breeze because this is when the boom will

87

have the greatest tendency to lift. The lighter a boat's boom, the tighter should be the vang adjustment to hold the boom down.

The value of a vang during a jibe has already been pointed out. It will ensure against a goosewing. Some large boats with cabin trunks, however, cannot carry a vang secured at the base of the mast (see fig. 6-8), because there is not enough space under the boom or the boom vang will foul the cabin top. In such a case, the vang must be fastened off-center to a through-bolted fitting to leeward on the side deck. When this is necessary, the vang must be adjusted every time there is a change of sheet trim. Obviously, it must be removed before jibing.

It is often advantageous to carry the vang set up tight when beating in a good breeze. The vang will sometimes bend a limber boom down near its middle to help remove draft, and on many boats it will help tighten the jibstay which is definitely advantageous when beating. If the boat has a fixed, nonadjustable, mainsheet lead, a vang rigged to the side deck will help pull the boom outboard and give about the same effect as could be achieved with an adjustable traveler. In fairly light breezes when the sheets are slacked, the vang is often carried in order to tighten the leech and remove sail twist, but usually it should not be carried to windward in light airs. At this time the mainsail should have maximum draft, and the vang will tend to flatten the sail. Figure 6-8 shows that a slight twist in a sail is desirable, because the wind near the head of a sail usually has a greater velocity than that at the foot. This causes the apparent wind aloft to be farther aft. Nevertheless, most sails, when trimmed for reaching in anything but light airs, have far too much twist and need at least some tension on the vang.

Handling and care of sails. Although sail construction and fitting details often vary with different boats, the procedure for *bending* sails (putting them on) is basically the same for all boats. When bending on a jib or staysail, start with the tack, which is fastened to the *stem head fitting* (a metal fitting with eyes at the top of the stem) or some other eye fitting at the lower end of the jibstay. The tack is secured with a *shackle* (a U-shaped fastener) which is usually closed with a screw or twist pin or spring-loaded piston (see the *snap shackle* in figure 6-2G). The jib is usually hooked to its stay with *piston hanks* or *snap hooks* (see figure 6-2) unless it is *set flying* (set without being hooked to a stay), or it is used with a slotted headfoil (as shown in figure 6-2I). When snapping on the hanks or hooks, start at the sail's tack and work towards the head being sure that the hanks all face the same way so that they are not twisted. Then attach the sheets to the clew (with bowlines, normally, unless the sheets have clew shackles) and shackle on the halyard. After the sheets are run through their lead blocks, figure-eight knots should be tied in the very ends of the lines to prevent them from accidentally being pulled back through the blocks.

On most boats the mainsail is held to the mast and boom by one of two means: slides on a track (shown in figure 6-2), or with grooved spars. When the spars are grooved, the sail's *bolt rope* (a rope sewn to the edge of the luff and foot) is fed into the boom groove as the clew is pulled aft, and then the bolt rope is fed into the mast groove as the sail is hoisted. In some cases, small plastic cylinders are fastened to a sail's luff or foot and these are fed into the grooves. In any event, in bending on the luff of a mainsail, it is usually necessary to start with the head and work down towards the tack. Also it is necessary to work from clew to tack when bending on the foot. The last edge of the sail (luff or foot) to be bent should first be run through the hands to see that the sail is not twisted before the bending is completed. Next the battens should be inserted. They should be shorter than their batten pockets by an inch or more. A sail equipped with batten pockets should not be used without the battens being inserted. Before hoisting the mainsail, be sure to set up the *topping lift* (the line which supports the boom when the sail is not hoisted). Failure to have the boom lifted up high when the sail is being hoisted or lowered may result in a crew member or deck gear being struck by the boom, and also it can over-stretch the sail's leech. After the sail is entirely hoisted, slack off the topping lift so that it gives no support to the boom. On some small boats without topping lifts, the boom can be lifted by hand.

Although Dacron sails are tougher and can stand more abuse than the cotton sails of former days, they are still vulnerable to certain mistreatment. Chafe is often a problem with synthetic sails because the stitching does not sink down into the cloth but lies on the surface where it is susceptible to being rubbed. Any area of a sail which is constantly chafed should be protected with a reinforcing patch. Sun rot is also a problem, especially with nylon. Sails which are left bent on should be furled, *stopped* (tied with cloth straps called *stops* or elastic shock cord), and protected with *sail covers* (specially fitted cloth covers which are lashed or snapped around the furled sail and its boom). Sail covers should not be entirely closed at the bottom, because lack of air inside the cover will encourage mildew, even on synthetic sails.

When furling a sail, pull the entire sail over to one side of the boom. Grab the leech of the sail and pull it aft so that the battens lie flat or parallel to the boom. Then bundle up the loose sail and neatly roll it up on top of the boom. After the roll is as tight as you can get it, secure it to the boom with stops. Before the sail is covered, slack off the outhaul.

If the sails are taken off and bagged, be sure the battens are removed as they can be broken or permanently bent inside a bag. Don't bag a wet sail. Let it dry first. Sails can be dried by hoisting them while moored, but only if the breeze is very light. The violent flapping and flogging of sails in a wind can be very harmful to them. Before racing sails are bagged, it is a good idea to fold them to minimize wrinkles. Fold a sail so that a few unavoidable creases run horizontally. Horizontal creases will least disturb the airflow from luff to leech.

When sailing is done in salt water, sails should be washed fairly frequently to remove salt crystals which become lodged in the material. A salt-caked sail usually does not set well, because the salt absorbs any moisture in the air even on a seemingly dry day. Sail washing should be done fairly gently and never with a detergent.

One of the greatest sources of damage to a sail is the cotter pin. This is a thin, bent metal pin that is put through a hole in a threaded screw fitting to prevent it from becoming unscrewed (see figure 6-14). Cotter pins have sharp ends which can easily snag and tear a sail. All these pins should be thoroughly wrapped in waterproof adhesive tape, and they should be inspected regularly to see that they remain taped. Another frequent source of sail damage is from cigarette or pipe ashes. Synthetic sails will not burst into flames, but they can be holed from sparks very easily.

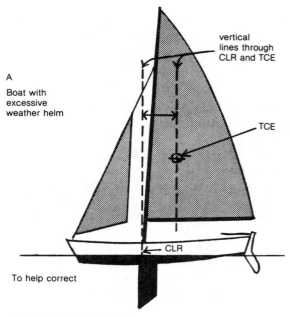

A
Boat with
excessive
weather helm

vertical
lines through
CLR and TCE

TCE

CLR

To help correct

1 prevent heeling to leeward
2 move weight aft
3 raise centerboard slightly
4 rake mast forward
5 trim jibsheet (pull it in) or set larger jib
6 reduce area of mainsail or have it recut
   to reduce draft (fig. 6-3) near after edge

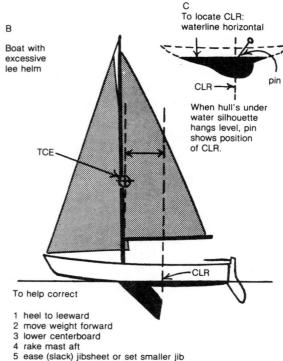

B
Boat with
excessive
lee helm

TCE

CLR

C
To locate CLR:
waterline horizontal

CLR

pin

When hull's under
water silhouette
hangs level, pin
shows position
of CLR.

To help correct

1 heel to leeward
2 move weight forward
3 lower centerboard
4 rake mast aft
5 ease (slack) jibsheet or set smaller jib
6 enlarge main and/or tighten its
   leech (after edge)

6-9. Helm balance.

Balance. As previously mentioned, helm balance has to do with the ability of a boat to hold a straight course when her helm is left alone. If she tends to head up into the wind, she has a *weather helm;* if she heads away from the wind, she has a *lee helm.* A boat's helm balance primarily depends on the relationship of the *center of effort* (CE) of her sails to the *center of lateral resistance* (CLR) of her underwater profile. The point at the geometric center of the side view of a sail is commonly referred to as the center of effort, and a combination of the centers of effort of each

sail concentrated at a single point, or the center of effort of the entire sail plan, is often called the *total center of effort* (TCE). The CLR is the central point on the hull's underwater side at which the boat can be pushed sideways (at right angles to her centerline) without turning. The fore-and-aft position of the CLR may be found by cutting from cardboard the silhouette of the immersed hull and hanging it in a level position from a pin, as shown in figure 6-9. Almost all boats are designed with the TCE slightly "leading" or ahead of the CLR, because it has been found that this gives the best average balance when considering all conditions of sailing. The amount of lead is generally from 5 to 20 percent of the boat's waterline length.

Although the fact that the TCE is forward of the CLR would apparently produce lee helm, several other forces acting on the boat tend to produce weather helm. For example, when the sheets are eased and the boat heels, the TCE is to leeward of the CLR, and this creates a moment arm that

6-10. Luffing the mainsail in a puffy breeze. Slacking the sheet relieves weather helm for two reasons: it helps keep the boat on her feet, and it moves the center of effort farther forward. In a steady breeze of this strength, the mainsail should be reefed, and possibly a jib with less overlap should be carried.

turns the boat to windward, thus giving her a weather helm.

Every boat should be *tuned* (properly adjusted) to carry a slight weather helm in all but the lightests breezes. A slight weather helm makes it easier for the helmsman to feel his boat, and also it is a built-in safety device; if the helmsman should happen to leave or lose his grip on the helm, the boat will automatically round up into the wind where she will lose headway and gain stability.

Furthermore, it has been found that a slight weather helm when beating actually boosts a boat to windward. If a rudder which is attached to the trailing edge of a keel is held at an angle of from three to five degrees from the boat's centerline, depending on the design, the keel-rudder combination will act as a hydrofoil and create a lateral lifting force. This is illustrated in figure 6-11. Of course, too much weather helm can be very harmful, because a rudder which is held over too far will partially stall and create a great amount of drag. When this happens the rudder acts partially as a brake. Also, boats with spade rudders should be balanced to carry very little weather helm, because these rudders cannot alter keel lift.

Improper balance is seldom extreme in a one-design class boat or boats designed by recognized naval architects, as are all Naval Academy boats, but many individual boats have minor helm faults which can be corrected by various minor adjustments. These are shown in figure 6-9. Most of the adjustments, raking the mast, raising or lowering the centerboard, moving crew weight, and setting larger or smaller sails forward or aft, change the boat's balance by changing the relation of the CLR to the TCE, as can be seen in the diagram.

There is a possibility, however, that one or two of these adjustments may be harmful to the boat's speed even though her helm is improved. For example, setting a smaller jib in light air to help correct a lee helm might cause a loss of speed. Therefore, care should be taken to see that helm balance is not improved at the expense of over-all performance. The first correction to be made when a boat is improperly balanced is to change the angle of heel. The severe weather helm often experienced when sailing in a blow is due mainly to an extreme heeling angle. This can be lessened by *hiking* or putting the crew as far as possible to windward and also by carrying a slight luff in the mainsail while the jib is trimmed reasonably flat.

The last balance correction listed in figure 6-9 (correction #6) mentions the tightening or slacking of the mainsail's leech. A tight leech will increase weather helm, while a loose leech will decrease it. Drastic changes in the leech can only be made by a skillful sailmaker, and even then, the changes may not be completely successful. Improving a sail's leech by recutting should be attempted only as a last resort to improve an original faulty draft. Slight, temporary changes in the leech can be made by adjustments to the boom vang. Tightening the vang will tighten the leech, and slacking the vang will slack the leech. Sometimes an overly tight leech on a sail can be eased by manually stretching it after the sail has been unbent.

Figure 6-12 shows how balance should be maintained when sail is reduced for heavy weather. As the diagram explains, there are various methods of shortening sail and these will vary according to the boat's rig. *Reefing* is the method of reducing a sail's area by lashing its lower area to its boom or by winding its foot

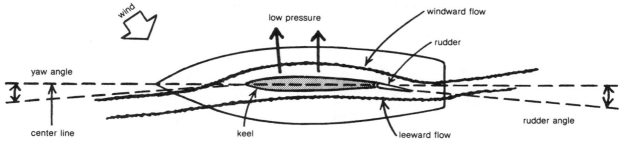

6-11. Keel-rudder hydrofoil action.

around the boom. It should also be remembered that reefing the mainsail not only reduces the angle of heel, but also moves the CE of that sail forward. Thus, reefing reduces weather helm in two ways. These procedures will be discussed in chapter 8. The purpose of figure 6-12 is to illustrate that the sail areas on either side of the TCE should be fairly equal when sail is reduced. In actual practice, however, most boats should carry more sail forward of the TCE as the wind increases in order to compensate for the excessive weather helm caused by extreme heeling.

Standing rigging. A boat's rigging can be divided into two categories: running and standing. Running rigging refers to the movable lines or wires used to set or adjust sails, and this rigging includes halyards, sheets, downhauls, outhauls, and topping lifts. Standing rigging, on the other hand, is more or less fixed, and this includes various stays and shrouds which support the mast and control its bending. On modern boats this rigging nearly always consists of wire rope, usually 1 × 19 construction wire (one solid strand of 19 wires) which is particularly resistant to stretch. Occasionally, solid rod rigging is used on racing boats, but many authorities feel this is not as reliable, because it is more subject

to fatigue failure—and failure is total, whereas the breaking of one wire in a 1 × 19 cable still leaves 18 wires for support.

Figure 6-13 illustrates two basic standing rigging plans with suggestions for tuning or adjusting the shrouds and stays. There are many standing rigging variations, but boats A and B in the diagram, *masthead* and *seven-eighths* rigs respectively, illustrate typical simple rigs and show the basic principles of tuning which can be applied to nearly all boats. Specific variations or departures from the norm, if any, will be pointed out when each individual Naval Academy boat is discussed.

Tuning the standing rigging can be a complicated and sometimes controversial procedure. We will not attempt a detailed study here but simply introduce the generally accepted rules. A common-sense rule is to adjust the shrouds so that the mast is held up vertically, at right angles to the deck, when the boat is viewed from her bow or stern. When the boat heels, of course, the mast will be supported by the windward shrouds only, and they will tighten, which will cause the leeward shrouds to slacken considerably. In this case, the mast will not be exactly at right angles to the deck, but it should be nearly so. From this same view (from the bow or stern),

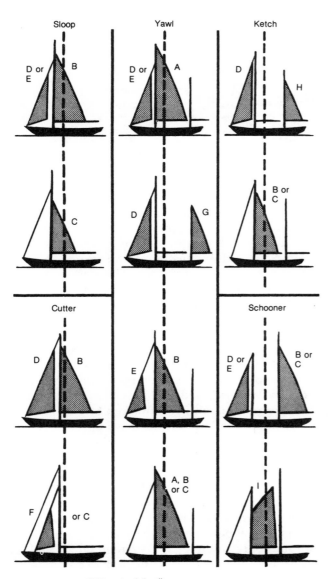

Broken lines are TCE under full sail.

A. full mainsail B. reefed main C. deeply reefed main D. jib
E. storm jib F. staysail G. mizzen H. reefed mizzen I. foresail

6-12. Balance with reduced sail.

the mast should be kept straight. This requires that the lower shrouds be kept slightly more slack than the upper shrouds, because the latter are longer, pass over a spreader, and therefore have more stretch when the boat heels. Lateral bends and "S" curves in a mast can be very harmful to the set of its sail.

Another fundamental of tuning is to keep the jibstay or headstay taut. This is essential to good windward performance. In order to keep these forward stays taut, the permanent backstay must be kept taut to counteract the pull of the forward stays; if the boat has running backstays, which pull directly behind the jibstay, these must be kept taut alternately when beating. Jumper stays on a seven-eighths rig (shown on boat B) should be kept taut if it is desired that the mast be straight when it is viewed from the side.

It has already been mentioned that there are certain occasions when masts are intentionally bent aft in order to alter draft. This is common practice with certain small-boat classes. The principle behind this bending or flexing of spars is shown by the bent mast (indicated by the dotted line) in figure 6-13. When a mast is bent so that its top bends aft and its lower portion, below the jibstay point of attachment, bows forward, then the sail is stretched fore and aft abaft the luff, and this flattens the draft. Boats with "bendy" rigs carry very full mainsails on straight spars in light airs or rough seas, but sail with bent spars in a good breeze to reduce the draft. If the boat is equipped with jumper stays and a permanent backstay, the former can be slacked while the latter is tightened to achieve a bend. In some very small boats with limber masts and few stays, bending the mast may be

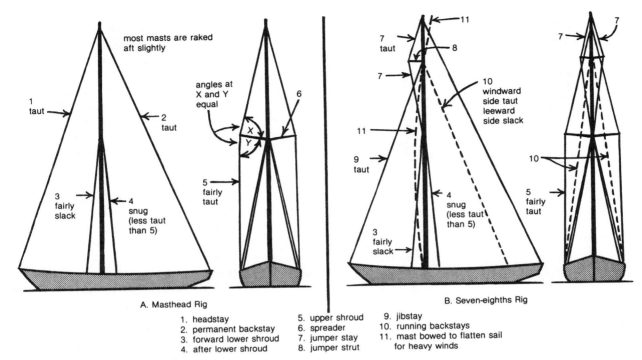

most masts are raked aft slightly

1 taut

2 taut

angles at X and Y equal

6

3 fairly slack

4 snug (less taut than 5)

5 fairly taut

A. Masthead Rig

11

7 taut

8

7

10 windward side taut leeward side slack

11

9 taut

4 snug (less taut than 5)

3 fairly slack

7

7

10

5 fairly taut

B. Seven-eighths Rig

1. headstay
2. permanent backstay
3. forward lower shroud
4. after lower shroud

5. upper shroud
6. spreader
7. jumper stay
8. jumper strut

9. jibstay
10. running backstays
11. mast bowed to flatten sail for heavy winds

6-13. Standing rigging and tuning.

accomplished simply by tightening the boom vang or sheet.

Mast bending works very well in many cases, but there should be a few words of warning. Sails must be specially cut for flexible spars. If the sail is cut for a straight mast, it will often be badly distorted if carried on a bent mast. A mast should rarely be bent in light airs as this is when full draft is needed. Also, it is usually not wise to attempt bending a mast which has a headstay to the masthead (shown on boat A in figure 6-13), because of difficulties in pulling the masthead aft without putting a compression bend in the mast, without changing the normal set of the jib, or without having a slack

headstay and upper shrouds because the top of the mast will be lower when it is bent. As a general rule, it is wise not to attempt bending the spars of any large cruising-racing yacht with a masthead rig. This could result in the loss of a mast.

Standing rigging is adjusted with turnbuckles (see figure 6-14). Once the shrouds are adjusted correctly, they should be left alone for most of the sailing season with only an occasional tightening if the rigging stretches; therefore, shroud turnbuckles should be locked with cotter pins as shown in the diagram. Don't forget to wrap the cotter pins with tape. Turnbuckles for stays, however, might need more frequent adjustment,

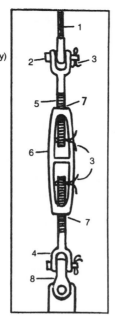

(1) shroud (2) clevis pin
(3) cotter pin (should be wrapped in tape)
(4) clevis (5) threads
(6) barrel (turn to tighten stay)
(7) some turnbuckles have locknuts here instead of cotter pins
(8) toggle (at the bottom of every turnbuckle on large boats at least)

6-14. A turnbuckle.

and it is often convenient to use turnbuckles with locking handles or wheels or hydraulic adjusters to avoid constant removal of cotters (see figure 6-14). Headstays and jibstays often have a lot of lateral movement due to the side pressure of a jib or staysail; thus it is especially vital on large boats that these stays are fitted with *toggles* as shown in the diagram. A toggle is a small fitting with a pin which makes a movable joint between the bottom of the turnbuckle and its eye, stemhead fitting, or other point of attachment. Without a toggle, the lower jaws of a turnbuckle are subject to breakage through metal fatigue.

The question of how tight to set up the rigging is an often debated one. Rigging that is too loose allows the mast to jump around and move too much in a seaway, but on the other hand,

rigging that is too tight often seems to kill a boat's speed, and it puts unnecessary strain and stress on the hull. Almost everyone agrees that the jibstay or headstay should be taut for windward sailing, but these should not be so taut that they put great strain on the stem or that they put compression bends in the mast. When tightening up the headstay, sight up the mast track on the after side of the mast to see that no bend is developing. Sight from aft forward and also from the side.

For most boats, shrouds should not be any tighter than they have to be to hold the mast nearly at right angles to the deck (when viewed from the bow or stern) when the boat is heeled. In other words, the mast should not be allowed to lean too far to leeward. As for the amount of rake in a mast (the amount it leans fore and aft when viewed from the side), most boats are designed to carry a slight rake aft. This usually makes the mainsail hang better (provided the after end of her boom is not too low) and it also causes the jibstay to stand better, allowing a minimum of sag. The question of rake, however, will depend primarily on the balance of the boat as mentioned in the last section. If the boat has too little weather helm or a lee helm, her mast should be raked fairly far aft. With too much weather helm, the mast should be almost vertical and in some rare cases raked slightly forward of the vertical.

A few last words of advice about rigging: a spreader should be adjusted so that the angles between the shroud and spreader above and below are exactly equal (see figure 6-13). Failure to do this can cause the spreader to slip which could result in the loss of the mast. Get in the habit of checking fittings for cracks, wear, or fatigue. Particularly, check lock nuts which often seem to come loose. Avoid, or at least be very cautious about making rigging adjustments while underway. Rigging on the leeward side is normally quite slack when a boat is heeled, and it is easy to adjust it too tight which can destroy the proper tune and put a great strain on the boat.

A summary of sail adjustments. In this chapter, a fair amount has been said about sail shaping and adjusting; therefore, a summary of the main points in outline form should be helpful. This will list the various adjustments for sailing to windward (beating) or off the wind (running and reaching) in different conditions of wind and sea.

To windward. In light airs or in rough seas, maximum draft is desirable. (Keep boat heeled slightly to leeward.)
- Slack outhaul and ease downhaul slightly.
- Ease sheets and lead mainsail from centerline of boat or slightly to windward for light airs but slightly to leeward in rough seas.
- Ease boom vang, but keep it tight enough to hold the boom steady.
- Keep mast fairly straight.
- Keep jibstay moderately taut.
- Open foot zipper if there is one.

In a moderate breeze with smooth water, draft should be reduced.
- Tighten outhaul and downhaul.
- Close foot zipper.
- Flatten sheets and lead main from centerline or slightly to leeward.
- Boom vang should be moderately taut.
- Mast may be bent moderately if rig is flexible.
- Jibstay should be taut.

In a strong breeze with fairly smooth water, flatten draft, avoid a tight leech, and keep boat from heeling excessively.
- Tight on downhaul or Cunningham and fairly tight on outhaul, unless seas are rough.
- Close foot zipper.
- Ease main but flatten jib.
- Lead main farther to leeward.
- Boom vang should be tight.
- Mast should have considerable bend if rig is flexible.
- Jibstay should be taut.

Off the wind. In light airs, full draft with most draft farther aft is desirable.
- Slack outhaul and downhaul.
- Ease sheets to point of luffing when reaching.
- Jib leads might be moved slightly farther forward.
- Open foot zipper.
- Boom vang should be only slightly taut unless boom is very light.
- Keep mast straight.
- On some boats the backstays may be eased.

In a strong breeze, slightly less draft is desirable.
- Ease outhaul and downhaul.
- Carry slight luff in main if there is a strong weather helm.
- Keep boom vang tight, but be ready to release it if the boom should start to dip in the water.
- Keep mast straight and particularly free from compression bends.
- Don't slack backstays.

Recent theory on rigging and sails. As a result of the most recent thinking by sailmakers, designers, handicap rule makers, and racing sailors, the following subtle changes or modifications to rigs and sails are in evidence: many new rigs have higher aspect ratios (they have become taller and more narrow at the foot); draft or camber in sails is somewhat deeper, more uniform from head to foot, and the greatest depth is farther aft; shrouds are being moved farther inboard; sheeting angles for jibs are becoming smaller; the mainsheet traveler slide is more often moved to windward of the boat's centerline; jib leads are often being moved slightly farther forward; and greater use is being made of staysails and *double slot* arrangements (one slot being between a jib and staysail and the other between staysail and mainsail).

One reason for the increased use of high aspect ratio rigs is the American acceptance of the International Offshore Rule (IOR) for handicapping racing-cruising boats. The rule has not only encouraged the use of taller rigs, but also relatively smaller mainsails and larger *headsails* (those sails set forward of the forward mast). A recent trend, however, is a return to seven-eighths and three-quarter rigs.

Today, sails are often cut with a deeper draft that is located farther aft, because the newest sail cloth is more stable (less subject to stretching out of shape) and a reasonably deep draft increases power. Having the sail's greatest depth farther aft increases pointing ability and often encourages the air flow to stay attached to the sail and thus delays stalling. Many of the newer mainsails have their greatest depth almost half way from the luff to the leech, while some Genoa jibs have their maximum draft 40 percent aft. Uniform draft curves from head to foot increase the effective area of a sail, and a typical modern jib has its foot as low as possible so that the deck becomes an aerodynamic end

plate or *fence* to prevent the high-pressure air flow on the windward side of the sail from escaping under the foot to the low-pressure leeward side. Jib leads are being set moderately far forward to encourage adequate draft curvature at the foot. This is done also to prevent the leech of high aspect ratio jibs from falling off excessively.

Genoa jibs on many of the newest boats lead to tracks set inboard of the rails, because many of these craft are exceedingly beamy by former standards, and also narrow sheeting angles permit high pointing. Of course, trimming an overlapping jib inside of the rail means that the shrouds must be set inboard somewhat (see figure 6-15). Boats with inboard shrouds often have two sets of spreaders in order that the spreaders can be short to permit the narrow sheeting angles and yet allow an ample angle between the mast and upper shroud. This latter angle should nearly always be at least 11 degrees to avoid extreme compression on the mast.

The mainsheet traveler slide is frequently positioned to windward of the boat's centerline in light to medium winds for several reasons. The more fully cambered jibs throw more backwind against the mainsail especially when they are sheeted at very narrow angles, and this means that the mainsail must be sheeted extra flat with its boom far inboard to avoid the backwind. Although the traveler slide may be somewhat to windward of the centerline, rarely if ever should the boom itself be pulled to windward, because then the after part of the mainsail attempts to push the boat backwards. When the slide is to windward but the boom is slightly to leeward of the centerline the boom lifts up somewhat, and this eases the mainsail's leech, which may help the air flow around the sail and relieve weather helm. Still another reason for sheeting the mainsail extra flat is to minimize backwind from a staysail carried with a high-cut Genoa jib or reaching jib when the boat is sailing close-hauled.

The carrying of special forestaysails with large jibs in light to moderate winds when beating or close reaching is a modern trend that has become quite popular in certain parts of this country. The primary purpose of light-air double headsail arrangements is to obtain a maximum of sail area at a minimum cost of rating in handicap racing. The practice generally is most

6-15. An Alan Gurney designed Islander 36 beating in heavy weather. Her inboard shrouds and deck track for the jib leads permit extra flat trimming of headsails. Notice the neatly laced reef in the mainsail. A lacing line may be wrapped around the boom as shown, but reef points should be tied under the sail's bolt rope whenever possible so that tension on the sail's foot can be more evenly distributed.

6-16. A Lapworth designed Cal 2-30 broad reaching with a radial-head spinnaker and Genoa staysail. This kind of staysail also can be carried effectively when beam reaching or close reaching under a high-cut jib, but it is not effective when running. The 15/16ths rig, with the headstay attached slightly below the masthead, is primarily for handicap rating advantages, but it also allows moderate flexing of the mast to flatten the main in a breeze.

suitable in areas where light winds and close-reaching courses prevail. In heavy winds when beating to windward, a conventional *double head rig* with a heavy staysail and small jib topsail, as carried by the Luders yawls (see chapter 8), is far more effective. The most effective light air double slot arrangement, however, is probably a very light Dacron drifter or reaching jib, sheeted as far as possible aft, set over a low-cut *Genoa staysail* (a staysail shaped like a Genoa) that is tacked about 25 percent of the distance from the stem head to the mast abaft the stem head and is sheeted quite far inboard of the rail (see figure 6-16). With such a rig the boat will not point high, but in very light airs the boat will make good progress to windward by virtue of her faster footing. It may not be advisable, though, to carry the rig on short windward legs where a lot of tacking is anticipated, because such tacking requires extra crew effort, and it often takes a while to get the two headsails properly trimmed so that they don't interfere with each other.

7. Small Sailboats

In the preceding chapters, we discussed the general principles of sailboat handling without going into the many variations of rigs, sails, and hulls in the different classes of boats. In this chapter, moving from the general to the particular, we will discuss the principal small-boat classes used, or formerly used, at the Naval Academy—the knockabout, the Skipjack, the 420, the Laser, and the Shields.

It is interesting to compare these boats, because each represents a slightly different concept of small, class-boat sailing. The knockabout is a modern fin keel/spade rudder boat primarily intended for elementary training and comfortable day sailing with a roomy cockpit and short rig. The Shields is also a ballast-keel boat, but is a modern racing type, sensitive, sophisticated, and designed to excel in windward performance. The Skipjack, the 420, and the Laser, on the other hand, are high-performance, light-displacement, modern, racing dinghies. Knockabouts make good trainers for the basic rudiments of sailing and preliminary big-boat handling. Shields boats are good trainers for keelboat racing, light-sail handling, and for developing helmsmanship and a fine "tiller touch." Skipjacks, 420s, and Lasers are good trainers for centerboard boat seamanship, racing, and special techniques, such as planing and sailing with flexible spars.

Knockabout sloops. Plans of the knockabout are shown in figure 7-1. As can be seen, she is a sloop-rigged day sailer, partially decked, with a large open cockpit. This kind of cockpit drains into the bilge, but the boat is equipped with a large-capacity fixed bilge pump (housed in a compartment just abaft the mainmast in the middle of the cockpit) for the removal of rainwater and spray. Some boats of this size or larger have *self-bailing* cockpits, with the *sole* (floor) level above the waterline and through-the-hull *scuppers* (drains).

With her short rig and cast-iron fin keel weighing 1120 pounds, having most of its weight concentrated in a bulb at the keel's bottom, the knockabout is a very stable boat that is nearly impossible to capsize. Furthermore, she has flotation and is unsinkable if she should happen to become filled with water. Of course, it is possible for any open sailboat to be heeled over, held down and swamped in choppy seas if she is badly handled. In a fresh, puffy breeze, knockdowns must be expected, and if the boat is not let right up, especially in rough water, she might possibly ship enough water to affect her stability. Such a predicament is extremely unlikely, however, if the knockabout skipper follows common-sense rules for heavy weather sailing—that is, if he reefs or shortens sail in very strong winds, luffs up in hard gusts (or bears off to a run when the wind is well abaft the beam), and slacks sheets when the rail buries. An effective feature for comfort and safety is the high coaming around the knockabout's cockpit, which helps keep waves from sloshing in when the boat is heeled.

The dimensions of these sloops are 24 feet 2 inches length overall, 17 feet 3 inches on the load waterline, 6 feet 3 inches beam, and 3 feet 6 inches draft. The knockabout is constructed of molded fiberglass, and her mast and boom are aluminum. She has a spade-type rudder (under-hung and not attached to the keel) made of bronze and fiberglass. Although her *working sail area* (the area of the mainsail plus a masthead non-overlapping jib) is a modest 218 square feet, it is sufficient for her easily driven, light-displacement hull. Produced by Tidewater Boats of Annapolis, the knockabout is a modification of the Rainbow class sloop, which was designed by Sparkman and Stephens. Changes over the original Rainbow include a larger cockpit, removal of a *cuddy* (small cabin-trunk shelter at the forward end of the cockpit), additional ballast on the keel, and a slightly modified rudder (see figures 7-1 and 7-2).

length overall	24'2"
length load waterline	17'3"
beam	6'3"
draft	3'6"
mast height	28'3½"
keel weight	1120 lbs.
displacement	2250 lbs.
working sail area	218 sq. ft.

7-1. The Knockabout, sail plan and lines.

The knockabout's jib is bent on with piston hanks that are snapped onto the headstay (see figure 6-2), and the mainsail is bent on with nylon slides sewn to the luff and a bolt rope on the foot that fit into grooves on the mast and boom. A cotter pin inserted into holes penetrating the mast groove just above the mainsail's tack prevents the slides from dropping out of the groove when the sail is lowered. The mainsail outhaul is a line that runs from a grommet in the sail's clew through an eye or shackle at the boom's end and then a short distance for-

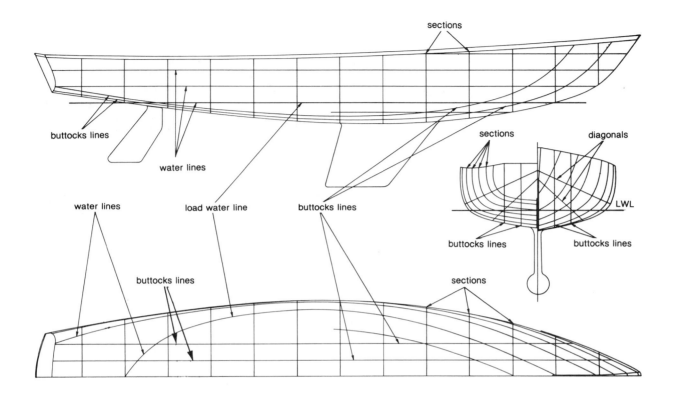

buttocks lines

water lines

water lines

load water line

buttocks lines

buttocks lines

sections

sections

diagonals

LWL

buttocks lines

buttocks lines

sections

ward to a cleat on the side of the boom. It is better to have the line run through a shackle rather than the small eye in order to reduce chafe. The boom also moves a limited distance up and down on a slide that fits into the mast groove, and its position is controlled by a downhaul line. The mainsail is hoisted until the head of the sail is at the bottom edge of a black band painted around the masthead; then the boom is pulled down with its downhaul, which is then made fast to a cleat near the base of the mast in order to adjust the sail's luff to the proper ten-

sion. As said earlier, tension will vary with the strength of wind. The luff should be tight in fresh breezes and slack in light airs but never so slack as to have very noticeable horizontal wrinkles along the luff. Before the sail is hoisted, however, four battens (stowed in the stern lazarette) must be inserted into pockets on the sail's leech. The battens are tapered and their thin ends are inserted first. The two longest battens go into the middle of the leech, while the short ones are at the sail's top and bottom.

The main boom is supported by a short wire

strop called the *boom support pendant*, that is attached to the permanent backstay. It is important that the boom is held high above the deck while the mainsail is being hoisted so that the leech will not be strained and no one will be hit on the head with the boom. A better arrangement would be a topping lift running from the boom's end to the masthead so that the sail could be hoisted and lowered with the boom broad off when necessary. With the short strop lift presently used, however, the boom must be held up by hand unless the boat is headed almost directly into the wind when hoisting or lower sail. Of course, during those operations it

7-2. A Knockabout sailing close hauled in front of the Robert Crown Sailing Center at the U.S. Naval Academy. Among the boat's virtues are her sizable cockpit that can accommodate a large crew and her short rig which makes her quite stiff.

it is nearly always desirable to have the boat headed directly into the wind, but there are times when such a heading is not possible, and then the boom should be unhooked from the strop and held by hand to one side of the boat in order that the sail itself can be headed, as closely as possible, into the wind. When hoisting the mainsail, look aloft and see that the battens do not foul the rigging and that everything up the mast is clear.

The jib halyard has a small winch on the port side of the mast. On the knockabouts winch handles are seldom carried because they are not really needed and, not being self-locking types, they can be lost overboard quite easily. In order to hoist the jib taut, therefore, it is necessary to *swig* or *sway* it up. This is a method of pulling on a halyard which may be described as follows. After the sail is hoisted until it is as taut as possible by pulling down on the halyard, several turns are wrapped clockwise around the winch. With one hand tightly holding the halyard as it comes off the winch, the jib hoister uses his other hand to grip the standing part of the halyard a foot or so above the winch, and he pulls it away from the mast. Then he hauls downward on the standing part and brings it back to the mast while slack is taken in at the winch. With two men, one can swig while the other takes in the slack. The jibsheets lead from the jib's clew to swivel lead blocks on each rail, then to small winches on each side farther aft, and finally to jam cleats just forward of the winches. Before getting underway, be sure the sheets are clear and that there are figure-eight knots in the ends of the jibsheets to prevent them from running through the lead blocks.

The mainsheet consists of a three-purchase tackle running from the boom's end to a deck swivel on the boat's centerline. There is no traveler, and the sheet is cleated in a cam-action jam attached to the lower end of the tackle. At the forward end of the boom there is a vang running from the boom several feet abaft the mast to the base of the mast similar to the vang shown in figure 6-6. The knockabouts do not have flexible rigs, and thus the vangs are not used for mastbending; they are used to hold the boom down and remove excessive sail twist when running and reaching as explained in the previous chapter.

With her short keel (short from fore edge to after edge) and spade rudder located at the after end of the load waterline, the knockabout is highly maneuverable and can turn within a small radius. At a considerable angle of heel, however, when the boat develops a significant weather helm, the rudder may stall and lose its grip on the water, at which time she is apt to round up inadvertently into the wind. To alleviate this, the mainsheet should be slacked to help prevent heeling and to move the center of effort farther forward, which will lessen the weather helm. If the boat begins to knock down and lose steering control while broad reaching, the helmsman should immediately bear off to a run so that stability will be regained and the rudder will not stall completely. When not allowed to heel excessively, knockabouts have good balance and they will even balance and sail reasonably well under jib alone.

Because of her light *displacement* (weight), a knockabout *forereaches* (carries way when shooting) for only a relatively short distance, especially when she is headed into a fresh breeze. Exactly how far she will shoot depends on the wind and waves, her speed, and how fast the rudder is turned. A dock, mooring, or *dolphin*

mooring post should be approached with ample headway for steering control, but at moderately slow speed. A *boat hook* (a pole with a blunt hook at its end) should be handy to reach the objective if the shoot is too short. If the boat is moving a little too fast, a crew member can slow speed by backing the mainsail, pushing the boom broad off against the wind so that it brakes the boat's forward momentum.

At the Naval Academy, the knockabouts are kept moored to seawalls at Santee Basin. Careful planning is required to get underway and land at these berths. Of course, exact procedure will vary according to the strength and direction of the wind. The boats are moored with their sterns to the seawall. They are moored by a heavy adjustable bow line, which is referred to as the *outhaul mooring line,* and a fixed stern line, referred to as a *stern fast.* This mooring arrangement is shown in figure 7-3. At the south seawall, the outhaul line runs from the boat's bow bitt through a large block on a dolphin about 60 feet out from the seawall and from this block back to the seawall where it is made fast to a large iron ring. At the north seawall the arrangement is the same except the bow line is fixed to a block attached to an anchored buoy. In order to board a knockabout, her stern must be pulled in to the seawall. This is done by hauling in on the stern fast as the outhaul is eased (slacked off but with tension on the line). Immediately prior to getting underway, all halyards and sheets should be carefully checked to see that they won't foul when sails are hoisted, and halyards as well as the sheets should have figure-eight knots in their ends.

When getting underway with the wind from astern, the jib may be hoisted first, and the knockabout may be run out from her berth

7-3. Arrangement for mooring. This photograph shows the dolphins, outhaul mooring lines, stern fasts, and manner of securing the lines to iron rings on the seawall. Sails are being bent on prior to getting underway.

under jib alone. The stern fast is unsnapped and left on the seawall and the outhaul mooring line is coiled up and left on top of the dolphin as the boat moves past. The helmsman should keep the boat headed directly out at right angles to the seawall until well clear of the dolphins, and then he should round up toward the wind while the mainsail is hoisted.

If the wind is abeam or from ahead, a knock-about should be propelled from her berth by a simultaneous push and pull before sail is hoisted. A crew member on the stern should push from the seawall as a crew member on the bow pulls on the outhaul. When there is a strong head wind, a great deal of force should be exerted to propel the boat well clear of the dolphins so that sail can be hoisted before she drifts back towards the seawall. Remember the basic principles of heading into the wind when hoisting sail, hoisting the aftermost sail first (the mainsail in this case), and backing the jib to make the bow fall off in the desired direction.

When returning to her berth (see figure 7-4), the knockabout should be landed at her dolphin bow first, at a slow speed, and with the dolphin ending up on the starboard bow. If the wind is from ahead, blowing from the seawall, the boat is luffed into the wind with sails shaking some distance from the dolphin in order to kill headway. In this situation, it is generally advisable to lower the jib prior to landing in order to slow the boat, give better visibility to the helmsman, and give more freedom of movement to the man on the foredeck. If the wind is on the beam or abaft the beam when the boat is headed directly towards the seawall, it is best to sail to windward of the dolphin, luff up and lower the main, and then sail downwind under jib alone toward the dolphin. If it is not blowing hard, the jib may be dropped just before reaching the dolphin, but if it is blowing hard, the boat should be sailed downwind toward the dolphin *under bare poles* (with all sails down). Remember that a knockabout will not go to weather as well under jib alone, so stay to windward of the dolphin.

After the crew member on the bow has caught the dolphin and taken the coiled-up outhaul line, he belays it to the bow cleat. Then all sail is lowered. The proper orders are: "Let go the main (or jib) halyard; douse the main (or jib)." The boat is then pushed into her slip on the port side of her dolphin. A crew member on the stern reaches for the neighboring boat's outhaul line with a boat hook, and then the knockabout is turned around end for end so that her stern is

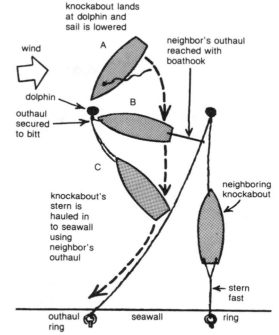

7-4. Knockabout mooring.

brought back to the seawall. The stern fast is secured, and the boat has then assumed her original moored position. Before leaving the boat, battens are removed from the sails, sails are bagged and stowed under the forward deck to keep them dry, lines are belayed and coiled, and the bilge is pumped dry.

In heavy weather, a knockabout's sail area may be reduced by reefing. The need for reefing should be determined by a careful evaluation of weather conditions before getting underway, because it is much easier to reef before sail is hoisted and in the calm waters of a mooring area. There are no hard and fast rules for when to reef, but generally a knockabout should be

109

reefed when the wind blows about 18 knots (see Beaufort Scale, appendix H). This will depend somewhat on the experience of the skipper. A novice skipper should reef sooner than a veteran sailor with previous knockabout experience. If it should breeze up after a knockabout has left her mooring area, the skipper should slack his mainsheet and carry a moderate luff in the mainsail. But if the boat still buries her rail and takes a lot of spray into the cockpit, it is definitely time to reef. A knockabout is probably stiffer than most boats of her size and type.

Knockabouts are provided with a simplified form of *roller reefing* whereby the boom can be rotated by hand to roll the foot of the mainsail around the boom, thus reducing the sail's area. The forward end of the boom has a square projection or spindle which fits into a square hole in the gooseneck fitting. To reef, the boom must be pulled aft far enough to remove the spindle from its hole, then the boom is rotated by hand until the sail is wound around it the desired amount, and finally the spindle is reinserted in its hole so that the sail will not inadvertently unwind. Of course, the halyard must be eased off as the boom is being turned. More will be said about roller reefing in the next chapter.

Knockabouts should be sailed with a minimum of two in the crew (the skipper plus two crew members) or a maximum of six. The sloops are provided with life jackets which are stowed in the stern lazarette.

Skipjacks. The Skipjack is no longer used at the Naval Academy, but it is a typical high-performance dinghy, and it serves well as an example to illustrate the techniques involved in sailing this type of boat. Her dimensions are 14 feet 7 inches in length overall, 5 feet 3 inches

beam, 300 pounds displacement, and she is sloop-rigged with 125 square feet of sail. Her hull is fiberglass and the spars are aluminum. These boats were designed and built by Newport Boats at Gloucester, Virginia.

A Skipjack is illustrated in figure 7-5. There are two transom bailers, one on either side of the rudder. These are small, round holes covered by hinged flaps. The flaps are held closed by a piece of shock cord and a lanyard that is fastened to a jam cleat within reach of the helmsman. The Skipjack is very buoyant, and her cockpit floor is above the water level; thus when

7-5. The Skipjack. This photograph of a Skipjack sailing in a moderate breeze shows the skipper and crew with their feet well under the hiking straps. This will enable the men to lean far backwards for effective hiking during strong gusts. Notice the skipper handling the mainsheet with one hand and the tiller extension with the other. Note that the extension is kept nearly at right angles to the tiller. The crew is reaching inboard with his right hand to help haul in the mainsheet.

water accumulates in the cockpit, the bailers can be opened to let the water run out.

Being an unballasted centerboarder, the Skipjack obviously can capsize; but having ample foam flotation under her gunwales, she will float high on her side when overturned. In addition, there is foam in the mast to help keep the boat from turning turtle. Righting a Skipjack is quite easy. Usually it is not necessary to lower sail. The bow is brought around near the wind and a crew member climbs on the centerboard. The crew counterbalance each other and scramble over the sides or stern after the boat is righted. Bailing is not necessary with the self-draining cockpit. (See chapter 2 for the basics of capsizing and righting.)

As with any small centerboard dinghy, the Skipjack depends on crew weight for much of her stability. The boat is provided with *hiking straps* (web straps secured inside the boat on the bottom) in order that the crew and skipper may put their feet under these straps and lean far out to windward when the boat heels excessively. The inboard edge of the side decking is rounded for comfortable hiking, and the helmsman is provided with a *tiller extension* (a bar that pivots from the end of the tiller), which allows him to steer while sitting far out to windward. The tiller can be adjusted fore and aft to a limited extent by sliding it through the head of the rudder. A pin in the after end of the tiller keeps it from sliding out of the rudder head. Hiking should be an almost instinctive reaction for the small centerboard dinghy sailor. These boats should be kept as flat (without heel) as possible except in very light airs, when they should be heeled slightly to leeward.

The Skipjack is nearly always rigged as a sloop, but she may be converted to a cat rig (sometimes called *una-rig*) if the mast is stepped forward and the jib is dispensed with. The boat is provided with several choices of fore-and-aft positions for the mast step. Ordinarily, when sloop-rigged, the mast is stepped in the aftermost position, but if permanently cat-rigged, the mast is stepped in the extreme forward position. If temporarily sailing under mainsail alone, however, it is not necessary to restep the mast. The boat will balance reasonably well under mainsail alone with the mast stepped aft.

Skipjacks use the bendy or flexible rig. Standing rigging consists of a jibstay and, at each side, a single shroud which is secured at the gunwale about one foot abaft the mast. These shrouds are held from the mast by spreaders which are hinged to move fore and aft to a limited extent. The rigging should be carried quite slack. Mast bend is achieved by bowsing down the mainsheet and vang which will pull the top of the mast aft and bow the lower part of the mast forward to flatten the sail. Mast bend is obtained with the mainsheet when the traveler slide is almost directly under the boom. The vang consists of a tackle, the upper block of which is fitted with a wire and a small swaged cylinder. This cylinder fits into a keyhole slot on the underside of the boom about two feet abaft the mast. The lower block of the boom vang is attached to a ring at the base of the mast. With this particular type of vang, cleating is not necessary. The hauling part or *fall* of the tackle is hauled up to tighten the vang, and then it is pulled down to lock or jam the line. Notice that the mainsheet is led from a bar traveler crossing the cockpit nearly amidships. This gives the helmsman good control over the sheet, and it can flex the boom in its middle to help remove sail draft. An amidships traveler, however, means that athwartship lead adjustment is considerably less than if the traveler were located under the boom's after end. Furthermore, to hold the boom near the boat's centerline when beating in light airs, it is frequently necessary to move the lead to windward of the centerline. When beating in a fresh breeze, the traveler should be adjusted so that the boom's end will lie approximately over the corner of the transom.

A unique feature of the Skipjack is the use of full-length mainsail battens. These are flexible slats of fiberglass which run from leech to luff. Their purpose is to hold out an extra large roach and to allow some draft change through batten adjustment. The deeper a batten is inserted, the greater the sail's draft. The end of each batten has several holes through which a metal snap pin on the leech is inserted. For average conditions, the pin is inserted through the fourth hole from the batten's end, leaving three holes exposed. In a light breeze, the batten could be inserted farther, while in a strong breeze, it might not be inserted as far. When the sail is unbent, the battens are not removed. The sail is simply rolled from head to foot, or vice versa.

The mainsail's clew outhaul consists of a simple lashing, and the boom is fitted with a downhaul to alter tension on the luff. Halyards are wire and rope combinations. After sail is hoisted, the wire parts of the halyards carry the full sail-supporting loads. The halyards do not belay to a cleat, but are secured by locking one of several small cylinders swaged to the wire under a slotted hook on the mast. When the jib is properly hoisted, the wire sewn into the luff of the sail takes the full load and causes the jibstay to go slack. In order to get the jib halyard taut, it is often necessary to make a loop in the halyard a foot or so above the mast step and then to stand on this loop until the appropriate swaged cylinder is pulled down to the slotted hook on the mast. Jib leads have a fore-and-aft adjustment only, and usually the correct adjustment lies near the center of the short track located on the side deck.

The sloop-rigged Skipjack carries a two-man crew (skipper plus a crew member). Teamwork is required to sail any boat effectively, but this is especially true with this type of boat. The crew member does most of the hiking and shifting of weight for the purpose of correcting the angle of heel so that the skipper can be in the most comfortable and convenient position to concentrate on his helmsmanship. The skipper hikes or moves his weight inboard only if it is really necessary. The boat should be kept at a more or less consistent angle of heel. During a puff the crew should hike, but during the lulls he should move inboard or even to leeward in light airs. In heavy winds, of course, both skipper and crew must hike to keep the boat flat.

Duties of the crew are: to trim the jib, tend the centerboard, adjust the vang and downhaul, hike, shift his weight fore and aft to affect hull trim, keep a lookout for other boats, and be alert for any maneuvering situations that should be called to the skipper's attention. When the boat is on a beat, the jib should be trimmed flat most of the time except in light airs and in rough seas, at which times it should be eased. Cam-action jam cleats are provided for the jibsheets. The sheet is belayed by pulling it down into the cams, but a tug upward will release it quickly. The centerboard is lifted with a tackle which may be adjusted from either side of the boat. The board is held down by a stout rubber cord. When the boat is on a run, the board is pulled all the way up, but when on a beat it is usually all the way down. On a reach, the board should not be down any farther than is necessary to prevent the boat from making excessive leeway. Opinions differ somewhat as to the proper board adjustment when jibing a light dinghy in a breeze. Most authorities agree that the board should not be all the way down because these boats have a tendency to trip on their board, which will encourage a capsizing. Many consider it dangerous

7-6. A Skipjack planing. Notice that the crew have their weight well aft to keep the bow up and that they are hiking to keep the boat flat. The boom is bowsed down with the vang, and the sails are being watched to see that they remain full as the apparent wind draws ahead when the boat picks up speed.

to carry the board all the way up because of side slipping and the tendency of the boat to roll and yaw in a heavy seaway. As a general rule it is the best policy, when jibing in a breeze, to carry the board about a quarter of the way down or slightly farther up.

Duties of the skipper are: to steer, handle the mainsheet, instruct the crew as to sail adjustment when necessary, look around frequently to keep a lookout and size up maneuvering situations, operate the bailer when necessary, and of course, make the major decisions during a race or in an emergency. When steering with the tiller extension, the extension arm must be kept almost at right angles with the tiller, because if the angle becomes extremely obtuse (the extension arm tending to make a straight line with the tiller), then the tiller might be unintentionally flipped in the wrong direction. The mainsheet should always be held in the skipper's hand unless it is temporarily jammed in the cam-action jam cleat in such a way that the sheet may be released instantly with an upward pull. The skipper should always hold the helm in one hand. This leaves only one hand for tending the sheet, and it becomes awkward when it is necessary to trim the mainsail in very much. It is sometimes necessary for the skipper to hold the sheet in his teeth while he slides his hand up the rope for a higher grip when pulling in the sail. In a fresh breeze it is often necessary for the crew to help with this operation. The helmsman's hands should usually be in constant motion slacking or trimming the mainsheet and/or moving the tiller to weave the smoothest course through the waves and to respond to puffs or lulls. When the boat is beating in a moderate breeze, the tiller should not be jammed over violently but it should be moved quite rapidly. In light airs, of course, a slower, smoother tiller action is used.

Planing in a small dinghy is an exhilarating experience. This is when the boat lifts up and breaks away from her speed-retarding wave system. Requirements for planing are a strong breeze and a light displacement hull having a flat run aft. Following seas are extremely helpful. A plane is usually attained most easily when sailing between a broad and a beam reach. To get on a plane the helmsman waits for a puff, heads up slightly if sailing low, and quickly trims in his mainsheet. As the boat begins to heel and pick up speed, he bears off but may have to trim in his sheets, because the apparent wind has been drawn forward due to the increased boat speed. At the same time, the skipper and crew should hike out to keep the boat flat and follow the rule for sailing to leeward: head up in the lulls, off in the puffs. The crew should be moved aft during a plane. This is particularly true when the bow begins to dig into the waves. The stern should not be allowed to bury, however. The boom vang is set up tight to remove sail twist, and the centerboard should usually be nearly all the way up. The jib should be kept full. On the other hand, the mainsail may be allowed to luff slightly when planing in a strong wind. A planing Skipjack is shown in figure 7-6.

Skipjacks may be reefed in a manner similar to the knockabouts, by a simple roller-reefing arrangement. The boom is pulled aft so that it disengages from a square plug at the gooseneck, and then the boom is rotated by hand so that the foot of the sail is wrapped around the boom. Roller reefing will be discussed in more detail when we describe the Luders yawls in the next chapter. Skipjacks are seldom reefed, however, because they can be sailed effectively under mainsail alone, and when racing they usually need maximum sail off the wind for planing purposes. It seldom pays to reef on a short upwind leg of a race course because of the time involved in the reefing operation. In such conditions, the boats can nearly always be kept flat by letting the main luff and by feathering. In a really strong breeze, races are usually canceled.

420 Dinghies. The Skipjacks have been recently replaced for intercollegiate competition at the Naval Academy by a slightly smaller and lighter class of dinghies known as 420s. These boats are very similar to the Skipjacks, but there are minor differences in rigging details as well as in their dimensions. The 420 was designed by a Frenchman, Christian Maury, and the class has had international acceptance as a racing dinghy and standard training boat. Her dimensions are: 13 feet 9 inches length overall, 5 feet 3 inches beam, 216 pounds displacement (minimum sailing weight), 3 feet 2 inches draft (with the centerboard down), and 110 square feet of sail area. The hull is fiberglass with integral molded side tanks for buoyancy that are well rounded for comfortable hiking, and her spars are of aluminum alloy (see figure 7-7). As a sloop, the 420 sails with a crew of two; however, like the Skipjack she has two mast steps so that she may be sailed as a catboat *single-handed* (crew of one). At the USNA the forward step has now been removed, and the dinghy is sailed only as a sloop.

A 420 is handled in a similar way to a Skipjack, and most of the advice given on sailing technique pertaining to the latter boat also applies to the former. There are a few subtle differences, however, in that the 420 is slightly

7-7. The 420 dinghy. Notice how the full-length upper batten holds out the leech to give the sail a substantial roach. The luff telltales on the jib seem to indicate that the sail is stalled as a result of being trimmed in too flat.

more sensitive, being a little quicker when turning and accelerating. She also will plane sooner because of her very light weight. Draft control for the mainsail is slightly different, because the 420 has only one full-length batten at its head to hold out the roach curve. Camber is not controlled so much by regulating the insertion of the battens as by the more conventional means of spar bending and tightening the luff. The mainsail is fitted with a Cunningham cringle (small hole just above the tack) so that a line may be rove through it and then lashed to the tack for stretching the luff extra tight in a fresh breeze. In light to moderate breezes, luff tension is controlled with a sliding gooseneck that is locked in the desired position with a spring-loaded piston controlled by a wing lever.

A 420 is sometimes fitted with a *trapeze* (a wire attached to the mast aloft used to support a hiking crew member), but the device is not used on boats at the Naval Academy. Toe straps for hiking, similar to those used on the Skipjacks, however, are fitted to the bottoms of cockpits on Academy boats. Other systems very similar to those used on Skipjacks are the standing rigging, centerboard lift, boom vang, midships bar traveler, and transom bailers. The bailer flaps are held shut with shock cords, and they must be pulled very tightly closed to prevent water from leaking in when the bottom of the transom is submerged. USNA 420s do not have transom bailers.

Laser. The single-handed dinghy raced in intercollegiate competition is the popular Laser. This cat-rigged, high-performance boat was designed in 1970 by Bruce Kirby. The first production boat was finished in 1971 with Ian Bruce as the builder and Hans Fogh as the sailmaker. The Laser's dimensions are: 13 feet 10½ inches length overall, 4 feet 6 inches beam, 130 pounds displacement (minimum sailing weight), 2 feet 4 inches draft (with the centerboard down), and 76 square feet of sail area. The hull is fiberglass, while the spars are of aluminum alloy. The hull has 350 pounds of positive flotation built in to

115

provide buoyancy. As with the 420 and Skipjack, the Laser is an unballasted centerboard boat fitted with a hiking strap and a tiller extension to allow the transfer of crew weight outboard. The rig is flexible but has no stays or shrouds. (See figure 7-8.)

Rigging the Laser is a simple job requiring only a few minutes. The mast is made up of two lightweight sections which slide together. The luff of the sail is sewn together to form a sleeve which slides completely over the assembled mast, and two Dacron straps at the top of the sleeve hold the sail aloft. The sail is fitted with three battens which are normally sewn into their pockets. After putting the mast together and attaching the sail, fit the mast into a loose step near the bow. Next rig a Cunningham line to a jam cleat just forward of the centerboard trunk, as shown in figure 7-9.

Since the mainsheet is rigged permanently to the boom and traveler (a light line that can be slacked or tightened with a jam cleat), ease the sheet completely off to allow the sail to luff while completing the remainder of the rigging operation. Fit the forward end of the boom onto a pin protruding from the gooseneck on the mast. Hold the boom up, walk aft, and secure the clew of the sail to the boom with the clew outhaul. Lead the outhaul forward along the boom and make it fast in its jam cleat. A small clew tie-down, consisting of a piece of *small stuff* (light line) led through the clew, is tied around the boom. This keeps the foot of the sail along the boom regardless of the foot tension set by the outhaul. The final step in rigging the sail is to attach the boom vang. The vang consists of a tackle attached to the mast by a clevis pin and securing ring. The top block of the vang tackle has either a swaged cylinder or a metal pin

length overall	4.23m	13' 10½"
length waterline	3.81m	12' 6"
beam	1.37m	4' 6"
sail area	7.06	76 sq ft
weight	56.7kg	130 lb
positive flotation	158.7kg	350 lb foam

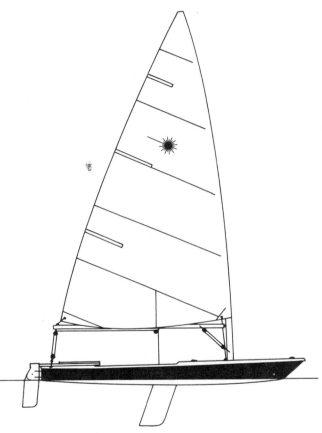

7-8. The Laser.

which slides into a keyhole slot on the bottom of the boom.

With the Laser's transom hanging out over the water's edge, attach the rudder to the transom

116

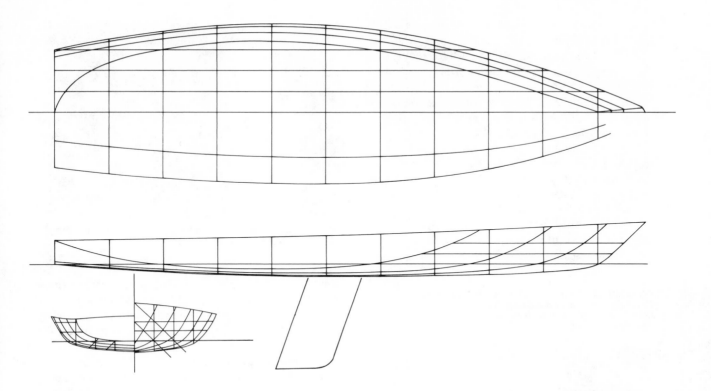

by fitting two *pintles* (pins) into *gudgeons* (brackets). Slip the tiller with its extension into the rudder head and secure it with a cotter pin. Rudder depth can be controlled with a small line that runs from the rudder through the rudder head, but since the rudder should always be fully extended while sailing, pull the rudder downhaul taut and secure it to a jam cleat mounted on the side of the tiller.

Now place the Laser in the water and insert the centerboard in its trunk. The top of the board has two rubber stops which prevent the board from sliding through the trunk. Most Laser sailors drill a small hole in the top of the

board at the forward edge. A length of shock cord with a hook at its end is tied through the hole, and the end may be hooked to the mast or the Cunningham fairlead. The shock cord prevents the board from falling out in the event of a capsize and also holds the board up when on a reach or run. To facilitate board positioning, it is a good idea to drill another small hole in the after end of the board and insert a rope handle.

The Laser is a highly maneuverable boat that responds rapidly to her helm and changes in wind velocity. With her light weight and high performance characteristics, any errors in sail shape, sail trim, weight distribution, or

117

helmsmanship is immediately evident as other boats rapidly pull away.

Roll tacking and roll jibing are two techniques that every racing dinghy sailor should master. While the techniques take a great deal of practice to perfect, once they are mastered the racing sailor will realize immediate results in faster, more controlled tacks and jibes.

Figure 7-10 shows the sequence for roll tacking the Laser. The same basic technique is also used successfully in the 420 and Skipjack. When preparing to tack, trim the sheet in hard, ease the tiller to leeward, and hike to weather. Your after foot should be free of the hiking strap in preparation for moving to the other side. As the boat heads up, allow the boat to roll towards

7-10A. Laser roll-tacking sequence. From close-hauled the tiller is pushed to leeward.

7-9. Laser Cunningham and vang. By tying a loop in the Cunningham line and leading the line back through the loop and the fairlead on deck, you get a 2 : 1 purchase to control luff tension.

you. When the rail you are sitting on touches the water, the luff of the sail will become soft. Push the tiller all the way to leeward, push off against the side of the cockpit with your forward foot, and duck as you move across the boat. Immediately hook your new forward foot (former after foot) under the hiking strap. In light or medium winds be careful not to hike out too quickly; let the boat get going on her new tack. The tiller should now be behind your back. Transfer your grip on the tiller and sheet to the other hand behind your back as you sail off on the new tack. Hike quickly and hard if the wind is fresh. Roll tacking gives the boat an extra boost to weather as well as keeping the speed up. The sail should never actually luff; it should quickly snap over to the new tack.

Roll jibing begins with the Laser sailing on a dead run with the sail well out, the board about two-thirds of the way up, and the boat heeled to weather. The sailor in figure 7-12 is rolling the boat to weather as he pushes the helm to

7-10B. The sailor hikes to weather rolling the boat toward him.

7-10C. The boat is head to wind, the tiller hard over. The sailor ducks under as the sail snaps across on the new tack.

7-10D. The sailor should be transferring the tiller and sheet behind his back.

7-10E. With the crew's weight outboard, the boat heads off from head to wind as a new tack is started.

weather. As the boat rolls, the boom will lift slightly and the sheet should be jerked hard and the stern turned through the wind. Since the natural tendency of the boat is to round up to windward, the helmsman must steer the boat "down" (away from the wind) as he eases the

sheet out on the new tack. The result is a course alteration in the shape of an "S". It is particularly important to get the boom up and jerk the sheet to prevent the sheet snagging on the transom. If this occurs the sail will be over-trimmed and the boat will have a marked tendency to round up. In a breeze this can easily lead to a capsize. The position of the centerboard is also very important. If the board is all the way down, the boat can trip over the board and capsize. If the board is all the way up, the boat will be out of balance and lose directional stability during the jibe. The result is that it is difficult to steer the boat "down" at the completion of the jibe and again a capsize can result.

The following is a summary of helpful hints which will be useful when sailing the Laser.

Light winds

Helm—Make slow, very smooth alterations in course. Do not pinch the boat when beating to windward. Let her foot to keep the speed up. On a run bear off in a puff, head up in the lulls.

Weight—Keep weight well forward, but be careful not to bury the bow. Heel to leeward going to windward; heel to weather on the runs.

Sail Shape—Clew tie-down should be tight against the boom. Ease the outhaul and Cunningham to get maximum draft. Since mast bend is controlled by sheet tension and the vang

7-12A. Laser roll-jibing sequence. Sailing on a dead run, the boat is heeled to weather as the tiller is put over.

7-11. Navy's All-American sailor Paul Van Cleve scrambles to prevent his Laser from capsizing after attempting a roll tack in a stiff breeze. In heavy winds it is not necessary to roll tack. Simply put the tiller over, trim the sheet, and hike out quickly on the new windward side as the boat comes through the wind.

rather than by stays and shrouds, the sheet should be trimmed in hard and the vang set up almost as tight as possible. Although this induces mast bend and tends to flatten the sail, it moves the draft aft. When going to weather the sheet should be eased slightly to allow the boat to foot. On a reach or run ease the vang slightly to ease the leech.

Traveler—Ease the traveler bridle a little to allow the boom to rise. Be careful not to allow excessive leech twist. Easing the traveler will also make the tiller action easier.

Centerboard—All the way down when going to weather. On a run get the board all the way up. Put it down about one-third just before a jibe.

Medium air

Helm—Respond quickly to wind shifts. Be careful not to overcorrect and jam the tiller over, as this will stall the rudder. Keep the boat pointing and sailing flat when going to windward. Once again, when on a run bear off in the puffs, head up in the lulls.

Weight—Keep your weight forward and hike

7-12B. As the stern passes through the wind, the tiller is pushed to weather and the sheet is jerked hard.

7-12C. As the sail jibes, the sailor ducks under and begins to bear off.

7-12D. The sailor continues to bear off. Note the correct position of the tiller behind the sailor's back.

7-12E. The Laser is heeled to weather on a run. The Cunningham and clew outhaul should now be eased to get more draft in the sail.

to keep the boat flat. Heel the boat to weather on the runs. If marginal planing conditions exist, move your weight quickly forward when coming off a wave. Also, give the sail a few rapid trims. If the boat gets up on a plane, shift your weight aft to keep the bow out, but do not bury the stern.

Sail Shape—Keep the shape basically the same as for light air. Tighten the outhaul and Cunningham to flatten the sail slightly. Keep the draft in the middle of the sail.

Traveler—Tighten the traveler as much as possible to keep the leech straight. Just before a jibe many good sailors ease the traveler to allow the

7-13. Righting technique for Laser.

traveler block to move freely across the boat.

Centerboard—Keep the board all the way down when going to weather unless the water is becoming sloppy, in which case move the board up about 2 inches. On a reach adjust the board to keep the boat *tracking* (holding a steady course). On a run the board should be all the way up.

Heavy air

Helm—Respond quickly to wind shifts and puffs. When going to windward keep the boat pointing. If you cannot keep the boat flat in the hardest puffs, head up slightly to gain distance to weather rather than allowing the boat to heel excessively (this is called feathering). If the boat is stopped by seas, bear off slightly and foot.

Weight—Hike hard and keep the boat flat. On reaches and runs, shift your weight aft when on a plane.

Sail shape—Get all sail controls as tight as possible. You can twist the vang to get extra tension and mast bend. The sail should be flat with the draft well forward.

Traveler—Have the traveler as tight as possible. Again, it helps to ease it slightly before a jibe.

Centerboard—Put the board all the way down when going to weather. On a run it may be necessary to put the board down slightly while planing to help the boat track. Be sure to get the board down less than half way before a jibe.

Capsize—It is not necessary to lower the sail on a Laser in order to get it upright after a capsize. The following technique will get the boat upright and sailing without spending time swimming the boat head to wind. Step up on the centerboard as shown in figure 7-13. As the sail clears itself of water and the boat begins to

come upright, step off the board and "hug" it hard with both arms. Go under the boat holding on to the board. Swim out on the weather side, crawl aboard, trim, hike, and sail away. Another method, perhaps easier, of righting a Laser is shown in figure 7-13.

Miscellaneous tips for Laser sailors.
• Keep the mast step clean. Soap chips make a good lubricant.
• When hiking on a long leg, cross your feet under the strap to give one leg a rest.
• Rig a short piece of shock cord at the after end of the hiking strap to keep it up. This makes it easier to hook your foot after a tack. Also rig a short "backup" securing line to the strap in case the primary securing line breaks.
• Wax the boom and mast to ease outhaul and Cunningham action.

• Use tape around the tiller to prevent any "play" in the rudder head. Use tape and twine to make a grip at the end of the tiller extension.
• Make sure that the battens are exactly the correct length and that they are sanded smooth or fitted with plastic end tips.
• Get extra purchase from the Cunningham by rigging a loop in the line as shown in figure 7-9.
• Install telltales. These may be ribbons taped to the sail or yarns threaded through the sail so that telltales show on each side at a distance of about 18 inches abaft the luff a little lower than halfway up the sail and also slightly higher than halfway up. In addition, yarns or ribbons are often attached to the leech at each batten. These telltales will indicate when the sail is stalled or when it is on the verge of luffing. Try to sail with the telltales streaming directly aft. If the leeward luff yarns are hanging down or twirling, the sail

is stalled and you can point higher or else ease the sheet; if the windward yarns are twirling, the sail is luffing and you should bear off or perhaps trim in slightly. Incidentally, luff yarns are also effective on jibs, but they are usually located farther forward, perhaps a foot or less abaft the luff, because there is no mast forward of the sail to disturb the air flow (see figure 5-6).

• Some Laser sailors mount wind direction indicators (a feather or Windex vane) atop the mast or on the bow. If the Windex is on the mast, care must be taken not to make any holes that would allow the mast to fill with water and thereby cause the boat to turn turtle in the event of a capsize.

The Shields Class. In 1963, five Shields class sloops were donated to the Naval Academy by

7-14. Rounding the mark during a Laser race. NA 1 is properly heeled to windward, while NA 4 is not. NA 8 is preparing to roll jibe around the mark.

length over all   30   feet 2½ inches
length water line   20   feet
beam   6   feet 5¼ inches
draft   4   feet 9 inches
sail area   360   square feet

7-15. The Shields one-design class sloop and sail plan.

7-16. A Shields sloop reaching with her spinnaker. Note that all the Shields are now fitted with a traveler.

Mr. Cornelius Shields, one of America's most famous yachtsmen. This class was designed by Sparkman and Stephens to specifications suggested by Mr. Shields. Since Mr. Shields was an organizer, founder, and champion of the well-known International One-Design class, it is not surprising that the Shields sloops bear a resemblance to the Internationals. The Shields boats are built of fiberglass by the Chris-Craft Corporation. Their dimensions are: 30 feet 2½ inches

length over-all, 20 feet on the waterline, 6 feet 5¼ inches beam, and 4 feet 9 inches draft. They carry 360 square feet of sail on aluminum spars.

Figures 7-15 and 7-16 illustrate Shields sloops. Notice that their standing rigging plan is basically similar to the seven-eighths rig shown in figure 5-10, except that the Shields does not carry jumper stays or struts. It is interesting that the original rigging plans for the Shields called for jumpers, but evidently it was felt later that the boat did not need these extra stays. Obviously, the simplest rig that can control the mast effectively is the best. Superfluous rigging causes tuning complications, windage, and extra weight aloft, which is harmful to a boat's stability. Also, the elimination of jumper stays permits the use of a jib that is slightly longer on the luff when this is considered desirable.

This sloop rig might be termed semiflexible. The spars are not bent nearly as much as those of the Skipjack, 420, or Laser, but the Shields mast is bowed somewhat in a breeze. This bowing is done by tightening the permanent backstay, which may be adjusted from the cockpit. Unlike the jibstay and shrouds, which have a turnbuckle, the backstay runs through the afterdeck, and is attached to a tackle which lies under the deck and may be controlled from the cockpit's after end. It is customary to tighten the backstay when beating to windward in a breeze, but to slack it when running. The single pair of lower shrouds are usually carried quite

7-17. The mooring arrangement for the Shields Sloops. Notice such details as the boom vang and halyard lead blocks at the base of the mast. All Shields sloops now have travelers, as shown in figure 7-16.

slack for two reasons: to keep the mast straight laterally and, since the lowers are slightly abaft the uppers, to allow the mast's middle to bow forward when the backstay is tightened. The mast should be raked aft very slightly. If a plumb line were dropped from the after side of the masthead, the plumb bob should lie about six inches abaft the base of the mast at the deck.

Sails are of Dacron, and they are fitted with conventional short battens. When sailing in a fresh breeze, it is necessary to ease the mainsheet and let the mainsail luff slightly; in a strong breeze, the mainsail must be reefed. USNA Shields have been fitted with "jiffy" or slab reefing. (This method of shortening sail will be described in some detail in the next chapter.) The lead blocks for the mainsheet were formerly fixed at the deck, but now there is a sliding lead on a traveler. Jibsheets have leads on tracks which allow athwartships as well as fore-and-aft adjustments. Halyards and sheets are provided with winches for extra power; winches will be discussed in more detail in the next chapter.

Halyards are controlled from the forward end of the cockpit, with the main halyard and winch under the deck, while the jib halyard is on the port side above the deck. Lines belayed on deck at the forward end of the cockpit include the halyard, lift, and downhaul for the spinnaker. (Spinnaker handling will be discussed in chapter 9.) The boom is equipped with a powerful vang, and this is especially important for sail shaping, because the Shields has a large mainsail and a lightweight boom. The boom is also fitted with an adjustable downhaul.

A Shields sloop is delightful to sail, especially on the wind in a moderate breeze. With her short keel and cutaway forefoot, she turns rapidly and has a sensitive helm. When properly tuned, she balances well with just a slight weather helm when moderately heeled. She responds to every touch of the tiller and can be worked to windward effectively using the technique discussed in chapter 5. The Shields is heavier than the knockabout, and she gives a feeling of power when beating against a chop. Her narrow hull knifes through the waves without appreciably being slowed by them. Her moderately light weight and large sail area make her a good performer in light air, despite the fact that she carries no Genoa jib. On account of her ample keel ballast, she is quite *stiff* (resistant to extreme heeling) in a breeze. She heels fairly easily to a certain point, but then rapidly gains in stability. Although it is possible (but not likely) for her to swamp, she is unsinkable. Flotation tanks fore and aft and in the bilge are said to be sufficient to buoy up the swamped boat with as many as thirteen people aboard, although normally she carries only three or four.

Shields sloops are moored in a manner similar to the knockabouts (see figure 7-17), and roughly the same basic problems are faced when getting underway or landing. The Shields are somewhat more maneuverable, carry more way, and handle better under jib alone than do the knockabouts. Neither class has self-draining cockpits, but the Shields are equipped with cloth cockpit covers to keep out rain water when the boats are moored.

127

8. Luders Yawls

In addition to having a fleet of small sailing craft, the Naval Academy owns and maintains 12 nearly identical 44-foot Luders yawls. These offer the midshipmen a unique opportunity for training in large ocean-racing sailboats. These boats carry a full complement of light sails, and they may be used as a class (racing against each other), or they can compete against comparable boats of different designs under a handicap system. A safe and seaworthy design, the Naval Academy yawls have been raced in many ocean races, even across the North Atlantic.

These yawls were designed for the Naval Academy in 1939 by the Luders Marine Construction Company of Stamford, Connecticut. The original 12 boats, the last of which was completed in 1943, were built of wood. Commencing in 1963, however, the wooden yawls were gradually replaced with fiberglass versions. Although hull forms and rigs are nearly identical, there are certain differences between the wooden and fiberglass yawls. For instance, the wooden boats are engineless, while the fiberglass boats are fitted with diesel power; the

old boats have wooden spars, while the new ones are fitted with aluminum masts and have improvements in the rigging, some of which will be discussed later. Accommodations below have been changed considerably, and the new boats carry slightly more keel ballast than the old boats. At present, the Naval Academy has fiberglass yawls only, but the original wooden yawls are being used at various naval stations.

The dimensions of the Luders yawls are as follows: length overall, 44 feet 2½ inches; length water line, 30 feet 1 inch; maximum beam, 10 feet 10½ inches; draft, 6 feet ⅜ inch; mainmast height from deck to masthead, 52 feet 3 inches; displacement (light) (fiberglass), 22,260 pounds; keel ballast (fiberglass), 9,850 pounds; keel ballast (wood), 9,000 pounds; and working sail area (main, mizzen, and forestaysail), 722 square feet.

Figure 8-1 shows a Luders yawl under sail. The shape of the Luders hull may be seen in figures 8-2 and 8-4. The interior layout for the fiberglass yawls is shown in figure 8-5, and that for the wooden yawls in figure 8-6. The sail and

8-1. The Luders yawl under shortened sail. The yawl *Frolic* under the well-balanced rig of mainsail and forestaysail. The photo was taken in 1953. Since then, anchor windlasses (shown on her foredeck) have been removed. The forestaysail halyard needs setting up, the main topping lift wants some slack, and the mizzen might be furled a bit more securely.

deck plans for the fiberglass yawls are shown in figure 8-7.

Yawl rigging. Figure 8-7 also shows the rigging of the Luders yawl. The rig is basically a masthead plan with a headstay and an opposing permanent backstay on the mainmast. At a distance of about 15 feet from the *truck* (top of the mast) on the mast's fore side a forestay is attached. The forestay has two functions: to support the forestaysail, and also to help prevent fore-and-aft bending below the headstay. Runners (running backstays) are attached to the mast at the same point to prevent the mast from bowing forward at the forestay's point of attachment.

Originally the yawls were designed to carry jumper stays and struts to eliminate the need for running backstays, but jumpers would have interfered with the tacking of large headsails, and it was decided that runners would be used.

Actually these stays are not used at all times but only when it is blowing hard enough to bend the mast or when the forestaysail is set. Likewise, the forestay is not usually set up in a light to moderate breeze. When not in use, it is released from its deck fitting by a lever and is brought aft, slack, and clipped to the shrouds. In this position, it will not interfere with the tacking of a large Genoa jib. The aluminum masts are stiffer than the wooden ones; therefore, on the new yawls, forestays and backstays are usually not needed except when a Genoa is carried in a fresh breeze. The need for these stays varies with individual boats. Some masts are more limber than others. The proper time for setting up these running stays should be determined by sighting up the mast. If it is bowing more than very slightly or pumping in a seaway, set them up. Don't take a chance on breaking the mast.

At their lower ends the running backstays on the wooden yawls have *whips* (a tackle in which only one block is used. See figure 8-7). One end of the whip has an eye which fits on a hook secured to the deck, while the whip's other end is adjusted with a lever. On the fiberglass yawls, a tail of ¾" dacron braid is led through a snatch-block attached to a pad eye located on deck between the primary and secondary Genoa winches. From there the runner may be led to either winch. When the runners are in use, naturally the one to leeward is slacked, while the one to windward is tightened with its lever or winch. However, when the runners are not in use, the eye ends of the whip are released from their hooks and the stays are brought forward, slack, and are secured to the after shrouds. The shrouds are provided with snap shackles for holding the runners.

The mizzenmast on a wooden yawl is provided with a backstay that is set up with a *pelican hook* (a hinged hook that is held closed with a sliding ring). A mizzen backstay is usually not set up unless the mizzen staysail is carried in a moderate breeze. This sail has a strong tendency to pull the mast forward. Of course, the backstay must be released when tacking or jibing. Fiberglass yawls have the chainplates for the mizzen after shrouds located much farther aft than on the wooden yawls; therefore, on the new boats, mizzen backstays are really not necessary. The mizzenmast is fitted with a jumper stay running over a strut; it keeps the top of the mast from bending aft.

8-2. Hull of a fiberglass Luders yawl. The lines of the yawl show a successful compromise between an able, seakindly, fairly heavy displacement hull and one that is easily driven. The slack bilges (having a gradual as opposed to a sharp curve) and moderate deadrise lessen wetted surface for speed and give an easy motion in a seaway. These factors make for a boat that will heel quite easily initially, but that will become increasingly stiff as her ample keel ballast becomes effective at higher angles of heel. The keel is of sufficient length to give good directional stability, but it is sufficiently cut away forward to reduce wetted surface and to assure reasonably quick helm response. The keel is also of ample draft to assure good performance when beating to windward, and the deep draft allows the keel ballast to be placed low where it is most effective. With their long overhangs, moderate freeboard, graceful sheer, and sleek underbody, the Luders yawls are among the most aesthetically pleasing of sailing yachts.

8-3. A new rudder design for the Luders yawls. The new rudder is more efficient partly because there is more area at the bottom where the water is less aerated. Also, tank tests have shown that the sharp corner has a beneficial effect on the efficiency of the lateral plane. Yawls fitted with the new rudder are easier to control downwind, and windward performance may be slightly improved in moderate to fresh winds. The rudder design before change is shown on right.

Looking at the rigging plan from the bow or stern, we can see that the mainmast has two sets of spreaders and has intermediate shrouds as well as upper shrouds and two sets of lower shrouds. Although the rigging seems complicated, it involves the same tuning principles as were discussed in chapter 6. The upper shrouds should always be kept taut, while the intermediates are slightly less taut, and the lowers are still less taut. The after and forward lowers are adjusted to keep the mast straight. Obviously, this is a masthead rig and the sails are cut for a straight mast; thus, the mast should be kept straight, both fore and aft and athwartships, at all times. The headstay and backstay should be

quite taut for efficient windward sailing. It is a good idea to tighten these stays slightly before a race but to slack them off again after the race. This keeps the strain off the boat most of the time. The yawls are designed to carry their masts with a slight rake aft of about 16 inches, which gives them a slight weather helm. Of course, this may vary slightly with individual boats because of differences in trim and the condition of the sails.

Most of the running rigging consists of one-half-inch Dacron sheets and a combination of wire and Dacron for halyards. There are six halyards on the mainmast: one for the fore-staysail and spinnaker staysail which runs

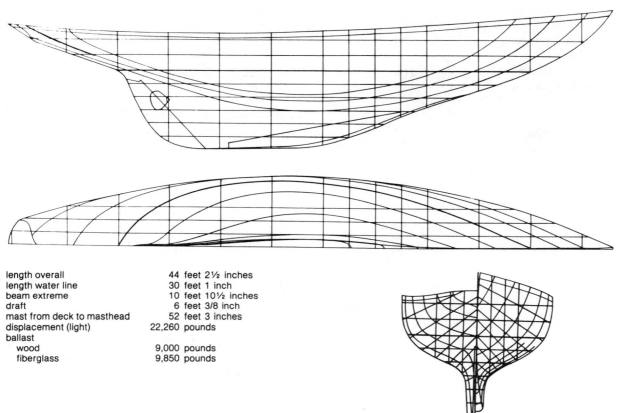

length overall	44	feet 2½ inches
length water line	30	feet 1 inch
beam extreme	10	feet 10½ inches
draft	6	feet 3/8 inch
mast from deck to masthead	52	feet 3 inches
displacement (light)	22,260	pounds
ballast		
wood	9,000	pounds
fiberglass	9,850	pounds

8-4. Luders yawl, lines.

through a block just below the point of attachment of the forestay, a main halyard, two masthead jib halyards running through mast sheaves (pulleys set into the masthead as shown in figure 8-8) on the fiberglass yawls, and two spinnaker halyards running through blocks hung just above and forward of the point of attachment of the headstay. Also, there is a spinnaker pole lift which runs through a block hung on the fore side of the mast some distance below the upper spreaders. All these lines belay at the base of the mast. The wooden yawls have a double purchase or tackle arrangement for their main halyards and a Number 2 ratchet main halyard winch on the mast. The halyard is wrapped three or four times around the winch after the sail is almost hoisted. The fiberglass boats, however, have a different main halyard arrangement. Until very recently, these halyards were all wire which wound up on reel winches, similar in principle to fishing line reels. Presently, however, the yawls have main halyards that are wire with Dacron tails and their winches are non-reel, number 16 Barients. The operation of winches will be discussed near the end of this chapter.

There is also a difference between the wooden and fiberglass yawls in their sheeting arrangements for most sails. On the former, there are adjustable forestaysail leads consisting of slides on tracks mounted on the side decks. On the fiberglass boats, forestaysail sheets are led to one of two pad eyes on each side to which lead

blocks are fastened. Both wooden and fiberglass yawls have mainsheet travelers abaft the cockpit, but on the wooden boats, the sheet runs along the underside of the boom to a block near the gooseneck, and then it is led back to a cleat and winch atop the cabin house near its after end on the starboard side. On the fiberglass boats, however, the sheet is led internally through the boom to a block at the gooseneck, and then back to a cleat and winch atop the cabin house near its after end on the port side.

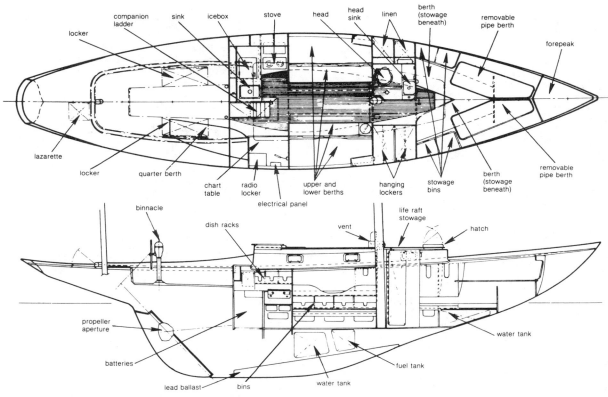

8-5. Luders fiberglass yawl, accommodations plan and inboard profile.

Genoa sheets are essentially the same for all boats. These sheets lead outside the shrouds through blocks on adjustable slides that attach to tracks mounted on the rails. They are then taken to winches through *turning blocks* (blocks used to change the direction of a line), as shown in figure 8-9.

The mizzen running rigging includes the mizzen halyard, which has a Number 10 Barient winch on the starboard side of the mast. Both the wooden and fiberglass yawls have mizzen staysail halyards, but only the wooden boats have a Number 2 winch on the port side of the mast for this halyard. The fiberglass boats are fitted with a cleat only for making fast the staysail halyard. All yawls have a triple-purchase mizzen sheet that leads to a winch mounted on the lower, after side of the mizzen mast. The sheet's cleat is just below the winch. The mizzen staysail sheet is led through a block at the end of the mizzen boom and belays to a cleat on the boom.

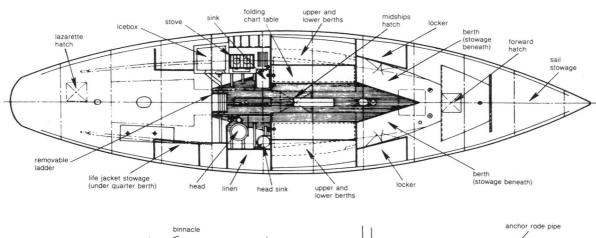

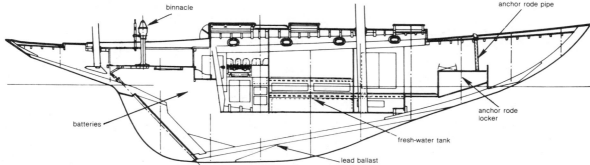

8-6. Luders wooden yawl, accommodations plan and inboard profile.

8-7. Luders fiberglass yawl, sail, rigging, and half-deck plans.

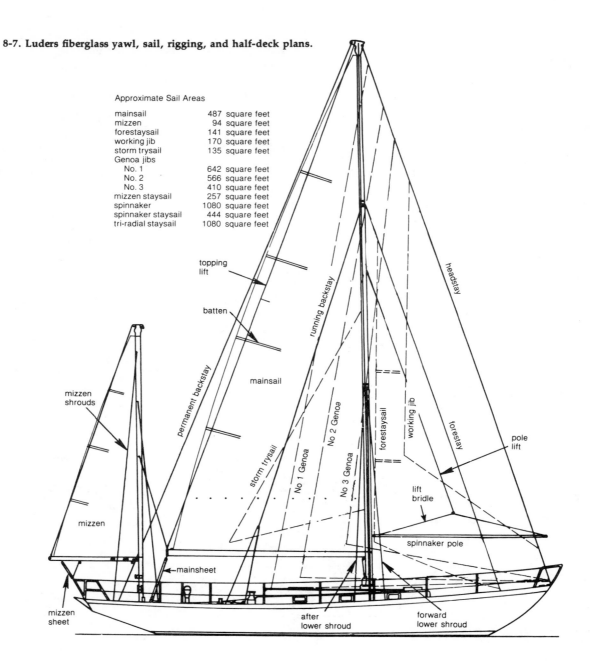

Approximate Sail Areas

mainsail	487	square feet
mizzen	94	square feet
forestaysail	141	square feet
working jib	170	square feet
storm trysail	135	square feet
Genoa jibs		
No. 1	642	square feet
No. 2	566	square feet
No. 3	410	square feet
mizzen staysail	257	square feet
spinnaker	1080	square feet
spinnaker staysail	444	square feet
tri-radial staysail	1080	square feet

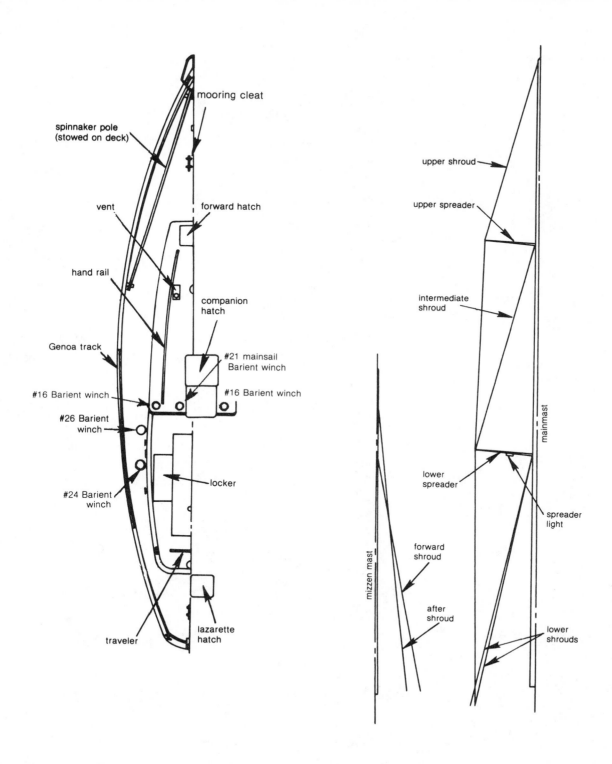

8-8. Luders fiberglass yawl, mainmasthead detail.

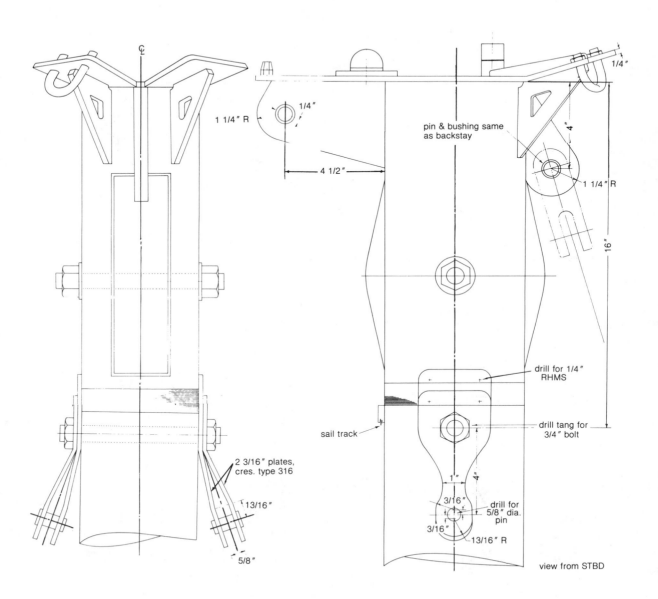

1 1/4" R

1/4"

4 1/2"

pin & bushing same
as backstay

1/4"

4"

1 1/4" R

16"

drill for 1/4"
RHMS

sail track

drill tang for
3/4" bolt

2 3/16" plates,
cres. type 316

13/16"

1"

4"

3/16"

drill for
5/8" dia.
pin

3/16"

13/16" R

5/8"

view from STBD

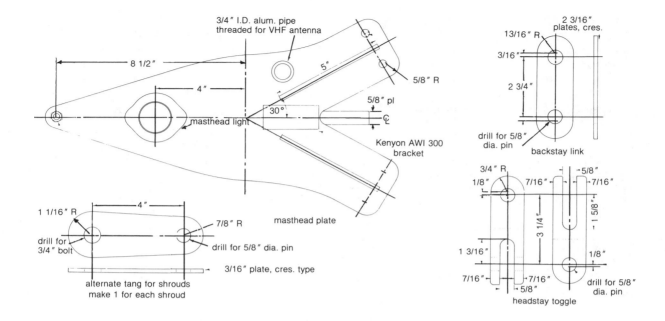

Yawl sails. Yawl mainsails are made of heavy Dacron and have an area of 487 square feet. They are usually left furled and stopped on the boom when the boats are not in use. The sails are secured to their spars with tracks and slides. On the wooden boats the main boom's gooseneck may slide up or down on the mast, and all luff tension adjustments are made with the boom downhaul. The fiberglass boats have a fixed gooseneck, and luff tension adjustments are made with a combination of a *jack line* (a line fitted through the bottom ten slides of the luff), a Cunningham line, or halyard tension. The sail is hoisted until the top of the headboard

(the plate in the head of the mainsail) is even with the bottom of the black band at the masthead, and then the downhaul is adjusted to give the proper luff tension appropriate to the wind velocity or a particular point of sailing. When sighting aloft to align the headboard with the black band, remember that you are sighting from directly beneath, and the extreme perspective will make it appear that the headboard is higher relative to the band than it really is. Once a mainsail is hoisted to its proper height, it is often possible to mark the halyard with a piece of tape which can be aligned with another tape mark on the mast for future reference. It is important to hoist the mainsail as high as possible for two reasons: in light airs there is usually more wind aloft, and the maximum distance between upper and lower black bands may be utilized fully to tighten the luff in a fresh breeze.

The clew outhaul on the main boom of the fiberglass yawls consists of a slide on a track mounted along the top of the boom. The outhaul line runs from the slide internally through the boom and exits along the forward starboard side of the boom. The mainsail clew on any yawl should never be pulled abaft the forward edge of the black band at the boom's end. Never forget to *slack the outhaul* of any furled sail left bent on

8-9. A fiberglass Luders yawl on the wind. This close view of the *Fearless* working to windward full and by shows the Genoa sheeting arrangement. Note that the sheet runs through the sliding lead block on the track on the rail, through a turning block abaft the lead block, and then forward to the large winch. To get extra power, the crew can then lead the sheet across the boat to the weather winch. The helmsman is sitting to leeward where he can get a clear view of the jib. Observe the dinghy in her chocks and secured by crisscrossed straps. The mizzen might set a little better if its topping lift were slacked.

its boom. Before hoisting or lowering the mainsail, be sure that the boom topping lift (see figure 8-7) is set up, and that it is slacked off when underway. Sailing with a taut topping lift is nearly always harmful to the set of a sail.

Mainsails on the wooden yawls are reefed in the conventional way, as shown in figure 8-10. Notice that before the sail is reefed there is a row of eyelets with lanyards (short lines) hanging from them. These are called *reef points,* and they hang down on each side of the sail. In line with the reef point eyelets at the luff, there is a reinforced hole in the sail called the *luff cringle* and at the leech a similar hole called the *leech cringle.* When reefing the sail, these cringles are lashed down to the boom with short, stout lines called *earings.* Each yawl is supplied with a clew and tack earing. The luff cringle should be lashed down before the leech cringle is pulled aft. The clew earing must not only hold the leech cringle down, but the line must pull the cringle aft as well. The earing should run from the cringle aft through the clew outhaul fitting (or some other reeving point at the boom's after end), and then be led forward to the cringle again. The sail is hauled aft until it is tight along the boom, and then the leech cringle is lashed down to the boom with the remaining end of the earing. After both cringles are lashed, the loose lower part of the sail below the reef points, which is called the *bunt,* is rolled up neatly and placed on top of the boom where it is tied with the reef points. Notice in figure 8-10 that the reef points are not tied around the boom, but they pass between the boom and the sail. Were they tied around the boom, unequal tension on different reef points could cause harmful stretching or even tearing of the sail.

If reefing is done while underway, the main-

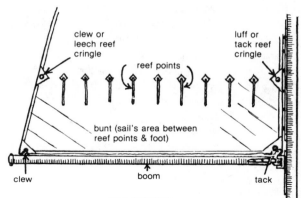

FULL MAINSAIL

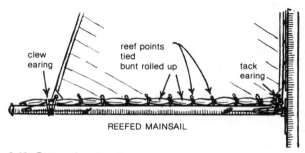

REEFED MAINSAIL

8.10. Conventional reefing.

sail can be lowered entirely. The topping lift is set up, the boat is luffed into the wind, and the sail is lowered. This requires that the boat be a sufficient distance from the *lee shore* (downwind shore) before the operation is begun because the boat may make considerable leeway while the reef is being tied in. The boat can jog along under jib and mizzen until the reef is tied in. While reefing, the boom should be in its crutch and the mainsheet must be *bowsed down* (pulled tight) to hold the boom in place. Since some yawls are equipped with more than one row of reef points, it is very important, before hoisting sail, to check that all the tied reef points are

141

from the same row. A sail could be seriously torn if some points were tied from the first row while others were tied from the second. If a mainsail is not equipped with reef points but only a row of eyelets, then a long, continuous reefing line may be rove through the eyelets and around the foot of the sail or around the boom. If a reef is taken in using the conventional points method, it is often easier and the sail flaps less if it is lowered, but racing boats seldom if ever lower their mainsails. Also, in rough seas when there is a large Genoa set, lowering the main can put excessive strain on the mast. To reef without lowering sail, set up the topping lift and sail close-hauled with a slight luff in the mainsail; ease the halyard until the luff cringle comes down to the boom, set up the tack earing and then the clew earing, tie in the reef points, hoist the sail until the luff is taut, and slack the topping lift.

Shaking out (untying) a reef is usually easier than tying one in. This is one reason why it is better to reef before getting underway when there is doubt as to the need for reducing sail. Should it be found, when underway, that conditions don't warrant a reef, it is not difficult to shake it out. This can usually be done without lowering the sail. First the topping lift is set up. Then the reef points are untied, the clew earing is cast off, and finally the tack earing is unlashed. The helmsman then luffs slightly and another crew man stands by the halyard to hoist the sail up hard as soon as the tack earing has been released.

The fiberglass yawls were equipped with roller reefing until 1976. With this reefing method, the mainsail is rolled up on its boom, which may be rotated with a gear and crank handle at the gooseneck. Figure 8-11 shows a worm-gear

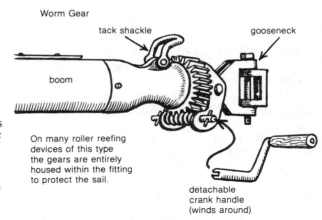

Worm Gear
tack shackle   gooseneck
boom

On many roller reefing devices of this type the gears are entirely housed within the fitting to protect the sail.

detachable crank handle (winds around)

8-11. Roller reefing.

roller reefing mechanism similar to that formerly used on the Navy yawls. For clarity, the illustration shows the gears exposed, but in actuality they lie within a metal housing so that the sail will not get caught in the gears. With roller reefing, sail is rarely lowered entirely before reefing. The halyard is simply eased off as the crank is turned. The bottom four slides on the mainsail are attached to the jack line. Before reefing, the jack line is unrove from the slides allowing them to remain on the track when the sail is wound around the boom. If a deeper reef is required, the upper slides must be removed from the track, one at a time, when they are pulled down to the bot om of the track by the boom's rotation. It is ne arly always necessary to have one or two crew members pulling aft on the sail's leech near the clew, in order that the roll be kept smooth all the way along the boom. The mainsheet is attached to a swivel fitting at the end of the boom. Someone should check to see that this fitting is swivelling smoothly as the boom is turned. When unrolling a reef, the pro-

142

cedure is reversed. The boom is turned in the opposite direction unwinding the sail, while the halyard is taken up and the slides are fed back onto the track and the bottom slides are secured to the sail.

In 1976 the Navy fiberglass yawls received new aluminum booms which converted the reefing to a "jiffy" or "slab" reefing system. The sail is lowered onto the boom and secured with a single earing and hook, and the bunt is gathered and tied up with small stuff through reef eyelets. With this system the yawls have a flattening reef, first reef, and second reef.

The flattening reef does little to reduce sail, but it removes excessive draft, particularly in the lower third of the sail. To set the flattening reef the mainsheet is eased while the flattening reef line is winched in until the leech cringle lies close to the boom. The luff of the sail is not adjusted for this reef.

The reef lines or earings which control the leech of the sail are led internally through the boom. The after part of each line exits the boom around a turning block, passes up through a reefing cringle in the leech, and then is led back to the boom where it is made fast. The forward part of the reef line leaves the boom at the gooseneck as shown in figure 8-13. Also note the internal mainsheet. The reef line is then led to a fairlead block, through a jam cleat, and to one of the #16 Barient winches at the aft end of the cabin house.

When the reef line is winched up, the leech of the sail is held firmly along the boom as seen in figure 8-14. The luff of the sail is secured through the use of a grommet (cringle) in the luff and one of the two hooks at the gooseneck, one hook for each of the two full reefs.

The steps for inserting a full reef are shown in

8-12. The Luders yawl *Swift* with a shallow reef rolled in her mainsail. Notice how the boom vang must be attached with a claw ring. The reef is not sufficiently deep to necessitate removing all the slides from the jack line. The mizzen is furled primarily to relieve weather helm.

figure 8-14. Two crew members are at the mast, the mainsheet is ready to be eased, and a crew member is ready to winch in the reef line. As shown in figure 8-14a, the mainsail is luffed and the main halyard eased until the first reef cringle along the luff is lowered to the hook. (As the sail is luffed the helmsman should bear off to keep up boat speed.) The luff cringle is placed over the hook (figure 8-14b), and the halyard is taken up to obtain the proper luff tension (figure 8-14D). Simultaneously, the crew member on the reef line has winched in until the leech cringle is against the boom. When both the luff and leech are secured, the reef line is stopped off in the jam cleat, the mainsail is trimmed, and the helmsman heads up to a close-hauled course. The crew then begin inserting small stuff through the reef points to complete the reef. A well-trained crew

143

8-13A. Luders fiberglass yawl slab or jiffy reefing sheave box. From left to right: first reef line; mainsheet; flattening reef; second reef line. All lines are lead internally along the boom.

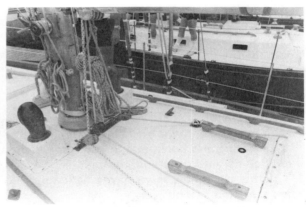

8-13B. Deck layout showing reefing arrangement. From starboard to port: the second reef line is coiled and hanging just beneath the sheave box; the flattening reef line is lead aft through a jam cleat.

should be able to set a reef and get the boat back to a close-hauled course in 15-20 seconds.

The mizzen on a Navy yawl is quite similar to the mainsail except, of course, that it is much smaller, with an area of 94 square feet. For this reason it is not provided with any means of reefing. The clew outhaul is a slide on a track controlled with a purchase, but the gooseneck is fixed, so luff tension must be controlled with the halyard. The mizzen's primary function is to act as a balancing sail. When the sail is sheeted in flat, weather helm is increased, but when the sheet is eased, weather helm is lessened. Because the mizzen is usually backwinded by the mainsail when sailing close-hauled, some sailors feel that the mizzen is of little value on a beat. Actually, it has considerable value as a balancing sail, however, particularly in light airs, giving the boat a little weather helm. As said previously, this helm is important to give the keel hydrodynamic lift and especially to give the

helmsman a "helm feel." In a strong breeze, when weather helm is excessive, the mizzen can be lowered, and this will nearly always relieve the boat's strong tendency to round up into the wind. One of the advantages of the yawl rig is that in a sudden squall the mainsail may be lowered and balance will be maintained under forestaysail and mizzen. Also, unless the boat is heeled excessively, reasonable balance can be had under mainsail and forestaysail, or even under mainsail alone, if it is desired that the jib and mizzen be lowered (see figures 6-9 and 8-1).

The forestaysail is a fairly small (141 square feet), heavy sail with battens, and it is hanked on to the forestay. It is the basic, working headsail on a yawl. Usually this sail is set in a strong breeze only, or when squalls threaten, or when a yawl is undermanned in a moderate breeze. The most usual sail combinations that include the forestaysail are as follows:

• Main, mizzen, forestaysail, and a high-cut

144

working jib hanked on to the headstay. This combination of sails forward of the mainmast is known as the double head rig, and it is sometimes carried when beating to windward in a fresh breeze. This combination can be very effective. Some boats with a double head rig carry a larger high-cut jib called a *yankee* in moderate weather.

• Main and forestaysail, or reefed main and forestaysail. The latter is an especially well-balanced plan for a strong breeze.

• Mizzen and forestaysail for a sudden squall.

• Forestaysail alone in a strong gale. If the boat is heeled severely, this sail will balance the boat reasonably well even though it is well forward of the normal total center of effort (see figure 6-9).

• Forestaysail set in combination with a Genoa jib, mainsail, and mizzen in squally weather, so that if a squall hits, Genoa and mainsail may be dropped quickly and the boat will be under a very short, balanced rig.

Light sails used on the yawls include three sizes of Genoa jibs, spinnakers (to be discussed in the next chapter), spinnaker staysails, mizzen staysail, and drifter. The large Genoa, called the number one Genoa, with an area of 642 square feet, is the "work horse" of a yawl in light weather. It supplies the principal driving power in a light breeze on all points of sailing, except when the wind is abaft the beam—at which times the spinnaker comes into prominence. The number one is probably carried more often than any other sail except the main and mizzen. (See figure 8-16.)

The newest number two is the next smaller size Genoa, and it has an area of 566 square feet. This is carried when the wind is too strong for the number one. When jibs should be changed will depend on whether the boat is being raced or cruised, whether the main is reefed, how many

and how skilled are her crew, the cut and condition of the particular jibs involved, and the stiffness of the boat. To be very general, however, when the boat is racing the number one should probably be replaced with the number two when the wind velocity is between 17 and 20 knots.

When a boat begins to be overburdened with the number two Genoa, the number three should be used. The latest version of this sail has an area of only 410 square feet. In a breeze which would warrant carrying this sail, perhaps 25 to 35 knots, there would be an option between the number three and the aforementioned double head rig. In heavy seas, the latter might be preferable, because the lower-cut Genoa often takes heavy spray and solid water against its foot and this could obviously damage the sail. Notice, however, that the new number three shown in figure 8-7 is cut with a high clew to minimize damage from the bow wave. Another factor to take into consideration is the trend of the weather. If it seems likely that the breeze will increase and develop into a gale, the double head rig will be preferable because the forestaysail is already set and the jib can be quickly doused if the wind becomes overpowering. When it comes to carrying only one headsail in a gale, the forestaysail is nearly always easier to manage than a long-tailed overlapping jib.

The drifter has been discussed very briefly in chapter 6. It is a light-weather sail, and therefore it should have a lightweight sheet so that its clew will lift in the slightest zephyr. If it is cut high in the foot, its sheet can be led to a block on the end of the main boom when sailing between a beam reach and a close reach, so that the sail is trimmed a maximum distance outboard (see figure 6-1). Of course, when racing with the wind abeam or abaft the beam, the

8-14A. Yawl reefing sequence. The skipper assigns crew positions and makes sure that everyone understands their job.

8-14B. The mainsail is luffed and the halyard eased off until the reefing grommet is fitted on the hook above the gooseneck.

drifter is not carried because this is when the spinnaker is the most effective sail. These two should rarely be carried simultaneously, because they will interfere with each other's wind. Drifters are rarely carried on a beat except, perhaps, in the very lightest airs. On the wind, it is usually better to carry a lightweight number one Genoa, because the boat will not be able to point very high with a drifter.

The yawls carry three spinnaker staysails, the first of these is a "low boy" having an area of 250 square feet. This sail is carried on broad reaches and runs, although frequently it is blanketed by the mainsail on a nearly dead run. It is designed to fill the area beneath the spinnaker. A new very large spinnaker staysail was added in 1977. This sail has an area of 444 square feet and is most effective on a reach. Having a very long luff, the staysail is set on a jib halyard and tacked down with a tack line to a pad eye on the foredeck. Since this is such a large sail, it must be properly trimmed to prevent spoiling the airflow to the spinnaker, which could cause the spinnaker to collapse. The third staysail used with the spinnaker is a "tall boy" with an area

of 250 square feet. This sail is most effective on the closer spinnaker reaches. It is also set on a jib halyard and tacked to the foredeck with a tack line.

The mizzen staysail can be an effective sail on certain points of sailing; its area is 257 square feet, as opposed to the mizzen's 94 square feet. The most effective point of sailing for the mizzen staysail is the broad reach. When the wind draws abaft the quarter the sail begins to be blanketed by the mizzen, but when the wind draws forward of the quarter the staysail begins to backwind the mizzen. The mizzen staysail can almost never be carried on a dead run, and it can rarely be carried effectively when sailing higher than a beam reach. On this latter point of sailing, it not only backwinds the mizzen, but it is backwinded by the mainsail, and it also blankets the lower after corner of the mainsail. The mizzen staysail is tacked down to a pad eye located on the windward side of the cabin top, or just inboard of the weather shrouds. Remember always to secure the tack to windward of the boat's centerline. The sail must be hoisted to leeward of the permanent backstay. Its sheet

8-14C. The reef line is taken in after the tack is secured.

8-14D. The cockpit crew winches the first reef clew cringle down to the boom. The halyard starts back up.

8-14E. When the luff tension is correct, the sail is trimmed.

8-14F. The yawl under one reef in the mainsail, mizzen, and number-two Genoa. The reef line and leech line should be adjusted to eliminate the stretch lines along the leech.

runs outside the mizzen shrouds, through a block on the end of the mizzen boom, and inboard (see figures 6-1 and 8-17).

As when trimming any sail on a reach, the mizzen staysail's sheet should be kept eased to the point where the sail begins to luff. In addi-

tion, there should be an ample slot between the leech of the staysail and the lee side of the mizzen. The clew of the staysail should never be pulled close to the mizzen boom when the mizzen is hoisted because of the problem with backwind. When pulling in on the staysail

8-15. The Navy boat *Ranger* showing her flattening reef. Notice how the reef lines lead internally through the boom. The helmsman is sitting where he can get a clear view of the jib's circular telltale window. Instrumentation includes apparent wind direction and speed indicators, inclinometer, and log. Rubber hoses on the lifelines allow the crew to lean against the wires in comfort.

sheet, always watch the mizzen to see that it does not begin to bulge from the staysail's backwind. When this bulge occurs, the staysail's sheet must be eased or else the mizzen must be lowered. Occasionally it pays to lower the mizzen when it blankets the mizzen staysail or when the latter backwinds the former, because

the staysail has the larger sail area. Once the mizzen staysail is basically well trimmed, it is often best to make fine trim adjustments with the mizzen sheet. Since the staysail sheet is led to the mizzen boom, then obviously the mizzen sheet will also affect the staysail's trim. Making the adjustments with the mizzen sheet will keep the slot between staysail and mizzen wide, and also the staysail will be led the maximum distance outboard. When sailing close to a beam reach, be sure the staysail's luff is taut. When jibing, the mizzen staysail must be lowered and removed entirely before the main boom swings across. Then the staysail may be reset on the new tack, again with its tack to windward and the halyard to leeward of the backstay.

The mizzen spinnaker is cut like a spinnaker but is set and sheeted like a conventional mizzen staysail. Unlike a conventional spinnaker set on the mainmast, the mizzen spinnaker is not equipped with a pole that holds the sail out to windward; therefore, the mizzen spinnaker is particularly subject to being blanketed by the mizzen when the wind is far aft. On a run it often pays to lower the mizzen to avoid this blanketing. Although by tightening its luff the conventional mizzen staysail can be carried when sailing almost as high as a beam reach, the mizzen spinnaker, with its full cut, cannot be carried that close to the wind. In a fresh breeze, the mizzen spinnaker should be allowed to lift to the maximum extent. This means that the sheet and tack should be eased liberally. When the sail is well lifted, it also often pays to slack the halyard slightly to let the head of the sail move away from the mizzen's wind shadow.

Stowable gear and equipment. Before getting underway in a Navy yawl (or any boat), it is im-

148

portant to know the location of her gear and equipment. For obvious reasons, all stowable gear should be returned to its proper location. Heed the old expression, "a place for everything and everything in its place."

Figure 8-5 shows the accommodation plan of a fiberglass yawl. The arrangement of the wooden yawls is similar (see figure 8-6), except that on these boats, the head is located aft on the starboard side, adjacent to the companion ladder. Of course, the fiberglass yawls have much more

practical and comfortable accommodations for the crew.

Locations for stowable gear are as follows:

• Life jackets are evenly distributed throughout the boat in order that they may be reached from anywhere regardless of the type of emergency that requires them.

• Two life rings are carried aft in holders attached to the stern pulpit. These rings should never be lashed in their holders.

• Sails are stowed forward under the foredeck in the wooden yawls, but on the forward bunks or in bins under the cockpit seats to port and starboard in the fiberglass yawls.

• Sheets are kept near the sail stowage area. In the wooden yawls, sheets are stowed in the labeled areas on either side of the mainmast. Genoa sheets are forward to starboard, spinnaker sheets aft to starboard, forestaysail sheets forward to port, and spare sheets and halyards aft to port. On the fiberglass boats, sheets are on the port side under the cockpit seat.

• *Snatch blocks* (removable, side-opening blocks) on the wooden yawls are stowed in drawers under the galley sink. When detaching a block from its pad eye, keep the sheet rove through the block until it is detached and has been moved inboard, so there is no possibility of dropping it overboard.

• Winch handles are stowed in drawers in the same area as the snatch blocks on the wooden boats. When under sail, if the handles are not in use, they are always kept in special holders in the cockpit.

• Snatch blocks and winch handles on the fiberglass boats are stowed in bins or drawers under the amidships bunks on the port and starboard sides.

• On all boats, reefing earings and sail stops

8-16. The number one Genoa jib. This picture shows the sail from two different views. Most Genoas have concave leeches (reverse roaches), because they are not fitted with battens. This leech curve is especially important with the Luders yawls in order that the leech will clear the upper spreaders. On the *Resolute* (starboard tack), the Genoa's foot seems to be stretched overly taut against the shrouds. This might be relieved by moving the lead farther forward, provided that the knot or splice in the sheet is not pulled into the lead block. In this light breeze, she might foot a little faster with the mainsheet started an inch or two.

are stowed in this same area, in the forward port drawers.

• These same drawers hold the tool kit, sail repair kit, and lead line.

• The fog horn is stowed in this area, although some yawls have it mounted on the cabin top.

• Flares are kept in the bottom locker of the navigator's table for easy access.

8-17. The mizzen staysail. Although this yawl is able to carry her mizzen staysail, it is probably doing her little good, because the apparent wind direction is too far forward, and the sail is trimmed so flat that it is seriously backwinding the mizzen. Note that the upper spreaders are sagging dangerously. Each spreader should bisect its shroud angle. (See chapter 6.)

• The first aid kit is stowed in a shelf on the forward bulkhead near the head (on the port side).

• Fenders, a *fender board* (a plank hung over the side outboard of the fenders to protect the topsides when lying alongside a pier), a *bosun's chair* (a wooden or canvas seat used to haul a man up the mast), and certain cleaning gear is kept in the *lazarette* (space under the hatch on the after deck abaft the cockpit).

• Other cleaning gear is stowed in the galley.

• One Danforth anchor (about 40 pounds) is kept forward in the sail locker. An anchor line is stowed in the lazarette.

• Three fire extinguishers are on board: one in the forward cabin, one in the galley, and one in the port sheet locker. These are dry chemical extinguishers, and each crew member should be familiar with their operation. They should be checked frequently to be sure they are pressurized adequately.

• The inflatable rubber life rafts on the yawls are stowed on the cabin house aft of the mast when the boat goes offshore.

Until recently, each Luders yawl was equipped with one dinghy, a 7-foot 9-inch, unsinkable Dyer Dhow. Although these boats are no longer used at the Naval Academy they are perhaps the most common dinghy used by private yachts. Such boats are primarily used for convenience in going to or from a yacht when she is anchored or moored offshore in a harbor away from home. However, a dinghy is also handy for such jobs as carrying out a kedge anchor in the event of a grounding, and the sailing model is great fun to sail in a small harbor. It can also be used as a lifeboat in calm weather, but it can only hold three or four people.

When not in use, a Dhow is usually carried upside down on the cabin top. The dinghies are lashed to special *chocks* (wooden blocks specifically designed to hold a boat or other equipment in place so that it will not shift during an extreme angle of heel or in rough weather). Usually one continuous line, often the boat's *painter* (bow line), is used to lash a boat in her chocks. If the painter is used, it is run through the eye in either forward chock and then the line is passed over the boat's bottom to the after chock on the opposite side. Here the line is passed through the chock's eye, back over the boat's bottom, through the handgrip hole in the boat's skeg, and through the eye in the other after chock. The line is then passed over the boat's bottom to the forward chock on the opposite side, and here the line is secured with two half hitches. It is a wise precaution to finish off this knot with a slippery hitch (see figure 2-11) for quick release in an emergency. As can be seen in figure 8-8, the lashing line will make a criss-cross pattern over the dinghy's bottom.

Oars, oarlocks, and a bailer should be lashed inside the dinghy.

A Dyer Dhow, weighing slightly less than 70 pounds, can easily be lifted aboard a yacht by two men. One man can lift the dinghy by her painter while another can lift her with a stern line made fast to the metal ring at her stern. An upward pull on these lines by two men at the yacht's rail will not only lift the dinghy but tilt her over so that her lower gunwale can be rested on the yacht's rail. From here she can easily be lifted over the lifelines, turned upside down, and placed on her chocks. When a dinghy is brought aboard in this manner, the yacht's topsides should be protected with fenders or lines draped over the side.

If a heavier boat is brought aboard, the main halyard can be used for lifting purposes. First a bridle is rigged from the stern ring to the bow ring, and then the halyard is shackled on to a loop in the center of the bridle. The bridle's loop should be in such a position that the boat is balanced or horizontal when she is lifted clear of the water. Obviously, a great deal of power can be had with the halyard when it is put on a winch.

The Dyer Dhows are cat-rigged and are fitted

8-18. The Dyer dhow. Crew weight is placed well so that the boat is not trimmed excessively by the stern. Notice that the mainsheet has fouled on its traveler on the fully shown boat.

with a removable rudder and dagger board. The boats have very small sails and are a bit sluggish in light airs, but in a moderate to fresh breeze they are quite responsive and great fun to sail. (See figure 8-18.)

The Dhow's sail is attached to a spar which is hooked on to the top of a short mast. First the mast is stepped and then the sail is bent to the spar by sliding the sail's luff rope into a groove on the after side of the spar. Next the spar, with sail attached, is lifted up and hooked to the top of the mast. The sail is loose-footed and secures to the boom with a hook at the tack and a short outhaul at the clew. The boom's forward end has jaws which fit around the mast. The mainsheet is snapped to the traveler and rove through the sheet blocks.

The rudder is hooked to a vertical rod on the transom and the dagger board, stowed under the thwart, is slid down its well. Then the boat is ready to sail.

Handling the yawl under sail. Although it is possible to sail a Navy yawl single-handed, the Naval Academy requires that there be a minimum crew of four. When sailing with this minimum, one man obviously will be at the helm. Another man should be assigned to the cockpit area forward of the helmsman to tend the jibsheets and sheet winches. The third man should be assigned to the foredeck to tend to the mooring line and halyards, and clear the jib if necessary when tacking. The fourth man should lend a hand either on the foredeck or in the cockpit. Sailing shorthanded requires careful planning ahead. The skipper should try to anticipate any difficulties that could arise as a result of having a small crew. A forestaysail or easy-to-handle jib should be carried in most cases.

The ideal racing crew for a Navy yawl generally numbers between seven and ten members (the fiberglass yawls have sleeping accommodations for nine). The yawls may be sailed with less than seven but not at maximum efficiency under all racing conditions, unless the crew is exceptionally skilled and experienced. When a crew numbers more than ten, some members are superfluous and they usually get in the way of each other and the working crew as well.

A crew should be divided into two groups, a foredeck crew and an afterguard. The latter group is concentrated in or near the cockpit, and it consists of the skipper who is the principal helmsman, a relief helmsman who may tend the mizzen and mizzen staysail, a navigator who may double as a mainsheet tender or help with other sheets or backstays, and the winch men. The foredeck group has a foredeck captain or person in charge of all activities forward of the mainmast, and he has at least two assistants. This forward group is particularly busy when the spinnaker is set.

The wooden yawls were moored offshore on permanent anchors. When under sail in a large heavy boat without an engine, such as a Luders yawl, it is usually much easier to leave and return to a mooring than to leave and enter a slip similar to those in which the knockabouts and Shields are kept. Fiberglass yawls are kept in slips, but because of their auxiliary power they are not difficult to maneuver. Maneuvering under power will be discussed in chapter 12.

Leaving and landing at a mooring under sail was discussed briefly in chapter 5, and of course the same basic principles apply to the Navy yawls. The skipper should size up the weather, estimate wind strength and direction, and determine which sails will be carried before boarding his yawl. This will prevent any apparent indecision on the skipper's part and allow him to give instructions to the crew immediately after going aboard. Any inexperienced crew members should be checked out on their particular duties and on the operation of deck gear they will handle. The mizzen is hoisted first, and it is sheeted flat so that the boat is held head to wind. Next, the mainsail is hoisted. But prior to this operation, both running backstays should be secured forward against the shrouds so that the mainsail will not foul them. Before casting off the mooring line, the mizzen may be backed (pushed to windward). This will cause the stern to move in the direction opposite to the sail. In other words, if the mizzen is pushed to port the stern will move to starboard, and the bow will fall away from the wind to port. When the bow has fallen away slightly, the jib may be hoisted. Care should be taken that the jib does not get aback in the wrong direction. After the mooring line's eye is taken off its bitt, the eye may be taken to the windward side of the bow and walked a short distance aft to ensure that the yawl will sail off in the desired direction. Then the mooring line is cast off, the jib is trimmed flat, or backed if necessary, and the mizzen is slacked until the yawl is on her proper course. Before casting off, be sure the halyards are coiled and all sheets are clear.

When picking up the mooring, the yawl is headed into the wind. It is usually the safest policy to approach the mooring about two or more boat lengths to leeward of it on a beam or close reach at low speed with the sails luffing. If it is found that the speed is too slow, sails may be trimmed in a little; if the speed seems too fast, sheets can be slacked. When nearing the moor-

ing buoy, the bow is turned slowly into the wind while all sheets are slacked. The mooring *pendant* (line) is picked up with a boat hook. If the boat should have slightly too much way, then the main boom may be pushed up to windward so that the sail will act as a brake. Be sure the runners are secured forward.

Another, but less desirable, mooring approach can be made directly downwind. The boat is sailed before the wind down to her mooring. She passes one or two boat lengths away from the buoy, leaving it on the windward side. When the buoy is less than half a boat length abaft the stern, the helm is put hard to leeward and the boat rounds up sharply coming to a nearly dead stop. Remember that a slowly turned rudder does little to kill speed, but a rudder jammed hard over acts as a brake.

It is usually best not to pick up a mooring with a Genoa jib set, because this sail restricts visibility and causes confusion on the foredeck when its long tail thrashes around as the boat heads into the wind. The mooring can be approached with a small jib or forestaysail set or without any headsail (under main and mizzen, or mainsail alone). If the mizzen is set, its sheet must be slacked off to maintain balance. After the buoy is picked up, the mizzen sheet should be pulled in to hold the boat's bow to the wind. Sails are doused from bow to stern, with the mizzen being the last sail lowered.

The procedures for tacking and jibing were discussed in chapter 5. It is important that all crew members understand the basic principles of these procedures, because maneuvering a Navy yawl requires teamwork. Before tacking the skipper alerts his crew to stand by to come about. The crew take their stations. One or two men should take a position along the foot of the jib to run the foot forward during the tack. A man stands by to release the jibsheet and set up the running backstay if it is in use. Two men stand by the windward Genoa sheet winch that will be used to bring the jib in on the new tack. Another man stands by to pull back on the jib's clew when it is first being trimmed in, and this same man can then release the leeward running backstay if it is set up. It is usually easier to adjust the traveler before tacking. Be sure that every man has a station and knows his job.

At the command *hard-a-lee*, the helm is put over. The jibsheet is slacked when almost head to wind, and it is eased off. It is not suddenly released, because this will noticeably slow the boat and kill her momentum. The skipper often tells the man on the sheet when to release it. If the runners are being used, the man who releases the sheet can set up the new windward backstay. Some authorities advise setting up the runner before the jibsheet is released, because at this time it is often possible to get the stay very taut. The men stationed at the foot of the Genoa carry it forward while the bowman gathers in the slack. If the forestay is set up, the jib must be fed through the space between the forestay and headstay. When the boat swings past the head-to-wind position, the jib will be blown through the space between the stays, so the helmsman should momentarily bear away sharply onto the new tack to make the jib blow through quickly. After this, the helm is turned more slowly to give the sheet trimmers maximum help in winching in the jib. Of course, if the backstays are not in use, and especially if the forestay is not set up, tacking is a much simpler job.

Jibing involves essentially the same crew activity as tacking, except that not as many men are needed to handle the jib and two men are needed to tend the mizzen and mainsheets. The man on the mainsheet has an especially important job because the mainsail is quite large and its boom has considerable weight. In a breeze, he must be sure that the sheet is pulled all the way in when the boom crosses over the boat's centerline, and he must never ease the sheet until the new leeward running backstay has been slacked. The helmsman does not actually turn onto the new tack until the mainsheet tender is ready and has the main boom amidships. At the word *jibe-ho*, the helmsman turns the bow to leeward so that the boom swings across onto the new tack.

It is important that all crew members be thoroughly familiar with the operation of winches. Crew members who are inexperienced should be given rudimentary winch instruction soon after boarding a yawl, because the improper operation of a winch can be dangerous and cause injuries. As previously mentioned, main halyards on the fiberglass yawls are now operated with number 16 Barients. With the wire halyards having Dacron tails, it is important to see that at least four turns of wire go around the winch. Never wrap the wire-to-rope splice around a cleat, as this could weaken the splice.

It might be well to include a few words about the operation of reel winches, even though they are no longer used on the Luders yawls, because they are so common on other boats. Many seamen consider the screw pin and toggle type of brake release (see figure 8-20) safer than the pull handle type, because if the screw pin is very carefully and slowly turned, there is seldom a necessity to insert the winch handle when sail is lowered or the halyard is slacked. Less modern types of reel winches had brake handles that

8-19. Standing by to come about. Notice the difference between the sheeting arrangement and Genoa winch for the fiberglass yawl (figure 8-9) and the wooden yawl shown here, which has the large winch aft. When the boat tacks, the man forward will help the jib around the mast and pull aft on the clew. The tailer is ready to put one or two turns around the winch, while the cranker is standing by with the winch handle.

could, on rare occasions, be tripped accidentally. Often, when the halyard was under great strain, the winch handle had to be used to ease the halyard's tension before the sail was lowered or the luff was slacked to adjust the sail's draft. According to the winch manufacturer's advertising literature, the screw pin brake can be released gradually and there is no need to ease off tension with the winch handle. One word of warning, however; some screw pin releases may slack off more quickly than the manufacturer's claims lead you to believe. If the handle must be used, it must be gripped firmly, because more than a few injuries have been caused by the handle slipping out of the operator's hand. Keep heads and arms well clear of the handle, and re-

member that tension on the halyard often can be eased by slacking the downhaul.

Another advantage of this screw toggle brake is that sail can be hoisted with the brake on so that if the handle should happen to slip out of the operator's hand the winch will not spin around.

Other winches on the yawls are conventional top-action (with handle at the top) ratchet or geared winches. With these winches, several turns of a sheet or halyard are wound around the winch and the winch is turned around with its crank handle while the line's tail (that part of the line between the winch and its free end) is pulled upon. A tension must be kept on the tail or else the line will slip on the drum. The man or men who pull on the tail are often called *tailers* and their job is *tailing the sheet*. With winches on the Navy yawls, and on nearly all American boats for that matter, *lines are wound around the winches in a clockwise direction*. (See figure 8-21.)

The yawls are equipped with powerful geared winches for the Genoa. Good teamwork is required to trim this jib rapidly when tacking in a breeze. When the jib swings over and begins to fill after the boat has tacked, the Genoa sheet tailer winds two or three loops of the sheet clockwise around the winch; then he pulls in on the sheet, hand over hand, as quickly as he can before the jib completely fills. The helmsman should be bearing away very slowly. When the tailer no longer has strength to pull in the sheet by hand, he wraps another turn or two around the winch, and the cranker (the man who cranks the winch) inserts the crank handle. The cranker then cranks the winch, turning the handle all the way around making complete circles until he no longer has the strength for this, and then he ratchets with the handle, or moves it back and forth so that the winch turns spasmodically. Winch cranking can be a tiring task if tacks are frequent, so it is usually wise to have the cranker and tailer alternate or to have other crew members spell the cranker. If the line begins to slip on the drum as it is being winched in, the cranker must quickly remove the handle, while the tailer puts another turn or two around the drum.

Some sheet winches are two-speed with a direct drive that gives fast speed and a low gear that slows the drum speed but increases power. Low gear is obtained by reversing the rotation direction of the winch handle. Ratcheting is obtained by flipping a switch on top of the winch handle. There is even a three-speed winch with an extra low gear that can be engaged by rotating a switch on top of the winch. Of course, low gears are only used for the last few feet of trim when there is too much strain to flatten the sail with higher gears or direct drive.

The following are a few tips on handling winches. Handles are always removed when the winch is not being used. When winching in a sheet, never throw on too many turns at first, as they can override each other and jam. When easing off a winch under strain, carefully unwrap one turn at a time while keeping tension on the tail; then ease off slowly until most of the strain has been relieved. When taking turns off a ratchet halyard winch, keep tension on the tail in such a way that it is pulled at right angles to the drum axis or else at a slight angle toward the mast, otherwise the line is liable to slip off the drum. When winching in a jib after tacking, be sure the windward sheet is completely clear to run through its lead blocks. When winding a wire-to-rope splice around a winch (some halyards are part wire and part rope), see that

8-20. Reel winch for the main halyard. Notice the screw toggle brake release on the left side of the winch base, the handle lock switch, and the step-up rim to take the last few turns of wire in order to prevent them from jamming into less tightly packed earlier turns. Recently, Barient added the following warning to its reel winches: "Set brake before cranking" and "Remove handle before releasing brake."

the splice is not left bent around the winch. This can harm the splice and cause wire snags to appear through the rope. Crank the winch a little farther, until the splice clears the drum. Never wrap the splice around the cleat, and never stand or sit with your head near a winch handle while it is being cranked, because the handle could slip out of the operator's hand. Be very cautious about placing fingers near a winch drum under

156

strain. Be particularly cautious with wire on a winch. And once again, don't forget that a line is wrapped around a winch in a clockwise direction.

When sailing a yawl off the wind, especially during a race, a main boom vang is often used. This consists of a tackle that fastens to a strap which is put around the middle part of the boom. The bottom of the tackle does not secure at the base of the mast but at various points on the side deck, depending on the trim of the sail. This type of vang is sometimes called a *go-fast*. The lower part of the vang should never be secured to the Genoa track as this could pull the track up, but the vang can be hooked to any through-bolt fitting, such as a pad eye or the base of a lifeline stanchion. Naturally the vang must be removed before jibing.

When sailing a yawl (or any boat), a lookout must be kept at all times. Of course, this is primarily the helmsman's responsibility, but when a low-cut Genoa jib is set, it is very difficult for the helmsman to see off the lee bow. Therefore a lookout should be stationed to leeward where he can see under or around the jib. The lookout should make constant reports to the helmsman concerning the location of approaching boats or obstructions that lie in this "blind" sector.

Electrical and water systems of the wooden Luders yawl. Although the wooden Luders yawls are no longer at the Naval Academy, they are still being used at various naval installations. Therefore, it is appropriate to describe here their electrical, and fresh- and salt-water systems, since detailed knowledge of these systems is required of any wooden-yawl skipper.

The electrical system of the wooden yawl has two 6-volt wet-cell batteries connected in series to obtain 12 volts. These batteries are located in a lead or fiberglass battery box (to protect the boat from acid) abaft the companionway ladder. These batteries provide power for cabin lights, running lights, spreader lights, the binnacle, and a Kenyon light (in boats where Kenyon speed indicators are installed). The cabin lights are controlled by switches on the fixtures, in addition to switches on the control panel located abaft the companion ladder. The appropriate switch on the control box must be turned on before the fixture switches will work. The other lights are controlled solely by the switch on the control panel. On deck, two electrical jacks are provided for connecting emergency running lights and spotlights. When not in use, these jacks should be capped to ensure that salt water does not short the circuit.

The fresh-water system has two 50-gallon tanks, located under the lower bunks amidships. Connecting valves are located beneath the cabin sole and are reached by removing a portable section of the cabin sole. The tanks are filled from the deck. The fresh-water fill pipe deck plate is on the port side amidships. The boat's tool kit should include a spanner wrench for removing the plate. Each tank has a vent on its top. There are two fresh-water pumps in the boat, one at the galley sink and one at the head sink. The head sink drains into the toilet bowl. The galley sink drains via a globe valve, pump, and sea cock overboard through the hull. The ice box drains via a separate valve into this same drain line, so that the pump below the ice box can be used to empty either the ice box or the sink. To do so, the appropriate valve must be open, and the valve not in use should be shut. Both these valves are in the locker next to the ice box.

8-21. Genoa sheet winch in operation. Notice that the tailer is keeping the sheet low, almost at right angles to the winch axis, so that the crank clears the sheet when the crank is turned all the way around. The cranker is adjusting the switch on top of the handle which controls ratcheting on the two-speed winch. The man forward of the cranker is helping to trim the jib quickly by pulling aft on the clew.

beneath the cockpit and is operated from the cockpit. The intake strainers for both these pumps are in the bilge beneath the companionway. Both these pumps discharge through the hull through sea cocks, which should be opened for use and shut immediately afterwards. A sea cock is opened by paralleling the handle with the piping; when the handle is perpendicular to the piping, the valve is shut. All through-hull fittings on the Luders yawls are equipped with sea cocks, and familiarity with their location and use is a must. If a bilge pump seems hard to operate, first check to make certain that the discharge valve is open. Second, check the intake strainer in the bilge to see if it has been clogged. For this very reason, it is important to keep all foreign matter out of the bilge. On some of the wooden yawls, a third bilge pump is installed. It is a high-capacity diaphragm pump located beneath the cabin sole. The intake for this pump is beneath it in the bilge, and it discharges over the side via a length of fire hose led out through the hatch. This length of fire hose and the handle needed to operate the pump should be stowed with the pump. If they are lost, the pump cannot be operated.

The head has two sea cocks, one at the hull on the intake side (this one is the smaller of the two), the other at the hull on the discharge side. The intake (hull) valve is beneath the cabin sole next to the head, and the discharge valve is in the locker just outboard of the head. Both must be open to use the head. To operate the head,

Before using any pump, check that both intake and discharge valves are open. If the intake valve is shut, only useless effort is expended, but if the discharge valve is shut, *pumping can rupture the pump or discharge line.*

Included in the salt-water system is the piping for the bilge pumps, cockpit scuppers, and the head. On all the boats there are two bilge pumps. One is located just abaft the head, to starboard of the companionway. The other is open the valves, depress the pedal on the foot-operated intake valve, and pump. This action pumps water both in and out. After the head has been pumped clear, pump ten more strokes to clear the discharge line, then release the foot pedal and continue to pump until most of the water has been removed from the bowl. In a rough sea, remove all water from the bowl. Before leaving, *shut the valves. Never* put solid objects or large quantities of paper in a marine toilet, as they will not fit through the rubber diaphragms. These rules apply to most marine toilets, but if there is any question about operation, ask before using one.

The cockpit scuppers drain overboard through pipes located beneath the cockpit. These pipes are fitted with sea cocks at the through-hull fittings which are abaft the ice box on the port side and under the quarter berth on the starboard side. These valves should always be left *open* so that the cockpit will drain.

As has been mentioned, it is good practice to shut sea cocks that are below the water line, if not after every use, at least when securing the boat. The reason for this is that pumps and the head often will siphon water back into the boat after use. Occasionally a boat has sunk while the owner was ashore because the head or bilge pump discharge sea cock had been left open.

All of the Luders yawls are equipped with alcohol-burning galley stoves. To the uninitiated, these stoves are hard to operate and seem dangerous. An alcohol stove must be filled before it is operated. Be very careful not to spill the alcohol while filling the stove. Once the tank is filled and the cap secured, the tank must be pressurized. There is a pump for this purpose and a pressure gauge which is very clearly marked. When the tank is full, it is very easy to

over-pressurize the tank. Be sure to watch the gauge while pumping. Also, remember that pressure must be maintained during use. This will require occasional pumping while the stove is in use.

After the stove has been filled, it must be primed. First some alcohol must be collected in the small basins below the burners. This is done by opening the burner valves *very* briefly. About three seconds will be all that is necessary. If the valves are left open too long, raw alcohol will spill onto the tray under the stove and when the stove is lighted there will be a conflagration. If alcohol has spilled, wait for it to evaporate before lighting. If a flash fire does occur, as it will whenever excess alcohol is allowed to collect on the tray beneath the burners, it can often be put out by smothering with a towel or garment. Water can be used to extinguish an alcohol fire if care is taken to see that all the fire is thoroughly extinguished and not merely washed to a new location. Be sure to use enough water to prevent smoldering. Do not use the dry-chemical fire extinguisher unless it is necessary, because it will cover the galley with a white powder that takes hours to clean up.

The alcohol in the basins under the burners is lighted to heat the burners. After the burners have been adequately pre-heated, when the valves are opened, the alcohol will vaporize before reaching the burner and will burn as a gas.

If a proper gas flame cannot be obtained, turn off the valves and start the whole process of priming again.

Diesel auxiliary engines. The fiberglass yawls are equipped with a four-cylinder Westerbeke Model Four-107 diesel engine (see figure 8-22). These engines are direct drive and have hydrau-

air breather

oil fill cap

fresh water
pressure cap

12v alternator

fresh water
surge tank

fresh-water pump

sea-water pump
(may be belt driven)

8-22. The Westerbeke Model Four-107 diesel.

lic transmissions. The engines are controlled from the cockpit by Morse single-lever controls (see figure 8-23). These engines are reliable and easy to operate, as are the controls, but there are a number of *essential* checks that must be made prior to operation in order to ensure continued reliability. Remember, the more you know about the operation of the auxiliary, the less likely it is to give you trouble. The checks that are necessary for the Westerbeke are similar to checks required before getting underway with any auxiliary. In every case, the cooling system,

oil level in the engine, fuel supply, and shaft lock, if there is one, should be checked.

The Westerbeke engine has a self-contained fresh-water cooling system. The fresh-water tank is atop the forward end of the engine and must be checked before starting. It should be filled to three-quarters of an inch below the opening. The fresh water, which recirculates, is kept cool by a heat exchanger on the after end of the engine, which in this system uses salt water. In addition, the salt water cools the lubricating oil heat exchanger and the exhaust pipe. The

160

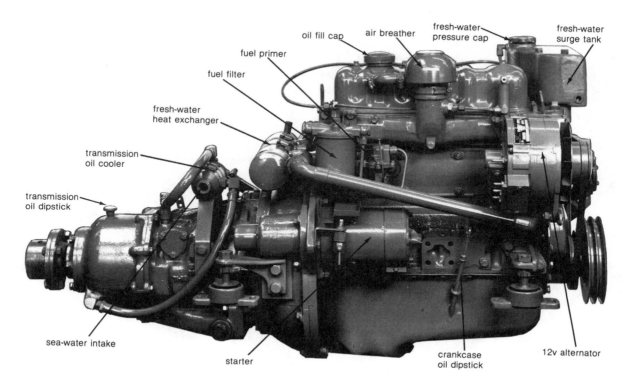

oil fill cap air breather fresh-water pressure cap fresh-water surge tank

fuel primer

fuel filter

fresh-water heat exchanger

transmission oil cooler

transmission oil dipstick

sea-water intake

starter

crankcase oil dipstick

12v alternator

salt-water cooling system has two valves, an intake and a discharge, and *both must be open when the engine is running.* The salt-water intake valve is abaft the engine shaft coupling on the port side. The discharge valve is in the exhaust line and is in the lazarette. The discharge valve should always be shut when under sail in a seaway, because it then keeps salt water from entering the engine via the exhaust line. Both valves are shown in figure 8-24.

The lubricating oil sump on the Westerbeke has a maximum capacity of five quarts of oil. For proper engine operation the oil level in the sump must be kept between four and five quarts. The engine sump dipstick must be pulled and

inspected to ensure that the lubricating oil is at the required level. The dipstick on the Westerbeke is on the starboard side of the engine, down quite low. Be sure to push it all the way into the sump when checking the oil level. As already mentioned, the engines are equipped with hydraulic reverse gears. Because of this, the reverse gear has a separate oil sump which must also be checked. The reverse gear dipstick is on top of the gear box at the after end of the engine on the port side. If oil is needed in the main sump, only Navy symbol 9250 oil or a high-quality, heavy-duty, 30-weight detergent oil should be used. The gear box uses special, light, hydraulic oil, and *only* this should be used if oil

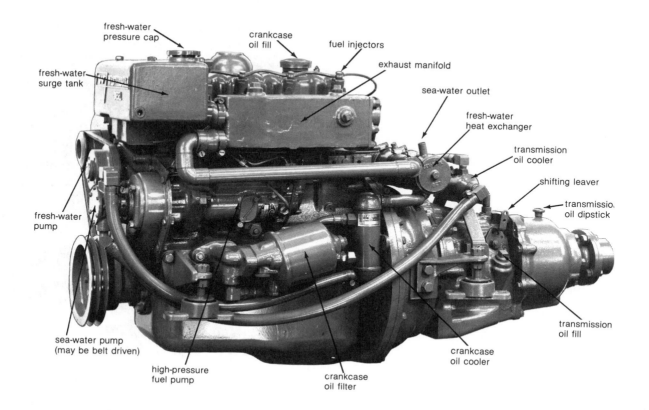

fresh-water
pressure cap

crankcase
oil fill

fuel injectors

exhaust manifold

fresh-water
surge tank

sea-water outlet

fresh-water
heat exchanger

transmission
oil cooler

shifting leaver

transmissio.
oil dipstick

fresh-water
pump

transmission
oil fill

sea-water pump
(may be belt driven)

crankcase
oil cooler

high-pressure
fuel pump

crankcase
oil filter

is needed. These dipsticks are located as shown in figure 8-22.

Fuel is supplied by one 40-gallon tank, which is amidships below the cabin sole. As indicated in figure 8-24, it is the forward one of the two tanks in this area. It is reached by lifting the forward removable section of the sole in the main cabin. The fuel gauge is on top of the tank or at the side of the companionway ladder. The fuel tank is filled from the deck. The fill pipe deck plate is forward in the cockpit. The valve in the fuel supply line is on the bulkhead abaft the companionway just forward of the first fuel

strainer; it should be left open. On boats with a gasoline auxiliary, because of the very explosive nature of the fuel, it is good practice to shut the gasoline supply valve when leaving the boat. More on this subject will be discussed in chapter 12.

One last item remains on the check-off list. This is the shaft lock, which is used to keep the propeller in a vertical position for minimum drag when sailing. It must be released before the engine is run. It is on the shaft beneath the cockpit. Once these items, (1) fresh-water tank, (2) salt-water exhaust and intake valves, (3) oil

8-23. Engine controls on the Luders yawl.

supply in sump and reverse gear, (4) fuel gauge, and (5) shaft lock, have been checked, you are ready to start the engine.

The first step in starting the engine is to energize the electrical system. This is done by switching the battery selector switch from "off" to position "1" or "2." The battery selector switch is abaft the companionway. It is a Perko circular switch, and it determines which of the yawl's two 12-volt batteries is going to be used for power. The switch is illustrated in figure 8-25. One should note that between positions "1" and "2" on the switch is a position marked "ALL." When the switch is moved to this position, power is drained from both batteries simultaneously. 'The "ALL" position should not be used unless neither battery has sufficient power by itself to start the engine. If both batteries must be used to start the engine, switch to position "1" or "2" immediately after starting, as any short circuit in the electrical system will discharge both batteries if the selector switch is left on "ALL."

The next step is to prime the engine. This is

done by pushing the hand prime pump shown in figure 8-22 three or four times. A diesel cannot be flooded, so overprime rather than underprime.

The rest of the starting operation is conducted from the cockpit. The engine is put in neutral, by putting the Morse control handle in the vertical position. This control is both gear shift and throttle. It is on the starboard side of the cockpit and is illustrated in figure 8-23. Once in neutral, the knob below the handle must be pulled out to disengage the gear shift, and then the throttle is advanced forward about one-half speed. The starter is a button which must be depressed. The starter switch is on the panel at the after end of the cockpit, or on the starboard side of the cockpit. This panel is illustrated in figure 8-25. As soon as the engine starts, move the throttle back to the idle position and let the engine warm up for at least five minutes. Remember to push in the knob below the handle to engage the gear shift. To start the engine in cold weather, it must be preheated. This is done by pushing in the button labeled "preheat" and holding it in for about 15 seconds. After the engine is heated, start in the normal manner. In each yawl, there are starting instructions posted in the cockpit near the starting panel.

Once the engine has started, check the oil pressure. The gauge is in the instrument panel at the forward end of the cockpit, and should read 40 pounds or more. Then check over the stern to see if water is coming out of the exhaust. If it is not, the salt-water cooling system is not working properly. If the oil pressure is low, or if water is not being pumped out the exhaust, shut down the engine immediately.

While running the engine, periodically check the oil pressure and the water temperature. The

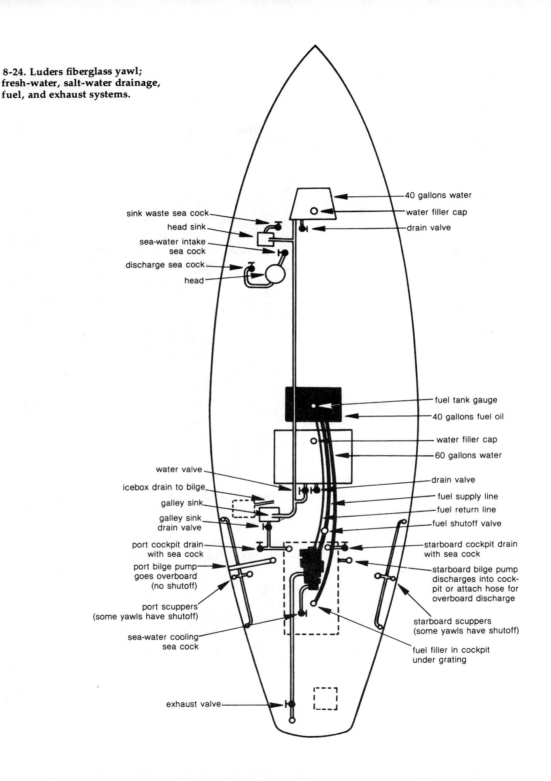

8-24. Luders fiberglass yawl; fresh-water, salt-water drainage, fuel, and exhaust systems.

sink waste sea cock

head sink

sea-water intake sea cock

discharge sea cock

head

40 gallons water

water filler cap

drain valve

fuel tank gauge

40 gallons fuel oil

water filler cap

60 gallons water

water valve

icebox drain to bilge

galley sink

galley sink drain valve

drain valve

fuel supply line

fuel return line

fuel shutoff valve

port cockpit drain with sea cock

port bilge pump goes overboard (no shutoff)

port scuppers (some yawls have shutoff)

sea-water cooling sea cock

starboard cockpit drain with sea cock

starboard bilge pump discharges into cockpit or attach hose for overboard discharge

starboard scuppers (some yawls have shutoff)

fuel filler in cockpit under grating

exhaust valve

water temperature gauge is beside the oil pressure gauge. The oil pressure should never go below 40 pounds, and the water temperature should never go higher than 190°F. *Never run the engine faster than 3,000 RPM.* Proper cruising speed for the Luders yawls is six knots at about 1,800 RPM. It should be noted in Table 8-1, that for engine RPMs greater than 1,800, fuel consumption goes up much faster than speed. When running the engine for several hours or more, shut it down periodically, and check the oil.

To secure the engine, put the throttle in neutral and pull out the engine "STOP" handle. Remember to push the stop handle back in, because it cuts off engine fuel and unless it is reset, the engine cannot be restarted. Once the engine has stopped and when power is no longer needed, switch the battery selector switch to the "OFF" position. Check fuel, oil, and fresh water to ensure that the engine will be ready for use when next needed.

Table 8-2 has been included to help troubleshoot the Westerbeke diesel engine. It does, however, offer many suggestions to the owner of any diesel-powered auxiliary who is trying to determine the cause of engine malfunction. It is for use primarily by trained mechanics, but also includes probable faults that can be checked by even the most inexperienced operator. The most common causes of engine failure—low battery, loss of cooling water, and dirty fuel (dirt or water in the fuel)—have been underlined.

On the Westerbeke engine, overheating is often a problem. Overheating can be caused by closed salt-water cooling system valves or an empty fresh-water tank. Often overheating is caused by the malfunction of either the fresh-or salt-water pump. These pumps are mounted on the front of the engine and are belt-driven. If the drive belts are too loose, they will not function. There are adjustments on both pumps that can be altered to increase tension.

Electrical and water systems of the fiberglass Luders yawl. In addition to knowing how to run the engine on the fiberglass yawls, the skipper and crew must know the location of the valves in the fresh- and salt-water systems and the switches in the electrical system (see figures 8-24 and 8-25). The fiberglass yawls carry 100 gallons of fresh water in two tanks, one in the forepeak with a capacity of 40 gallons, and one amidships in the main cabin aft of the fuel tank under the cabin sole with a capacity of 60 gallons. On some boats both tanks are filled via the tank in the main cabin and are vented on the bulkhead over the starboard berth in the main cabin. The tanks are interconnected by opening both valves on the supply line. These valves are at each tank. They must be open when filling the tanks, or the forward tank will not fill. On other boats, the forward tank must be filled separately from a fill pipe on top of the tank. Each tank has a drain at the bottom which must be shut to prevent the water from running into the bilge. The system has two pumps, one at the head sink and one at the galley sink. Both these sinks drain overboard through a sea cock in the hull. The valve in the head is below the sink. The valve for the galley sink is located in the port cockpit locker and is also the valve for the port cockpit scupper. For this reason it must be left open. To keep sea water from backing up into the galley sink when under sail, there is an additional stop valve in the sink drain line in the locker just below the sink. This valve should be shut when the sink is not in use.

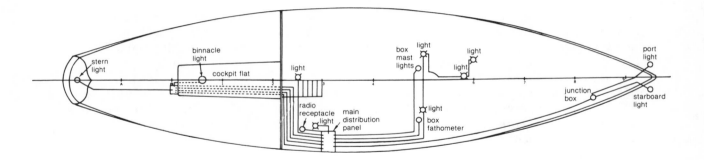

8-25. Luders fiberglass yawl, electrical system.

The icebox drains into the bilge. Since there is no check valve installed in the drain line it is important to keep the bilge free of water.

The fiberglass yawls have two manually operated bilge pumps installed. The intake strainers are in the bilge beneath the companionway ladder. The port pump is a GUSHER 10 (discharges 10 gallons per minute) and is located inside the port sheet locker in the cockpit. The starboard pump is a GUSHER 25 (25 gallons per minute) which is located over the navigator's berth. There is an access port for each pump on either side of the cockpit. The starboard pump may also be operated from below decks. Both pumps discharge through the side above the waterline. While there is no sea cock installed, the diaphragm in each pump acts as a check valve to prevent water from backing up into the bilges when the yawl is heeled.

The marine toilet in the head is installed with sea cocks on both intake and discharge lines. The intake valve is beneath the sink, and the discharge is in the locker behind the toilet. The operating procedure for the head is the same as that for the wooden yawls. It should be noted that the fiberglass yawl heads have a hand-, rather than a foot-operated intake valve.

Power for the electrical instruments and lights aboard the fiberglass yawls is supplied by two 12-volt storage batteries located aft and to starboard of the engine. The engine is equipped with a 60-amp, 14-volt, battery-charging alternator-rectifier system. This system rapidly charges the batteries until they reach capacity and then shuts itself down and provides only a trickle charge to keep them fully charged. All control switches and fuses are installed in the control panel above the navigator's chart table on the starboard side of the main cabin, with the

Engine RPM	Speed in Knots	Fuel Consumed in Gallons Per Hour
1,000	3.0	0.39
1,500	4.5	0.48
1,750	5.5	0.57
2,000	6.0	0.66
2,250	6.3	0.75
2,500	6.5	0.82
2,750	6.6	1.00

Table 8-1. Luders fiberglass yawl, performance characteristics under power.

exception of the engine starter, binnacle, and engine panel light switches, which are in the cockpit.

Battery-powered equipment aboard the fiberglass yawls includes cabin lights, running lights, spreader lights, masthead lights, stern light, anchor light, binnacle light, fathometer, and radio. The entire system is diagrammed in detail in figure 8-25.

Boarding and securing procedures. The following are rough check lists of what should be done after a yawl is boarded, before getting underway, and what should be done before securing or leaving her.

Before getting underway.
• Check the bilge. Pump it into the harbor only if you are certain there is no oil in the bilge. The Naval Academy and most marinas have pumping stations for removing oily water from the bilge.
• See that the head is almost dry and that both its water intake and discharge valves are shut.

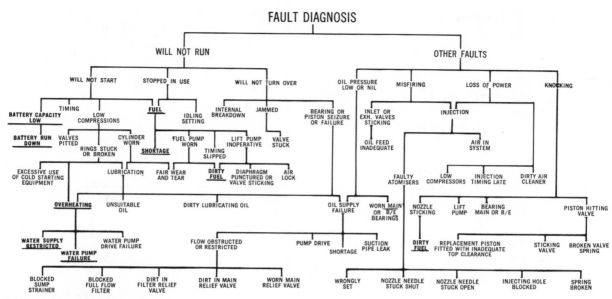

Table 8-2. Troubleshooting the Westerbeke diesel.

• See that halyards are clear aloft and that sheets are bent and led properly.

• Remove the *binnacle* (the compass housing) cover and wheel cover and stow these below.

• Set up the topping lift and detach the boom strap. Stow this and the boat hook below.

• Bend on the desired jib and check to see that it is correctly bent.

• Break out winch handles and place in their proper holders.

• If aboard a fiberglass yawl, see that the engine's fuel and water valves are opened and that the main battery switch is on. Check oil and cooling water.

• Unstop furled sails and tighten their outhauls just before hoisting.

• See that all loose gear below is properly stowed and that all opening lockers are closed so that gear will not spill out when the boat heels.

• See that ports are shut unless it is a calm, hot day with clear weather.

Before leaving the boat.

• Be sure mooring pendants are properly secured on the bow cleat. It is wise to put a short, stout lashing through the mooring pendant eye and the center part of the cleat, so that even should the eye jump off the cleat, it would be held by several turns of lashing.

• If on a mooring, put up the anchor light.

• If moored in a slip, secure the boat so that she lies straight fore and aft in the slip and as nearly as possible in the slip's center. Be sure that there is some slack in the mooring lines to allow for a change in tide, and that the lines are properly secured with tail ends coiled.

• Pull boarding plank in and leave it on the

pier. Coil the hose over its proper rack.

• See that bent sails are properly furled, well stopped, and that outhauls are slacked. Tie down the heads of furled sails.

• See that sails are properly bagged and stowed. Wet or torn sails should be bagged and taken ashore to be dried or repaired.

• Halyards should be secured in such a manner that they do not chafe the rigging or mast. On the Luders yawls all headsail halyards are led forward to the foredeck and secured to the bow pulpit and stanchions. Another method is to pull them somewhat away from the mast by lashing them to the shrouds with short lengths of line, often called *gilguys*. They should be securely belayed to their proper cleats. The main halyard should be unshackled from the head of the mainsail and shackled into a rubber strop or cloth *belly band* provided for the purpose, which is led under the main boom at about its midpoint.

• The mainsheet should be taut enough to hold the boom steady.

• The mizzen topping lift should be set up enough to tilt the mizzen boom slightly upward, and then the mizzen sheet set up taut enough to keep the boom from swinging. A drooping mizzen boom makes the boat look droopy, while a topped up mizzen gives her a cheerful look.

• Lines should be coiled and, if not removable, should be hung up off the deck.

• All removable sheets, blocks, winch handles, and other gear should be stowed in their proper places.

• Set up runners, but not overly taut. No line should be pulled overly taut. Some allowance should be made for shrinkage in wet weather.

• Strike and stow ensign and burgee.

• Replace covers on the wheel and binnacle.

• See that the main electrical and other switches are off and that the engine is properly secured (if on a fiberglass yawl).

• See that the bilge and sink are dry and that the bilge pump discharge valve is shut.

• The head should be clean and the intake and discharge valves shut.

• The icebox should be drained, and all ice, food, and beverage should be removed. Prop open the icebox door.

• All lockers below should be opened to allow adequate circulation of air. All deck ventilators should be turned the correct way. The aft end of the companionway should be left open, but other hatches and ports should be shut, except the port in the head. The after end of the lazarette hatch should be propped open about three inches.

• Secure lower extension berths in outboard position.

• A yawl should be left shipshape and in a cleaner condition than when she was boarded.

• Remove all trash, sweep down cabin sole, clean out sinks, wipe off bunk cushions, and wash down decks. Use hoses and fresh water when available, but otherwise use a bucket and Bay water. If possible, hose down topsides to remove salt deposits. Stow cleaning gear.

• Note any discrepancies—negative reports are required—in the log and sign it (please print). Don't forget to enter engine hours. Leave the log aboard on the chart desk.

Most of the essential information on the Luders yawls has been covered in this chapter, but other subjects related to these boats will be discussed later. Chapter 11, ''Distance Racing,'' will cover emergencies such as man overboard and rigging failures. It will also discuss the changing of headsails and heavy weather sailing.

9. The Spinnaker

Description. The Luders yawls, Shields sloops, a few knockabouts, and the Naval Academy ocean racers are equipped with spinnakers. These sails are essential for racing and are often difficult to handle; therefore, this entire chapter will be devoted to them.

The spinnaker derives its name from the fact that the first version of the sail was carried by the British yacht, *Sphinx*. It is said that rival crews called the sail a "Sphinxer" and sometimes referred to it as "Sphinx's Acre." These names soon evolved into our present term for the sail.

The modern racing spinnaker, the type carried on the Navy boats, is properly termed a parachute spinnaker. It is shaped like a ballooned isosceles triangle, the upper corner of which is called the head and the lower corners both called clews. When set, the sail is supported at these three corners only. Either clew may be fastened to the end of a boom called the *spinnaker pole*, which is carried on the fore side of the mast, and the clew on the pole would then actually be called the tack. The clews are inter-changeable; that is, either may be used as the tack, depending on whether the sail is set to port or to starboard. Figure 9-1 shows a typical parachute spinnaker with its lines and fittings. The line attached to the tack and pole is called the *after guy* (or often just *guy*), while the line attached to the clew is the sheet. Of course, the head is supported by the halyard. Another line shown in the illustration is attached to the pole to hold it down and forward, and this line is called the pole *downhaul* or *foreguy*. Still another line shown in the illustration is the *pole topping lift*, or simply *lift*, and this holds the pole up.

Pole adjustments. At its inboard end, the pole is attached to a slide on a track that is fastened to the fore side of the mast. The outboard end of the pole may swing forward until it touches the headstay or aft until it touches the forward shroud. The after guy controls the pole's fore-and-aft position. When beam reaching, the pole is carried all the way forward; when running, the pole is all the way aft. But when broad reaching, the pole is about halfway between the run-

171

9-1. The parachute spinnaker.

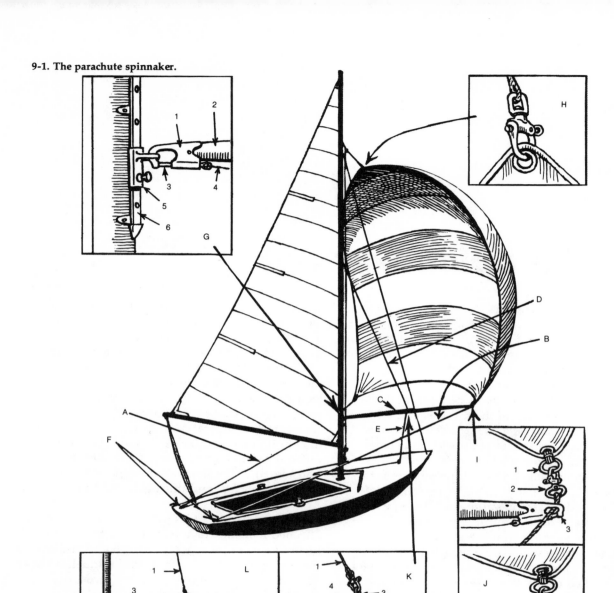

172

A   Spinnaker Sheet
B   Guy (sheet & guy
     lead outside shrouds)
C   Spinnaker Pole
D   Pole Lift
E   Pole Downhaul (foreguy)
F   Sheet and Guy
     Lead Blocks
G   Pole Fitting and Slide
     (1) pole fitting (at each
     end of pole)
     (2) pole (3) spring loaded pin
     (4) lanyard (pull to open pin)
     (5) adjustable slide
     (6) track (on mast's fore side)
H   Spinnaker Halyard Swivel
     Shackle (at each end of halyard)
I   Spinnaker Tack
     (1) metal ring lashed to

tack grommet (optional)
(2) Swivel ring shackle
(same arrangement
at clew)
(3) pole snapped on guy
J   Alternate Method
     (pole snapped to ring
     on shackle)
K   Middle of Pole
     (1) lift (2) downhaul
     (3) wire or rope strop
     (4) eye strap
     (5) continuous lanyard
L   Alternate Method
     (1) lift (may lead to end of
     pole for dip-pole jibing)
     (2) downhaul (3) bridle
     (4) lanyard

matter what the point of sailing. Most spinnakers cannot be carried effectively when the true wind comes from forward of the beam or when the boat is on a point of sailing that is slightly higher than a beam reach.

The pole may be raised or lowered at either end. The height of the outboard end is controlled with the lift, and the inboard end is controlled with the adjustable slide on the mast track. Given a good breeze, a well-designed parachute spinnaker will lift, and it should be encouraged to do so. The pole should be carried as high as possible when the 'chute is lifting, but the tack should not be allowed to lift much higher than the clew. In other words, the tack and clew should be kept at about the same level, almost parallel to the deck or horizontal when the boat is not heeled. Then also, the pole should

ning and beam-reaching positions. These positions are illustrated in figure 9-2. Notice that the pole is always about at right angles to the direction of the apparent wind. This holds true no

9-2. Fore-and-aft spinnaker pole positions.

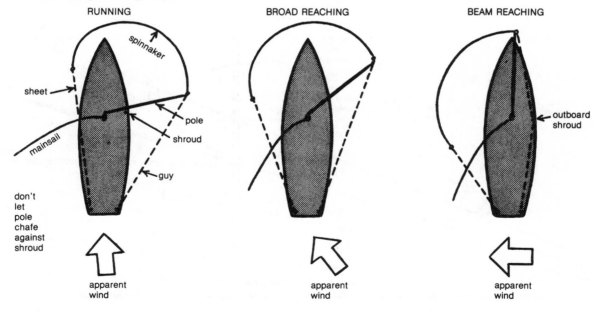

RUNNING

spinnaker

sheet

mainsail

pole

shroud

guy

don't
let
pole
chafe
against
shroud

apparent
wind

BROAD REACHING

apparent
wind

BEAM REACHING

outboard
shroud

apparent
wind

not be cocked up very much with its outboard end a great deal higher than its inboard end.

Proper up and down pole positions are shown in figure 9-3. In a light breeze, the pole should make an approximate right angle with the mast with the inboard end at the highest position that will keep the tack level with the clew. In very light airs, the clew will not lift; therefore, the inboard pole end must be kept low. As the breeze freshens, the inboard end can be pushed higher up the mast until, in a moderate breeze, the pole is at the top of its track. If the clew is lifting sufficiently in this much breeze the pole can be raised with the pole lift until the outboard end is slightly higher than the inboard end. As the breeze continues to freshen, the pole's outboard end can be lifted until the pole comes in line with the angle of the after guy, as shown by position B in the diagram. In this position, the sail

is lifted and the pull of the after guy doesn't exert an extra strain on the downhaul or the pole lift. Position A, shown in the diagram, is usually bad even when the spinnaker lifts in a fresh breeze. Although the pole is lifted, its outboard end is too close to the mast, putting an extra strain on the downhaul which already has a great deal of upward strain from the lifting 'chute. It is advantageous to keep the pole's outboard end away from the mast so that the spinnaker is held out in cleaner air, away from the blanketing effect of the mainsail. In a very strong breeze, the spinnaker should be kept flatter for better steering control, and so this calls for a lower pole setting at both the inboard and outboard ends.

The spinnaker pole may be rigged with its lift and downhaul in one of two ways. Both of these ways are illustrated in figure 9-1. Illustration K

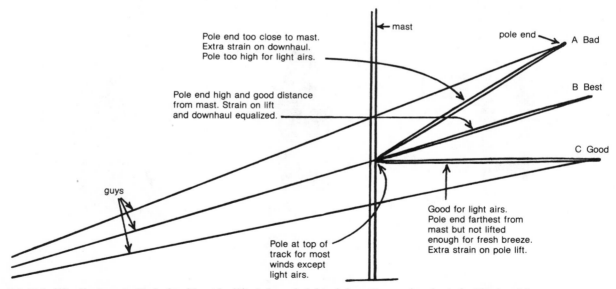

9-3. Pole lift adjustments. Tack should not be lifted above height of clew. Keep spinnaker's foot horizontal.

174

shows the lift rigged to the middle of the pole with the downhaul at the under side of the pole, directly beneath the lift. Illustration L shows the downhaul rigged from the outboard end of the pole and the lift attached to the middle of a *bridle* or wire span running from one end of the pole to the other. Of course, the lift may also be rigged directly to the pole end if the method of jibing called dip-poling (see figure 9-12 and accompanying text) is used exclusively. A pole rigged by method L is usually somewhat easier to handle, especially when jibing. This arrangement is often used on small boats and sometimes on fairly large boats in a moderate breeze. The other method, K, however, is most often used by large boats and in a strong breeze. With this arrangement there is less chance of breaking the pole. In a strong breeze, the spinnaker usually exerts a strong upward pull which can bend the pole up if the downhaul is secured in the pole's middle. This can be counteracted by putting the after guy into a forward lead, but usually the most effective way to stop the upward bending is to secure the downhaul to the pole's end. The bridle transfers the pull of the lift from the pole's middle to its end. No matter how a pole is rigged, it is wise to have the lift fastened directly above the pole downhaul. Navy Shields sloops are rigged with the bridle as shown by L in the illustration, but the large Navy boats are normally rigged with the lift secured directly to the pole end.

Setting the spinnaker. There are three common ways to set a spinnaker: by stopping it, setting it from a turtle, or setting it from its bag. Actually, however, the latter two methods are practically the same. The turtle is a special container which holds the folded or bundled spinnaker on deck prior to hoisting. These containers are often quite varied in design, depending on the fancy of each particular skipper or foredeck captain. One type of turtle is shown in figure 9-5. Notice that the three corners of the sail emerge from the container's top, which is held almost closed with a piece of elastic shock cord (sometimes rubber is used). Each corner is rigged to its proper line: the head to the halyard, the guy to the tack, and the sheet to the clew. Figure 9-5 shows the pole hooked onto the guy (the line itself), but the pole may be hooked onto the ring of the swivel shackle as shown in figure 9-1J. The first method (the pole on the guy) is preferable for short races in sheltered waters, but the second method (the pole on the ring) may be better for distance and offshore sailing because there is less chafe.

When setting the 'chute from its bag, the bag becomes a simplified turtle. About the only difference between the bag and the turtle is that the latter is more elaborate, and it is usually (though not always) designed to be secured forward of the headstay or jibstay as shown in figure 9-5. Sometimes the turtle is equipped with snap hooks which snap on to the bow pulpit if the boat has one. When the spinnaker is set from its bag, however, it is usually secured to the foredeck abaft the headstay. The bag must have a lanyard at its bottom so that it can be lashed to the bow cleat or some other fitting on the foredeck. Figure 9-6 illustrates the usual manner of rigging the spinnaker bag. The sail's three corners hang out of the bag's top, which is closed with the bag's draw string and tied with a slip knot. Immediately prior to hoisting the spinnaker, the slip knot is pulled to release the sail. Notice that figure 9-6 shows the jib hoisted. Usually, the jib is not lowered until after the

9-4. Luders yawls flying their radial head 'chutes. Notice the bridle for the pole lift and the downhaul or foreguy attached to the pole end. In this much breeze and on this point of sailing, the spinnakers seem to be drawing well with the large Genoas hoisted, but they might draw better with the jibs lowered.

176

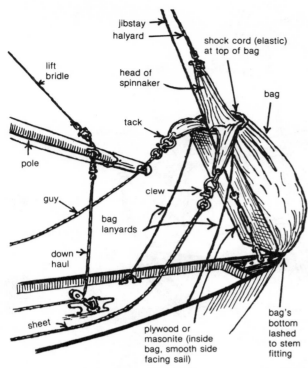

9-5. A turtle (for medium-size boat). Spinnaker ready to hoist (pole to port). Be careful that the leeches are not twisted around each other when sail is put into bag. Spinnaker may be hoisted while jib is set, but after spinnaker is up, jib is normally lowered.

Labels on figure:
jibstay
halyard
shock cord (elastic) at top of bag
head of spinnaker
lift bridle
bag
tack
pole
clew
guy
bag lanyards
down haul
sheet
plywood or masonite (inside bag, smooth side facing sail)
bag's bottom lashed to stem fitting

spinnaker has been hoisted, at which time the jib is *quickly* dropped, so it will not blanket the spinnaker.

As figure 9-6 shows, with dotted lines, that part of the halyard which fastens to the sail's head must lie to leeward of the jib. The hoisting part of the halyard is, of course, to windward of the jib, next to the mast. The halyard's end that snaps on to the head must be put to leeward of the jib by running it aft, outside the shrouds, to

the sail's leech. Then the halyard is put behind the leech and the halyard's end is worked forward under the foot of the jib until it is opposite the spinnaker bag where the end can be snapped onto the sail's head. Putting the halyard to leeward of the jib by running the line forward and around the headstay will often cause the halyard to make a wrap around the stay. More will be said about this later when we discuss spinnaker problems. Always look aloft to see that all is clear before hoisting the spinnaker.

It should be noticed in figure 9-6 that the after guy runs around the headstay and to leeward of the jib tack where it is snapped onto the spinnaker's tack. If it is desired that the pole be snapped to the guy's shackle ring, then the spinnaker's tack corner must be carried to leeward of the jib and around the headstay where the ring can be fastened to the pole's outboard end which is resting up against the headstay. The sheet leads outboard of the lee shrouds and snaps into the clew.

On large boats with *lifelines* (lines forming a safety railing around the outboard edge of the deck), it is especially important to check the sheet, guy, and halyard which are to leeward of the jib to make sure they are not fouled in the lifelines. The spinnaker sheet, guy, and halyard are always led *over*, or outboard of the lifelines.

It is very important that the spinnaker be "made up" or properly prepared before it is stuffed into its turtle or bag prior to hoisting. This preparation consists of folding the two spinnaker leeches together before the sail is bagged so that the sail will not be twisted when it is hoisted. A simple method is to dump the loose sail on the cabin sole where it is protected from the wind; then starting at the head, each

177

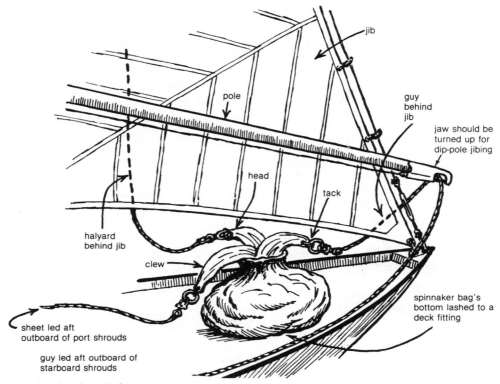

jib

guy behind jib

jaw should be turned up for dip-pole jibing

pole

head

tack

halyard behind jib

clew

spinnaker bag's bottom lashed to a deck fitting

sheet led aft outboard of port shrouds

guy led aft outboard of starboard shrouds

9-6. Setting the spinnaker from its bag.

leech is located and folded one against the other. The man doing this works his way down towards the sail's foot, *flaking down* or folding the sail accordion style with the leeches together. When almost at the foot, the two clews are separated and pulled out in opposite directions. The loose bulk of the sail is stuffed into the bag followed by the folded leeches. The head and the two clews are left hanging out of the bag or the turtle's top with the head in the middle between the two clews. On large boats when the spinnaker is being hoisted, a man should "see" it out of the bag or turtle. He should let the spin-

naker run through his hands or arms while looking aloft to see that the sail does not foul on a stay or spreader and that it does not become twisted. More will be said about this when we study spinnaker problems later in this chapter.

The remaining method of setting a spinnaker is to hoist the sail while it is rolled up and tied with light stops. After the sail is hoisted, the stops are then broken. This method is illustrated in figure 9-7. In former days, before the advent of the turtle, stopping a spinnaker was the usual practice, but now this is not often done except on a big boat in a strong wind. In most in-

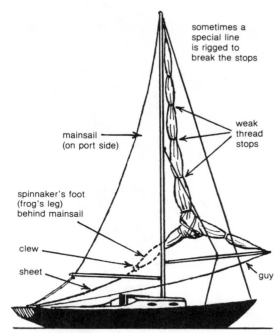

sometimes a
special line
is rigged to
break the stops

weak
thread
stops

mainsail
(on port side)

spinnaker's foot
(frog's leg)
behind mainsail

clew

sheet

guy

9-7. A stopped spinnaker. Pull on sheet to break it out.

stances, using a turtle or bag is simpler and quicker.

When a spinnaker is stopped, its leeches are put together in much the same manner as when preparing the sail for a turtle. The sail should be stretched tight between its head and foot, and then the loose part of the sail between the leeches is rolled or bunched up so that it makes the appearance of a long, thin, sausage. A rolled sail is usually more difficult to break out than one that is bunched. The sail is then stopped tightly at about every two or three feet with rotten twine or light cotton thread which may be broken very easily. The tighter the twine is tied the easier it may be broken. It is usually a good practice to make "frog's legs" at the foot as

shown in figure 9-7. As can be seen, the lowest stops are not put around the two leeches but around the foot and leech so that each clew forms the end of a leg. It is important that the upper stop not be tied too close to the spinnaker's head because this stop is often difficult to break. Upper stops are usually tied with one turn, while lower stops may have two. The lower the stop, the more force can be applied to it by a pull on the sheet.

Occasionally a special line is tied under the stops in such a way that the line may be pulled from the deck after the sail is hoisted to facilitate breaking the stops. Usually, however, a breaking line is not necessary. The leg stops can be reached and broken by hand, and a hard pull aft on the sheet will break the higher stops. When the stops begin to break, the wind will fill out the lower portion of the sail and help break the upper stops. The important thing in preparing a spinnaker for hoisting (whether it be in a bag, turtle, or stops) is to have the leeches running continuously together in order to assure that the sail is not twisted.

After the sail is hoisted, in a moderate or stronger breeze, ease the halyard slightly (about 12 to 18 inches) so that the head is blown slightly out and away from the mast. In light airs, however, the head should be as high as possible.

Spinnaker trim and helmsmanship. There are two ways a boat can be sailed with the spinnaker set. The first is to trim the sail properly and leave it alone while the helmsman changes course to conform with changes in the velocity and direction of the wind. The second is for the helmsman to hold a steady course while the spinnaker's trim is changed to match every change in the wind. On most top racing boats, however, a combination of these two techniques is used.

When the first method is used, the helmsman must be able to watch the spinnaker's luff (the forward edge from masthead to the outboard end of the pole). When the sail begins to collapse, he must quickly alter course. When sailing between a beam reach and a broad reach, the helmsman bears off if the spinnaker starts to *break* (to luff, beginning to collapse). But if the boat is running and the spinnaker begins to collapse, it is often difficult for the helmsman to know which way to turn. The sail could be luffing on account of a wind shift that is more on the beam, or the sail might be blanketed by the mainsail because of a shift that comes from astern and puts the boat by the lee (see chapter 5). This can become a real problem even for an experienced sailor in a rapidly shifting wind. The best way to overcome the problem is to look at the windward telltales or a masthead wind indicator. These will tell which way the wind is shifting. The helmsman should remember that the pole should be kept at right angles to the apparent wind. Of course, the wind indicators will give the apparent wind direction; thus, when an indicator makes an acute angle (less than 90 degrees) with the pole, the helmsman should *head up* to make the angle 90 degrees, but when the indicator makes an obtuse angle (more than 90 degrees) with the pole, he should *bear off* to make the angle 90 degrees. This is explained in figure 9-8.

An experienced helmsman can often (but not always) tell what is causing a spinnaker to break by simply looking at the sail. If it suddenly shakes and begins to collapse all over, it is probably blanketed by the mainsail. But if the sail first curls or bulges in near the luff edge, then

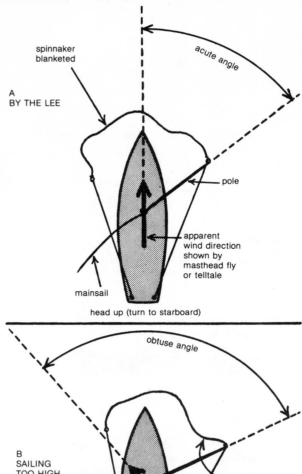

9-8. Spinnaker helmsmanship.
Masthead flys often swing from side to side if boat is rolling severely. In such a case it is usually better to watch the telltales.

180

the sail is probably luffing because of being on a point of sailing that is too high for the sail trim. The feel of the wind on the back of his neck aids the helmsman also. Nevertheless, many experienced sailors have caused a complete spinnaker collapse by steering the wrong way at the first sign of the sail's breaking. This can usually be avoided by referring to the wind indicators. In shifty conditions, it is sometimes wise to station a man near the telltales who can call their direction to the helmsman with the words "beamy" or "by the lee," or some such designation.

The second method mentioned (changing the sail's trim for shifts while the helmsman holds a straight course) requires a lot of action and coordination on the crew's part, because the guy as well as the sheet must be constantly tended. The responsibility for preventing a spinnaker collapse lies primarily with the sheet tender instead of the helmsman.

At most times it is best to use a combination of the two methods discussed, whereby the helmsman alters course to keep on the fastest point of sailing while a man stands by the sheet to prevent a collapse in the event of a sudden wind shift. With this technique, the fore-and-aft pole position is not often changed. The most frequent adjustments are with the helm and sheet. The helmsman should sail according to the principles discussed in chapter 5. He should bear off in the puffs and head up in the lulls, and unless there is a good reason for not doing so, he should *moderately* tack downwind. It is nearly always harmful to run dead before the wind with the spinnaker set, because this is a slower point of sailing and there is the danger of the spinnaker collapsing from being by the lee. Of course, the helmsman should steer as low as possible but with the sails, especially the spin-

naker, drawing at maximum efficiency. On a yawl, the mizzen staysail can be an effective guide to the helmsman. If he steers too low, this sail will collapse because of being blanketed by the mizzen. A simple rule of thumb for sailing a yawl downwind is to sail as low as possible without collapsing the mizzen staysail.

Principles for trimming the spinnaker sheet are essentially the same as for any other downwind sail. The sheet should be eased as far as possible without the sail beginning to bulge in at the luff. The sail should actually be carried "on edge," with the luff just beginning to curl. The man who tends the sheet is the key to successful spinnaker sailing. Since the wind and the boat's heading change almost continuously, he must follow with almost continuous experiments to try to ease the sheet more and more until the luff curls too much, then quickly trim in just enough to straighten the curl, then try to ease it out again, and keep on repeating this cycle. He must be stationed far enough forward so that he can watch the luff of the sail continuously. At times he may be able to put several turns around the winch with the sheet and then lead it forward to a position just forward of the main boom. At other times, on a large boat such as a Navy yawl, he may stand at the shrouds and reach outboard to the sheet to give it frequent inward tugs while another sheet trimmer backs him up aft at the winch. If the man at the shrouds cannot reach the sheet with his hand, he may use a short piece of line looped over the sheet. This short line is sometimes called a *snatch line* or *jerking line*. The man at the shrouds should watch the luff continuously and give the sheet a jerk when the luff edge begins to curl too much. In light airs, light sheets with lightweight shackles (or no shackle at all) should be used so that the clew will lift as high as possible. This sheet should be played by hand every moment.

When running, the spinnaker sheet should be led far aft where it is a maximum distance outboard. On many boats this lead point is at the top corners of the transom, but on the Navy yawls and Shields the lead blocks are somewhat farther forward because these boats have such narrow sterns. When reaching, it sometimes pays to lead the spinnaker sheet through a block at the end of the main boom in order to move the lead outboard. This has been effectively done on the Navy yawls. In strong winds it is usually best to lead the sheet farther forward.

Jibing the 'chute. There are two principal methods of jibing a parachute spinnaker: the *end-for-end* method and the *dip-pole* or *free-wheeling* jibe. Since the 'chute is symmetrical with leech and clew being identical, the sail can merely be shifted bodily from one side of the boat to the other without turning it around leech for leech.

The first jibing method mentioned, end-for-ending, requires that the spinnaker pole be reversible, that there be identical fittings on each end of the pole. Actually, the vast majority of poles are made this way. Opinions vary as to which is the best method of jibing. But generally speaking, end-for-ending seems to be more suitable for small boats and even medium-sized boats in light airs when the lift and foreguy are rigged from the middle of the pole (as in figure 9-1K). Dip-poling is more often favored on large boats, especially when jibing in a fresh breeze and when jibing from a broad reach on one tack to a broad reach on the other tack. End-for-ending is most often done on the Shields sloops but dip-poling is usually done on the Navy yawls.

Figure 9-9 explains the end-for-end spinnaker jibe. The procedure is divided into three steps. In the first, Step A, the guy and lift are slacked slightly. The pole should be about horizontal and low enough to be within easy reach of the foredeck man. The inboard end of the pole is unhooked from the mast, and in Step B, this same pole end is hooked onto the spinnaker sheet or swivel shackle. At this point, midway in the jibe, the pole is attached to both lower corners of the spinnaker, the sail is directly ahead of the bow and is kept full, the pole is at right angles to the boat's centerline, the boat is headed directly before the wind, and the main boom has been pulled in amidships. In the final Step C, the pole end that was formerly the outboard end is detached from the sail and is hooked onto the mast while the new guy is being eased off and the new sheet is trimmed in as the boat turns onto her new course, and finally the lift is readjusted.

One advantage of this jibing technique is that it is usually not difficult to keep the spinnaker full and drawing during the entire operation, because the clews are held apart by the pole. Nevertheless, it is important that the helmsman turn from one tack to the other very slowly. He should hold the boat dead before the wind until he is sure that the foredeck crew has everything under control and that the guy and sheet tenders are ready to slack and trim. Also, the mainsail should be held amidships and jibed very slowly in a light breeze; because if it is slacked too soon, it will blanket the spinnaker and perhaps cause the 'chute to collapse before it is properly trimmed for the new course.

A spinnaker pole of the type in figure 9-1 is frequently rigged with a continuous lanyard or trip line which connects the pull pins of the

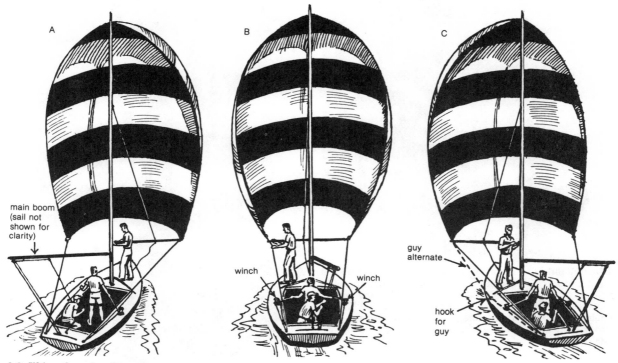

9-9. Jibing the spinnaker.

A. Lift and guy slacked slightly. Foredeck man unhooks pole from mast. On small boats one man can handle sheet and guy. Each line should be led to and snubbed on (wrapped around) a winch.

B. Sheet slacked slightly. Pole end snapped on sheet. Pole now on both corners of sail and at right angles to wind. Helmsman holds boat before wind and jibes the main. On some small boats foredeck man can work in fore end of cockpit.

C. Pole unhooked from former guy. New guy (port side) is slacked. Pole end hooked to mast. New sheet trimmed in. On small boats, guy can be hooked down forward near shrouds (shown by dotted line) to hold pole down eliminating need for downhaul.

pole-end fittings as shown in the illustration. With this arrangement, the foredeck man can release the sail from the end fitting by pulling the lanyard at any point on the pole.

Although it is customary to dip the poles of Navy yawls and they are usually fitted with lift bridles, the yawls can be jibed using the end-for-end method when they have poles with proper jaws at both ends. This can be very effective in a light breeze, especially when jibing from a run on one tack to a run on the other tack. The procedure is the same as shown in figure 9-9 except that two men should be used to disconnect and connect the pole with the mast and another man is needed to help connect the new guy to the pole end and disconnect the former guy. The

183

9-10. Bell fitting for the wooden Luders yawls. The pole end fits and locks into the bell, which is hinged to an adjustable slide on the track secured to the fore side of the mainmast. The lock release lever is shown on the side of the bell. The knob at the bottom of the slide pulls out to control a spring-loaded pin, which locks the slide in the desired position on the track.

wooden yawls are equipped with bell-shaped fittings on the spinnaker track slide (on the fore side of the mainmast). (See figure 9-10.) The poles have tapered ends which fit into the bells and are locked in place with spring catches. As previously said, the downhauls are attached to the outboard pole ends. When end-for-ending one of these poles, a minor problem is encountered in that after the jibe has been completed, the downhaul will be attached to the inboard end of the pole unless the line is shifted sometime during the jibe which, of course, is not desirable because it gives the busy foredeck crew an additional chore. A simple solution is to keep a downhaul fastened to each end of the pole.

9-11. Spinnaker pole fitting on mast of a fiberglass Luders yawl. The jaws at the end of the pole fit around the pin in the bracket. Inboard pole height is controlled by adjusting the position of the fitting using the block and tackle arrangement fitted to the slide. Two jam cleats are provided to prevent the line from slipping.

A dip-pole jibe is shown in figure 9-12. With this method, the outboard end of the pole is unhooked from the after guy or tack shackle, and the lift is slacked in order to lower (almost to the deck) the outboard pole end which is then passed under the headstay and across to the boat's other side where it is attached to the spinnaker's new guy or other clew. This method usually requires the inboard end of the pole to be slid up to the highest position on the mast track so that the pole will be short enough, when its outboard end is lowered, to clear the headstay. When dip-pole jibing, the spinnaker sheet and guy should be eased. The man who stands by the pole lift should trip the outboard end of the pole with the tripping lanyard, and perhaps another man will be needed to help remove the tack from the outboard pole end fitting. The pole is dipped by slacking the lift and it is swung inboard and ducked under the headstay. A man grabs the old sheet that will become the new guy and hooks it to the outboard end of the pole. Tension should be put on the new sheet immediately to prevent the sail from collapsing. At one point during this jibing procedure the spinnaker is, of course, completely detached from the pole. This is a crucial time and the helmsman must be careful not to put over his helm too suddenly before the pole is attached, the sheet trimmed, and the main boom is swung over. Also the mainsail should not be slacked off so rapidly that it blankets the 'chute while it is guyed far forward and before the helmsman heads up onto his new course.

Dip-pole jibing is usually the best method in a strong breeze because the pole does not have to be removed and refitted to the mast, a considerable task in a blow. In heavy weather, on big boats especially, an extra pair of sheets can be bent to each spinnaker clew. This will greatly facilitate the handling of the sail because it gives extra lines to control the sail, and during the

dip-pole jibe, the pole can be attached to the extra sheet when it is slack and inboard, within easy reach. This extra sheet to which the pole is fastened then becomes the new guy after the jibe has been completed.

On small boats during a race, consideration should be given to keeping extra weight off the foredeck. To some extent this is even true with boats as large as the Navy yawls. When jibing, therefore, no extra crew should be on the foredeck, because this can have a harmful effect on the boat's fore-and-aft trim. On a Shields sloop, one man should rig the spinnaker, getting it ready for hoisting. He may stand on the foredeck when jibing, but as far aft as possible, near the mast. End-for-end jibing, especially when done with a tripping lanyard on the pole, usually keeps weight on the foredeck to a mini-

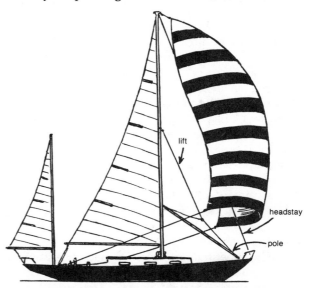

9-12. Dip-pole jibing. Yawl at mid point during dip-pole jibe. Pole end released from guy, lowered, passed under headstay, and hooked to former sheet (new guy).

185

mum. There are conflicting schools of thought on whether the sliding pin on the pole-end fitting should be up or down. This is a matter of personal preference. The pole is usually easier to engage and disengage from the mast during an end-for-end jibe if the pin is down (as illustrated in figure 9-1), but it is much easier to trip the end fitting with its lanyard to release the guy or tack if the pole is upside down with the sliding pin on top. Since dip-poling is used on the larger Navy boats, the pole should normally be carried with the jaws up on these boats.

Handing the spinnaker. *Handing* or taking in the spinnaker is not difficult if the job is done properly and carefully, but poor helmsmanship and sailhandling during the lowering operation can mean trouble aplenty. In nearly all cases, the Genoa or some other jib is set before the spinnaker is taken down. This will provide continuous sail power during a race, and the jib will help blanket the spinnaker and thereby make it easier to handle when it is being lowered. After the jib is hoisted, the guy is slacked all the way forward until the pole lies against the headstay or jibstay. Then the spinnaker's tack is released from the guy snap shackle so that the sail's luff flies free.

It is better to head the boat nearly dead before the wind when the tack is released in order that the spinnaker is blanketed to the greatest extent. At this point, a man or two is standing by the clew and sheet. When the men on the sheet are ready, a man on the halyard slowly lowers the sail. The sheet tenders, who are usually stationed abaft the main shrouds, pull in on the sheet and gather in the sail as it is lowered, either smothering the sail to keep it from blowing overboard or stuffing it out of the way (see figure 9-13). It can

9-13. Dousing the spinnaker. The tack has been released from the pole end, and the sail is being handed under the lee of the mainsail. The crew is keeping the sail tightly muzzled so it cannot fill with wind, which is especially important when it is blowing hard.

often be stuffed under the fore end of the cockpit on a Shields sloop or down the companionway hatch on a Navy yawl. The halyard man must be sure he doesn't lower the spinnaker faster than it can be taken in; otherwise, the sail will blow overboard and possibly scoop up water which could tear the sail and make it very difficult to haul it back aboard. In the rare instance that no jib is hoisted, the boat should be headed dead before the wind so that the spinnaker can be lowered in the lee of the mainsail.

A frequently encountered spinnaker-lowering situation occurs when approaching a leeward turning mark during a race, when the next leg of the course is closer than a beam reach. The 'chute should be lowered in advance of reaching the mark. Unless sailing with an experienced crew who have worked together, it is far better to be too soon than too late getting the spinnaker off. If the mark can be approached on a broad reach, the Genoa can be hoisted early to substitute for the 'chute, and not a great deal of speed will be lost if the jib is not blanketed by the mainsail. When jibing around the mark, try to jibe early or else hoist the jib, lower the spinnaker, and then jibe. If the mark is rounded sharply and the boat heads onto a close reach before the spinnaker has been lowered, the sail will blow quite far aft when its tack is released from the guy, and the dousing operation may be difficult because the 'chute will be partly out of the mainsail's wind shadow. In this case, the 'chute must be brought in under the after end of the main boom. On a yawl, great care must be taken to see that the sail does not foul the mizzen mast or its rigging. This has happened. When the 'chute is being lowered, it should be gathered in by the clew edge of the sail. Hand only one leech. If both leeches are pulled on, the sail will fill with wind and become very difficult to handle. The man lowering the spinnaker should always keep a turn of the halyard on its cleat or winch so that the sail can not get away from him.

Spinnaker problems. In certain conditions of wind and sea, spinnakers can cause many problems even when they are reasonably well handled. Many experienced offshore sailors feel that the modern 'chute is not a completely safe and seamanlike sail to carry at sea. There is no doubt, however, that it is a very fast sail, and a boat racing without a spinnaker has little chance of doing well in a downwind race. Furthermore, troubles can be minimized with practice, careful sail handling, advanced planning, and a general knowledge of what to expect.

The most common spinnaker problems with brief solutions or suggestions as to how to avoid them are as follows:

• *The hour glass*—This is a spinnaker twist about halfway between head and foot that prevents the middle of the sail from filling, but above and below the twist, the sail balloons out in such a way that it gives the appearance of an hour glass (see figure 9-14). It is usually caused by improperly preparing the sail before hoisting or by not spreading the clews as the sail is hoisted. The best way to prevent the twist is to see that the *leeches* are not twisted about each other when the sail is bagged, turtled, or stopped. Also, as said before, a man should see the sail out of its turtle or bag during the hoisting. He can often clear a twist before it develops by tugging on a leech. In addition, the sheet trimmer should keep tension on the sheet as the sail goes up. If an hour glass occurs near the spinnaker's head, the twist might be removed by

9-14. An hourglassed spinnaker. Crew members are pulling on both leeches in an attempt to make the swivel at the sail's head turn. The twist is so low, however, that it is doubtful that this attempt will succeed. The sail will probably have to be lowered to clear it, or if the breeze is light, the tack and clew could be detached and the lower half of the sail untwisted.

tugging on the sheet or leech or by jerking on the halyard, because there is always a swivel at the head that might turn to allow the sail to untwist. An hour glass near the middle or bottom of the sail will probably necessitate its lowering and untwisting by interchanging the tack and clew.

• *A fouled halyard*—Spinnaker halyard blocks are mounted on a swivel above the headstay (or jibstay with a seven-eighths rig). The halyard will either lie entirely on one side of the stay, or will straddle the stay (with one part of the halyard on either side of the stay). Some spinnaker halyards have snap shackles at both ends, but the usual 'chute halyard on a Navy boat has a shackle at one end of the line only. If a single-shackle halyard straddles the headstay and the shackle end of the line lies to leeward of the stay, then, as explained earlier, the leeward part of the halyard should be taken to leeward of the jib by passing the line aft around the jib's leech. Do *not pass the leeward part of a spinnaker halyard around the headstay to get it behind the jib,* because this will cause the halyard to wrap the stay. On the other hand, if this halyard's shackle end lies to windward of the stay, then the shackle end of the line must be taken forward where it is passed around the headstay to the jib's leeward side. Of course, it is then passed under the foot of the jib, and the shackle is snapped onto the spinnaker's head. With a double-shackle halyard (a shackle on each end) straddling the headstay, one has a choice: to take the *leeward part* of the halyard *aft,* around the jib's leech, or take the *windward part forward* around the headstay. In the first case, the hauling part of the halyard is to windward of the headstay, and in the second case, the hauling part is to leeward of the stay. The latter solution is better in the interest of chafe prevention when the spinnaker is carried for lengthy periods.

One method of simplifying halyard preparation is to fasten the halyard's shackle end (or both shackles on a double-shackle halyard) to the bow pulpit ahead of the jib on a Navy yawl. It is then in a position to be easily rigged on either tack. However, it is not advisable to leave the halyard permanently hooked to the pulpit, because the whipping line will cause some windage and turbulence which will interfere with the jib's luff when beating to windward. The spinnaker halyard should be hooked forward only just prior to setting the 'chute.

Some good general rules for rigging the halyard are: *Determine well in advance of setting the spinnaker on which side the sail will be carried.* Of course, this is determined by noting the wind direction and estimating what the spinnaker carrying course will be. Another vital rule is *always to look aloft just prior to hoisting the spinnaker to see that its halyard is clear.* See that the line is not wrapped around the headstay, and see that the block above the stay has properly swivelled.

• *Spinnaker knockdowns*—In a fresh breeze, it is not uncommon to see boats with spinnakers set take sudden *knockdowns* (extreme heelings) to either windward or leeward. (See figures 9-15 and 9-16.) Quite often these knockdowns will cause a loss of rudder control because the rudder will be acting in more of a horizontal than a vertical plane. A knockdown to windward can cause an accidental jibe, while a leeward knockdown can cause the main boom to break if it is broad off and vanged down. Either kind of knockdown can make the boat broach to or turn, out of control, broadside to the wind and seas.

The most seamanlike solution to this problem is to take the spinnaker off when there is real

9-15. Spinnaker knockdowns to leeward. This picture illustrates examples of the troubles that can be had when trying to carry spinnakers in too much breeze. Obviously, both boats are overpowered, and they would have been safer—and would be sailing faster—with boomed-out jibs. The lead boat appears to have tripped on her main boom while it was vanged down. This could break the boom. The spinnaker pole has escaped its bell fitting and is flailing dangerously. The mizzen is trimmed in flat making it very difficult for the helmsman to bear off. The after boat should have slacked her spinnaker sheet and borne off. The mizzen staysail is doing no good and is only adding to the confusion.

danger of a knockdown. In a race when competitors are carrying 'chutes successfully, however, it is desirable to carry the spinnaker as long as possible. It if often difficult to determine the exact time the spinnaker should be handed. To a large extent this will depend on the experience and skill of the crew and on the condition of the boat. By and large, when the boat is at hull speed, when she is yawing and rolling violently, when there is a steep following sea, or when extreme heeling commences and the helm is very hard to control, the spinnaker should be

9-16. The Luders yawl *Lively* under reefed mainsail and tri-radial spinnaker takes a roll to weather. Weather knockdowns can be prevented by heading up slightly, moving the sheet lead well forward, and overtrimming the spinnaker in gusts.

doused. Under these conditions the boat will be safer, handle much easier, and perhaps will not lose any speed carrying a poled-out Genoa jib. When poling out a jib, the spinnaker pole is rigged to windward, the jib is kept blanketed by the main, and then the jib's clew is hauled out to the pole's outboard end.

If caught by a sudden puff which causes a knockdown to leeward when the spinnaker is set, release the sheet to spill the wind from the sail. Be sure, however, that the end of the sheet is knotted so that it won't run out of its lead blocks. It is often wise to rig two sheets, one with a few feet of slack, so that when the taut sheet is slacked, the loose sheet will take the strain but still allow the spinnaker to go out enough to spill its wind. With a knockdown to leeward, the helmsman should try to bear off immediately so that the boat will gain stability.

If caught by a sudden puff that causes a windward knockdown, the sheet should be flattened quickly and the boat headed up, if possible. This kind of knockdown can be avoided by overtrimming the spinnaker sheet and by not sailing too low, by reaching instead of running.

• *Breaking the spinnaker pole*—Breaking a pole is not a common occurrence, but it does happen occasionally. As previously said, the lift bridle arrangement with the downhaul or foreguy secured to the pole's end is generally considered the strongest rig. However, with this arrangement, there is still a great compression load on the pole when it is guyed far forward because the after guy pulls almost straight aft.

One solution to this is the *reaching strut* which is often used by large boats on distance races but seldom on short, closed-course races. This strut is a short extra pole which is rigged to windward to hold the guy a few feet out from the windward shrouds. While the pole is guyed forward, the strut sticks out horizontally at a near right angle to the boat's centerline. The length of the strut is equal to approximately three-quarters of the boat's maximum beam. The strut lies against the fore side of the forward shroud and it is usually lashed to the shroud. The strut's inboard end hooks onto a pad eye or similar fitting on the mast, while the outboard end usually has a large sheave to accept the guy. Advantages of the strut are three-fold: to keep the pole from pressing too hard against the headstay, to reduce compression on the pole, and to prevent the guy from chafing against the outboard shroud. On the other hand, the strut does cause extra complications on the foredeck, and both setting it up and removing it take extra time; so it is not always used on short races in protected waters, especially if the boat has outboard shrouds that hold the guy fairly far away from the boat's centerline.

Whether or not the strut is used, care must be taken to see that the pole does not exert too much pressure against the headstay. The guy must be kept tight enough to hold the pole just off the stay even on a beam reach. In a strong wind the outboard pole end should be lowered slightly for two reasons. First, if the pole does hit the headstay, due to the guy stretching, the lateral strain will be near the pole's end where

the spinnaker will not have the leverage to break the pole (by pulling it sideways against the stay). Secondly, by keeping the pole end low, the after guy will pull the pole down to help counteract the strong upward pull of the spinnaker. Of course, in winds less than those which threaten to break the pole, the spinnaker should be allowed to lift for the greatest efficiency and drive. But in strong winds it is best to control and tame the 'chute somewhat by over-trimming the sheet and lowering the pole.

• *The spinnaker wrap*—One of the most difficult troubles to clear up is the spinnaker headstay wrap. This is most likely to occur in a seaway when the spinnaker has collapsed and its loose middle section lies against the headstay. Occasionally, a current of wind from the side will cause the loose folds of the sail to start spinning around the headstay. The boat's motion from the seas will often initiate or add to the twisting. This is most likely to happen if the sail collapses from sailing by the lee, during a jibe, or as the 'chute is hoisted without the jib being set. Of course, if the jib is kept up until after the spinnaker is hoisted and sheeted, then there is little chance of a wrap. The 'chute cannot wind around the stay as long as the jib is hoisted. For this reason many ocean racers carry *spinnaker nets* which are basically jibs made from big-mesh nets instead of cloth. In fact, the British often refer to spinnaker nets as *phantom jibs*. Nets vary greatly in design, but they are usually composed of the least number of lines or tapes that will do the job of preventing a wrap. Of course, a cloth jib should not always remain hoisted because it may blanket the spinnaker.

Spinnaker nets are seldom used in short races or in protected waters because the nets take time to rig, and they are easy to tangle. Many small boats carry one or two *antiwrap lines* which are permanently rigged. An antiwrap line (usually of shock cord) is one permanently fastened to the mast at about a third or more of the mast's length down from the masthead (if the boat has a masthead rig). This line is slightly shorter than the distance from its point of attachment on the mast to the masthead. The other end of the line (the end not attached to the mast) is fastened to a sliding ring on the headstay. When no jib is set, the line hangs loosely between the mast and the stay where it will help prevent a spinnaker wrap; but when the jib is hoisted, the ring slides up to the top of the stay, and the line will be stretched tight against or near the fore side of the mast. Of course, effectiveness is increased if two such antiwrap lines are used.

With boats rigged like the Navy yawls, the forestay may be set up, and a jib halyard may be wound back and forth between the forestay and the headstay so that the halyard makes a kind of net. This is not recommended for short races but only on long spinnaker courses and when there is danger of a spinnaker wrap. At all other times when the spinnaker is carried, the forestay should be detached and secured to the shrouds. The foredeck should always be kept as clear as possible (stripped of anchors, boathooks, etc.) to minimize the possibility of lines becoming fouled.

Once the spinnaker becomes wrapped, it is usually very difficult to clear. The first action to take is to jibe over as soon as the wrap occurs, so that the wind current which caused the wrap will come from the opposite side. After jibing, the boat should be held almost dead before the wind. She should not be let up to a broad reach. This may promptly cause the sail to unwrap, but if not you may be in for some trouble. Sometimes the wraps can be cleared by sailing by the lee and then luffing the boat in a series of swoops that reduce the wraps one turn per swoop. But if this doesn't work and the sail is badly wrapped, a man may have to go aloft in a bosun's chair to clear the twists.

Some general tips on spinnaker wraps are as follows. Try to avoid letting the sail collapse against the headstay, especially in a seaway. Keep the jib set until after the spinnaker is hoisted and trimmed. Try to keep the spinnaker full when jibing. After the jib has been lowered, unshackle its halyard and bring it aft to the mast, because if a wrap occurs, the sail can get pinched between the stay and halyard. Also, the halyard may have to be used to hoist a man up in the bosun's chair. When there is danger of a wrap, keep tension on the spinnaker's sheet or pull on the leech, or both; anything that can be done to flatten the sail will be helpful. If the sail begins to wrap, a sharp change of course may stop it, but if not, jibe over and perhaps the sail will unwrap.

Recent spinnaker theory. In recent years some subtle improvements have been made in the design of spinnakers. Many of these sails have become more highly specialized for particular points of sailing and certain strengths of wind. Great strides, especially, have been made in the development of reaching spinnakers, and some of the newest designs can be carried when the boat is sailing considerably higher than a beam reach.

Specialized reaching spinnakers vary from flat, crosscut 'chutes to *spankers* (symmetrical jib-like spinnakers with narrow shoulders—see figure 9-17) to the more recent *star-cut* reachers (figure 9-18). The latter design has cloth panels

9-17. Contrasting spinnaker types. Two Britton Chance designed 30-footers racing with different spinnakers. The lead boat, a Chance 30-30, is flying a conventional cross-cut 'chute, while the following boat, a PT-30, is carrying a type of spanker. Notice the high-aspect ratio rigs favored by the IOR handicap rule and the double-spreader rig, clearly seen on the PT-30, which allows inboard shrouds without much sacrifice to the shroud angle. The outboard rudder moves the center of pressure aft, but it may be more prone to ventilation (sucking air down from the surface) at times.

that radiate inwards from each corner towards the center of the sail to form a star-shaped pattern. This radial construction minimizes bias stretch (distortion from pull that is diagonal to the direction of the cloth's weave) and thus allows the sail to better hold its shape on a reach. The first spankers usually had mitered seams at the clews, and the sails were carried jib-style with the outboard end of the pole lowered to the stem head to tighten and thereby straighten the luff (rules forbid detaching the sail from the pole and tacking it to the stem). Many newer spankers, however, are designed to be carried with the pole fairly low but horizontal, so that the sail's tack is slightly forward of the headstay, and, although there is some sag in the luff, it will have a flatter draft curve forward to allow reasonably high pointing. On many spinnakers over-tightening the luff will cause very deep draft forward which will be detrimental to close reaching. As a rule, when reaching it is well to experiment with the pole level on every individual sail to test its pointing abilities, because optimal shaping of the sail will depend on its particular cut. Spinnakers intended for close reaching, being made of medium weight cloth, having narrow shoulders aloft, and being cut relatively flat, are also highly suitable for running in strong winds.

Those 'chutes intended for running or broad reaching in light airs are made of the lightest weight nylon, one-half ounce or three-quarters ounce, depending on the size of the boat. Such spinnakers are cut with deeper draft, and, except for those intended for drifting conditions, they have fairly broad shoulders aloft. In very light airs, the pole is carried quite low but horizontal, partly to deepen the draft curve from the luff to leech. In medium winds, however, the

9-18. The Navy boat *Patriot* flying a tri-radial spinnaker. The radial seams at the head and clews help prevent bias stretch and thus distortion on a reach. The round patch just above the numbers is for the attachment of a retrieving line, which helps in handing the 'chute. With the retrieving line, the 'chute is lowered in the usual manner behind a jib, but it is normally not necessary to release the tack initially, because the sail is hauled down by the line attached to its middle, and this will effectively spill the wind.

194

pole is raised and the sail is allowed to lift all it can, and the shoulders are encouraged to spread apart. When only one spinnaker is on board, it must quite obviously be a very versatile sail, reasonably good in all conditions. Such a 'chute might be a three-quarters-or 1.2-ounce *radial head crosscut* (having horizontal panels in the lower half and vertical radial panels in the upper half) with only moderately deep draft and substantial shoulders. Another versatile 'chute is the *tri-radial*, which is crosscut in the middle but has radial panels at all three corners.

Staysails carried under spinnakers also are becoming more specialized. Sailmakers and expert sailors do not always agree about what staysail is most effective for each set of conditions, but by and large, taller staysails with shorter foot lengths are now being used. Very tall, narrow sails often called *tallboys* or *ribbon staysails* are tacked to the windward rail not far forward of the mainmast when running (see figure 9-19). For broad reaching with the apparent wind about on the quarter or somewhat farther forward, a low spinnaker staysail with a long foot (similar to the one illustrated in figure 6-1) is probably more effective to minimize blanketing the spinnaker. On this same point of sailing some boats carry *topless* or *baldheaded staysails* (those having their tops cut off to avoid blocking off the spinnaker's wind). Most broad-reaching staysails are tacked down a third or more of the distance from the stem head to the mainmast abaft the stem head. When the wind is closer to being on the beam or slightly forward of the beam, larger, taller staysails can be used, and generally they are tacked down farther forward. An effective sail for this point of sailing is a large Genoa staysail (a staysail shaped like a Genoa jib) with its tack about a quarter of the

stem-to-mast distance aft and its luff about parallel to the headstay. On a very close spinnaker reach in moderate winds and smooth water, a full-size Genoa or reaching jib often can be

9-19. A C&C 35 flying a cross-cut 'chute and tallboy staysail. Notice the battens in the tallboy to stabilize its leech. The sail might be tacked down a little farther to weather. The mainsail is well vanged and its luff slacked to increase draft and move it aft, but the sail might be hoisted a bit more for better advantage in such light air.

carried under the 'chute to give a very noticeable increase in speed. Double slot arrangements with large staysails or jibs under the spinnaker are most effective when *penalty poles* (spinnaker poles longer than the distance between the stem head and mast) are carried. Also, it will pay to ease the spinnaker halyard a foot or so in fresh breezes to get the 'chute as far as possible away from the jib.

Summary. A brief summary of the main points in this chapter in list form may be helpful. Sev-

9-20. Hoisting the 'chute on the former Navy boat *Guerriere*. The spinnaker bag is secured quite far abaft the stem, and the sail is being hoisted under the foot of the jib. This may help prevent hour-glass twists, because it allows the clews to be spread a maximum distance apart while hoisting. Care must be taken, however, to see that the sail does not drag in the water too much.

eral of these points are illustrated in figure 9-21. If any of the tips are not clear, they should be looked up in the preceding text where they are dealt with in more detail.

Spinnaker tips.

• Plan ahead. Lay out sheet and guy, prepare the 'chute, and set up pole with lift and downhaul well in advance of hoisting.

• Bag, turtle, or stop spinnaker with both leeches untwisted.

• Look aloft before hoisting. Be sure halyard is not wrapped around the headstay.

• Be sure that the sheet, guy, and halyard are led over the lifelines.

• Consider hooking spinnaker halyard on bow pulpit while getting the sail ready to hoist.

• Hoist spinnaker behind the jib whenever possible, and hoist fast.

• Ease halyard slightly in a moderate or stronger breeze unless spinnaker begins to osciliate, in which case halyard should be *two-blocked* (hauled all the way up).

• Start trimming the sheet immediately while the 'chute is being hoisted.

• Keep pole at right angles to apparent wind.

• Keep tack and clew at same level.

• Keep inboard end of pole high in a moderate breeze but low in a light air.

• Keep pole horizontal in a light air but cocked up slightly in a moderate breeze.

• Keep pole's outboard end low in a strong breeze.

• Keep spinnaker "on edge" with the sheet.

• Station the sheet trimmer where he can see the luff.

• Use a sheet snatch line in a strong breeze.

• Make maximum use of wind indicators when steering with the 'chute set.

• Avoid sailing low, or by the lee.

9-21. A spinnaker problem. NA 2 is successfully hoisting her 'chute behind the lee of the jib, but it appears that NA 9 has not kept her spinnaker blanketed, and the halyard has gotten away from the crew doing the hoisting. The spinnaker should be pulled aboard by one sheet only; otherwise it will act like a sea anchor.

• Use a combination of course changing and sheet adjusting when sailing with the 'chute in a shifting breeze.

• Use the mizzen staysail as a guide to spinnaker steering.

• Jibe the mainsail slowly when the 'chute is being jibed.

• Consider dip-poling when jibing from reach to reach or in a strong breeze.

• Consider end-for-ending pole when jibing

197

9-22. Setting the 'chute after rounding the windward mark. It is the safest policy, especially in a fresh wind, to keep the spinnaker blanketed until after it is fully hoisted. Crew members who are not busy should check for lines dragging overboard.

from run to run or in a moderate breeze on a small boat.

• Keep excess crew off the foredeck.

• Slack the sheet during a spinnaker knock-down to leeward, slack the main, and head off.

• Flatten sheet during a windward knock-down. Also head up and/or guy the pole farther forward.

• Lower the 'chute in the lee of a jib.

• Cast off tack and hand the 'chute by one leech only.

• Keep a turn around the winch or cleat with the halyard when the 'chute is lowered, and lower slowly.

• Continue steering before the wind, if possible, until the 'chute has been entirely lowered.

• Keep the pole from bearing hard against the forestay.

• Consider using a reaching strut and some form of spinnaker net when distance racing in a rough sea.

• When beginning to lose helm control, douse the 'chute and pole out a jib.

10. Basic Racing

Although there are many excellent seamen who seldom race, there is no doubt that sailboat racing is a sport that develops and sharpens all the aspects and skills of good seamanship—team work, organization, the power to concentrate, the ability to make quick decisions, and the desire to learn and improve. Volumes have been written on racing, and we cannot hope to cover all the fine points of the subject in one chapter. We have already put a good deal of emphasis on a very important aspect of racing, however—that of getting the best speed and performance from a boat through helmsmanship, sail trim, and the duties of the crew. Therefore, a large part of competitive sailing has been dealt with. What remains to be covered may be roughly divided into three parts: racing rules, starting, and course tactics.

Introduction to racing. When a group of sailboats race against each other as individuals (not as a team), there can be two forms of competition: handicap or class (sometimes called one-design) racing. The latter is boat-for-boat racing between nearly identical boats. In this case, the boat with the fastest *elapsed time* from start to finish, or the first boat over the finish line, wins the race. In handicap racing, however, boats of different sizes and types compete against each other. The larger, faster boats are given time handicaps. Under this system, each boat is given a *measurement rating* that attempts to predict her speed potential. This rating is assigned a time allowance in seconds per mile. To find out how much time a particular boat would receive from a larger, higher-rated boat, subtract the allowance of the larger boat from the allowance of the smaller one, and multiply this difference by the distance in miles of the particular race. The winning boat is the one with the best *corrected time,* or the best time for sailing the course after handicap corrections have been made.

While many small boats are raced as a class, the Navy yawls may be raced either as a class, when racing among themselves, or under a handicap system when racing against boats of different sizes and designs. The yawls are presently rated under the Delta Class measurement rule when racing on the Chesapeake Bay. Under this rule each boat is assigned a rated length after certain vital dimensions and characteristics have been physically measured. These measurements include: load water line length and the overall length, beam, draft, and sail area. These various measurements are applied to the Delta rating formula, and the result is the boat's rated length. The yawls also race in the PHRF (Performance Handicap Racing Fleet) which is an arbitrary form of handicapping, and ratings are assigned in seconds per mile.

Race courses are of two general types: the point-to-point course and the closed course. The former is literally from one geographic location to another. This type of racing may turn out to be a reach, beat, or run the entire way, or it may be some combination of these points of sailing depending on the wind direction with respect to the particular course. Certain aspects of this kind of racing will be discussed in the next chapter. Unlike the point-to-point course, the closed course has its start and finish in the same, or approximately the same, location. This type of race is deliberately planned to have a variety of points of sailing, and at least one beating leg is considered essential. Most closed courses are *windward-leeward, triangular,* or some combination of the two.

The simplest windward-leeward course has its first leg a near dead beat to a windward turning mark and then a run back to the starting point. Some windward-leeward courses have an initial short windward leg to the mark, then a long run to another mark to leeward of the starting line, and finally a short beat back to the starting area which then becomes the finish line. In a triangular course, three major marks are involved so as to make each leg of the course the side of a triangle. This kind of course is usually arranged so that one leg is a beat, another a run, and the other a reach. Combinations of windward-leeward and triangular courses make the *Gold Cup, Modified Gold Cup,* and *Olympic* courses. The Gold Cup is a windward-leeward followed by a triangular course, the Modified Gold Cup is a triangle followed by a windward-leeward course, and an Olympic is a triangle followed by a windward-leeward course with an extra windward leg.

A first look at the racing rules. The principal racing rules in this country and those under which all Navy boats race are the International Yacht Racing Union Rules as adopted by the United States Yacht Racing Union (USYRU). Included in these rules are the right-of-way principles for all converging situations. Remember that these are not rules of the road. The USYRU rules govern boats racing among themselves only.

It is important for all racing skippers to know the rules. Of course, the newcomer cannot be expected to know all the fine points of the rules or the outcome of all protests resulting from different interpretations of the rules, but all skippers should at least be thoroughly familiar with the main points expressed in Part IV of the USYRU rules, which is "Right of Way Rules, and Rights and Obligations When Yachts Meet." This and other parts of the rules are printed verbatim in appendix C. Knowledge of these rules not only gives the racing skipper confidence to exercise his judgment and to make split-second decisions, but his knowledge considerably lessens the chance of a dangerous collision on the race course. Racing terms used in the rules are defined in Part I of the USYRU rules and this is also printed verbatim in the appendix.

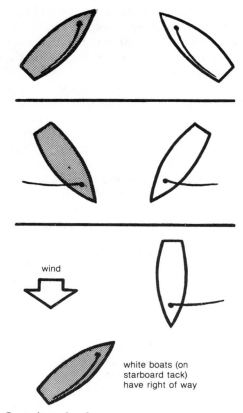

wind

white boats (on
starboard tack)
have right of way

10-1. Opposite tack rule.

It is most important first to learn the Basic Rules, Numbers 36 and 37 in Part IV of the USYRU rules; Number 36 is the *opposite tack rule,* and Number 37 is the *same tack rule.* Rule 36 is the most simple basic rule, and it states that: "A *port-tack* yacht shall keep clear of a *starboard-tack* yacht." There are but three exceptions to this rule. First, if you have crossed the starting line too early and must return to restart, you do not have the right of way even if on the

starboard tack. This is expressed in Rule 44.1 (a). The second exception has to do with overlapping boats when rounding or passing a mark, and it is expressed in Rule 42.1 (a). We shall discuss the subject of rounding marks later in this chapter. The other exception has to do with yachts re-rounding after touching a mark (see Rule 45).

Rule 37 deals with boats converging when they are on the same tack. This states that: "1. A *windward yacht* shall keep clear of a *leeward yacht.* 2. A yacht *clear astern* shall keep clear of a yacht *clear ahead.* 3. A yacht which establishes an *overlap* to *leeward* from *clear astern* shall allow the *windward yacht* ample room and opportunity to keep clear." In defining clear astern, clear ahead, and overlap, the rules say, "A yacht is *clear astern* of another when her hull and equipment in normal position are abaft an imaginary line projected abeam from the aftermost point of the other's hull and equipment in normal position. The other yacht is *clear ahead.* The yachts *overlap* when neither is *clear astern;* or if, although one is *clear astern,* an intervening yacht *overlaps* both of them. The terms *clear astern, clear ahead,* and *overlap* apply to yachts on opposite *tacks* only when they are subject to Rule 42, (Rounding or Passing Marks and Obstructions)." The term proper course is defined as follows: "A *proper course* is any course which a yacht might sail after the starting signal, in the absence of the other yacht or yachts affected, to *finish* as quickly as possible. The course sailed before *luffing* or *bearing away* is presumably, but not necessarily, that yacht's *proper course.* There is no *proper course* before the starting signal." (Words printed in italics in the quoted parts of the rule, are terms that are defined in Part I of the rule. For those terms not already defined, see appen-

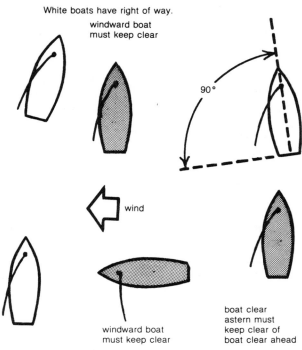

White boats have right of way.

windward boat
must keep clear

90°

wind

windward boat
must keep clear

boat clear
astern must
keep clear of
boat clear ahead

10-2. Same tack rule.

dix C.) Examples of the opposite tack rule and the same tack rule are shown in figures 10-1 and 10-2. More will be said about the racing rules later in this chapter.

The start. The start is often the most difficult and unnerving part of a race, especially for the novice skipper; but in a short race, getting a good start is tremendously important. Races have been won and lost at the start.

The starting line is an imaginary line between two points, usually a mark and an orange flag on a committee boat. The mark may be a fixed channel marker or buoy or a special mark, often a siz-

able orange inflatable buoy, temporarily put into position by the organization sponsoring the race. The committee boat may be any kind of craft with a mast from which flags and shapes (usually balls, cylinders, or cones) can be hoisted. The boat must be large enough to accommodate several members of the race committee from the sponsoring yacht club. Usually, but not always, the starting line marker is placed so that it is passed on the same side as the course turning marks are passed. In other words, all marks are usually left on the same side. Course instructions are usually given in the form of a race circular mailed or handed to each contestant before the race; often the course is given at a preliminary skipper's meeting, or sometimes the course is posted with large signs on the side of the committee boat. In the latter case, the signs are often a combination system of single letters or numbers, and the system is explained in the race circular.

The ideal starting line is one that is set approximately square (90 degrees) to the wind. If there is any variation, the left-hand end of the line should be set slightly closer to the first mark than the right-hand end. This variation should rarely exceed 5 degrees, with the first leg of the course (the direction to the first mark) being nearly a dead beat to windward. This is theoretically possible to achieve with a closed-course race, but it is usually not possible on a point-to-point course unless the wind happens to blow from exactly the right direction. Of course, the first mark may not always lie dead to windward, but it is important that the line be about square to the wind. The object of such a line is that neither end of the line is favored, so that competitors will not be bunched or jammed together at one end. If the current or some other factor makes one end of the line more attractive, then the line should be slanted slightly away from the right angle to the wind in order to make both ends equally attractive. This principle holds true on reaching and running starts as well. It is highly desirable to have the starting boats evenly spread out along the line no matter what the point of sailing. Windward starts are preferable, because all the boats rarely arrive at the first mark at almost the same time, as so often happens with reaching and running starts.

Even on a closed course, the ideal starting line is often very difficult to set because of last minute wind shifts which cause the line to be slanted away from the 90-degree angle to the wind. In fact, even though the race committee makes a great effort to set a perfect line, more often than not one end will be slightly more favored than the other.

The following system is customarily used to start a race: at precisely ten minutes before the start, a *warning* signal is given from the committee boat. This signal is given audibly, with a gun or horn, and at the same time it is given visibly with the hoisting of a flag or shape. Exactly four minutes later, the warning shape, which is usually white, is hauled down; and one minute later another signal is given audibly and visibly with a gun or horn and the hoisting of another flag or shape. This is called the *preparatory* signal and the flag or shape is usually colored blue. Four minutes later, the preparatory shape is hauled down; and one minute after this, the *start* signal is given with the hoisting of the starting shape or flag, usually colored red, and the sounding of the horn or gun. Actually, the visual signal gives the exact time of the start, because a starting gun can misfire.

Racing skippers try to reach the starting line just as the starting signal is made. The ideal or perfect start is one that is made at the favored spot on the line, with the boat sailing at top speed and just touching the line as the signal is

10-3. Getting ready to start. Everyone seems to be in his proper position with the timer informing the helmsman of time remaining, the bow man keeping a lookout and sighting down the line, and other crew members standing by the sheets.

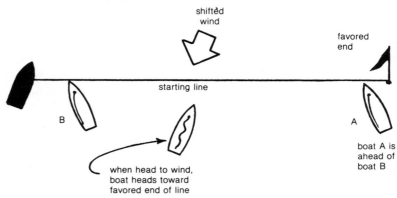

a lifting shift for starboard tack boats

shifted wind

favored end

starting line

B

A

boat A is ahead of boat B

when head to wind, boat heads toward favored end of line

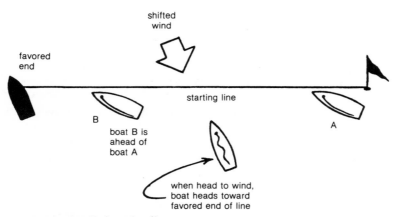

a heading shift for starboard tack boats

shifted wind

favored end

starting line

B

A

boat B is ahead of boat A

when head to wind, boat heads toward favored end of line

10-4. Favored end of starting line.

hoisted and the gun is fired. Of course, this is an ideal that is very difficult to achieve.

Choosing the favored spot on the line is one of the keys to successful starting. There is a simple rule for choosing the favored end when the line is not square to the wind. With the boat near the center of the starting line, luff up until the boat is headed directly into the eye of the wind, and the bow will point closer to one end of the line than the other. *The end that is closer to the boat's heading when she is head-to-wind is the favored end of the line.* This is illustrated in figure 10-4. A boat making a well-timed start at the favored end is always ahead of boats making well-timed starts anywhere else on the line. In choosing the favored end, however, one has to be careful about a last minute wind shift which might favor the opposite end. If you are ahead but to leeward of a competitor, you gain if the shift is a header, but you lose if the shift is a lift. This can be seen in figure 10-4.

Notice in the diagram, the starting boats are on the starboard tack. This is a fundamental rule. *Start on the starboard tack,* because you have the right of way and can force port tack boats about in converging situations. Of course, there are exceptions to every rule, and occasionally a perfectly timed port tack start will pay off. But there is no question that starting on the starboard tack is the safest policy, and it is most certainly recommended for beginners.

When choosing the favored starting spot on the line, there are factors to be considered other than what position will put you ahead of your competitors at that particular moment. The racing skipper must decide where he wants to go immediately after the start. He may, for example, wish to go offshore if the current is favorable and there appears to be a better breeze away from the land, or he may want to tack inshore to get into smoother water and to escape a foul current. If he knows where he wants to go, he must plan the kind of start that will allow him to reach his strategic course in the quickest time. For instance, if he starts to leeward on the starboard tack but wishes to stand inshore on the port tack, he might be boxed in or trapped by boats to windward that could prevent him from coming about. In this hypothetical case, it might be the better plan for him to take a late start to windward so that he could go over on the port

tack immediately after crossing the line.

Another tremendously important consideration is where the starter should go to get clean, undisturbed wind. A boat's speed can be greatly harmed by the disturbed air (backwind and wind shadows) from other boats, and this is particularly true in the vicinity of a crowded starting line. A boat that makes a well-timed start at the line's favored end will usually get clean air. At the windward end of the line (when on the starboard tack of a windward start), a boat can usually get clear wind even if she gets a bad start, because she can promptly tack into undisturbed wind soon after crossing the line. If she gets a bad start at the line's leeward end, she may not be able to tack, but she may be able to bear off slightly and foot into clean air. Of course, if all the starting boats are headed, this will put the leeward boat in the most favored position. In the event that the line is square to the wind and the starters are bunched at each end, there might be cleaner air in the middle; but when starting in the line's middle, it is usually difficult to bear off into less disturbed air and also difficult to tack for clean air.

Figure 10-5 shows just how a boat can disturb the air of other boats in her vicinity. The black boats in the diagram have their wind disturbed by boat A, while the white boats have their wind clear. Notice that black boat 3 is getting some backwind even though she is to windward of A. This is due to the draft curve of A's mainsail which deflects the backwind to windward. To clear her air, black 3 should pinch up in an attempt to work farther to windward of A. Black boat 2, to leeward, is sailing in A's wind shadow. To clear her air, black 2 should try to drive off slightly to leeward with eased sheets until she sails out of the wind shadow. Black

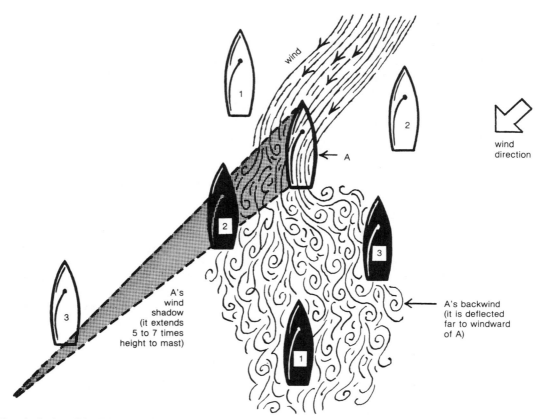

wind

wind
direction

A

A's
wind
shadow
(it extends
5 to 7 times
height to mast)

A's backwind
(it is deflected
far to windward
of A)

10-5. Disturbed air. White boats have their wind clear with respect to boat A. Black boats' winds are disturbed by boat A.

boat 1, dead astern of A, is getting backwind and also disturbed water from A's wake. The chances are that she cannot pinch up or drive off enough to clear her air without dropping far astern. Probably, her best alternative is to tack. If her skipper wants to remain on the starboard tack, then he can tack again as soon as he gets into undisturbed air. White boat 1 in the diagram is in the most enviable position, because she is actually lifted slightly by the deflected air flowing to leeward of A's jib. White 1 is said to

have a *safe leeward position.* Of course, she has her wind clear and is throwing backwind against the lee side of A's sails.

Once the starting spot on the line is selected, the next problem to cope with is how to hit the line with sufficient headway when the starting gun is fired. There are five fundamental techniques for arriving at the line as the starting signal is made: (1) the timed start, (2) sitting on the line, (3) running the line, (4) the dip start, and (5) the barging start (see figure 10-6). There

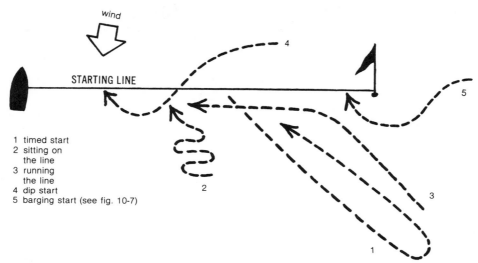

wind

STARTING LINE

1 timed start
2 sitting on
  the line
3 running
  the line
4 dip start
5 barging start (see fig. 10-7)

10-6. Five types of starts.

are certain special occasions when any of these techniques or a combination of some of them might be used, but by and large, the timed start is generally the most effective and the safest, for large boats at least.

The most commonly used method with this kind of start is known as the Vanderbilt system. This system suggests that you cross the line on the port tack heading in the wrong direction (away from the first turning mark) while, as nearly as possible, beam reaching with very roughly 2 minutes to go before the starting gun. A timer, a crew member with a stopwatch, takes the time as you cross the line and notes the time remaining until the starting gun. You add the time it takes to turn (tack or jibe) to the time remaining and divide by 2. This figure gives the proper time to begin your turn to head back for the starting line. Theoretically, you should return to the line as the gun fires.

An example is shown in figure 10-7. The boat crosses the line going the wrong way when there are 2 minutes and 20 seconds to go (until the start). The skipper estimates that it will take him 10 seconds to tack. He adds 10 seconds to 2 minutes 20 seconds and divides by 2, which gives 1 minute 15 seconds. He sails the boat on a steady course until there is 1 minute 15 seconds to go, and then he tacks and heads straight back to the spot where he formerly crossed the line. In the absence of a current, interference from other boats, and if the wind is steady, he should reach the line at gunfire. This method usually works well when there are not a great number of boats racing. A crowded starting line can throw off the timing because of necessary course alterations. Also, strong currents and light or spotty winds can disrupt this kind of start.

The second starting technique, sitting on the line, is sometimes used when racing small, light dinghies—420s or Lasers, for instance. In this case, a skipper approaches the line early, per-

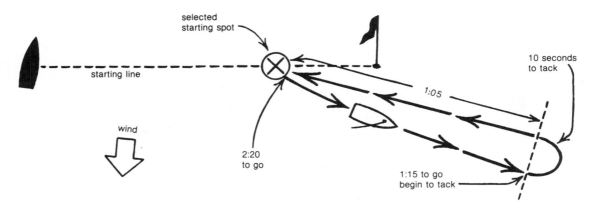

selected
starting spot

starting line

wind

2:20
to go

1:05

10 seconds
to tack

1:15 to go
begin to tack

10-7. A timed start.

haps a minute before the gun, lets his sails luff to kill speed, and then trims them in immediately prior to gunfire. This can be dangerous when right-of-way boats establish an overlap to leeward. This starting method is not recommended with large, heavy boats (Navy yawls, for instance), because they are slow to pick up speed after the sails are trimmed. Even in small boats that will accelerate rapidly, care must be taken that speed is not altogether killed, because then the boat has no rudder control. If there is open water around the boat using the sitting start, she might be sailed on a slightly weaving, up and down, course while her sheets are only slightly slacked.

The other three starting techniques should be used rarely and with great caution. When running the line, a boat arrives at the line early and to windward of the desired starting spot. Her sheets are then eased, and she reaches along parallel to the line until just before the gun fires at which time her sheets are trimmed and she is headed up onto her proper course. This method has the advantage that the boat has good headway when she hits the line as the gun is fired.

The method is dangerous, however, because boats to leeward have the right of way. Never attempt this unless there is plenty of open space to leeward; and if attempting it, always keep a constant lookout to leeward for converging boats. Also, run the line a safe distance away from the line.

The dip start can also be dangerous. In this case, you stay on the wrong side of the line and dip back across to the right side of the line just before the gun fires. This start is sometimes used when there is a strong foul current (flow of water against you) and when the other starters are late getting to the line. The dip starter must be very cautious and dip into a clear open spot, for he usually has no rights. This kind of start is certainly not recommended for beginners at a crowded start, especially in large boats.

The barging start is also dangerous. When a boat illegally barges, she attempts to force her way between the starting mark and another competitor as illustrated in figure 10-8. However, it is perfectly legal to start on the wrong side of the danger line, as boats B are doing in the diagram, provided there are no boats close

210

or overlapping you to leeward. The danger lines shown in the diagram represent the course to the first mark for a reaching start and the close-hauled course for a windward start.

In order to understand the barging start thoroughly, it is necessary to learn Racing Rule 42, which deals with rounding or passing marks or obstructions. Rule 42.1 covers various rounding situations when boats are overlapped, the Rule 42.4 is the Anti-barging Rule. In most cases, when two boats are overlapped rounding or passing a mark, the outside boat must give the inside boat room to pass the mark on the correct side. An important exception is the Anti-barging Rule which says that the windward boat *cannot* claim room from an overlapping leeward boat. The rule goes on to say, however, that the leeward boat may not sail above her course to the first mark on a reaching or running start or luff above a close-hauled course on a windward start after the starting signal has been made. Before the signal, the leeward boat may sail higher, and if she is close enough to the mark, she may squeeze out windward boats after the signal provided she doesn't sail above her course to the next mark or above close-hauled on a windward start. Of course, this prohibition against luffing applies only before reaching the starting line and after the starting signal has been made.

The following is a list of tips for getting good starts:

• Get to the starting area early (a half hour before your start or earlier if other classes are starting ahead of you).

• Study the race circular, the wind, current, and position of starting line.

• Luff head-to-wind to determine favored end of the line.

• Just before starting, sight along the line at an

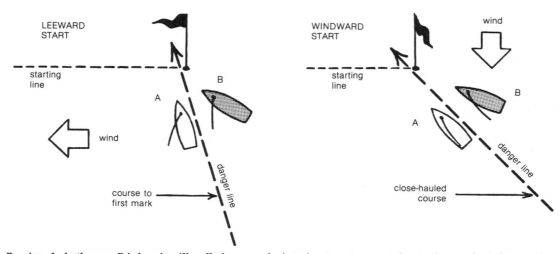

10-8. Barging. In both cases *B* is barging illegally because she is trying to get room at the starting mark. *A* does not have to give room to *B,* but *A* cannot head above her course to the first mark (or her close-hauled course when beating) after the starting signal before she had crossed the starting line.

object on shore to establish a range and thus facilitate judging your distance away from the line when boats block your view of the line's other end.

• Run the entire length of the line and time your run.

• Decide where you want to go after the start. (This should be based on such factors as wind, current, and where you think your competitors will go.)

• Try to determine the most probable area of undisturbed air. (This may be done by watching your competitors to see which end of the line they favor and by watching them make practice runs at preselected starting spots.)

• Stay close to the line especially in light airs.

• If other classes are starting ahead of you, watch their starts closely to see which boats profit and which do not in their various starting tactics, but stay clear of them.

• Use a timed start in most cases.

• The timer should start his stopwatch at the warning signal and call out the time remaining to the helmsman.

• If you are a little late for the start, properly trim your sails immediately, bear off slightly, and drive for the line.

• If it seems you will be a little too early slack sheets and/or luff up slightly to kill speed.

• Never kill speed to the extent that it affects helm control.

• Start on the starboard tack unless there is no doubt that you will be entirely clear on the port tack or can find a gap through the starboard tack boats and if there should happen to be a great advantage to starting on the port tack.

• If the windward end of the line is favored on a windward starboard tack start, plan to start not exactly at the mark but a boat length or two

to leeward of the line's windward end. In this position, there is little chance of your being forced into a barging position by boats to leeward.

• If the leeward end of the line is favored on a windward starboard tack start, plan to start not exactly at the mark but a slight distance to windward of the leeward end; otherwise, a heading wind shift might keep you from fetching the leeward mark. Also, if the committee boat is at that end, you may, at the last moment, become trapped in what is often called the "coffin corner." A boat in this predicament cannot bear off at the last moment because she may hit the committee boat; she cannot tack if there are boats close to windward because she will then be on the port tack with no rights, and Rule 41.1 says that a yacht tacking must keep clear of a yacht on a tack.

• If headed when approaching the coffin corner, do not try to pinch by the mark; but bear off, jibe around, and pass under the stern of the starboard tack boats.

The foregoing discussion of starting has been primarily concerned with the windward start, the usual start for closed courses. The next chapter will deal with distance racing involving point-to-point courses, so in this chapter there will be little more said about the tactics of reaching and running starts.

Basic course tactics. After the start, we are concerned with three general factors: boat speed, the fastest course, and the whereabouts of competitors. Of course, boat speed depends on what has already been discussed—helmsmanship, tuning, sail adjustment, and boat handling. The fastest course primarily depends on the wind and current if we discount the presence of other competitors. As the race progresses, competitors will have a definite influence on strategy, but to begin with there should be a basic preliminary plan, and this should mainly be based on wind and current. This section, therefore, will first touch on wind and current tactics and then on tactics relative to the competition.

Many sailors use the words current and tide interchangeably, but actually tide is the alternating, vertical rise and fall of water, while current is the horizontal movement of the water. Tidal currents are the currents caused by the tides. Before every race, the current should be looked up in the *Tidal Current Tables*, which give the velocity of flow and the time of *slack water,* maximum *ebb,* and maximum *flood* in the general locality of your race. Slack water means no flow, while ebb means to flow outward and flood means to flow inward. Current tables should not be relied on absolutely because certain weather conditions can throw them off. The flow of water should continually be checked visually, by looking at buoys, fish stakes, channel markers, anchored boats, crab or lobster pots, and so forth. Tall objects that are anchored, such as spar buoys, tend to lean in the direction of flow. Stationary objects in a strong current will leave a definite wake and appear as though they were moving through the water. Anchored boats in light air will often swing into the current so that their bows will point in the direction from which the current is flowing. Incidentally, if we speak of a southerly wind we mean that the wind is blowing *from* the south, but a southerly current means that the current is flowing *towards* the south.

Figure 10-9 shows how land and bottom contours affect the current. In deep water and particularly in channels, the current flows fast, but

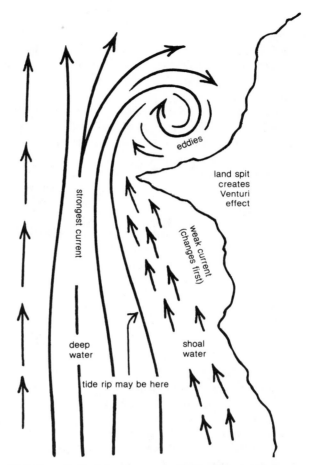

10-9. Current. To determine current's direction, watch buoys and fixed objects in water such as fish stakes. Buoys usually lean in the direction of flow. Current causes buoys and fixed objects to make rippled wakes.

the flow is slow in shallow water. The current changes first in shoal areas, however. If we have foul current (against us), then we should usually sail near the shore where the water is shallow, but if the current is fair (with us), we should probably go offshore where the water is deep. Of course, we also want to go where the current will first change to favor us. The current is often accelerated when it flows past a point, land spit, or constricted channel because of the venturi principle; and behind a point or spit there will often be eddies or contrary flows as shown in figure 10-9. Tide rips are streaks of ruffled waters that usually mark the dividing line between a fast current and a slow current moving in the same direction or two currents moving in opposite directions. Usually it is wise to stay out of the rip, but obviously you should stay to the favorable side of the rip.

When beating to windward against the current, try to take the tack that will allow a directional change of the current to push against the lee side of your bow. This is called *lee-bowing* the current and will give the boat a push to windward. Sometimes a lee-bow current can be had by tacking into the mouth of a river when the river's current meets the main current (of the bay or principal body of water) at a wide angle. This is illustrated in figure 10-10.

When sailing across a current, nearly at right angles to the current, allowance must be made for its sidewise push. If we continually aim our boat directly at the mark or destination, our course will resemble an arc, but if we steer above the mark (toward the direction from which the current is flowing), our course will be closer to a straight line. Obviously, the latter course is the shortest, and the stronger the current the higher above the mark we should steer. This course can often be determined by ranging the mark against the shore. If the mark does not appear to move against the shore, the boat should arrive precisely at the mark.

Wind is far more difficult to predict than cur-

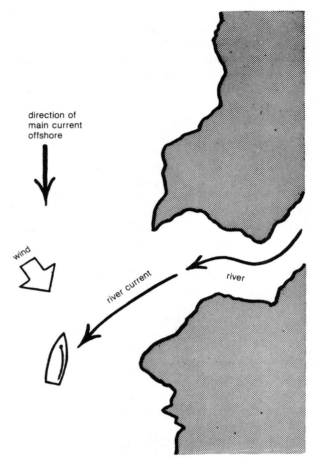

10-10. Lee bow current.

rent. It is always a good plan to get the latest weather report before a short race and to obtain frequent weather reports during a distance race. But no one knows better than a sailor that these reports are not entirely dependable. Quite often the reports are accurate, but the weather does not follow the predicted timetable. An expected breeze may arrive hours later than expected, a front as much as a day later than predicted, and so on. Also, something resembling the predicted weather may be taking place high above us, but there may be entirely different conditions at our location on the earth's surface. Forecasts of the general weather pattern are of far greater significance for the offshore, distance racer than for the closed-course, round-the-buoys racer. A two hours' difference between a predicted and an actual wind change may not be crucial during a race that lasts five days, but the same time lag will be crucial on a three-hour race. The short-distance racer is interested in the local weather only over a limited period of time—the time it takes to get around the course.

The local weather picture is very much influenced by the geography and topography of the land. The uneven heating of land and water cause the diurnal and nocturnal land-sea breezes. In the daytime, on a hot summer's day, the land heats up considerably more than the water. This causes the hot air over the land to rise and leave a partial void which sucks in the cooler air from over the water; thus, we have a sea breeze. On the other hand, after dark the land begins to cool, and the thermal activity is reversed with the warmer air over the water rising and the cooler land air being sucked towards the sea. In this case we have a land breeze. Sea breezes are most likely to be strong in the late afternoon on a clear, hot day after a cool night, while land breezes often occur late at night or in the early morning. Land and sea breezes are affected by such factors as the directional changes of the shoreline, the clearness of the weather, and the surface of the land. Flat plains, beaches, pavements, and open fields heat up faster than wooded areas. The land and sea breezes usually do not dominate the prevailing winds but only

exert an influence on them. For instance, if a south wind (the most frequent summer breeze in the Chesapeake area) has been blowing steadily and a sea breeze comes in from the east, the

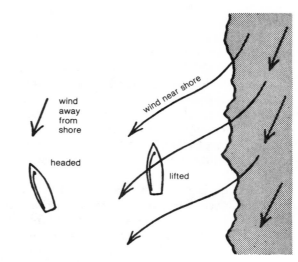

10-11. Shore slants.

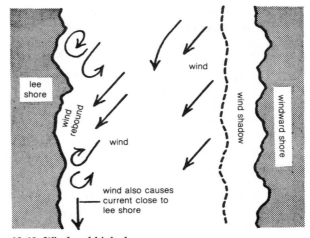

10-12. Wind and high shores.

215

two winds will most likely combine to form a southeaster.

Away from the shore, a wind blowing diagonally to the longest dimension of an elongated body of water will generally shift direction so that it blows parallel to the body's longest dimension. Near the shore, however, the wind will often slant out so that it blows more at right angles to the shore line. This is shown in figure 10-11. Notice that the wind near shore has bent in a more easterly direction. The boat away from shore experiences a header as the wind bends back to its original direction, but this may only be true on a narrow body of water such as the Chesapeake where the wind bends back to follow the long axis of the bay.

A boat beating near the shore can often get a lift from this shore slant as can be seen in the diagram. However, if the windward shore is high (with high banks or many trees) it should never be approached closely because of its wind shadow (see figure 10-12). Even high lee shores should be approached with caution because the wind can rebound, causing turbulence and even an adverse current near the shore. Needless to say, charts should be carefully examined before approaching any shore to avoid running aground. Wind shifts will often occur near the mouth of a river because of the wind bending to blow directly into or out of the river. Crossing the river diagonally, the wind tends to shift so that it follows the course of the river.

In light airs look for streaks of wind on the water. The skipper should be concentrating on his sailing continually; so it is often a good idea to assign the puff-watching job to a capable crew member. When the wind is spotty, do not worry about sailing a direct course, but get into the breeze even if at first it appears you are going quite far off course to do so. Very often when the breeze is light, zephyrs will not come to you; you must go to them.

In heavy winds look for smooth water on the windward leg. There is nothing that will slow a boat more than driving into a steep head sea. Usually the smoothest water will lie under the windward shore. Current will make a difference in the seas also. When a strong current sets against the wind, the seas become very steep.

When a threatening thunderhead is seen in the west on a hot, calm afternoon be prepared for the worst, but tack towards the cloud. Those boats closest to the squall when it hits will get the wind first. Don't take chances with an ugly looking storm, however. Be ready to drop the sails in an instant. If the storm appears to be a severe frontal type, if it is particularly dark and ragged, and particularly if it has a preceding roll cloud or if weather reports have given warnings of severe thunderstorms, reduce sail and take all precautions. But head towards the storm.

Of particular importance to the racing sailor is an understanding of wind shifts. He cannot predict exactly when the wind will shift, but he can be in the right place to take advantage of it. Constantly steady breezes are rare. Of course, some are steadier than others. Winds that blow across the land are often shifty. In the Chesapeake Bay area, the southerly is generally the steadiest breeze, while northwesters are the least steady. Nevertheless, even southerlies can fluctuate in direction to some extent.

The following are three general rules for beating in a shifty wind: (1) take the tack which brings you closest to the windward mark, (2) tack on each major header, and (3) don't sail out to the lay line (or fetch line) until close to the windward mark. The first rule is explained in

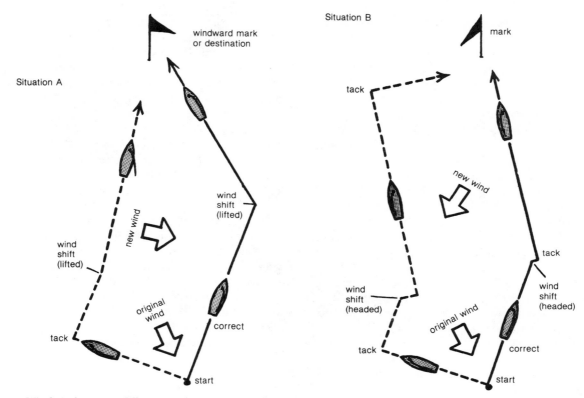

10-13. Windward strategy. Whenever a boat is severely headed by a wind shift, she should tack.

figure 10-13. It can be seen that the boat taking the close tack to the mark profits whether lifted or headed by a wind shift. If well lifted, the boat sailing the correct course can fetch the mark without tacking; and if headed severely, the boat tacks and can fetch on the opposite tack. Although the illustration shows how taking the close tack to the mark pays off when beating in shifty winds, the same principle applies when tacking downwind. Take the best sailing angle course (the downwind tack that lets the sails

draw at maximum efficiency) which brings you closest to the mark. If the wind shifts so that it is flat aft, you can jibe and head directly for the mark on an efficient sailing angle; and if the wind shifts the opposite way (so that it is closer to the beam), you can head directly for the mark on an efficient angle without jibing.

Figure 10-13 also illustrates the second rule, tacking on major headers. This is clearly shown by the boat sailing the correct course in situation B. This strategy, however, will vary somewhat with the kind of boat that is being sailed. Small, light boats that pick up speed very quickly after tacking can be tacked far more often than large, heavy boats that are complicated to tack (the Navy yawls, for instance). With a large boat, a great deal of time is often lost tacking, so tacks should be limited. The tacking-on-headers strategy still holds true for a large boat, but care should be taken to see that she is well into a major, definite shift before tacking. It is especially damaging to tack a large, heavy boat too often in very light airs.

The third tactical rule for beating in shifty winds is to stay away from the lay line until close to the mark. If you sail out to the lay line far from the windward mark, any shift is bound to hurt you. When you are heading for the mark on the lay line, a lifting shift means that you have overstood the mark, and a heading shift means that you have wasted at least part of the time you spent reaching the lay line.

Although these aforementioned tactical rules apply most of the time, all rules have exceptions. For example, it might pay not to take the close tack to the mark first if this meant you had to sail in the backwind of boats ahead of you or if there were better wind and current on the other tack. Before forming any final tactical judgment, look at the whole situation and take every influencing factor into account.

Up to this point, our discussion of basic tactics after the starting gun has been concerned with sailing the fastest course as though there were no other boats in the race. The presence of competitors, however, creates tactical situations of a different sort which we might term competition tactics.

Most competition tactics involve *covering* situations. When one boat covers another, the cover-ing boat keeps herself in a relatively advantageous tactical position with respect to the other. To cover another boat, you must be ahead or at least even with her. Actually, there are two ways of covering a competitor—with a loose cover and a tight cover. The latter method has to do with keeping close to a competitor and maneuvering into a position where you can give her disturbed air (either backwind or wind shadow). The loose form of covering means that you simply try to stay in such a position with respect to your competitor that he gets no beneficial wind or current that you won't get also. Unless you have only one important competitor to beat (as in a match race or if you are tied in a series standing), it is generally wiser to use loose covering tactics. *Because if you become preoccupied with one boat, the rest of the competition may leave you behind.* Loose covering tactics are based on a simple principle: *keep between your competitor and the next mark.* With this strategy, you will not do the competitor any particular harm unless he gets close enough to be affected by your disturbed air, but you will have reasonable assurance that you will be able to hold your lead position when boat speeds are the same.

With a tight cover on a beat to windward, you try to attain the safe leeward position or else put your competitor in your wake where he will not only get disturbed air but will be affected by your wake. These tactics are quite often used with small class boats, but they are often not practical in large handicapped boats. In handicap races, the boats are not equal in speed or ability to point. Thus, if a leading boat were trying to tight-cover a faster more close-winded boat, the latter could not be held back; and if it were the other way around, with the faster boat ahead, she would simply leave the slower boat

10-14. Rounding the mark. This photograph clearly shows the wakes of the yawls *Alert* (No. 2) and *Dandy* (No. 7) as they round a nun buoy. No. 2 is trying to blanket her rival, while No. 7 counters by luffing (the course to the next mark lies well off the port bow of both boats). If No. 7 had made a wider approach, then cut closer to the buoy's leeward side and afterwards headed as high as she could without breaking the spinnaker, she might have discouraged the blanketing tactics attempted by No. 2. Notice that No. 7 is able to keep her spinnaker full while No. 2 cannot, because No. 7's spinnaker tack has been slacked off so that it is a considerable distance from the end of the pole. This technique, however, is forbidden under both the IOR and USYRU racing rules.

behind. In races involving small, light-displacement boats, it is common practice to tack under a competitor's lee bow so that the tacking boat attains a safe leeward position and can throw disturbed and deflected backwind against her opponent's sails. But this is a dangerous maneuver with large, heavy boats, because they are slow to gain headway after tacking. The rules forbid tacking too close to another boat (Rule 41.1); furthermore, the boat that has not tacked will carry good momentum and will probably pass right by the boat that has tacked just ahead.

Occasionally two boats become engaged in a tacking duel when the boat that is being covered tries to tack away from the covering boat. In this case, the covered boat attempts to break away from the leading boat's backwind by tacking, but the lead boat counters by tacking in an attempt to blanket her rival and keep her covered. The leeward boat tacks again, and the windward boat also tacks again to cover. Such tacking duels come under the heading of becoming preoccupied with one competitor and should be avoided unless it is a match race (only two boats racing).

When a boat is being overtaken by a boat close to windward, the lead boat may luff to prevent the overtaking boat from passing (see figure 10-14). The rules define luffing as, "Altering course towards the wind until head to wind." The maneuver is explained under Rule 38, Same Tack—Luffing and Sailing above a Proper Course after Starting. This rule should be studied carefully in its entirety.

"Luffing Rights" are given in the first part of the rule, 38.1. This says that, "After she has *started* and cleared the starting line, a yacht *clear ahead* or a *leeward yacht* may *luff* as she pleases,

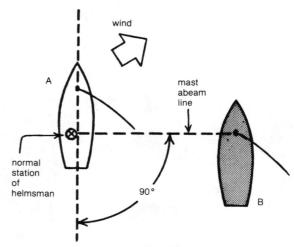

10-15. Mast abeam. *A* is passing to windward of *B*. Before reaching this mast-abeam position, *B* could have luffed. Now, or if *A* pulls farther ahead, *B* cannot luff. If *B* is the faster boat and is attempting to pass to leeward of *A, B* cannot luff even if she draws ahead of the mast-abeam line so long as this overlap exists.

subject to the *proper course* limitations of this rule." Proper course limitations are explained in rule 38.2: "A *leeward yacht* shall not sail above her *proper course* while an *overlap* exists if, when the overlap began or, at any time during its existence, the helmsman of the *windward yacht* (when sighting abeam from his normal station and sailing no higher than the *leeward yacht*) has been abreast or forward of the mainmast of the *leeward yacht*." The "mast abeam" line is illustrated in figure 10-15. When the leeward boat is ahead of the mast abeam line, she may luff, but behind this position, she cannot luff. Ordinarily, when a leeward boat luffs one to windward, the windward boat must respond by luffing also in order to avoid contact. If the leeward boat luffs when she is abaft the mast abeam line, however, the windward boat may not be able to luff without throwing her stern into the leeward boat's bow.

Competition tactics become very important at turning marks, because this is where the competitors often bunch together. When you are converging with other competitors on a windward mark to be left to port, try to approach the mark on the starboard tack. The reason for this obviously is that the starboard-tack boat has the right of way, and if she can fetch the mark, she will not have to tack again whereas a port tacker will have to tack around the mark. When the mark is to be left to starboard, however, a port-tack boat can often beat a starboard tacker around if the port tacker slows down slightly to allow her bow to be crossed by the other boat; then while the starboard tacker must partially kill her way with an additional tack, the port tacker can simply drive for the mark. This is explained in figure 10-16.

In most cases when rounding a mark with other boats, try to maneuver to be on the inside at the mark so that you have the right of way. (See fig. 10-18.) However, if you plan to squeeze into the inside position on a boat ahead of you, be very careful not to establish your overlap when the boat ahead is very close to the mark.

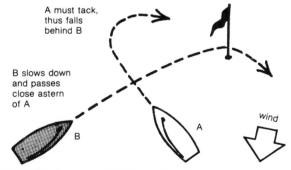

A must tack, thus falls behind B

B slows down and passes close astern of A

B

A

wind

10-16. Windward mark left to starboard.

Rule 42 deals with rounding or passing marks or obstructions, and should be studied carefully. Rule 42.3 says in part that a yacht clear astern may establish an inside overlap and be entitled to room only when the yacht clear ahead is outside two of her overall lengths of the mark.

There is a definite technique to rounding marks. A turn which is too sharp will kill your boat's way; thus, the turn should be fairly gradual. This is truer for big boats than for small ones. If you are not overlapped by other boats, do not approach the mark very closely when first beginning to make your turn, but cut close to the mark after the turn has been almost completed. This is important when turning onto a windward leg, in order that boats behind cannot sail up on your windward quarter in an attempt to go to weather of your backwind. You should try to keep boats following you directly behind you or slightly to leeward. When turning onto a leeward leg, keep to windward of your close competitors so that you can blanket them. Be very careful not to touch the mark when passing or rounding it. The penalty for this is rerounding (Rule 45, appendix C).

The following is a list of tactical and strategy tips to be used on the race course:

• Make use of the current tables.

• Observe current constantly during the race by watching buoys, stakes, marks, etc.

• Whenever possible take advantage of a lee-bow current. The lee-bow effect is advantageous relative to a competitor only if the current changes direction.

• Stay in shoal water when the current is against you; conversely, stay in deep water and channels when the current is with you.

• Try to take advantage of eddies and counter currents behind points or near river mouths.

221

• Stay where you get a favoring current for the maximum length of time, and stay where you get a foul current for the minimum length of time.

• Stay to the most favorable side of a tide rip.

• Allow for sideways push when crossing a current.

• Do not always play the current at the expense of wind strategy. Unless the current is strong, it may be better to go where there is the best wind.

• Obtain marine weather forecasts before the race, but don't depend absolutely on the forecasts, especially during a short race.

10-17. 505s at the turning mark. It appears that the lead boat has gotten on a plane quickly with the help of the crew on the trapeze to help keep the boat on her feet. Normally, it is best to make a wide approach to the mark and then cut close as you are leaving it.

- Look for the influence of a sea breeze during the afternoon of a hot, clear, summer day; look for the influence of a land breeze in the early morning.
- On calm days play the wind streaks. Go to them; don't wait for them to come to you.
- On hot, calm summer days, look westward for rising cumulus clouds that could develop into thunderheads. If a thunderstorm develops, be cautious, but in most cases work towards the storm.
- When the wind blows diagonally across a shore, look for wind slants. Also look for slants near the mouth of a river.
- Do not sail too close under a windward shore because of the shore's wind shadow.
- Make a study of local weather. Take mental or actual notes of local conditions during each race. These conditions often repeat themselves.
- In a strong breeze and rough sea, look for a smooth lee near the windward shore.
- In shifty winds when beating, take the close tack to the mark first.
- Tack on major headers.
- Do not sail out to the lay line until close to the windward mark.
- Do not tack more than is necessary, especially in a large boat.
- Constantly keep track of your competitors, particularly the best ones.
- Use loose covering instead of tight covering tactics most of the time unless in a match race, or unless you are tied in a series.
- Keep between your competitors and the next mark whenever possible.
- In most cases, do not engage in tacking duels or prolonged luffing matches, especially when running or reaching.
- Keep your wind clear.

10-18. Shields sloops at windward mark. No. 4 has an overlap and is entitled to buoy room. No. 7 has not established an overlap in sufficient time, so she has had to head up to keep clear of No. 4.

- If well clear of a competitor, consider tacking under his lee bow if you are sailing a small, light boat, but don't try this in a large, heavy boat.
- When beating, luff to prevent a boat from passing close to windward, but don't luff if you are abaft the mast abeam line.
- Approach a windward mark that is to be left to port on the starboard tack in most cases.
- Round a turning mark fairly slowly so that you do not kill your boat's speed.
- Do not sail close to the mark when first beginning to turn, but cut close to it after nearly

completing the turn if turning onto a windward leg.

• Try to round a mark in such a way that competitors behind are placed in your backwind on windward legs and competitors abeam or ahead are in your wind shadow on running or reaching legs.

• Try for the inside position at a mark.

• Learn the racing rules.

• Stay out of trouble. Try to avoid crowds of boats jammed together, and anticipate conditions or maneuvers that could lead to a collision.

• Don't be a wild, tactical gambler. Play the percentages. If you are behind, don't split with the rest of the fleet on the wild hope that you might get a break, when you are fairly certain you would be doing the wrong thing.

• If converging on the finish line with other boats, try to be on the starboard tack.

• Head for the closest end of the finish line.

11. Distance Racing

Distance racing and night sailing are, for the most part, done by seaworthy cruising-racing yachts, racing on a handicap basis, usually under the International Offshore Rule (or the Delta or PHRF rule for Luders yawls). The Luders yawls and other large boats at the Naval Academy participate in several night races on the Chesapeake Bay and quite a few ocean races. Among these are the Skipper Race, the Gibson Island to Cedar Point Race, the Naval Academy Sailing Squadron race to Oxford, the Chesapeake Lightship Race, the Gibson Island to Cape May Race, the Cape May to Newport Race, the Newport to Bermuda Race, the Annapolis to Newport Race, the Marblehead to Halifax Race, the Transatlantic Race, and the Transpacific Race. In addition to conventional racing, there is the Circumnavigation of Delmarva Training Cruise, an exercise in seamanship, navigation, and sailboat handling held every May in preparation for the Summer Sail Training Program. Details of the training cruise and the exercise drills to be done are given in appendix D.

Safety at sea. The primary consideration in any night race or ocean race should be safety. It is easier than you might think to lose a man overboard at night in a rough sea, and if accidents happen offshore, prompt help is all but impossible to get.

Lists of required yacht equipment are compiled for most ocean races. Most race sponsors now use the Offshore Rating Council lists shown in appendix F. These lists include such safety equipment as: fire extinguishers, a suitable first-aid kit with instruction book, double lifelines with through-bolted *stanchions* (vertical posts supporting the lifelines), bow and stern *pulpits* (metal railings), a *radar reflector* (folding, geometric shape made of light metal which is hoisted in the rigging), a suitable binnacle and light, running lights meeting legal requirements, flares and a *Very pistol* (flare-shooting gun), at least one large life ring equipped with water light, whistle and dye marker, a properly buoyed pole weighted so it will float upright with a highly visible flag at the top at least eight feet above the water, extra water, two compasses, one fog horn, two waterproof flashlights, two anchors, two chains or rodes, safety belts for each crew member, rafts capable of taking off the entire crew, proper covers for all openings, navigation instruments, rigging cutters, a spare tiller or suitable auxiliary steering arrangement, etc. Of course, many of these items should be aboard your boat whether or not you are going to sea. Exact equipment requirements for an ocean race must be obtained from the sponsoring yacht club. Remember, however, that equipment required is not all the equipment needed. A great deal of preliminary planning should go into preparing for a long ocean race. Plans should be made to meet all possible emergencies, and a complete set of tools and spares for almost every part of the rigging and fittings should be carried.

Some of the equipment listed above deserves brief comment. The large life rings should be placed in holders, usually on the lifelines, near the helmsman, since there is always a man stationed at the helm. Never lash a life ring to its holder. The horseshoe life buoy is generally thought to be the best type (see figure 11-1). The buoyed pole with a counterweight and flag is a very important item at sea where there are large waves, because the flag can be seen above the wave tops. The pole should be attached to a life ring, and if a man falls overboard, both pole and ring are thrown over the side instantly. The weighted pole will also tend to prevent the life ring from drifting excessively. It is always wise to attach a small *drogue* (a canvas, cone-shaped sea anchor) to a life ring even if it is attached to a pole, in order to decrease drift. Obviously, water lights attached to life rings are essential at night. Electric water lights vary in design, but the usual type is equipped with a battery-

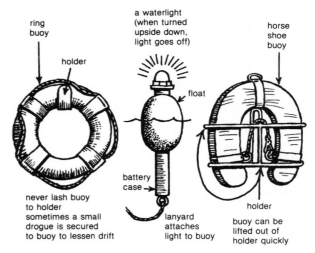

11-1. Lifesaving devices.

powered light that shuts off when it is hung upside down (near the life ring on the lifelines, or on the stern pulpit). The light is buoyed and weighted in such a way, however, that when it is thrown overboard, it rights itself and turns itself on (see figures 11-1 and 11-2).

Safety belts or harnesses are indispensable for the crew in rough weather at sea, especially at night. It is generally agreed that the best belt is one that fits on the chest and is equipped with shoulder straps. Attached to the front of the belt is a short, stout line, sometimes called a *tag line*, with a large snaphook at its end. The belted crewman snaps the hook onto a convenient part of the rigging or a fitting when he needs to work with both hands. The crew should always use safety belts when they leave the cockpit at night and when in the cockpit in a rough sea.

The radar reflector is very important at night and especially in fog. Its purpose is to warn large ships, or any radar-equipped vessel, of your presence. Obviously, the reflector is essential in or near shipping lanes.

The crew of an ocean racer should always be conscious of the watertightness of the hull. In bad weather or even in fair weather, a boat can be rolled over on her beam ends by a sudden squall. If ports, ventilators, and hatches are not closed and *secured,* the boat can quickly fill with water and perhaps sink. This has happened. Sea cocks and valves on all through-hull openings should be shut in bad weather. Hinged cockpit seat-locker lids should be latched shut, because during a severe knockdown, they can fall or float open. Portholes and hatches should be dogged down in bad weather, and vulnerable ventilators should be provided with a quick means of closing, even if they are only covered with small canvas bags.

Of course, all stores and equipment should be properly stowed so that they cannot go adrift in any kind of a knockdown. It is especially important that heavy gear, and particularly any loose ballast in the bilge, is wedged in place or secured so that it cannot possibly shift position during the most severe heeling. Care should be taken to see that gear cannot fall against pipes, electric wires, or the handles of sea cocks.

Every man in the crew of an ocean racer should know where all the vital gear is stowed. He should also be thoroughly familiar with the operation of emergency equipment such as flares, fire extinguishers, and lifesaving devices. He must know the proper and safe way to operate winches, and he must be thoroughly familiar with the rigging. A new crew member should study the halyards, sheets, leads, and cleat locations so that he can find them quickly in the dark.

11-2. Close quarters. This photo shows a close view of the yawl's stern pulpit, the ring buoys resting in their holders, and the inverted waterlight abaft the port ring buoy. Notice that the aftermost slide on the mizzen has parted its lashing.

Before sailing in an ocean race, a boat should be thoroughly surveyed and inspected. Most sponsoring yacht clubs require a superficial inspection, but most such inspections are far from complete. The hull should be checked for dry rot, seams carefully inspected to see that they are tight and well caulked, metal parts and fittings checked for fatigue or corrosion, the fastenings of fittings should be checked, the nuts on keel bolts should be tightened, the sea cocks especially should be checked to see that they operate properly, and so forth. Electrical equipment, wiring, piping, water systems, and all mechanical gear must be checked.

The spars and rigging should receive particular attention. Look for hairline cracks or signs of wear and strain in turnbuckles, tangs, or any metal parts of the rigging. Look for the shifting of tangs, for bent bolts, worn pins, or any deformation of wood or metal. See that all tracks

229

on the mast, deck, and rail are securely fastened. All tracks should be through-bolted wherever possible at major points of stress. Also, wherever possible, all cleats and other fittings should be through-bolted. Inspect the spreaders and the masthead very carefully. See that the spreaders are securely fastened and that wire halyards cannot possibly jump out of their sheaves. Double-check the spinnaker halyard blocks and swivels, because these take tremendous strain. It is always wise to have spare halyards rigged in case one parts from chafe. See that all stays and shrouds are fitted with toggles. Also see that most halyards or at least the essential ones are fitted with downhauls (light lines attached to the halyard ends so that they can be pulled down in case a halyard shackle breaks or the head pulls out of a sail and leaves the halyard end aloft).

As said before, an important inspection that relates to speed rather than safety is an examination of the boat's bottom surface; the hull should be as smooth and fair as possible. Slime and marine growth on the bottom, especially barnacles, are disastrous to boat speed. A foul bottom can make a difference of many hours on a distance race. Before racing in a major ocean race, the boat should be hauled and her bottom cleaned. Particular attention should be given to the bottom of the keel as this is an area that is often neglected. If the boat cannot be hauled, the crew should scrub her bottom with stiff brushes (or with a towel if the paint is soft). Before racing, be sure to see that the two blades of the propeller are lined up directly behind the keel, in the position of least drag. The shaft should be marked so that the propeller position for sailing can be noted by looking at the shaft from aboard the boat. Quite often this position can be noted by looking at the shaft keyways. If the propeller is out of position, it can be corrected by turning the shaft by hand. Once in position, the shaft must be locked (with the gear shift or shaft lock) to prevent inadvertent turning. Folding propellers should be aligned in such a way that the pin on which the blades hinge is exactly vertical so that the blades will not fall open when the boat heels.

Emergencies. *Man overboard*—If an ocean racer is properly inspected and equipped, and if her crew takes common-sense safety precautions, it is not likely that emergency situations will arise, but nevertheless, certain emergencies should be prepared for.

Every crew member should be given instruction on what to do if a man falls overboard, and if possible, a man overboard drill or two should be practiced before the start of an offshore race. In most cases, a boat under sail should be jibed when returning to a man who has fallen overboard. This is usually the quicker, more effective maneuver, and the reason for this is shown in figure 11-3. Of course, if the boat were running dead before the wind when the man fell overboard, there would be an option between jibing or tacking, and the latter might be easier and safer. Another exception to the jibing rule might be if a boat were running or reaching with a spinnaker, a boom vang, or a mizzen staysail set. Of course, these should quickly be removed before jibing or tacking. Another exception is in a strong breeze and rough sea, when care must be taken that the boat does not get too far to leeward of the man.

When a man falls overboard, whoever sees him first should shout, "Man overboard," at the top of his lungs to alert the rest of the crew. The man nearest to the life ring or buoyant cushion

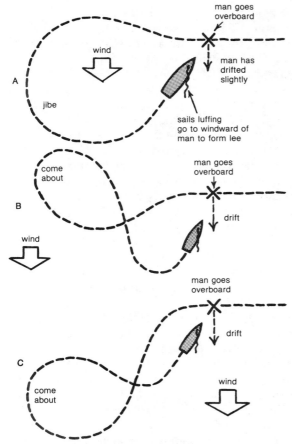

11-3. Man overboard. Shout "man overboard!" to your crew. Throw life buoy. Have a crew member keep eyes on victim. Jibe in most cases.

A. Correct maneuver under sail. Hang looped or knotted lines or ladder over leeward side to assist man getting aboard.

B. Alternate maneuver for heavy weather.

C. Alternate maneuver for heavy weather. If under power, throw gear into neutral temporarily and swing stern away from victim so that he will not be cut by prop. When picking him up, go close to windward of him, put gear in neutral, and drift down to him.

should immediately throw it over the side near the man, but must take care not to hit him. Another crew member should keep his eyes on the man (or water light at night) and point to him continuously. All hands should come on deck, and other crew members should make the boat ready for jibing or tacking, taking care especially to slack the running backstay. The helmsman should note his compass course and the time of the accident so that a return course to the victim can be figured, if this becomes necessary.

The man overboard should be approached as shown in the diagram at a slow speed with luffing sails. Notice that the man is pulled aboard on the boat's leeward side so that the boat's hull forms a lee and so that the boat will drift toward the man, rather than away from him. Lines looped and hung over the side can assist the man to reboard the boat. A crew member with a boat hook and another with a heaving line should stand by. Other crew members can stand by to back the sails to slow the boat as the man is brought aboard. When the man is too exhausted to help himself on board, he might be scooped up in a sail hung over the side, or he might be lifted with a tackle such as the boom vang rigged to the main boom (see appendix D). If he needs artificial respiration, use mouth-to-mouth resuscitation. This is now almost universally accepted as the best method.

Of course, during a race you will be under sail when the man goes overboard, but you may wish to start the engine to help maneuver. Don't forget to remove the propeller lock, and be careful not to let any lines that were trailed overboard foul the propeller. When picking up the man, you must be careful to keep the propeller away from him. Go to windward and drift down on him with the engine in neutral.

Fire—Some thought should be given to fire at sea. Of course, the Navy yawls are relatively safe in this respect with their diesel engines. Fuel for these engines does not have the explosion potential of gasoline, but nevertheless a close check should be kept to see that there are no drips or leaks in the fuel lines or tanks. Bilges ought to be clean. Do not allow grease and oil to accumulate in the bilge, as this can become a definite fire hazard.

A potential fire hazard on many boats is the galley stove. The Navy yawls are equipped with relatively safe, gimbled alcohol stoves, but certain precautions should be taken. Garments and towels should not be hung too close to open flames, woodwork and painted surfaces around the stove must be protected or insulated from flames, the stove should be kept clean and grease-free, and care must be taken when filling or priming not to spill fuel. A dry chemical fire extinguisher is hung near the stove. Minor fires can be smothered with a towel or by pouring salt on the flames. Some people advocate pouring water on flaming alcohol, but this could be dangerous when the boat is heeled, because a small amount of water may simply float the burning alcohol and the fire may flow to a new location. If water is used, be sure to use plenty of it, because alcohol fires have a tendency to smolder and reignite. If the cook has a good harness to hold him in his cooking location, there will be less chance of his spilling foods or being thrown against the stove in rough weather.

The following paragraphs on kerosene stoves and LP gas stoves were reprinted with permission from *Sea Sense* by Richard Henderson, published by International Marine Publishing Company, Camden, Maine.

Kerosene stoves, which are similar to the alcohol type we have been discussing, are also quite safe, but they require a fire extinguisher (rather than merely water) to put out a flare-up that is out of control. Regardless of the fuel, however, a fire extinguisher should always be mounted in or near the galley. The ABYC (American Boat and Yacht Council) does not recommend wick-type burners, because their performance may be adversely affected by the boat's motion. All accepted standards warn against the use of gasoline for stove fuel aboard boats. With any kind of stove, the woodwork around it, especially overhead, should be well protected with asbestos and sheet metal. Also, it is important to keep all stoves clean, because accumulations of grease from cooking can be highly flammable.

Many boats are fitted with liquified petroleum (LP) gas stoves because of their convenience in not needing to be primed. These appliances can be extremely dangerous if they are not properly installed and carefully handled. They should be given the same respect as a gasoline engine and its fuel system, because LP gas and the gasoline vapors have the same dangerous characteristics; both are heavier than air, and both are potentially explosive. In some respects, LP gas, which includes propane and butane, may be even more hazardous than gasoline, because it is easily diffused and is difficult to dispel by overhead ventilation, and, furthermore, it is relatively odorless. In fact, the ABYC and NFPA (National Fire Protection Association) recommend the odorizing of LP gas used on boats. It is therefore important that LP gas cylinders be carried on deck or in a ventilated deck box fitted with a drain at the bottom which leads overboard. Thus, any possible leakage of gas will escape well clear of the boat's interior. LP gas systems should have a pressure gauge to allow a periodic (at least biweekly) convenient means of checking for leaks. The pressure should be read with the main cut-off valve and the cylinder valve open, while the appliance valves are shut. If the pressure remains constant for ten minutes after the cylinder valve is shut, this indicates there are no leaks. Of course, a drop in pressure would indicate a leak. The application of soapy water to all connections is an effective means of locating the leak.

• Always keep the cylinder valve shut unless the appliance is actually in use. Be sure that the valve is shut in any emergency.

• See that the appliance valves are shut before the cylinder valve is turned on.

• When lighting the stove, apply the lighted match (or lighter) to the burner *before* its valve is opened.

• Watch the stove while it is being used to see that the flame does not go out. If it should go out (from a sudden draft, a pot boiling over, etc.), shut the valve immediately.

• In order to ensure that minimal gas will remain in the fuel line, shut the cylinder valve first and allow the fuel to burn out of the line before shutting the appliance valves.

• Test for leaks in the system, in the manner previously described, at least every two weeks.

• Never use a flame to look for leaks.

Obviously, precautions should be taken against smoking around flammable materials, against smoking in bunks, and so forth. A fire at sea is usually a lot more dangerous than a fire in one's home.

Rigging breaks—Another potential emergency for which the crew of an ocean racer should prepare is the breaking of vital rigging. At sea when sailing continuously for days at a time, rigging gets a lot more wear than one would ordinarily think. Metals can become fatigued from the constant motion, and lines that are rubbed can soon chafe through. Chafe is a major enemy at sea, and chafing gear must be applied to any running rigging where it touches anything. Chafing gear must be checked and adjusted continually.

If the headstay should part while beating, bear off immediately so that you are running dead before the wind. Don't lower the jib right away because its wire luff will help hold the mast forward. Set up the forestay at once, if it is not already rigged. Fasten one or two masthead halyards to the stem head, and tighten these halyards so that they pull the masthead forward. Lower the mainsail and reef it to the point where its head is no higher than the forestay's point of attachment to the mast. If a spare headstay is carried, then this may be rigged when the weather permits. Otherwise, perhaps the wire jib halyard can be rigged as a *jury* (makeshift) headstay. The upper end of the halyard might be held to the masthead with wire clamps, and in moderate or light weather a large jib could be hoisted with a spinnaker halyard. Needless to say, spares of turnbuckles of every size should be carried.

If any of the main shrouds should break on the boat's windward side, tack immediately so that the strain will be put on the opposite shrouds. This maneuver, quickly done, might save the mast. If the mast should happen to break (a very unlikely occurrence if the rigging is regularly inspected), the mast will usually fall over the side. In this case the broken spar should be hauled aboard as soon as possible because in rough seas, it can pound a hole in the hull. This is where the required rigging cutters will come in handy. At sea in heavy weather it is always a good idea to glance at the lee shrouds immediately before tacking to see that none are loose. Masts have been lost needlessly because of failure to check the lee rigging before tacking.

Should the permanent backstay break, round up into the wind at once. Simultaneously set up the running backstays and haul the mainsail in flat. Then lower the jib to take the strain off the head of the mast. If a jury backstay is rigged, don't set the spinnaker, as this can put a great strain on the backstays.

There is much less chance of breaking a stay if the rigging is thoroughly inspected. It is not enough to do this before going to sea. Inspections should also take place regularly while at sea. Once in a while, when weather permits, a man should be hauled up to the head of the mast in a bosun's chair so that he can check stays, mast sheaves, blocks, pins, tangs, splices, swages, halyards, etc. Hauling a man up the mast at sea when the boat is rolling can be a dangerous operation. Every precaution should be taken. It is important that the man going aloft is lashed into his seat in such a way that he cannot fall even if he is knocked unconscious.

A chafed rope halyard should be replaced long before it has a chance to chafe through. It is often possible to replace a halyard without going aloft by *marrying* the new halyard to the old one. (This is done by placing the ends of the two halyards together, end-to-end, and sewing them in that position.) Then the old halyard can be unrove from the deck, and the new halyard will follow the old one through the block.

Spinnaker halyards are particularly susceptible to chafe aloft, but this chafe can be reduced by taking the hauling part of the halyard to leeward of the headstay so that the halyard will not cross the headstay and chafe on it.

Helmsmanship at night. One of the keys to successful distance racing is the ability to keep a boat moving at her best at night. This is not easy. In the dark, some competent daytime helmsmen become disoriented, and sail trimming is often neglected.

On downwind courses at night, steering is done primarily by the compass. In this case, the helmsman usually tries to steer the straightest course; at least he should not let his heading wander excessively. It is not easy to steer a straight compass course with a following or quartering sea, when the boat has a tendency to yaw. The helmsman must attempt to "catch" the boat before she swings past her proper heading. The common mistake of beginners is to turn the helm too late and to overcorrect. This kind of steering takes practice and the helmsman's full attention.

Beginners often become disoriented when steering with a compass at night, because of the lack of distant visible reference points. On a clear night it is sometimes wise to pick out a star somewhere ahead that can be lined up with the mast or rigging for a check point. Sometimes a beginner becomes almost hypnotized by the compass so that it seems as though the compass card moves while the boat remains stationary. However, it must always be kept in mind that the card stands still and the *lubber line* (the mark or thin post on the compass bowl which corresponds to the boat's heading) is what really moves. (See figure 11-4.)

The binnacle light should not be too bright, because this can be blinding to the helmsman when he has to look away from the compass. Red binnacle lights are the least damaging to night vision. Those crew members in the cabin should be careful to use a minimum of light so

11-4. The wheel, binnacle, compass, anemometer, and apparent wind indicator on a Luders fiberglass yawl. The compass is clearly marked in degrees as well as points. Courses may be referred to by points, as for example, Southeast (SE), or by degrees, as 135°, which is more customary. The thin white line on the forward side of the compass bowl is the lubber's line. The knob on the starboard side of the pedestal locks the wheel when screwed in clockwise.

as not to blind the helmsman (and, of course, so that they won't disturb off-watch sleepers or use more electrical power than necessary).

When sailing to windward at night, the helmsman must depend to a lesser degree on his sense of sight and to a greater degree on some of the senses discussed in chapter 5—sound, feel, balance, and the helm touch. He must determine when the boat is moving at her best to windward by listening to the bow wave, sensing the liveliness of the boat, and feeling the balance of the helm. He senses when to bear off or head up by listening to the rattling of the sail slides, by

feeling any wind changes on his face, and by using his sense of balance in detecting any changes in the angle of heel.

Although there is less emphasis on the visual aspects of helmsmanship when sailing at night, the sense of sight should not be discounted altogether. When there is a moon, sails can often be seen fairly well. Also, the luff of a sail can be checked occasionally with a flashlight that is not overly bright. White ribbon telltales should be substituted for those of light thread. Although the compass is not used as much when beating, it should constantly be consulted both to see that you are sailing the generally proper course and to detect wind shifts. If you were headed southeast on the starboard tack, for example, you should be sailing roughly southwest on the port tack, barring any permanent wind shift. Also, of course, the navigator is usually interested in your "average" heading for his *dead reckoning* (the figuring of the boat's position by recording or estimating the distance over a known course). There is a normal tendency to pinch a boat at night, because the boat's speed is apt to seem greater than it actually is, and heavy night air can cause you to misjudge the wind strength. Of course, instruments are a great help to a helmsman at night, and these will be discussed in the next section.

When one helmsman relieves another, the new man coming on watch should have plenty of time to get oriented and to let his eyes become adjusted to the dark. The new helmsman should watch for several minutes before taking the wheel to see how the boat is being steered and to study how the compass heading averages. The helmsman to be relieved should give the new man all pertinent information, such as the course he is trying to make good, the location of other boats, the steering characteristics, what sails are set, what preventers are rigged, and any special problems that might arise.

Sails should constantly be trimmed at night just as they are in the daytime. It is easy to become complacent in this respect after dark, but boat speed will suffer far more than one might think from apathetic attention to trim. Sails can be checked by stationing a man forward to check the headsails (when weather permits), by shining a dim flashlight on the sails and luff yarns, or by the use of the spreader lights once in a while, and by noting the proper daylight trim points and lead positions. It is often a help to mark the sheets with pieces of white tape at proper positions of trim for various points of sailing.

When carrying the spinnaker at night, keep the wind well on the quarter, so there is little danger of the sail being blanketed by the mainsail. On this point of sailing in a good breeze, the sheet should be trimmed a little more than usual to guard against the sail collapsing at the luff. A man should be standing by the sheet at all times, ready to give it a quick pull in the event of collapse. Naturally, the helmsman should be ready to bear off when the sail first begins to break at the luff. The Navy yawls carry striped spinnakers and these are relatively easy to see or at least to interpret in the dark. When these sails begin to break, one can see a distortion in the contrasting striped pattern.

Instrumentation. Most modern ocean racers are fitted with mechanical or electronic instruments to help the helmsman achieve optimal sailing speed and efficiency. A typical list of instruments would include: a speedometer, apparent wind indicator, *anemometer* (wind speed indicator), inclinometer, and a depth finder. Of course, the latter might be considered primarily a navigation instrument, but it can also be helpful in attaining the best possible speed, because it shows the fastest course through shallow water when there are adverse tidal currents and through deep water when the current is favorable. Instrument dials are located in or near the cockpit where they can be viewed easily by the helmsman, and in many cases there are repeater dials below near the chart table in order that the navigator can also read the instruments.

Before proceeding further with this discussion, it should be said that instruments should not be considered a substitute for the instincts and judgment of a skilled helmsman. They should be thought of as aids only. In most cases, they should not be stared at continuously but merely checked frequently during daylight hours. There are many other things the helmsman ought to be looking at, such as the luffs of his sails, puffs on the water, waves approaching the windward bow, and nearby competitors during a race. Furthermore, overdependence on the instruments may partially atrophy a helmsman's feel of the boat and his "tiller touch," and this could not only adversely affect the boat's speed, but also take some of the fun out of sailing her. This is especially true in light airs when the instruments usually are least helpful. At night, however, a speedometer, inclinometer, and wind indicator are invaluable, and the helmsman should watch them attentively. The dials of these instruments should be illuminated with red lights, so that the helmsman will not be momentarily blinded when he looks away from them.

Speedometers come in a variety of styles. Some types register speed by measuring water pressure, either with a drag sensor such as a hinged, spring-loaded wand mounted on the boat's bottom or with a protruding, underwater pitot tube, although the latter type may be of limited value in rough seas or very light airs. Other speedometers use a free-turning rotator of the propeller (or impeller) or paddle-wheel type to indicate speed or distance traveled (figure 11-5). When distance alone or distance together with speed is recorded, the instrument is generally called a *log,* but sometimes the term log is used as a synonym for speedometer. Underwater parts of speedometers—rotators or sensors—can be linked to their indicators mechanically, hydraulically, or with a transducer that converts the physical movement of the submerged element to an electric signal which moves the indicator's pointer. It is advisable that a sensor or rotator be a removable type that can be withdrawn into the boat while she is afloat via a through-hull fitting provided with a valve or at least a watertight cap. In most salt-water areas, marine growth can rather quickly foul the underwater elements of speedometers or logs; thus, they should be cleaned frequently. Also, they should be protected from being fouled by floating seaweed with a streamlined weed deflector.

The real value of a speedometer, aside from its usefulness to the navigator in calculating distance traveled, is its ability to show differences in speed when sails are changed, sheets are retrimmed, or headings are altered. Some sailboat speedometers have indicator dials with expanded scales showing readings in tenths of a knot in order that very subtle changes in speed can be observed. It should be kept in mind, however, that speed changes result not only from the manner in which the boat is handled and sailed, but also from changes in wind veloc-

11-5. Two sailboat speedometers.

This type utilizes a rotator and transducer. The particular instrument shown is a self-powered Sims Yachtspeed. Notice that the underwater unit is designed to deflect seaweed.

The Kenyon KMX speedometer, a log measuring speed but not distance, which uses a strut or wand type underwater sensor. The control box has a switch that increases sensitivity and in effect expands the scale so that very slight changes in speed can be easily noted.

ity and sea conditions. During a race, therefore, it is important to judge speed by watching competitors as well as by looking at the speedometer.

Changes in wind speed, of course, may be observed on the anemometer dial. This is a useful instrument for determining the need for sail changes, but bear in mind that a boat's anemometer measures the velocity of the apparent wind, not the true wind. The former may be considerably stronger than the latter when beating to windward, but the contrary will be true when running before the wind.

Wind strength also can be judged by the vessel's angle of heel when beating or reaching, and small changes in heel can be noted by reading the inclinometer. This is usually a simple mechanical instrument that consists of a curved scale marked in degrees of heeling angle and a pointer, which may be in the form of a ball in a curved tube filled with liquid or a rigid plumb bob that hangs at right angles to the surface of the earth regardless of the boat's heel. Every sailboat has some angle of heel beyond which (on heeling further) she will begin to slow. With most conventional deep-keel ocean racers this angle might lie between twenty and twenty-five degrees, but, of course, it will vary with individual boats and often with different conditions of the sea or weather. Every effort should be made to determine the various optimum heeling angles, primarily by comparing the inclinometer and speedometer readings. Optimum inclinometer readings should very rarely be exceeded even if this means reducing sail.

Apparent wind indicators, sometimes called relative wind indicators, show the direction of the apparent wind. They consist of vanes, usually located above the masthead, electronically connected to dials located near the helmsman. These instruments serve the same purpose as masthead flies or wind socks, but the better electronic indicators have certain advantages. They obviate the need for helmsmen to stare aloft, and they are constructed so that wild oscillations of their wind vanes caused by pitching and rolling are damped. In addition, many indicators are provided with pairs of dials for easier reading on the beat when the detection of minute changes in the apparent wind angle is very important. Each pair of dials has a general indicator, which shows wind direction through 360 degrees (180 degrees on the left side of the dial and 180 degrees on the right) and a close-hauled indicator which amplifies the scale on the close-hauled headings, showing zero to 45 degrees on both the starboard and port tacks. The ideal close-hauled heading for a typical modern ocean racer might lie between 30 and 25 degrees in favorable conditions of wind and sea. Of course, just how high a boat will point effectively will depend on her hull design, rig, and the cut of her sails. Here again, the pointing angle should be compared with the speedometer reading while leeway is noted to determine optimal close-hauled angles. Leeway can be estimated when trying to fetch a mark and observing the mark's apparent movement against a shore or some other object in the background when the current is slack.

As said earlier, depth sounders are especially handy for boats racing in shoal waters against a foul current. The instrument performs the same function as an old-fashioned lead line, but it has the great advantage of giving more continuous readings with less physical effort expended. In simple terms, a depth sounder operates by bouncing high-frequency sound waves off the bottom of the sea and measuring the time it takes for them to reach the sea bed and return to the boat. A transmitter feeds electric signals to a transducer, usually mounted on the boat's bottom, which sends and picks up the sound waves. The return waves or echos are converted back into electric signals by the transducer, and they are amplified by a receiver and visually presented on an indicator or depth recorder. The latter system supplies a permanent record of depth on paper which is motor-moved at a constant rate under an inscribing stylus. A recorder can be of great value to a navigator in making a *chain of soundings* (finding one's position by matching a series of soundings to depths marked on a chart).

There are several types of nonpermanent indicators. Some types show depths in numbers (digits), but perhaps the most popular indicator is the one that has a flashing neon light at the end of an arm which rotates rapidly around a circular scale. The light flashes when the sound waves leave and return to the transducer, thus showing depth on the scale. With this type, however, a certain amount of interpretation of the indicator reading is required, because different types of bottoms will change the character of the flashes somewhat, and intervening subsurface flotsam or schools of fish will show a less deep and usually weaker signal than that bouncing off the sea bed. On some boats with long keels, there may be two transducers, one on each side of the boat, and in this case the leeward transducer should be used when the boat is heeled. Flashing light indicators on deck should be provided with sun shades for easy reading.

A final word on instruments is that the compass is not only indispensable to the navigator and to the helmsman for steering in poor visibility, it is also useful as a tactical instrument when beating to windward. As said in the last chapter, it often pays to tack on major heading wind shifts, but sometimes they occur so gradually that the helmsman, lacking clear landmarks, is not aware that he is being headed or of the extent of the shift. Obviously, an occasional reference to the compass can tell whether the boat is being headed or lifted and how much.

The crew. Although all racing is a team effort, in short races the skipper is the most important member of the crew. His start has a great bearing on the outcome, his quick tactical decisions largely form the strategy, and he usually has the helm for most of the race. In distance racing, however, there is less emphasis on the start and other members of the crew are more important. Most crew members must take their trick at the helm, and although strategy is the skipper's responsibility, other members of the crew are conferred with and consulted before major decisions are made. In fact, it is usually the judgment of the weather expert or the navigator that influences the skipper's decisions the most.

Signing on a qualified crew is vital to the success of a distance race. A few inexperienced crew members may be taken if there are an ample number of veterans aboard, but the novices should be thoroughly investigated for susceptibility to seasickness, and they should be given ocean racing instruction and training before the race. All new crew members, whether experienced or not, should be thoroughly familiar with every aspect of the boat. An attempt should be made to acquire a number of good helmsmen, because no one helmsman, regardless of his skill, should be allowed to steer for too long a period of time. If so, he will become

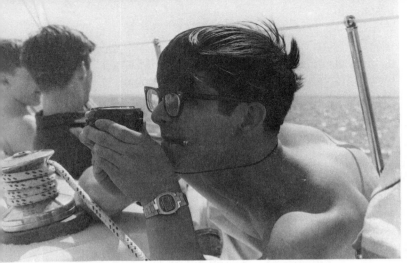

11-6. Learning the elements of navigation is an important part of boating. Here a midshipman navigator takes a bearing using a hand-bearing magnetic compass.

fatigued and lose judgment and effectiveness.

Certain members of the crew have definite specialities—for example, the navigator and the cook. Other members should be able helmsmen, sail handlers, and seamen; but even these men should have knowledge of, or should be encouraged to specialize in, one or more useful subjects. For instance, there should be a weather specialist, a medic, or one with a good knowledge of first aid, at least one member with mechanical and electrical aptitude, a carpenter, an expert on marlinspike seamanship, and so forth. Of course, the perfect crew is hard to find, but regardless of experience and skills the single most important ingredient for an ocean racing crew is probably enthusiasm.

When there are not other competitors around, it often helps to build up a sort of competition between watches to see which watch can log the greater number of miles or keep above a certain speed. Of course, such contests are not really meaningful and are contrived, to a large extent,

in the spirit of fun, but often they do help keep the crew on their toes.

On most ocean races, the deck watch is on duty four hours and off four hours. This is commonly referred to as the "two-watch" or "watch-and-watch" system. In order to avoid the rotation sequence that would bring the same watch on duty at the same times each day, one of the four-hour periods is divided into two *dog watches*. These are two-hour watches, customarily from 1600 to 1800 and from 1800 to 2000, for the specific purpose of alternating watch hours each day. Another popular watch schedule is the *Swedish system*, which divides the day into five watches: 0200-0600, 0600-1200, 1200-1800, 1800-2200, and 2200-0200.

This method gives six-hour watches during daylight, four-hour watches at night, and automatically alternates watches daily. Quite often the navigator is not required to stand watches, and in some cases the skipper does not stand regular watches. Each watch should have a capable watch officer.

Soon after the start of a long-distance race, although excitement is high, it is a good idea to settle down into a regular routine. It is important from the outset to combat fatigue. This is the ever-present enemy of the ocean racing sailor. Fatigue causes carelessness, poor judgment, and laziness which can lose races, cause accidents, and even endanger lives. An adequate crew should be carried so that the boat can be tacked and her headsails changed without rousing out the watch below. It is important that the crew get plenty of rest and sleep. If anyone has trouble sleeping, he might try using ear plugs or an eye mask or perhaps even a mild sedative. Ample food, sweets, and vitamin B1 pills provide energy.

240

Another enemy of the offshore sailor is seasickness. As said before, any person particularly prone to this malady should not be allowed on an ocean race, but most sailors, even veterans, can expect to be at least mildly afflicted at times. Many sailors are subject to stomach queasiness the first day or so at sea, and then they become accustomed to the boat's motion and feel well for the rest of the passage, unless exceptionally rough weather is encountered. It is generally agreed that greasy and acid foods as well as excessive use of alcoholic beverages should be avoided a week or ten days before the beginning of an offshore race. If you should begin to feel mildly seasick or queasy, stay as much as possible on deck in the fresh air, try nibbling on dry soda crackers or biscuits, do not use your eyes excessively for close work such as compass or chart reading, and keep warm and dry. In rough weather, smoking in the cabin, especially cigar smoking, should be forbidden. Care should be taken to see that odorless alcohol is used in the galley stove. The galley should be ventilated as much as possible commensurate with safety. There will be the least amount of motion in the aftermost bunks. Certain seasickness remedies such as Dramamine and Bonamine are a real help, but they should be taken before rough weather is encountered. Also, they are apt to make some people very drowsy.

The most valuable personal item for the offshore crew is good foul weather gear. This not only keeps him dry, but warm. It should be of medium weight and colored bright orange or yellow for best visibility. It is generally agreed that the jacket should open at the front with snaps or with zipper and velcro. This type is the easiest to put on and take off in rough weather and to doff if you should fall overboard. Boots are a great comfort in bad weather, but they should be short, light, have skidproof soles, and be designed so that they can be kicked off easily. There is a great tendency for the crew to peel off their clothes in fair weather, but overexposure to the sun should be avoided. This can not only produce bad burns, but it can be enervating. It is important for any sailor to carry a knife and wear nonskid deck shoes, but it is doubly important for the offshore sailor. Deck shoes not only help prevent skidding, but they also protect against stubbing toes.

Distance racing strategy. The strategy and tactics involved in a distance race are basically similar to those of a short race, but there are subtle differences. The start of a distance race is, of course, very important, but it is not as crucial as in a short, closed-course race around the buoys. In long ocean races there is a greater dependence on general weather forecasts. Navigation plays a greater role in the distance race, and there is less boat-for-boat racing or covering tactics. By and large, each skipper sails his own race.

Although the start is not as vital in a 600-mile race as in one 20 miles long, the start is always important. Distance races have been won and lost by minutes and even seconds. Nevertheless, it seems ridiculous to attempt a split-second start at the risk of fouling (as happened to one famous ocean racer) when there are perhaps four or five days of racing to come. The important thing is to start in clear air. More often than not, a distant point-to-point race will have a reaching start. In such a case, the smaller boats or late starters will often be subjected to the disturbed wind of the leaders. Don't follow in the wakes of those boats ahead unless they are far ahead. It is usually best to drive off or head up until you reach clear air. Quite often when there is a long starting line with competitors bunched at the windward end, it pays to try a leeward-end start with a "full head of steam." In this way, perhaps you can get a safe leeward position, and if you are overtaken by a large boat close to windward, you can usually bear off below her wind shadow. It seldom pays to split tacks on a reaching start. Even if your wind is disturbed temporarily, boats will soon disperse.

The general weather picture certainly must be carefully considered in a distance race. Weather maps should be meticulously studied before the race. Most ocean racers do not have the facilities, nor their crew the inclination, to pick up the vast number of radio weather reports (some of which are in code) necessary to draft their own complete daily weather maps during the progress of a race. However, forecasts based on the information available just before the start can predict weather over the following few days with reasonable accuracy. These predictions can be substantiated or modified by tuning in, as often as possible, to the regular forecasts on commercial stations, reports from airports, or WWV on distant ocean races.

On many long ocean races, contestants can benefit greatly from passing barometric lows (cyclones) which move in a general west-to-east direction in the middle latitudes. In the northern hemisphere, the winds rotate counter-clockwise around a low and blow inward towards its center. Lows usually follow more or less definite tracks, and by staying in the favorable quadrant of a low, of course, a boat can get the benefit of its favoring winds. Keeping a continuous record of wind direction and barometer readings can help determine where your boat is located with respect to the low. Of course, natural signs of the weather such as the color of the sky at dawn and dusk and especially the clouds should be studied.

Everyone knows that weather reports are not entirely reliable, and therefore they should not be depended upon absolutely. Don't make a drastic alteration in a normally sensible course to gamble on a probable weather change. If the risk is such that a predicted change which fails to materialize costs you only a few miles or even hours, it may pay to take the risk. But if the failure to materialize could seriously damage your chances of doing well in the race, don't take the risk. In other words, where the weather is concerned, don't climb out on a limb. Make slight alterations in the course in an attempt to take advantage of weather predictions, but don't risk everything.

Any course alterations on the *rhumb line* (the straight-line course on a Mercator chart) will not amount to any great change in the total distance to be covered if you are far from your destination, but a similar course alteration close to your destination will add considerably to the total distance remaining. Another thing to keep in mind if you are attempting to follow a rhumb-line course, is that your *present* rhumb line is a straight line from where you are, at the moment, to the finish line. Don't feel that you necessarily have to get back to the original (start to finish) rhumb line. This original course may have been the shortest one at the time of the start, but it is not the shortest later on in the race if you are not located on that line.

With some skippers, the desire to stick to the rhumb line becomes almost an obsession. Don't become overly concerned with a straight-line course especially in the early stages of the race. The important thing is to keep your boat moving even if it is not in the exact direction of the finish line. If, for example, you have a close-hauled course to the finish and you pinch up in an attempt to fetch, a competitor near you who cracks sheets and sails full and by on a non-fetching course will almost always beat you. The reason for this is that there will probably be a general wind shift later on that will either lift and allow your competitor to fetch, or else will head you both, allowing neither of you to fetch. In the latter case, this shift will put you directly astern of your competitor, because (as you will recall from the last chapter) a heading shift favors the leeward leading boat. The same principle often applies when you are reaching or running. If you are sailing a course which gives you an effective angle with the wind, especially when the spinnaker is set, don't worry about straying from the rhumb line, because the chances are that the wind will shift or change velocity later on. Use the wind you have to best advantage while you have it.

One of the keys to successful distance racing is the ability to maintain the best possible speed, not only by choosing the right course, but by paying constant attention to such factors as sail trim and helmsmanship. It is easy to let down on these matters when there are no other competitors in sight, but an attempt should be made to sail the boat just as though she were racing around the buoys. Not only sheets, but also outhauls, downhauls, and leads, should be adjusted for every wind change. It is of the utmost importance that the boat be reefed when necessary and that appropriate headsails are carried. There is a common tendency to procrastinate when it comes to sail changes; sails are usually reefed and unreefed too late, and headsails are not changed often enough. (See figure 11-7.)

When the wind moderates while you are carrying a Number 3 Genoa, it is easy to be lazy and rationalize that the wind will freshen again after a while, but in most cases the No. 1 or 2 Genoa should be set. If properly done, a headsail change does not waste much time. On a Navy yawl, or any double head rigged boat that does not have a double slotted head-foil (fig. 6-2I), the forestaysail is set as an interim sail to prevent excessive speed loss while the jib is down. Before the original jib is lowered, its two lower hanks are unsnapped and the substitute jib is hanked onto the headstay beneath the original jib. A new set of sheets are bent to the substitute jib and properly led. Then the original jib is lowered, and its hanks are unsnapped as it comes down. The halyard is quickly shifted to the substitute jib and this is immediately hoisted. In a strong breeze, it sometimes pays to stop the substitute jib with light thread, similar to the way a spinnaker is stopped. Then after the jib is hoisted, the stops can be broken by hauling back on the sheet, and the forestaysail may be lowered if so desired. On a short closed-course race, it is often not advisable to change jibs, because the time wasted is too great when compared with the time spent on a course leg; but on a distance race, the best sails for the conditions of the moment should be used, and this often means reasonably frequent sail changes.

One sail change that is important, even though it is not often required, is a change from a reefed mainsail to the storm trysail, or vice versa. On some boats, the slides on the luff of the trysail are fitted into a separate track alongside the track for the mainsail. The trysail track connects into the main track on the mast via a switch about four feet above the gooseneck. This arrangement allows the trysail to

11-7. Under reduced sail. The skippers of the four Luders yawls shown in this photo have all decided on different reduced sail combinations. From left to right these are: No. 2 Genoa, reefed main and mizzen; No. 2 Genoa and mizzen; No. 1 Genoa and trysail; and No. 3 Genoa and full main. The extreme left and right boats have the more effective rigs for beating to windward, and they seem to be sailing a bit faster than the other two boats.

be bent onto its track while the mainsail is still set, and then to be hoisted as soon as the mainsail is lowered below the switch and the main halyard has been shackled onto the head of the trysail. On three of the fiberglass yawls, the separate trysail track runs up the mast alongside the main track far enough so that the trysail can be set on its own track. Most of the wooden yawls and many private yachts have no separate track, and the mainsail must be unbent before the trysail is bent on. Recently, a number of the yawls have had gates added to their sail tracks so that the trysail can be left bent on under the

gate. When sail is reduced, the mainsail is lowered and its slides are run off the track through the gate, and then the trysail can be hoisted immediately after the halyard is transferred.

The trysail has a tack line that is shackled into the gooseneck fitting and allows the tack of the sail to ride up the mast about six feet when the sail is set.

Sheets are permanently attached to the trysail. The sail is normally sheeted like a headsail, with one sheet led on each side. The lead is through a block shackled into the base of the stanchion just forward of the forward mizzen shroud. Alternatively, the clew of the trysail may be lashed to the main boom after the mainsail has been lowered and the sail trimmed by using the mainsheet. In this case, the clew of the trysail must be lashed strongly aft, as well as down. Also, the main topping lift should be set up to take some of the weight of the boom.

The questions as to how hard to drive a boat and how long to carry on in bad weather are very difficult to answer. When these questions arise the skipper must carefully consider the trend of the weather, the behavior of his boat, the condition of the boat and her equipment, and the ability of his crew. If the weather appears to be growing worse, if the boat is becoming difficult to manage and there have been a number of gear failures and jury repairs, or if some of the crew are sick, tired, or inexperienced, then it is time to reduce sail drastically. As weather conditions get worse, sail should be reduced accordingly. At first you might shift to a smaller Genoa, then to a double head rig, with working jib and forestaysail, then take in the mizzen and reef the mainsail. A further wind increase might call for the storm trysail with the forestaysail, storm jib, and mizzen. If it blows even harder, you might reduce sail further to the double head rig and mizzen. This is the smallest rig under which the boat will perform well to windward. If even further sail reduction is necessary, you would have the choice of either trysail and forestaysail, or forestaysail and mizzen. The boat will handle well under either of these minimum rigs, but cannot be expected to drive to windward with so little sail. In prolonged exposure to heavy weather with rough seas, the trysail and forestaysail might be the preferable rig, because the sails are concentrated just forward of the center of effort, and the

trysail should help support the main mast and hold it steady, provided the sail is kept full and not allowed to flap excessively.

Under conditions that would warrant such sail reduction, the boat should be eased along and held on course as closely as possible. But if she shows any alarming tendencies to bury the lee rail, or broach to when running or reaching, or if she frequently takes solid green water on deck, she should be put on the easiest, most comfortable course, and slowed down even more.

Boat management in gale-force winds offshore. In the heaviest weather at sea, preparedness must be the first consideration. When it becomes evident that the weather is deteriorating and the vessel will face a real blow, the following precautions should be taken: don foul weather gear if it is not already being worn; put on safety belts and life jackets or flotation jackets (if safety belts will not fit around the jackets); dog all hatches and ports; stow unneeded deck gear below; lash securely all other gear remaining on deck; check stowage of all gear below; remove ventilators and replace them with screw caps (*Dorade*-type vents should be the last to be removed); insert heavy slides in the after end of the companionway; see that the bilge pumps are working properly; see that all gear which might be needed (flares, horn, flashlights, storm sails, heavy lines to be used as drags, etc.) is readily available; hoist the radar reflector; shut off all sea cocks except those on the cockpit and deck scupper drains; shut off the valve on the engine exhaust outlet; and set up backstays and forestays (provided they do not interfere with any sail that is being carried). Of course, seasickness remedies should have been taken, meals and hot drinks for thermos bottles should be prepared, and as much rest as possible should be obtained well in advance of the bad weather. Make every effort to keep clothing and blankets dry, perhaps by stowing them in plastic bags. Get ready for bad weather early; the simplest task on deck becomes extraordinarily difficult in a gale, and an undone rigging chore may lead to a serious casualty.

While sailing, as the weather gradually deteriorates, it is important that the condition of the vessel be checked frequently. See that the mast is not bending or whipping excessively, that lines or sails are not chafing, that gear is not breaking, and so forth. Periodically, check the amount of water in the bilge. If the boat appears to be taking a serious battering from the seas, she should be *hove to* (her headway nearly stopped with her bow held fairly close to the wind under counteracting sails). This might be accomplished under a storm trysail and a *spitfire* (storm jib) backed (trimmed to windward) with the helm lashed down. Finding the best means of heaving to will take a little experimentation. The boat should lie reasonably comfortably, and she should not be allowed to *forereach* (move ahead) with any speed (see figure 11-8). Do not allow the sails to flog in the wind, as they could easily become damaged.

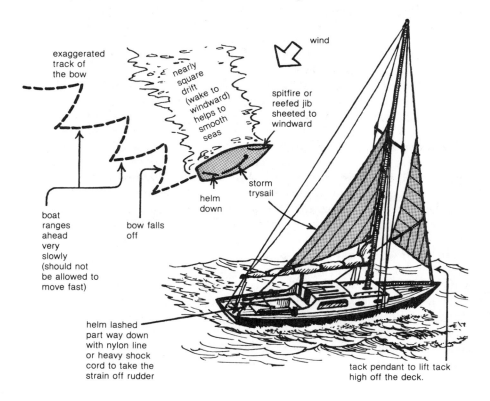

exaggerated track of the bow

nearly square drift (wake to windward) helps to smooth seas

wind

spitfire or reefed jib sheeted to windward

storm trysail

helm down

boat ranges ahead very slowly (should not be allowed to move fast)

bow falls off

helm lashed part way down with nylon line or heavy shock cord to take the strain off rudder

tack pendant to lift tack high off the deck.

11-8. Heaving to under sail.

If the wind freshens to such an extent that the boat no longer behaves well while hove to under storm sails, or if the sails are being damaged, it is advisable to lower them. Alternative storm tactics are *scudding* (running off before the wind under little or no sail) or *lying a-hull* (lying beam to the wind and seas under bare poles). In deciding which tactic to use, a major consideration will be the boat's position with respect to a lee shore. Obviously, scudding will take a boat quite rapidly towards a lee shore, so there must be ample sea room to leeward. Related considerations are that the boat should be headed away from the storm and away from shoal waters or a strong current flowing against the wind that could produce dangerously short, steep, breaking seas.

The tactic of lying a-hull is being used with increasing frequency by small sailing yachts in heavy weather offshore. It is essential that boats using this tactic are strongly built, are completely watertight, have reasonable freeboard, and have ample reserve stability. Excessive draft with a large lateral plane generally is not conducive to successful hulling, because it is important that the boat make a moderate amount of leeway in order that she can yield to the force of the seas. Also, a boat is apt to trip on a very deep keel and heel over excessively. Although a Luders yawl has a moderate lateral plane, she should make sufficient leeway at a moderate angle of heel when she is not allowed to make excessive headway. If her bow blows off so that she begins to forereach with speed, her helm should be lashed down. Some yawls will lie a-hull effectively with just the mizzen hoisted and sheeted flat, but in the heaviest winds this may require an extra strong and slightly smaller storm mizzen and perhaps a temporary mizzen

forestay. It might be possible to convert the mizzen staysail halyard into a temporary forestay if the top of the mizzen mast appears to be bending aft due to wind pressure on the sail.

In several respects, a Luders yawl should be quite well suited to the hulling tactic. For instance, she has a round bilge, a low cabin trunk, and small portholes, which afford high resistance to damage from knockdowns and seas taken on the beam. In addition, she has a tall rig which should afford sufficient windage to heel the boat moderately, minimizing the tendency to roll to weather. Excessive heeling that deeply buries the lee rail, however, could be dangerous. Also, it might not be advisable to lie a-hull in short breaking seas of the *plunging* type. These waves are the kind usually associated with shallow water that tumble or fall forward with considerable force. On the other hand, *spilling* type breakers, usually found in deep water (those waves that break gradually, only at the top of their crests, leaving trails of foam streaming behind) may be negotiated easily by a sailboat lying a-hull, especially when the seas are long with considerable distance between crests. The rolling motion of a boat while hulling can be considerable, and therefore the crew must be careful to hold tight in order to avoid being thrown off balance. It is essential to use bunk boards so that sleepers will not be rolled out of their berths. If the boat does not behave well lying a-hull, that is, if she takes repeated severe knockdowns or rolls too violently, using the scudding tactic might be advisable.

Scudding requires a helmsman to hold the bow off and keep the stern more or less square to the seas. The boat should be running under bare poles or possibly a very small storm jib sheeted flat to help hold the bow off provided the sail does not cause too much speed. Of course, some speed is necessary in order that the rudder can be effective, but a speed faster than that necessary for adequate steering control could be dangerous for the following reasons: the bow might be pushed deeply into a hollow in an irregular, confused sea, which might encourage a tendency to *broach to* (suddenly and inadvertently turn sideways to the seas) or else, in the very worst conditions, to *pitchpole* (turn end over end). The faster a boat is moving, the more dangerous a broach can be, because when the boat turns, her forward momentum is converted into a lateral force, which may cause excessive heeling. Furthermore, her forward speed lessens her ability to make leeway when she first turns sideways to the waves, and thus she will lack the same ability to yield to breaking seas that she would have if she were lying a-hull. Although broaching to at high speeds is not always dangerous in moderate winds and seas, in extreme weather conditions there is considerable risk. Another argument for scudding at low speeds is that a displacement hull such as a Luders yawl might create a fairly sizable hull resistance wave system at high speed, which could cause the stern to *squat* (sink slightly) or possibly could disturb the following seas and cause them to break over the stern. A further argument for running off slowly is that the boat spends less time on the crests of the waves, at which time she has less steering control and less stability because her ends are relatively unsupported by the water's buoyancy force forward and aft.

It is not always easy to slow a boat when she is rapidly scudding before great following seas, because she may tend to surf on the wave faces. The usual practice is to tow drags—long cables, docking lines tied together, extra sails (be sure they can be spared), fenders, buckets, and so forth. Incidentally, an automobile tire makes an excellent drag. Sea anchors such as the parachute type or the large conic type (a cone of canvas attached to an iron ring) are not often recommended for use in heavy weather by today's most experienced offshore sailors, except when it is imperative to slow a boat's drift towards a lee shore. These sea anchors can impose tremendous strains and overly tether a boat so that she cannot retreat from the force of the seas. When towing heavy lines astern, it is often helpful to the helmsman if they can be towed in bights with their ends made fast to the boat amidships near her maximum beam. Drags secured at the stern rail may hamper steering, because the pull will be far abaft the boat's vertical turning axis. Remember too, that enough speed should be maintained to create sufficient water flow against which the rudder can work effectively.

When scudding in steep following seas, there is always the possibility that the boat will be *pooped* (have the cockpit flooded by a sea breaking over the stern). Therefore, it is important that the cockpit well is small, there are ample drains, there is a bridge deck or high companionway sill, and very strong slides are inserted in the after end of the companionway hatch. The Luders yawls meet these requirements in most respects, except that it would be advisable to carry extra-strong storm slides that are completely watertight. Also, these yawls have considerable overhangs aft, and an occasional check should be made to see that the counter is not slamming excessively or flexing and leaking. Unlike the hulling tactic, scudding, of course, requires a man at the helm. It is essential that he is held securely to his post with a stout safety line (figure 11-9).

11-9. A sea coming aboard. This dramatic shot was taken by Norris Hoyt aboard the ocean racer *Figaro III* (later named *Foolscap*) during heavy weather in the mid-Atlantic. It clearly illustrates the value of a small self-draining cockpit on an offshore boat and also why it is important for the helmsman to be secured to the boat with a safety line in very heavy weather.

During the storm the navigator must do his best to keep track of the boat's position with dead reckoning or possibly with radio navigation. When scudding, the helmsman should try to keep track of his compass headings and also the speed on the speed indicator or distance on the taffrail log or other distance-recording device. When hulling, leeway will generally be about 1½ or 2 knots, and the boat will make some headway. It is important that one of the crew keep a lookout at all times, especially when near the coast or in steamer lanes.

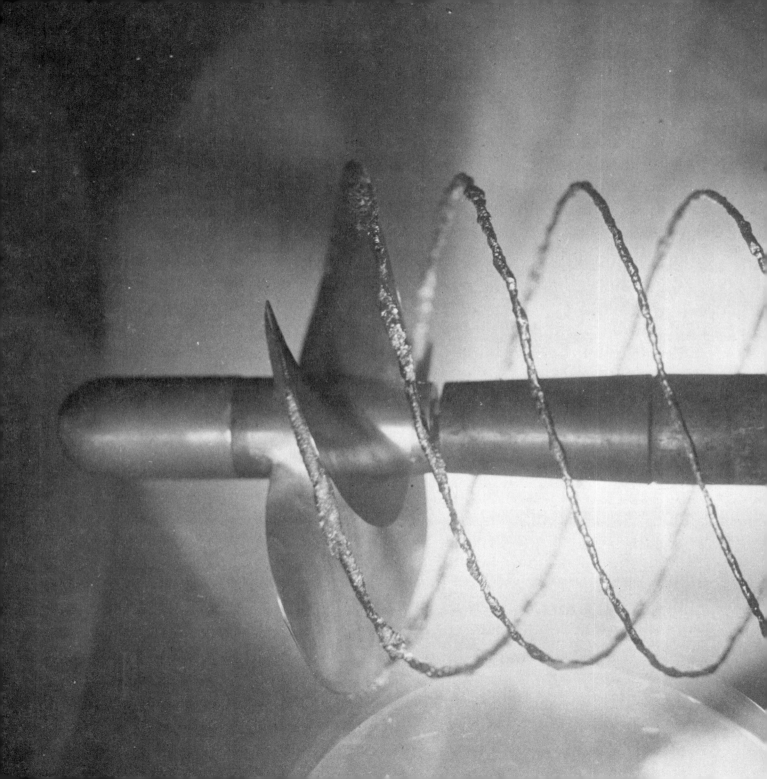

12. Boat Handling Under Power

The secret to success when handling a power-driven vessel is a thorough understanding of each of the forces affecting her travel. The Naval Academy uses several different types of power-driven vessels (see chapter 13) to teach midshipmen the principles of ship-handling. Whether the craft is a 14-foot outboard skiff, an auxiliary powered sailboat, or a 400-foot steam-powered frigate, these principles are the same. Once they are mastered, you are well on your way to becoming a competent boat or ship handler.

Uncontrollable forces. Every skipper must appreciate the significance of the effects of the wind and current. When they are understood, these forces can actually assist the skipper in completing a maneuver. Ignored, the wind and current can force even a powerful boat out of the channel and onto the shallows of a lee shore.

The shape of the boat both above and below the waterline determines the degree to which the wind and current act on the craft. A deep-keeled sailboat maneuvering under auxiliary power is pushed around quite a bit by the current. This is because there is so much underwater surface area that is exposed to this force. The effect of wind will depend on the height of freeboard and super-structures, wind velocity, and boat speed. On boats with very low freeboard the wind does not usually cause much difficulty except when the boat is traveling at very slow speeds. A modern motor cruiser with an ordinary "V" bottom and a high superstructure often reacts to the wind more than the current. (See figure 12-1 for representative hull shapes.)

While there is no fixed relationship between the wind and current, a good rule of thumb is that 1 knot of current will have about the same effect as 15 to 25 knots of wind. It is very easy to overestimate the effects of the wind and underestimate the effects of the current. It is important, therefore, to know the precise direction and strength of the wind and current. This will assist you in making the correct decision when handling the boat in restricted waters.

Often the wind and current will not be from the same direction, and in such cases it is best to

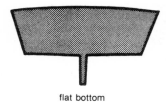

flat bottom

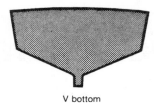

V bottom

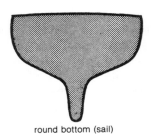

round bottom (sail)

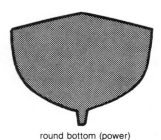

round bottom (power)

dock into the dominating force. For example, in a 10-knot breeze, you should dock into a 2-knot current, and, conversely, in a 25-knot breeze with a slight current of 1 knot or less, the docking should be made into the wind, if possible. The advantage of maneuvering into a strong current is that steerageway is maintained, while with a fair current you lose steerageway even though the boat is still making way over the bottom.

Most motor yachts, including the Naval Academy's Yard Patrol (YP) craft, are shallow draft with most of the "sail area" or *windage* (surface of the vessel exposed to the wind) well forward. When underway, but with no way on, the boats will tend to lie with the beam almost perpendicular to the wind (the bow will be blown downwind slightly more than the stern). If not understood, this can ruin a good landing at a dock. As the boat approaches the pier with her engines stopped, the force of the wind becomes more noticeable and the boat starts to present her beam to the wind. Large amounts of rudder are required to keep the boat on course. If it becomes necessary to add power to correct the boat's heading, the initial movement will be to continue downwind, not straight ahead. The reason for this is that as the boat is seeking to present its maximum sail area to the wind, the bow will "sail" downwind faster than the engines and rudder can force the boat's head up into the wind.

It is not possible to describe the maneuvers required in every combination of wind and current. Later sections in this chapter will present additional examples which will assist the beginner in understanding the effects of wind and current. There is, however, no better way to learn than to take your boat to sea and practice handling her under a wide variety of weather conditions.

Controllable forces. There are five controllable forces available to you while handling under power: (1) your engines, (2) the rudder, (3) mooring lines, (4) anchors, (5) and tugs or pusher boats. Of course a tug or pusher boat is only used for larger vessels, but you should always consider each of these forces when maneuvering any type of power-driven vessel.

Before beginning a discussion of these forces, a word should be said about safety and the proper operation of power boats. Too many serious accidents are caused by the failure of skippers to operate and maintain their engines in accordance with the manufacturer's instructions. Engines and engine compartments should be kept clean and dry. You should never allow fuel or lubricating oil to accumulate in the bilges of the boat. This is particularly important if the boat has a gasoline engine. Gasoline and air combine to form an extremely dangerous vapor that can easily explode and possibly destroy the boat. Fuel and electrical systems should be carefully inspected on a regular basis to ensure that hoses, pipes, and cables are securely fastened and that no deterioration has occurred which could lead to a fire on board. Battery stowage spaces should have adequate ventilation to allow the escape of gas which may build up during charging. Bear in mind that hydrogen gas (generated by the batteries) rises. All through-hull fittings, sea cocks, and hose clamps should be checked to make sure that there is no possibility of flooding.

There should be a set of operating instructions and a maintenance manual on board the boat for every piece of equipment. Midshipmen at the Naval Academy use two systems to ensure that boats are operated and maintained correctly. The first is called Engineering Operating Sequencing System (EOSS). This is a detailed check list system for starting and securing engineering equipment aboard large vessels. The same simplified system is effectively used, however, as a one-page check list on board smaller boats. The second system is the Planned Maintenance System (PMS). Each piece of equipment on board the boat has periodic maintenance checks. These checks range from a detailed technical inspection of the engines to the routine cleaning of air and fuel filters. Most manufacturers include instructions for the standard operation and recommended maintenance of their equipment. It is up to the conscientious boat owner to follow these recommendations so that he has a complete knowledge of all the equipment installed on board his boat.

Engines and rudder. The boat's engines are the most obvious source of power and sometimes cause the greatest difficulty to the novice as he attempts to "power" his way out of a tight spot. The expert *understands* his engines and knows how to combine them with other external forces to maneuver his craft skillfully into the tightest slip even during bad weather.

The engine drives a propeller which forces water astern when the engine is going ahead. This force not only drives the boat ahead, but it also acts on the rudder which is generally directly behind the screw. When deflected by the turned rudder, the wash from the propeller will move the stern of the boat in the direction opposite to that of the rudder (figure 12-2). It should

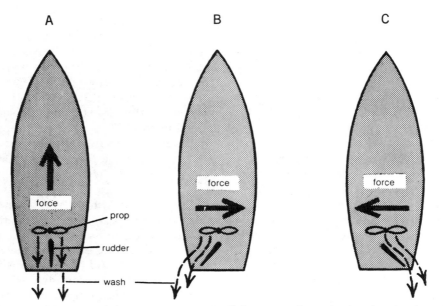

A   **B**   **C**

force

prop

rudder

wash

force

force

12-2. Effects of propeller wash on rudder of stationary boat. In all three cases the engine is going ahead. In case *B* and *C*, there is an ahead component in addition to the lateral one.

be obvious that if the engine is turning in the astern direction there is no wash directed onto the rudder. Thus, while the boat is easily maneuvered when going ahead, there is not as much control over her direction while going astern.

A second force generated by the propeller is a "side force", sometimes called *torque.* Figure 12-3 shows how this force is generated. Notice that there are two explanations, one having to do with the water being more aerated and thus less solid near the surface, and the other having to do with the fact that the projected area of the propeller pitch is greater on one side than on the other due to the shaft angle. On a single-screw boat with a "right-hand" propeller, one that turns clockwise when going ahead, the side

force will drive the boat slightly to port with the rudder amidships. When backing, the side force has a very pronounced effect on the single-screw boat. When there is no wind and as yet no sternway, the boat will back to port regardless of the position of the rudder. (Remember that there is no wash being deflected by the rudder). Until there is sufficient sternway on the boat, the rudder will remain ineffective and the side force generated by the screw will be the dominant force.

An important factor affecting the handling of a vessel is the location of her *pivot point* (the point about which she turns). When the vessel is underway, but has no way on, the pivot point is located along the axis of the center-line and some distance, usually between 25 and 40 per-

254

cent of the boat's length, abaft the bow. Figure 12-4 shows a vessel making a turn to starboard. Notice that the bow is slightly inside the path made by the pivot point while the stern is well outside this line. As the vessel gains headway the pivot point shifts forward. As the speed increases, the pivot point will shift slightly farther forward. When the boat backs down, the pivot point shifts aft.

Advance and transfer data is important in that it gives the boathandler information about the turning characteristics of his craft under various speeds and rudder angles. When the rudder is put over, say to starboard, the boat does not immediately pivot to the right and steady on the new course. The boat "advances" along the original course as shown in figure 12-5. Movement perpendicular to the original course is called transfer.

When one of the uncontrollable forces, wind, is present, the boat handles quite differently. Going ahead we have seen that the wind may force us off course but that this can be corrected with the engines and rudder. It is while backing that the wind and propeller side force can cause problems. As we have noted, on most boats "sail area" is forward of the pivot point. As the boat backs down, the wind tends to force the bow downwind while the force of the engine turning astern pulls the stern up into the wind. Figure 12-6A shows the course a single-screw vessel might make while backing into a berth with no wind. Here the side force causes her to back to port. Figure 12-6B shows the same boat making the same approach with a moderate wind coming from the starboard side. In this example the wind is partially canceling the tendency to back to port caused by the side force. Notice that in each example it is not until sternway is gathered that the skipper is able to control his boat with the rudder.

Mooring lines. Mooring lines are a valuable asset to the skipper when handled safely and properly by the crew. On a small boat a spring line rigged amidships can settle the boat neatly

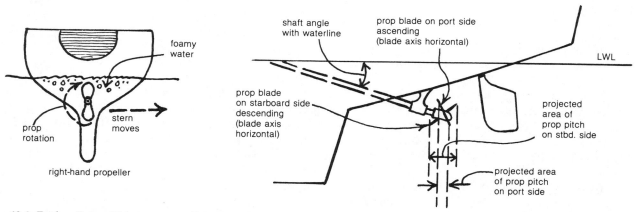

12-3. Explanations of torque or propeller side force.

255

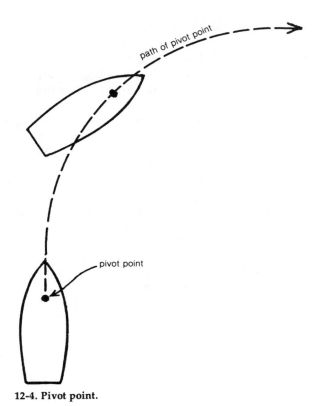

12-4. Pivot point.

Command	Meaning
"Hold the bow line"	Hold the bow line even if it risks parting the line.
"Check the stern line"	Keep a heavy strain on the stern line, but do not allow the line to part.
"Ease 2"	Ease tension on the number 2 line, but it should not be slacked.
"Slack 3"	There should be no tension on the number 3 line.
"Cast off"	Command to someone on the pier to cast off your lines.
"Take in ___"	Command to the crew to take aboard the lines cast off from the pier.
"Take a strain on ___"	Put tension on the line.

Table 12-1. Line-handling commands.

into her berth. If handled poorly, however, the bow can swing around suddenly and crash into the pier.

The advantage gained from mooring lines is that the position of the pivot point is known precisely. Figure 12-7 shows the use of mooring lines alongside a pier. In each case the pivot point of the boat is the point at which the line is belayed on deck.

Figure 12-8 shows the mooring line arrangement used on the 80-foot Naval Academy YP. Figure 12-9 illustrates the use of mooring lines

required to securely moor a much larger vessel such as a destroyer.

Safety on deck is an important consideration when handling lines on any vessel. Heavy strains are frequently placed on the lines as the boat maneuvers around the pier. When new line is obtained, the manufacturer's label should be carefully checked to ensure that the right line is being used for the job. A line that is too small for the loads placed on it may part suddenly and recoil with tremendous force.

The lines must be cared for properly if they are to last and perform safely under all conditions. They should never be allowed to chafe and become frayed. Sand, grease, rust, and chemicals can quickly ruin the most expensive mooring lines, and the lines should be inspected frequently for excessive wear or discoloration. If a line shows signs of deterioration, get rid of it; don't try to get through one more season with gear that might be unsafe.

The skipper and crew must communicate effectively if mooring lines are to be used to advantage. The command "Put that line over there!" leads to confusion and accidents even on small boats. The command "Hold the bow line!" means precisely that, even if it risks parting the line. Correct line-handling commands are simple, easily understood, and lead to smart, safe

maneuvers. Table 12-1 lists a few of the most common line-handling commands and their meanings.

Lines should be coiled, *faked down* (coiled flat, figure-eight fashion), or *flemished* (see fig. 12-10) so that they are ready for use at any time. This

12-5. Ship turning circle.

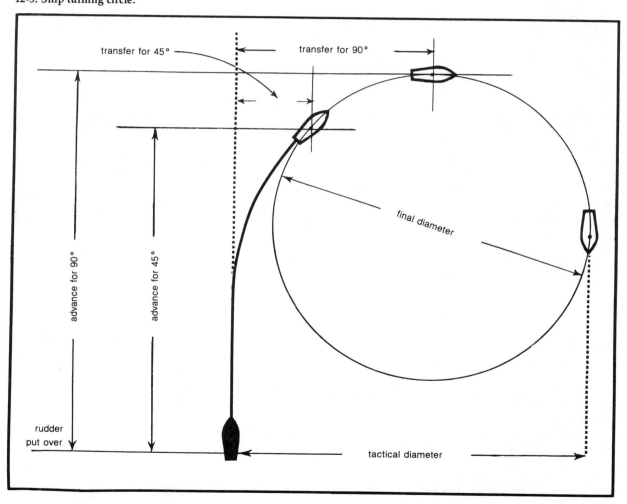

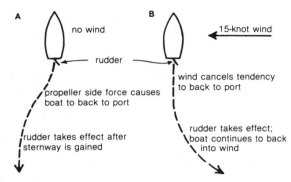

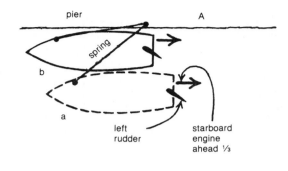

12-6. **Effects of side force when backing a single-screw vessel.**

also ensures that there are no lines that can foul the screw. The crew should also learn never to stand in a line's *bight* (slack or loop in the middle which will come taut when the line is put under strain). The line should always be tended with a turn around a cleat or bitt, and line-handlers should keep their hands one or two feet away from the cleat to provide a safety margin in case the line suddenly comes under strain and slips.

On most small boats the mooring lines are light enough to pass to the pier without the use of a *heaving line.* The heaving line is made of lightweight line and is fitted with a weight, usually a monkey's fist knot or a leather pouch filled with lead at the end of the line. However,

12-7. **Use of mooring lines when maneuvering alongside. (Arrows show screw wash.)**

A. **A bow spring can be used to bring a vessel alongside, in this case by going ahead on the starboard screw while using left rudder.**

B. **Twisting against a bow line with starboard ahead, port backing, and left rudder; once alongside, stop the twist and back starboard.**

C. **Twisting against a quarter spring is much less efficient, since the pivot point is aft near the screws.**

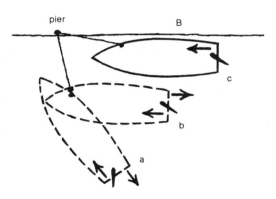

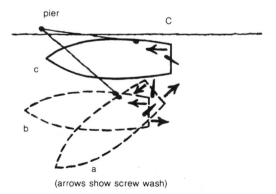

(arrows show screw wash)

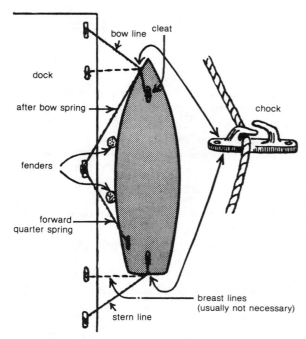

12-8. Dock lines.

use the anchor while maneuvering in the vicinity of a pier, because they claim that it is too much trouble. Actually, the opposite is true. Used correctly, the anchor provides excellent control at the bow with a minimum of effort.

As with mooring lines, the pivot point is moved to the hawse pipe or chock through which the anchor rode is led. With the bow under control, the stern can be easily maneuvered by using the engines and rudder, or by just letting the boat drift with the wind and current.

If strong wind and current are perpendicular to the pier, the experienced seaman prefers to moor on the lee side where the wind and current keep the boat away from the pier. If the approach must be made on the upwind side of the pier, an anchor will prevent the boat from crashing into the pier as it makes the landing. Figure 12-12 shows a wide approach in a single-screw boat. When abreast the desired berth, the headway is killed and the anchor let go on the weather bow. The rate of approach to the pier is controlled by a combination of paying out the anchor rode and exerting short, strong bursts of power from the engine.

If the same conditions prevail when getting underway, the anchor set to windward can again

a heaving line makes it easier to pass large mooring lines or a towing hawser from larger boats and ships. Figure 12-11 shows the proper way to prepare to use a heaving line. The line is neatly coiled and the coils evenly separated into the left and right hands. When you heave the line, both coils are released at once. The line will uncoil without forming knots or kinks. It takes a little practice, but soon you will be right on target with each throw. Don't forget to compensate for the wind when you take aim.

Anchors. The fundamentals of anchoring in open water were described in chapter 2. In this chapter we will discuss the use of an anchor in handling alongside. Many people are reluctant to

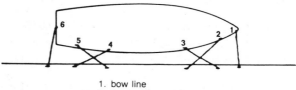

1. bow line
2. forward bow spring
3. after bow spring
4. forward quarter spring
5. after quarter spring
6. stern line

12-9. Mooring lines for large vessel.

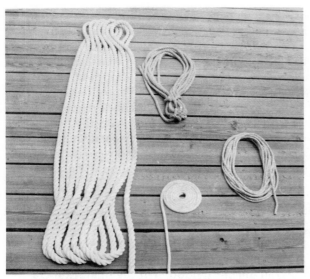

12-10. Lines faked down (left), flemished (lower middle), and coiled.

enough to keep the bow from "sailing" downwind faster than the stern. With the anchor controlling the bow, the engines and rudder are used to maneuver the stern during the landing.

Tugs and towing. The use of tug boats is generally restricted to large ships in crowded harbors or narrow channels. Occasionally, a very large yacht might use a "pusher boat" (a work boat with fenders) to assist in a difficult maneuver such as a Mediterranean moor. Most yachts of this size have twin screws, however, and as we will see later in this chapter, they can be easily handled by using their engines, rudder, lines, and anchor.

There is one maneuver in which your powerboat may do the work of a tug—that is, when towing a vessel in distress or a sailboat that is becalmed. Towing safely is not easy, and every step must be very carefully planned well in advance if you are to be successful.

When towing, there are no hard and fast rules. Analyze each situation before taking action, but never try to tow a capsized boat unless, perhaps, she has been righted. Assisting capsized boats will be discussed in more detail in the next chapter. If the vessel requiring assistance is not aground, you may approach her from either her windward or leeward side. When approaching from the windward side, you provide a lee for the disabled boat which may be helpful, but the boats will tend to be blown together while the tow line is passed. Usually the better approach is from the leeward side. Before starting your approach, be sure the tow line is made fast, properly led, and ready for passing. Make your approach at an angle across the bow of the disabled vessel, and pass the tow line to the disabled vessel as it's bow is crossed. Once the tow

assist in the maneuver. If the anchor has not been set, the only solution is to row an anchor out to weather. Once the anchor is set, the boat is warped around head to wind (or current) and powered up to retrieve the anchor before proceeding out of the harbor.

Another landing using an anchor is the Mediterranean moor. Figure 12-13 shows the steps for a single-screw boat making a stern-first landing using one anchor. Larger ships will use two anchors which are set as shown in Figure 12-14. This is a difficult maneuver, especially if there is a strong wind or current running parallel to the pier.

A final use of the anchor is to "snub" it underfoot when attempting a landing with an onsetting wind. The anchor is let go to windward so that it just touches bottom beneath the bow. In this case, the anchor does not hold; it drags just

12-11. Using the heaving line. Note the weighted monkey's fist knot at the end of the coil in the sailor's right hand.

line has been passed, pay it out slowly, allowing your boat enough slack to come up into the wind before taking a strain.

Coming head to wind is important, because it allows your boat to maintain her position while waiting for the tow line to be secured on the disabled vessel. Take great care while paying out the tow line not to let it foul your propeller.

If the tow line should foul the propeller, put the clutch in neutral immediately and try reversing the engine slowly. If this fails, the line will have to be cleared by a diver who can unwrap, or cut away, the fouled line. Another tow line will have to be passed, and it might be wise to anchor while the old tow line is being cleared.

When the tow line has been secured on the disabled vessel, take up the strain very slowly. It is at this point, when the inertia of the vessel under tow is greatest, that the danger of parting the tow line becomes critical. Increase speed slowly until both vessels have adequate steerageway. Maximum towing speed will be determined by wind and sea conditions and by the size of the vessels, but it should always be moderate. Remember that towing another vessel puts a double load on the engine and severely reduces the maneuverability of your boat.

The amount of tow line will vary with the sea condition. In calm water, several boat lengths should separate the boats, but in a rough sea, considerably more scope should be used. The more scope, the more spring and the less sudden

261

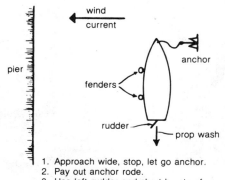

1. Approach wide, stop, let go anchor.
2. Pay out anchor rode.
3. Use left rudder and short bursts of power to keep boat parallel with pier.

12-12. Using an anchor to moor on a weather pier.

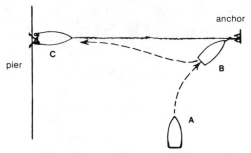

1. Approach parallel to the pier about 4 or 5 boat lengths away. When boat is opposite berth, turn rudder away from pier and back engine. After headway is checked, drop the anchor.
2. Continue backing and pay out anchor rode.
3. Steer with rudder after sternway is gained. Use engine ahead and a strain on the anchor rode to check sternway.
4. Pass two stern lines, place fenders on the stern.

12-13. Mediterranean moor.

strain on the tow line and towed boat. Although it is desirable to have the two boats in the same position relative to crests and troughs, the seas are seldom regular enough to achieve this.

Assisting a vessel that has gone aground presents many additional problems. First, you must determine how hard she is aground. Taking soundings around the boat with a lead line, or any light line rigged with a weight and marked with strips of cloth or string to indicate depth, will give the quickest indication of the depth of water around the boat. Also check the nautical chart carefully, and accurately fix your position. A thorough inspection below decks will determine if the boat has maintained its watertight integrity. If the boat has been holed, you should attempt to plug or repair any leaks before continuing action to remove the boat from a shoal. Successful repairs of this nature have been made using mattresses, life jackets, sails, boards, table tops, or wooden plugs. The idea is to slow the flow of water into the boat to the point that a bilge pump can keep up with any flooding. If she is high and dry, any efforts to dislodge her will end in parted tow lines or damaged gear. Offer to set an anchor to windward and let the tide take care of the rest. If, however, she is not too hard aground, you may render towing assistance with caution. Most often, the grounded vessel will be on a lee shore, with the wind pushing her farther onto the shoal. In this situation, your approach must be made directly downwind, and you must take great care not to run aground in the process. To prevent this, set an anchor well to windward and ease back towards the grounded vessel, using the anchor to hold the bow into the wind. Once the tow line has been passed, increase the strain gradually while still using the anchor to keep from being blown broadside to the wind. After the grounded vessel has been freed, pick up the anchor, and if the vessel can proceed under her own power, cast her off when she is ready. If not, take her in tow, remembering the precautions mentioned in the preceding section.

If the situation is reversed and you have run aground, there is an excellent chance that you

262

will be able to get off if you act quickly enough. If the boat has power, it should be used whether the boat is under sail or power at the instant of grounding. If under sail, lower the sails immediately. Try to back the boat off in the direction from which she came, as there is always good water astern. Put the engine in full reverse and move the entire crew, perhaps even the helmsman, to the bow. As most sailboats are deepest aft, this tends to lessen the draft. The wash from the reversed engine will tend to free the keel from mud or sand. The crew can help by rhythmically jumping in unison on the bow. If this procedure does not free the boat in a few minutes, do not continue it, because prolonged running of the engine in full reverse will overheat it. Whether this action gets the boat off or not, be sure to check the salt-water cooling system intake strainer for weeds and sand before proceeding. You may have to go overboard to check the through-hull fitting for the saltwater system.

If the boat has not been freed by the above method, other steps, such as kedging or heeling the boat, will have to be taken. Two points should be reemphasized. If you accept help from another boat, you must remain in charge of the situation as it affects your boat, and you should be ready to take immediate action to avoid having a would-be rescuer inadvertently damage your boat. In this regard, it is well to convey your exact intention to the boat rendering assistance before any maneuvering starts, as once engines begin to strain, communications may be difficult. Secondly, it is much better to wait for the tide to rise than to damage a boat while trying to get her off.

System of shiphandling. Midshipmen at the Naval Academy study an excellent book, *Naval Shiphandling,* by Captain R. S. Crenshaw. In this classic work on naval vessels, Captain Crenshaw provides a simple three-step system for shiphandling that is worth repeating. The beginner must understand that these steps are based on his having a very sound knowledge of his craft and how it reacts to a variety of weather conditions. Once these factors are understood, a systematic approach to each problem can begin. The three steps listed below are reprinted with permission from pages 6 and 7 of *Naval Shiphandling*.

1. Measure the situation. Measure the ranges and bearings important to the maneuver. Measure the ship's speed, the depth of water, the velocity of the wind.
2. Calculate the maneuver. Calculate the

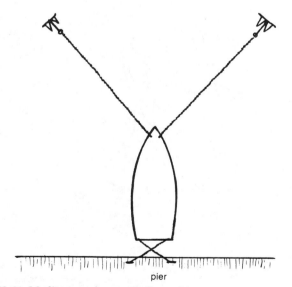

12-14. Mediterranean moor for large ship.

ranges at which to turn, the bearings at which the speed should be changed, the time to maintain a course.

3. Check and correct. As the maneuver progresses, continual revaluation of the situation is required. At each opportunity the accuracy of the maneuver should be checked and corrections made as required. There are too many variables to expect the initial solution to hold good throughout an extended maneuver.

Every experienced skipper instinctively goes through these three steps each time he maneuvers his craft. The beginner should make a conscious effort to remember the steps and learn boathandling as a precise science. Once again, shiphandling can be studied from books, but it can only be learned by practicing at sea.

Single-screw boats. In discussing the forces acting on power-driven vessels thus far, most of the examples have referred to a single-screw boat. This section will build on these examples. When the single-screw craft is thoroughly understood, the understanding of a twin-screw craft is a logical extension of this knowledge and experience.

Since the most difficult maneuvers for the shiphandler usually occur in restricted waters or around the pier, the following examples of docking situations should be studied carefully. In preparing for a docking maneuver, it is important that the entire evolution be worked out ahead of time, including an alternative plan to be used if the initial approach fails at any point in its execution. The experienced seaman always tries to keep himself from getting into a situation from which he cannot recover. He makes

elaborate preparations even for a simple maneuver. An anchor should always be ready for use in any situation where engine failure would endanger or embarrass the boat. Under some circumstances, a ready stern anchor may also be necessary. In every case, dock lines should be ready and led. Fenders should be out, but preferably not over the side until near the pier. Most important, the crew should be briefed on the skipper's plan and exactly what their individual jobs will be. Confusion at the last minute is the cause of most unseamanlike docking maneuvers. The crew, once briefed, should keep out of the skipper's way, and out of his line of vision.

As noted earlier, a single-screw boat (having a right-hand propeller) with rudder amidships tracks slightly to port when going ahead and

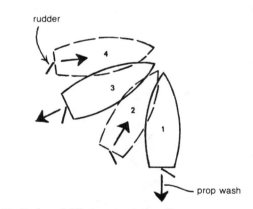

12-15. Back and fill, turn to starboard.

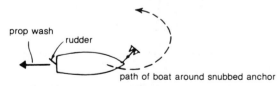

12-16. Snubbing an anchor.

264

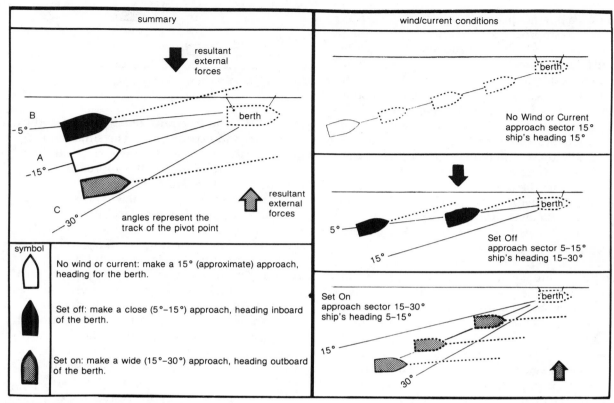

12-17. Landing approaches.

backs very noticeably to port with sternway. With this in mind, a few additional examples will provide a basic understanding of single-screw characteristics.

One of the operating parameters you should be familiar with is the turning circle of the boat. Knowing the boat's advance and transfer is enough in open water. But what if you have to turn the boat around in a very tight space, such as a harbor or narrow channel? It is not difficult, although it does take practice.

Turning to starboard is easier since the ten-

dency to back to port will assist the maneuver. Figure 12-15 shows how to "back and fill" in a tight spot. Notice that the rudder remains to the right throughout the maneuver. *Don't forget to determine the effects of wind and current.*

Turning to port is more difficult since each 10 degrees of compass heading gained while going ahead is quickly lost as the boat backs to port. Figure 12-16 shows a very easy method, using the anchor snubbed underfoot on the port bow.

When making a landing, it is easier to dock port side to the pier if possible. Figure 12-17A

265

shows a line of approach of about 15 degrees. Make the approach at the slowest speed possible. Continually think ahead and develop alternative actions so that you are prepared if you should suddenly lose power or rudder control.

Backing away from the berth while moored port side to the pier is more difficult than backing away would be if the boat were moored on the starboard side. The text accompanying figure 12-12 discussed a method of getting underway if there is a strong wind or current pinning the boat against the pier. If the wind is not very strong, the boat may be maneuvered by springing the stern away from the pier.

First, the bow line, stern line, and quarter spring are taken in; then a crewman with a fender is stationed forward to fend off the bow. The engine is put ahead slowly and the rudder put over toward the pier. The boat pivots slowly against the bow spring. Power is kept on until the bow comes in against the forward fender and the stern swings away from the pier. When the stern is well away from the pier, the engine is reversed smartly, the rudder is shifted, and the bow spring is taken in. If the wind is not too strong, the boat can be backed rapidly away from the pier. When the wind is strong, there is the danger that the bow will scrape along the pier before the boat can be backed clear. If this is the case, the rudder should not be shifted immediately, allowing the boat to back in a direction more parallel to the pier, until the bow is well clear. In this maneuver, it should be remembered that the torque effect of a right-hand screw tends to walk the stern to port. In all cases the boat should be backed smartly to avoid being blown back against the pier. Again, practice is essential.

Landing downwind can be one of the most

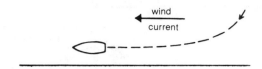

12-18. Approach for downwind landing.

challenging and frustrating maneuvers faced by beginners and experts alike. The situation is made even more difficult if the boat is running with a fair current during the approach. Needless to say, if there are no other boats alongside the pier, the problem is somewhat easier. Figure 12-18 shows a very flat approach in which you must take great care not to get the stern stuck out too far into the wind or current. You will have to maintain power throughout the maneuver since steerageway will be lost while the boat is still making some speed over the ground. Just as the berth is reached, you must undertake three actions quickly. Place the rudder hard left *and* back down hard. The left rudder will move the bow toward the pier, while the side force from the backing screw forces the stern to port. The result is that the boat slows down and moves parallel to the berth. Adjust the engine speed so that the boat's position is maintained. When the boat starts to back down, the crew must pass a line from the stern or port quarter to the pier. This keeps the stern into the pier and prevents the boat turning end for end which could occur had a bow line been passed first. This after spring line also allows the wind and current to settle the bow into the berth. Note that the engine, not the line, is used to kill headway.

If the same situation exists and the landing must be made with the boat's starboard side against the pier, again the stern line is the secret to success. You must make a very flat, slow approach. Just *before* reversing the engine, put the rudder over hard left to push the stern toward the pier. After the stern line is passed, reverse the engine to cause the boat to back to port and prevent the starboard quarter from striking the pier. If other boats are fore and aft of the desired berth during a downwind landing the approach should still be as flat as possible without risking a collision with the boats already moored. In some cases, of course, it may be possible to turn the boat around and bring her into the berth against the wind and current. Upwind landings are normally much easier.

Getting underway by backing clear or using the anchor with an onsetting wind was described earlier. Frequently the boat must get underway by going ahead. If the boat is on the leeward side of the pier, this is an easy maneuver. The spring lines are taken in followed by the bow and stern lines at the same time. Remember that the bow will blow downwind faster than the stern. It may be necessary to steer back toward the pier for a few seconds to keep the boat straight before proceeding out ahead. In any case, you should not make a sharp turn away from the pier until the stern is well clear. This could result in the stern striking pilings or boats moored at the pier.

Twin screw boats. Once you understand the forces involved in handling a single-screw boat, a twin-screw boat will seem relatively easy. The two shafts are offset some distance from the centerline and most boats have twin rudders, one directly behind each screw. The two screws rotate in opposite directions so that when going ahead the starboard screw rotates clockwise and the port screw counterclockwise. Each screw

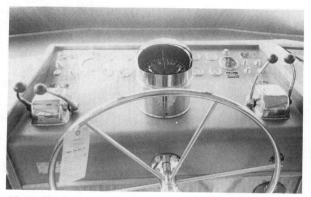

12-19. The helm and controls on a 42-foot, twin-engine, diesel-powered offshore yacht. Clutches are on the left and throttles on the right.

generates a side force, but since the directions of these forces are opposite, a twin-screw boat will track straight ahead and astern with the rudders amidships and no wind present (see figure 12-20). With the rudders amidships and only the starboard engine turning ahead, the boat will make a slow turn to port. This is a result of the side force and the offset screw. Conversely, the side force and offset propeller will cause the boat to track slowly to starboard when going ahead on the port screw with the rudder amidships.

Turning a twin-screw boat in a narrow channel or harbor is very simple. The boat is "twisted" around to starboard by placing the port engine ahead and the starboard astern. These two opposing forces act through a moment arm to the centerline of the boat, causing the boat to twist around in its own length. It is not necessary to use the rudder while twisting, although the rate of turn can be increased by placing the rudder over in the direction of the turn (see figure 12-21). Notice that only the port rudder is effective, since it is the only rudder

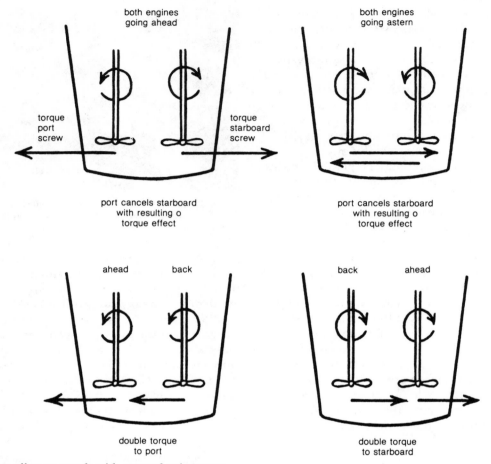

both engines
going ahead

both engines
going astern

torque
port
screw

torque
starboard
screw

port cancels starboard
with resulting o
torque effect

port cancels starboard
with resulting o
torque effect

ahead   back

back   ahead

double torque
to port

double torque
to starboard

12-20. Torque effect on vessels with opposed twin screws.

which has propeller wash being directed across it. Also, notice how torque helps accelerate the turn.

If there is wind present, the twin-screw boat will be affected in the same manner as the single-screw vessel. It will back into the wind since on most boats the "sail area" is concen-

trated forward of the pivot point. However, this is easily overcome by using the engines, the rudders, or a combination of the two. Figure 12-22 shows a twin-screw vessel backing into the wind when the skipper wants to go straight back toward point A. The course can be corrected by stopping the port engine or speeding

268

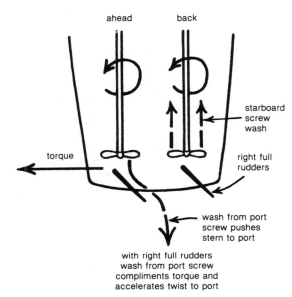

12-21. **Twisting a twin-screw boat.**

Labels in figure: ahead, back, starboard screw wash, right full rudders, torque, wash from port screw pushes stern to port, with right full rudders wash from port screw compliments torque and accelerates twist to port

Correction alternatives:
1. Stop the port engines; or
2. turn rudder left; or
3. speed up the starboard engine.

12-22. **Backing with twin screws.**

Labels in figure: prop wash from screws, actual course, wind, desired course, point A

up the starboard engine. The rudders can also be placed over full left to achieve positive course control since a twin-screw boat will respond quite well to the rudders when backing. Remember there is no dominating side force causing the boat to back to port.

Landing at the pier may be accomplished easily on the port or starboard side with the twin-screw boat. As the boat nears the berth during a port-side landing, and the headway slows, the rudder is placed right and the starboard engine is backed to kill headway and swing the boat parallel to the pier. The same procedure is followed if the landing is on the starboard side except that the rudder is turned left and the port engine is backed. The first line to be passed ashore is the after bow spring. It should not be used to stop the boat's headway. If the line is

"held" before the headway is killed, the bow will be brought too violently into contact with the pier.

Getting underway from the berth is normally accomplished by taking in the bow line, the forward quarter spring, and the stern line. The boat is then twisted about the after bow spring so that the stern is moved out into the stream. One of the crew should place a fender along the bow to prevent scraping the side during the twisting. Once the stern is clear, the bow spring is taken in and the boat backed smartly into the channel. If there is an onsetting wind it is important to get the line on deck and commence backing before the boat has a chance to settle back down on the pier.

If there is clear space astern (about four boat lengths) and the pier is solid, the boat can be backed out of the berth without a spring, using only the inboard engine. All lines are taken in and the boat lies on her fenders against the pier. The inboard engine is backed down smartly and the rudder is turned away from the pier. This forms a cushion of water for the bow. The inboard engine and outward turned rudder bring the stern away from the pier while the rapidly building sternway lets the bow ride the cushion

269

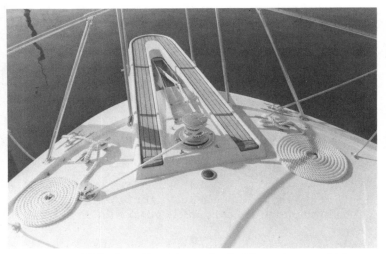

12-23. A small, retrieve-only electric capstan on a Hatteras 42-foot motor yacht. The motor controller is the rubber-covered button in the foreground. Note the neatly flemished mooring lines.

of water without striking the pier. Nevertheless, a fender should be used at the bow.

When going out ahead, the twin-screw boat can often be "walked" away from the pier by alternating twists. Care must be taken to maneuver slowly so that neither headway nor sternway is gathered. Once the boat is clear of the pier, both engines are placed ahead and the rudders control the course into the channel. An alternate method is to spring the bow out around a fender placed on the stern. With all lines taken in except the stern line, the engines are used to twist the stern into the pier while the quarter is protected by a large fender. This twisting action is not nearly as efficient as when twisting around the bow spring since the propellers are so close to the pivot point of the boat. When the bow is turned clear, the stern line is taken in, and the boat goes ahead on both engines. Do not turn

the boat away from the pier until the stern is well clear. The rudders must remain amidships or be turned slightly toward the pier to prevent the quarter from striking the pier as the boat gets underway.

Just as the sailboat skipper should practice docking under sail, the twin-screw boat skipper should practice handling his craft with two propellers and then with one propeller only. Use either the port or starboard screw under a variety of weather conditions. Also try steering using the engines alone. It takes some extra time for these practice sessions, but they are well worth it if you should suddenly lose an engine or suffer a steering casualty.

Backing into slip—single- and twin-screw boats. With the large number of boats on the water today most marinas offer slips instead of a berth alongside a dock. A slip is a space built at right angles to the pier with piles set to seaward as shown in Figure 12-24a. The slip may also have a small finger pier or catwalk built from the pier to facilitate access to the boat.

Entering a slip bow first is a simple procedure as long as you remember to maneuver slowly. There is little margin for error in most slips and having your engine fail as you approach the seawall can obviously be disastrous if the boat is moving too fast. To make the job of entering a slip easier most owners attach mooring lines permanently to the piles so that they may be picked up by hand or with a boat hook as the boat passes between the piles. Properly tended around cleats, the lines may be used to check the boat's forward progress in the event that there is a problem with the engine. If the boat is entering the slip with excessive headway, the load placed on lines, deck fittings, and the linehan-

270

12-24b. The flexibility offered by twin screws makes backing this boat into a slip a relatively easy task. The effects of wind and current may be overcome with the proper use of the engines and lines. Normally the rudder may be left amidships while the skipper uses the engines to maintain position as the boat is backed into the slip.

easier to offload passengers and gear over the stern. Backing into a slip with a single-screw boat may appear difficult at first, but with practice this becomes another routine maneuver. A thorough understanding of how your boat handles while backing in various wind and current conditions is necessary before entering a crowded marina. You should also take time to brief the crew on their duties and what you desire in the way of line handling or tending a fender.

When the wind is from dead ahead or dead astern the boat must simply be backed straight into the slip. It is when there is a strong beam wind or current that the process of backing into the slip can become a real challenge for the boat handler.

If your boat will only back straight down with the rudder over hard right, you should position it to windward of your slip before backing. This allows room to leeward as you maneuver at slow speed into position. Fenders should be rigged on both sides of the boat and your crew should be in position to handle lines without obstructing your view. As you enter the slip, the windward lines should be picked up first and the boat held up to weather until you are positioned fore and aft in the slip. The leeward lines may be passed and adjusted later.

There are some slips around which there is not enough room to position the boat to weather before backing in a strong beam wind. If this is the case you may have to back upwind at right angles to the slip. Since most boats back into the wind you should have excellent directional control. Maneuver the stern up to the windward

dler's hands may be too great to check the boat's forward progress.

If the slip does not have a finger pier, many skippers prefer to back into the slip since it is

271

pile. The leeward pile will now be amidships. Make sure that you have the crew hold a fender in between the hull and this pile to prevent damage to the sides. The boat now can be backed against a line led from the quarter to the leeward pile. This force, together with manually pulling the stern around the windward pile, will twist the boat into the slip stern first. You may now use slow bursts of astern power to bring the boat farther into the slip. Backing down will also keep the stern headed up into the wind rather than blowing down toward the slip to leeward. The crew must remember to constantly adjust the fender on the lee bow as the boat manuevers around the leeward pile into the slip. As the stern nears the seawall, the windward stern line is passed and the boat is held to windward in the slip.

Sailboats under power. The examples presented earlier apply to both motorboats and auxiliary powered sailboats such as the Naval Academy Luders yawls. There are, however, some significant differences that the skipper must be aware of when handling a sailboat under power.

To begin with, auxiliary engines are just that: a secondary source of power. The sailor should practice difficult maneuvers under power as well as under sail until he is completely comfortable with the boat under all conditions. Auxiliary sailboats have small propellers, because they have small engines and also because of the need to minimize drag when under sail. Many sailboats are equipped with *feathering* or *folding* propellers which fold into a streamlined shape when not in use. While these are excellent for reducing underwater resistance, they may not provide much power for a large sailboat.

Most auxiliary sailboats with long, deep keels will track straight with a beam wind much longer than a shallow-draft boat with a short keel. The large area of lateral plane reduces the amount of leeway or yaw when underway. Handling smaller centerboard boats which have either an outboard motor or a small inboard auxiliary can be very difficult in adverse weather conditions. The skipper should always plan ahead and allow a margin for error when there is a strong wind in the vicinity of the pier.

A final factor which is often remembered only after the skipper hears a loud and unpleasant noise, is that sailboats have standing rigging and spreaders to support this rigging. Look aloft when making an approach alongside another sailboat. You may have to adjust the boat's position forward or aft several feet in order to maintain safe clearance between the rigs.

Gasoline auxiliary engines. Although most Navy auxiliaries are diesel powered, gasoline engines are found on the majority of small- to medium-sized sailboats that are not owned by the Navy. The principal advantage of a diesel engine is that it uses a relatively safe fuel that will not readily explode. Also, diesels are generally considered more reliable due to the fact that they have no electrical ignition systems that can be affected by dampness. On the other hand, gasoline engines are considerably cheaper in initial cost, though their fuel is more expensive and is consumed faster than diesel oil. They are lighter in weight, and are less seriously affected by a major source of engine failure—water in the fuel. This is because fuel mixed with air is fed into the cylinders through a gasoline engine's carburetor, which is more forgiving of water than the injectors that introduce fuel to the cylinders of a diesel engine. Then, too, there is

12-25. A smart Alden ketch that might be described as an 80-20 motor-sailor type. This boat can perform very well under power as well as under sail. Note that everything on deck is neatly stowed. Sail handling is simplified with the roller-furling jib, self-tending staysail, and gallows frame which supports the main boom. The dinghy is conveniently carried in stern davits, but it might need stowing on deck in heavy weather at sea.

generally greater condensation in diesel tanks because some heated fuel is usually returned to the tank after it has been used for cooling purposes. As for the safety disadvantage of gasoline, engines using this fuel need not be dangerous so long as proper safety precautions are taken. These precautions will be discussed in some detail later in this section. The most commonly used gasoline engine in the typical small-to medium-sized U.S. auxiliary sailboat is the Universal Atomic Four, illustrated in figure 12-26. This is a compact, four-cylinder engine, designed specifically for marine use, that develops 30 horsepower near top speed, at about 3500 RPM. Average fuel consumption is approxi-

mately two quarts per hour at 1000 RPM, four quarts per hour at 2000 RPM, and six quarts per hour at 3000 RPM. On a light-displacement boat with a small propeller that causes little drag under sail, the engine's drive is usually direct, but on a heavy boat with a larger propeller, a reduction gear is often used with a ratio of perhaps two to one. In other words, with this ratio the engine will be turning over twice as fast as the propeller.

More often than not, these engines are cooled with sea water, but they may be had with a closed, fresh-water cooling system similar to that used with the Westerbeke diesel. The principal advantage of a closed system is that it prolongs the engine's life, especially in areas where the water is very salty or polluted with chemicals. Exhaust pipes should be water jacketed or well insulated to prevent the possibility of hot metal starting a fire. The exhaust system should have a high loop or "swan neck" in the line to stop sea water from being forced back into the manifold during heavy weather when the engine is not running. Of course, it is desirable that there be an outlet shut-off similar to that on a Luders yawl (see figure 8-24), but great care must be taken to see that the valve is open when the engine is running.

The fuel system of any gasoline engine should be very carefully installed so that no leaks can develop, as these could cause a definite explosion hazard. Some important points concerning the gas tank installation are shown in figure 12-27. Other points are that the tank should be grounded, the fuel line should lead from the top of the tank, and there should be a shut-off valve at the tank connection. Fuel lines should be well secured and protected from vibration by flexible connections at the engine. Furthermore, there

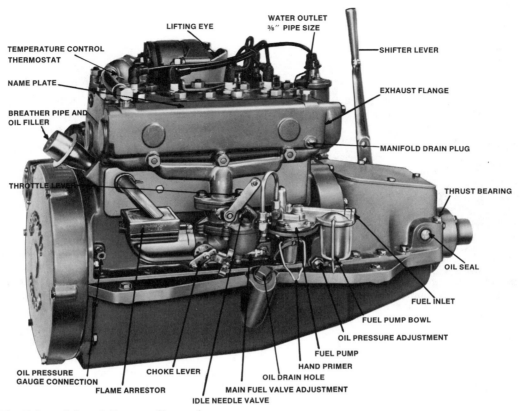

LIFTING EYE

WATER OUTLET ⅜″ PIPE SIZE

TEMPERATURE CONTROL THERMOSTAT

SHIFTER LEVER

NAME PLATE

EXHAUST FLANGE

BREATHER PIPE AND OIL FILLER

MANIFOLD DRAIN PLUG

THROTTLE LEVER

THRUST BEARING

OIL SEAL

FUEL INLET

FUEL PUMP BOWL

OIL PRESSURE ADJUSTMENT

FUEL PUMP

HAND PRIMER

OIL PRESSURE GAUGE CONNECTION

CHOKE LEVER

OIL DRAIN HOLE

FLAME ARRESTOR

MAIN FUEL VALVE ADJUSTMENT

IDLE NEEDLE VALVE

12-26 A. The Universal Atomic Four gasoline engine.

should be shut-off valves on the fuel line to allow the engine to be serviced without spilling fuel. Also, of course, there must be an adequate ventilation system meeting Coast Guard approval, and a sparkproof blower located high up in the air exhaust outlet.

Atomic Four engines, like the Westerbeke, can have Morse controls. It is preferable that cockpit controls be recessed so that they will not be fouled by lines or be bumped into accidentally, but one type of Morse control has removable handles that make recessing of the throttle un-

necessary. The throttle, which regulates the engine's speed and is often susceptible to being moved inadvertently, can be controlled very easily on the Morse model by turning its notched hub when the handle is removed.

Starting procedure for the Atomic Four or a similar gasoline auxiliary engine is as follows:

• Check the fuel in the tank to see that there is an ample supply. Turn on the fuel supply valve located at the tank and any other valve in the fuel line. These valves are usually manual lever types that can be opened by turning the handle

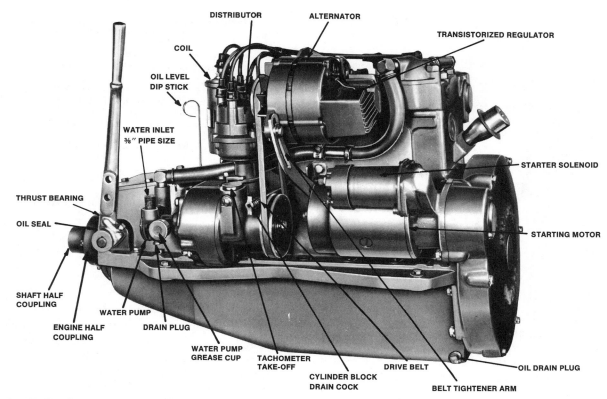

12-26 B. Opposite side view of the Universal Atomic Four gasoline engine.

Labels on figure:
DISTRIBUTOR
ALTERNATOR
TRANSISTORIZED REGULATOR
COIL
OIL LEVEL DIP STICK
WATER INLET ⅜" PIPE SIZE
STARTER SOLENOID
THRUST BEARING
OIL SEAL
STARTING MOTOR
SHAFT HALF COUPLING
ENGINE HALF COUPLING
WATER PUMP
DRAIN PLUG
WATER PUMP GREASE CUP
TACHOMETER TAKE-OFF
CYLINDER BLOCK DRAIN COCK
DRIVE BELT
BELT TIGHTENER ARM
OIL DRAIN PLUG

a quarter of a revolution. When the handle is perpendicular to the fuel line, the valve is closed, but when it is parallel to the line the valve is open.

• Open the sea-water intake valve and exhaust valve, if there is one, at the exhaust pipe outlet.

• Turn on the main electric switch. Usually this will be a three-way master switch similar to the Perko used with the Westerbeke, which has "All," "Battery one," and "Battery two" positions. Caution should be exercised in switching from one battery to the other when the engine is running because of the possibility of damaging the alternator. Don't pass through the "Off" position to change from battery one to two, and be sure the engine is idling if it is running when changing from one battery to the other.

• Before starting the engine, sniff the engine compartment for gas fumes. Turn on the blower and let it run for about five minutes. Sniff the air exhaust outlet for fumes before shutting off the blower. Be sure, incidentally, that the air exhaust hose runs from the deepest part of the bilge, because gas fumes sink to the low point.

275

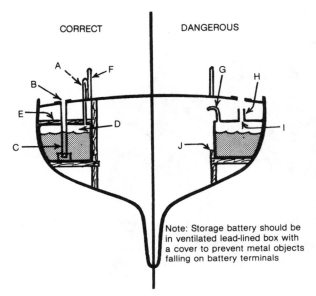

CORRECT   DANGEROUS

Note: Storage battery should be in ventilated lead-lined box with a cover to prevent metal objects falling on battery terminals

12-27. Gas tank installation.
A—Vent pipe above deck (opening bent down and facing aft).
B—Fill pipe connected to deck plate.
C—Fill pipe running to bottom of tank with well to form liquid seal.
D—Tank with baffles (avoid soldered seams). There should be a fuel line shut-off valve near tank with control outside tank's compartment.
E—Supports or straps at top as well as sides and bottom of tank.
F—Vent fastened to coaming or cabin side, but bent or looped to keep water out.
G—Vent pipe below deck. Fumes escape below.
H—Fill pipe not attached to deck plate. Gas can spill and fumes escape when fueling.
I—No fill pipe to bottom of tank. Tank can explode from ignited fill pipe.
J—Tank not adequately supported.
(Note: Storage battery should be in ventilated lead-lined box with a cover to prevent metal objects falling on battery terminals.)

If there is water in the bilge it may be high enough to block the hose's intake; thus the bilge must be pumped almost dry.

• Check to see that the shaft lock is released if the boat has one, and insert control handles if they are removable.

• After all possible fumes have been exhausted, put gearshift clutch lever into neutral (normally the vertical position), pull the choke rod all the way out (if engine is cold), place the throttle lever at one quarter open position, turn on the ignition, and start the engine. If the engine has not been run for a long time, fill the fuel pump bowl with the hand primer on the fuel pump (see figure 12-26) before starting.

• Immediately after starting the engine, push the choke in gradually until it is all the way in.

• Let the engine warm up at idling speed between 600 and 1000 RPM.

• Check the oil-pressure gauge and the exhaust outlet to see that it is emitting water. Oil pressure should show about 50 to 55 pounds for normal speeds when the engine is cold, but the pressure may go as low as 15 pounds at idling speed when the engine is hot. When the pressure is too low, check the oil level with the dip stick (see figure 12-26). If water is not coming out of the exhaust, stop the engine and check the intake valve to be sure it is turned on.

• When getting underway, shift into forward at idling speeds only. When going ahead the Morse shift lever is pushed ahead, and it is pushed aft when going into reverse.

• Should there be a lot of vibration after shifting into forward, shift back into neutral at once. Such vibration is often due to failure of a blade on a folding propeller to fully open. The usual remedy is to shift momentarily into reverse and then to shift into forward again. Allowing the vibration to continue can seriously damage the *stern tube* and *shaft log* areas (at the point where the propeller shaft penetrates the hull).

To secure the engine, simply shift into neutral, let the engine idle for a few minutes, and then turn off the ignition. The reason for letting the engine run for a short while at idling speed is to permit gradual cooling. A common mistake is to cut power suddenly when the engine is hot after it has been running at high speeds. Of course, this shuts off the cooling water, and residual heat builds up rapidly, which could be harmful to the engine, especially in locations where the water is very salty. Shut off the fuel valve, and before leaving the boat, turn off the main switch and cooling water intake.

Table 12-2 is a troubleshooting chart taken from the Universal Atomic Four engine manual. The chart covers almost every type of malfunction, and it will be most helpful to mechanics or at least mechanically minded owners with proper tools and spare parts. Unskilled boat owners should bear in mind a few simple principles when it comes to preventing engine troubles. Many problems that can be easily prevented or corrected by the owner will have to do with moisture, dirt, or corrosion—corroded battery terminals, water or dirt in the fuel, damp ignition system, and so forth. Keep the engine and all connections (mechanical and electrical) clean and tight. Keep the fuel tank almost full to discourage condensation, and see that a good marine-type filter is installed in an accessible location on the fuel line. See that no water can enter the gas tank air vent, and be sure that the fill pipe cap is leakproof. See that the engine compartment is leakproof but well ventilated. Change the oil at regular intervals, every 40 to 50 hours according to Universal's recommendation.

Most engine ailments, aside from the ones already mentioned, come from broken or worn parts. The answer to this problem is to carry spares. The Universal Motor Division (of Medalist Industries) sells an on-board spare parts kit that includes such items as distributor points and rotor, condenser, distributor cap, coil, an extra spark plug (there should be several), water pump seal and impeller with pin, fuel pump diaphragm kit, and an alternator belt. In addition, it is a good idea to carry an ignition spray (used to protect wiring against moisture), extra lube oil (SAE 30 for the Atomic Four), several lengths of insulated electrical wire, some extra hose and hose clamps, and a small "junk" box with screws, bolts, nuts, washers, etc. Also, of course, be sure to carry an engine manual.

Although it often takes a skilled mechanic to repair a malfunctioning engine, very simple remedial actions can work surprisingly often. These actions include tapping, tightening, and drying. Tapping with a hammer is done gently to the carburetor when its valves are clogged with dirt particles, and sometimes a stuck Bendix gear can be loosened by tapping the starting motor. Tightening can often provide better electrical contacts, stop fuel leaks, and improve compression (by tightening spark plugs and intake manifold connections). Drying the ignition system can be done most simply by wiping the spark plugs and their wires and the inside of the distributor with a clean, dry rag. If spark tests are performed as suggested in the troubleshooting chart, hold the high-tension (large) wires by their insulation to guard against shocks, and be especially careful that the engine compartment is clear of gasoline fumes. When draining the gas filter, carburetor, or fuel pump, be sure to close the appropriate fuel line valves, drain into a container, wipe up any spills, and thoroughly air

Table 12-2. Troubleshooting procedures for the Universal Atomic Four gasoline engine.

Trouble	Probable Cause	Correction
Starter will not crank engine	Discharged battery	Charge or replace battery.
	Corroded battery terminals	Clean terminals.
	Loose connection in starting circuit	Check and tighten all connections.
	Defective starting switch	Replace switch.
	Starter motor brushes dirty	Clean or replace brushes.
	Jammed Bendix gear	Loosen starter motor to free gear.
	Defective starter motor	Replace motor.
Starter motor turns but does not crank engine	Partially discharged battery	Charge or replace battery.
	Defective wiring or wiring of too low capacity	Check wiring for worn acid spots. See manual for proper size wire.
	Broken Bendix drive	Remove starter motor and repair drive.
Engine will not start	Empty fuel tank	Fill tank with proper fuel.
	Flooded engine	Remove spark plugs and crank engine several times. Replace plugs.
	Water in fuel system	If water is found, clean tank, fuel lines, and carburetor. Refill with proper fuel.
	Inoperative or sticking choke valve	Check valve, linkage, and choke rod or cable for proper operation.
	Improperly adjusted carburetor	Adjust carburetor.
	Clogged fuel lines or defective fuel pump	Disconnect fuel line at carburetor. If fuel does not flow freely when engine is cranked, clean fuel line and sediment bowl. If fuel still does not flow freely after cleaning, repair or replace pump.
Engine will not start (Poor compression and other causes)	Air leak around intake manifold	Check for leak by squirting oil around intake connections. If leak is found, tighten manifold and if necessary replace gaskets.
	Loose spark plugs	Check all plugs for proper seating, gasket, and tightness. Replace all damaged plugs and gaskets.
	Loosely seating valves	Check for broken or weak valve springs, warped stems, carbon and gum deposits, and insufficient tappet clearance.
	Damaged cylinder head gasket	Check for leaks around gasket when engine is cranked. If a leak is found, replace gasket.
	Worn or broken piston rings	Replace broken and worn rings. Check cylinders for ''out of round'' and ''taper.''
Excessive engine temperature	No water circulation	Check for clogged water lines and restricted inlets and outlets. Check for broken or stuck thermostat. Look for worn or damaged water pump or water pump drive.
Engine temperature too low	Broken or stuck the thermostat	Replace thermostat.

Table 12-2 continued.

Trouble	Probable Cause	Correction
Engine will not start (ignition system)	Ignition switch "off" or defective	Turn on switch or replace.
	Fouled or broken spark plugs	Remove plugs and inspect for cracked porcelain, dirty points, or improper gap.
	Improperly set, worn, or pitted distributor points. Defective ignition coil.	Remove center wire from distributor cap and hold within 3/8 inch of motor block. Crank engine. Clean, sharp spark should jump between wire and block when points open. Clean and adjust points. If spark is weak or yellow after adjustment of points, replace condenser. If spark still is weak or not present, replace ignition coil
	Wet, cracked, or broken distributor	Wipe inside surface of distributor dry with clean cloth. Inspect for cracked or broken parts. Replace parts where necessary.

Trouble	Probable Cause	Correction
Engine will not start (ignition system — Cont.)	Improperly set, worn, or pitted magneto breaker points (magneto models only)	Remove spark plug wire and hold within 3/8 inch of engine block. Clean, sharp spark should jump between wire and block when engine is cranked. If spark is weak or not present clean and adjust breaker points.
		Remove spark plug wire and hold within 1/8 inch of engine block. A clean spark should jump between wire and block when engine is cranked. Clean and set timer points. If spark still is not present when engine is cranked, replace coil.
	Improper timing	Set timing.
No oil pressure	Defective gauge or tube	Replace gauge or tube.
	No oil in engine	Refill with proper grade oil.
	Dirt in pressure relief valve	Clean valve.
	Defective oil pump, leak in oil lines or broken oil pump drive	Check oil pump and oil pump drive for worn or broken parts. Tighten all oil line connections.
Loss of RPM (Boat or associated equipment)	Damaged propeller	Repair propeller.
	Bent rudder	Repair.
	Misalignment	Realign engine to shaft.
	Too tight stuffing box packing gland	Adjust.
	Dirty boat bottom	
Vibration	Misfiring or pre-ignition	See correction under misfiring and pre-ignition.
	Loose foundation or foundation bolts	
	Propeller shaft out of line or bent	
	Propeller bent or pitch out of true	

279

Trouble	Probable Cause	Correction
Pre-ignition	Defective spark plugs	Check all spark plugs for broken porcelain, burned electrodes or electrodes out of adjustment. Replace all defective plugs or clean and reset.
	Improper timing	See engine manual.
	Engine carbon	Remove cylinder head and clean out carbon.
	Engine overheating	See correction under "Engine Temp" portion of this table.
Back-firing	Insufficient fuel reaching engine due to dirty lines, strainer, or blocked fuel tank vent. Water in fuel	See correction under "Engine will not start" portion of this table.
	Poorly adjusted distributor	See correction under "Engine will not start" portion of this table.
Low oil pressure	Too light body oil	Replace with proper weight oil.
	Oil leak in pressure line	Inspect all oil lines. Tighten all connections.
	Weak or broken pressure relief valve spring	Replace spring.
	Worn oil pump	Replace pump.
	Worn or loose bearings	Replace bearings.
Oil pressure too high	Too heavy body oil	Drain oil and replace with oil of proper weight.
	Stuck pressure relief valve	Clean or replace valve.
	Dirt or obstruction in lines	Drain and clean oil system. Check for bent or flattened oil lines and replace where necessary.
Sludge in oil	Infrequent oil changes	Drain and refill with proper weight oil.
	Water in oil	Drain and refill. If trouble persists check for cracked block, defective head gasket, and cracked head.
	Dirty oil filter	Replace filter.

Table 12-2 continued.

out the compartment and bilge before the engine is started or any electrical repairs are attempted.

Fire is an ever-present danger on any boat with an engine, whether gasoline or diesel powered. At sea, fire is a most dangerous emergency. Bilges should be kept clean. Never allow gasoline, diesel oil, or lubricating oil to accumulate. The engine room should be ventilated properly in accordance with the latest Coast Guard regulations. When the engine is running for long periods, inspect it frequently for fuel and lubricating oil leaks. To guard against broken fuel lines caused by engine vibration, flexible hose should be used between the engine and any unflexible connection. If a fire occurs, stop the engine and head off the wind to minimize relative wind velocity.

With a gasoline auxiliary, the times for *extra* caution are when fueling and when starting, especially starting after fueling or after a prolonged absence from the boat. (Figure 12-27 indicates proper and improper fuel tank installations.) Before fueling, shut off all power, turn off the stove, and stop smoking. Try to fuel up with the boat heading so that the tanks are to leeward of the companionway. Then the gasoline fumes will be blown away from the boat, *not* down below. Remember that gasoline fumes are heavier than air and will displace the air in the cabin and engine room. When fueling, keep the nozzle of the gasoline hose in contact with the fill pipe to prevent a possible static electric spark. A static electric spark can also be caused by running water, so do not fill water tanks at the same time or immediately after filling fuel tanks. Do not spill fuel, and be very careful not to overflow the tank. After fueling, air the boat and run the engine room blower for at least five minutes before starting the engine. The higher the humidity and the lighter the breeze, the greater the danger from accumulated gasoline fumes. Open the engine compartment and smell for fumes *in the bilge* before starting. Also sniff the blower vent.

When securing gasoline engines prior to leaving the boat, shut off the fuel at the tank. This ensures against significant leakage from the carburetor into the bilge while the boat is at the mooring.

When starting a gasoline engine after a long shut-down period, it is especially important to open the engine room hatch and smell for gasoline fumes in the bilge before energizing any of the systems. Most important of all, incorporate these precautions into a routine that is *never* varied. Overconfidence and haste are the most usual causes of boat explosions and fires.

Outboard and inboard/outboard drive boats.
The previous sections have discussed the handling characteristics of boats with inboard engines, rudders, and, for the most part, displacement hulls. In this section we will describe the characteristics of the most popular type of small boat found on the water today: the outboard drive. These boats generally are 12 to 24 feet in length and have aluminum or fiberglass hulls. Supplied with modern engines, these sturdy hulls provide simple, inexpensive boating pleasure. Power for these small boats is provided by either a gasoline outboard engine or an *inboard/ outboard* (I/O) drive. The outboard engine is mounted on the boat's transom as shown in figure 12-28. The I/O drive has the engine mounted inboard with the drive, or lower, unit located outside the hull at the stern (figure 12-29).

Before beginning a discussion of the handling of these boats, it is worth repeating that it is very important for the boat owner to understand fully the operation of the craft. United States Coast Guard statistics indicate that the largest percentage of boating accidents resulting in serious injury or death occur during operation of outboard or inboard/outboard boats. The hazards associated with gasoline engines are only partly to blame. One of the most frequent accidents is capsizing or swamping the boat as a result of overloading. Also, accidents frequently result from operating in weather conditions which are beyond the capability of the boat. Troubles of this nature can be avoided with a watchful weather eye and by maintaining and operating your boat in accordance with the manufacturer's recommendations. In addition, all required safety equipment should be on board and fully operational. To assist you in learning about your boat and how it operates, both the USCG Auxiliary and the U.S. Power Squadrons offer inexpensive safe-boating

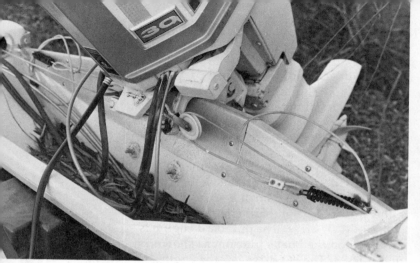

12-28. Outboard mounting and steering systems. The outboard engine is mounted to the transom of the boat using two screw clamps. The cables mounted to the spring-and-pulley arrangement inside the transom are linked to the steering wheel to provide a simple mechanical steering system. The bottom photograph shows a small outboard which has the throttle control installed in the hand tiller which is used to steer the boat.

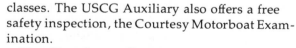

classes. The USCG Auxiliary also offers a free safety inspection, the Courtesy Motorboat Examination.

Handling the small outboard drive boat is not exactly like handling the larger inboards described earlier in the chapter. The beginner

should fully appreciate the differences before getting underway for the first time. Some obvious physical differences are in freeboard, displacement, and hull form. Figure 12-31 shows typical hull forms for boats from about 12 to 24 feet in length. A fourth type generally used for fishing or utility purposes is the flat-bottomed skiff shown earlier in figure 12-1. Each of these hulls has its own advantages and disadvantages, and you should find out which hull best suits your needs. Note that each hull is lightweight and has shallow draft. With the proper engine installed, these boats will get up on a plane very quickly in open water. Once on a plane and free of much of the water's resistance, speed increases rapidly. The speed produced by the planing hull and engines with high rotational speeds is another characteristic of the outboard boat. The boat will handle quite differently at planing speed than it does alongside the pier. Only practice on the water will tell you exactly how your boat handles through the wide range of speeds available.

Despite their light weight and shallow draft, most outboard boats are very stable prior to submerging their gunwales. They handle well in a moderate seaway and are normally equipped with positive buoyancy. This means that they will not sink unless perhaps very badly holed by collision. Some boats are somewhat tender initially, however, and they will respond quickly to any outside force such as a wave or shift of weight on board. For this reason, you should not step on the gunwales when boarding. The boat

12-29. A three-bladed prop on an inboard-outdrive boat. Note the steering arm which rotates the outdrive unit for steering control. Also note the twin trim tabs on either side of the stern. These are controlled from the cockpit to keep this planing hull craft at optimum trim.

will not "tip over" but it may roll toward you rapidly. This may cause you to lose your balance and fall overboard. To get on board, step, never jump, into the boat and move your weight to the centerline. The placement of passengers, as well as the battery, gasoline tanks, and other equipment, will have a significant effect on the boat's performance and handling. Normally, the boat should be trimmed so that her bow is up slightly, and of course she should not be listed or heeled.

Proper trim is very important if the outboard boat is to operate safely and achieve the performance intended by its designer. Not only must weight on board be properly placed, but also the outboard or I/O drive unit must be correctly aligned. Both vertical position and angle of the propeller have an important effect on the boat's trim and performance.

Another major difference between the inboard and the outboard boat is that the latter has no rudder. The entire engine, or drive unit, pivots so that the boat is turned by directing the propeller wash in the direction of the desired turn. This ability to turn by controlling the wash moves the position of the pivot point well aft.

Every outboard and I/O drive has a cavitation or antiventilation plate (see figure 12-32) installed just above the propeller. Antiventilation is the less commonly used but more accurate term, since the plate does not prevent propeller *cavitation*. (Cavitation is the formation of a partial vacuum along the tips of the propeller when it rotates at very high speeds, a problem not normally encountered on pleasure boats if the correct propeller for the boat and engine is used.) The purpose of the cavitation plate is to prevent the propeller from drawing air down from the surface of the water into the propeller blades.

12-30. A well-operated outboard motorboat. 1. Proper weight placement fore and aft, as well as athwartships. 2. Life jackets properly used. 3. Boat has oars in case of power failure, although the oars might be better stowed.

When air is sucked down, the propeller meets with much less resistance. This allows the engine to race at very high speeds which may damage the engine or drive shaft. When the transom is too high for the outboard being used, or if the engine is tilted too far aft, the cavitation plate cannot perform its function, since the propeller is too close to the surface. Ventilation can also occur if the boat banks excessively in a hard turn so that the propeller is brought close to the surface. Properly aligned, the cavitation plate should be about an inch or so below the keel or skeg.

Figure 12-33 shows a typical method of adjusting the angle of an outboard engine using a pin and hole arrangement on the mounting bracket. The propeller shaft should be adjusted so that it

is aligned horizontally with the surface of the water when the boat is on a plane. If the shaft is not adjusted so that the water flow runs parallel to the cavitation plate, the boat will either squat by the stern or hog down by the bow. Incorrect trim makes steering difficult and also slows the boat, since the planing hull is not meeting the water at the proper angle. Figure 12-29 shows trim tabs installed on the transom of an I/O boat. These are adjusted, usually remotely from the helmsman's position, to keep the boat in trim with various loading and sea conditions.

When the propeller shaft is correctly positioned, there is little if any propeller side force due to the shaft angle discussed earlier in this chapter. However, many high-speed engines do generate a noticeable pull on the steering as a result of propeller torque which is due perhaps to the lower blade being in more solid water (see figure 12-3). This is easily corrected by placing a small, adjustable vertical trim tab such as the one shown in figure 12-32 just below the cavitation plate. An alternative method is to offset the engine exhaust outlet. In both cases the slight amount of offset produces enough force at high speeds to counteract propeller torque and keep the boat tracking straight.

Handling a small outboard or I/O alongside a pier is somewhat easier than handling larger vessels, but even if the boat is moving at slow speeds, her trim, propeller alignment, and the location of her pivot point must all be considered. You will notice that a boat with shallow draft is pushed around easily by the wind. The skillful skipper will use the directed thrust of the propeller in combination with lines and perhaps even a small anchor in very difficult conditions to overcome the uncontrollable forces of wind and current.

12-31. Variations on the V hull.

shallow V

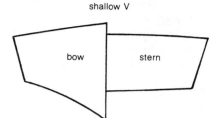

bow   stern

deep V

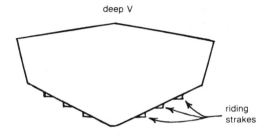

riding strakes

cathedral

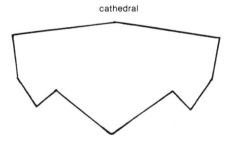

12-32. Outboard cavitation plate and trim tab. The top view shows the location of the cavitation plate above the propeller. The plate is properly called an "antiventilation" plate since it prevents air from being drawn down into the propeller from the surface. The bottom photograph shows the trim tab offset to port. This small steering correction counteracts torque developed by the propeller at high rotational speeds. The trim tab is also made of zinc. The zinc is sacrificed to galvanic corrosion, thus protecting the remainder of the lower unit.

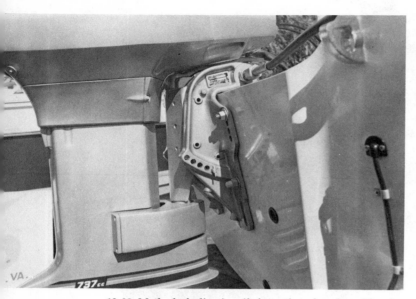

12-33. Method of adjusting tilt for outboard engines. The pin and hole arrangement built into the mounting bracket provides the means of adjusting the tilt of this outboard engine. The tilt of the lower unit should be set so that the bow rides slightly bow up (2° to 3°) at cruising speeds. Normally this will occur when the cavitation plate is positioned parallel to the keel. Improper engine tilt and poor weight distribution can cause the boat to trim down by either the bow or stern. In both cases the hull and engine will not perform at design efficiency.

A simple method of getting underway is to use a spring line as was described earlier and back clear of the pier. Bear in mind that the outboard drive boat has excellent handling characteristics while backing. Since these small craft are very light and are often handled by one person, an even simpler method is to take in all lines and push the boat away from the pier. This will give you enough room to maneuver. Turn the boat slowly away from the pier when going out ahead. An abrupt turn of the wheel will only force the stern into the pier.

Landing alongside a pier is accomplished in the same manner as with larger craft. Get your mooring lines and fenders ready well in advance. Approach the pier at an angle of 20 to 30 degrees. Here is where you will notice an important difference in the small outboard as compared with larger displacement hulls. Without a rudder and having a shallow draft, the boat will not hold her course very well when the engine is in neutral. By shifting back and forth from ahead to neutral you can easily maintain your heading at slow speed. As the bow approaches the pier, turn the wheel all the way towards the pier and apply just enough reverse power to stop the boat. This will also bring the boat parallel to the pier. You should be close enough to the pier to step ashore with the bow line.

Since the lower unit of the engine is completely exposed, it is generally preferable to enter a slip bow first. This protects the propeller and does not pose a problem when getting underway since, as we have noted, the outboard handles so well when backing.

In boats of any size you should always check the official weather forecasts before getting underway. Once clear of the harbor, be alert for changes in the weather which could produce high winds and seas. This is particularly important in boats of the size we have been discussing. Also, keep a careful eye on your fuel supply. While it may seem overly conservative, leave at least two-thirds of your fuel supply in reserve for the trip back home. A small outboard or I/O is not much fun in a storm and even less so without power to help ride out the blow.

If you are caught in a sudden storm, one option is to try to outrun it. Make certain that you have the required fuel and that you are headed for a safe harbor before picking this course of ac-

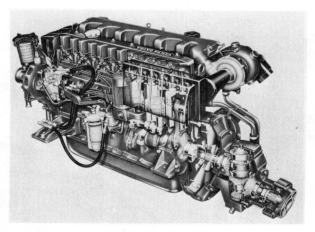

12-34. Contrasting uses of marine engines. Two uses of the same six-cylinder marine diesel are illustrated in the two top photographs. The top photograph shows a Volvo-Penta engine as it would appear in an inboard mounting. In the middle photograph, the engine is mated to an outdrive unit. Steering the inboard-outdrive (I/O) is accomplished by rotating the entire outdrive lower unit. Notice the cavitation plate and trim tab installed above the propeller in the two lower photographs. The bottom photograph shows a gasoline-powered inboard-outdrive marine engine.

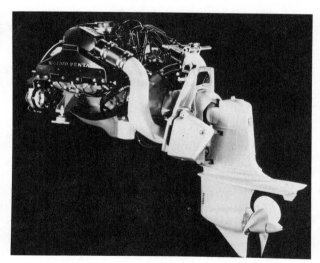

tion. If the seas pick up quickly and the boat is slamming badly from one wave to the next, slow the boat and head into the waves at a slight angle. The "Deep Vee" and cathedral hulls will be reasonably comfortable and will make headway against the storm. The shallow "V" and flat bottom boat will probably be better off idled down just enough to hold the boat's head almost into the waves.

When the storm is so bad that the boat cannot be comfortably controlled, it is time to set a sea anchor (see chapter 11). The sea anchor may be set either from the bow or stern. If you need to make distance to leeward but cannot control the

boat in the following seas, some lines or drags, such as boat cushions streamed astern, will help hold the stern into the seas. A word of caution should be added about going downwind in this manner. The transoms of most small boats are relatively low and the risk of taking a wave over

12-35. Emergency drills. Every good skipper takes the time to drill the crew in emergency procedures. In the top photograph midshipmen conduct man-overboard drills on board an MSL. Below, midshipmen learn the proper way to use CO_2 and dry-chemical fire extinguishers.

the stern is great. The boat could be "pooped" by a large wave, filling it with water as well as flooding the engine. The preferred method is to set the anchor from the bow if it will hold the bow into the wind and seas. By careful adjustment of the throttle the boat will either maintain her position or drift very slowly, for the most part sternfirst, to leeward. Finally, keep weights low in the boat and keep her pumped out as much as possible. Try to rig a spray dodger from a piece of cloth to keep water from coming over the bow.

13. Naval Academy Powerboats

After receiving their basic training in knockabouts and Luders yawls, midshipmen at the Naval Academy are given instruction in powerboat handling. Learning to handle a small, single-screw powerboat is important, because midshipmen often have occasion to run such boats at the Naval Academy and on summer cruises with the Fleet. Moreover, the midshipman or young ensign assigned to a ship for training or duty will soon find himself designated "Boat Officer," or, in effect, Officer-in-Charge of a boat, a position of great responsibility that requires a detailed knowledge of small powerboat seamanship and safety precautions.

The 80-foot, twin-screw, wooden yard patrol craft (YP) used at the U.S. Naval Academy closely resemble in handling characteristics and equipment many of the ships in the Fleet (see figure 13-7. They provide advanced seamanship training under conditions approximating those that will be encountered by the newly commissioned ensign at sea.

Professionally, YP training provides every midshipman with experience in seamanship, shiphandling, navigation, naval tactics and communications, naval phraseology, and standard shipboard procedures.

Naval Academy single-screw powerboats. In the spring of 1977 the Naval Academy acquired ten converted Mine Sweeping Launches (MSL). Prior to conversion the MSL was used as an assault minesweeper capable of clearing a variety of mines from an amphibious landing area.

The MSL is a 36-foot, shallow-draft, fiberglass boat (see figure 13-1). Power is provided by a General Motors V-6 diesel which develops 216 horsepower at 2800 rpm. With the minesweeping gear removed, the MSL is extremely light for its engine and large 32-inch, three-bladed propeller. As a result, the MSL is very responsive to rudder and engine commands.

The MSL is capable of carrying ten passengers including the crew. Normally, during training classes, the MSL is manned by a crew of five midshipmen and one instructor. Since the steering console also contains all engine and electrical controls, it is not necessary to have an engineer.

13-1. Handling alongside in the single-screw MSL.

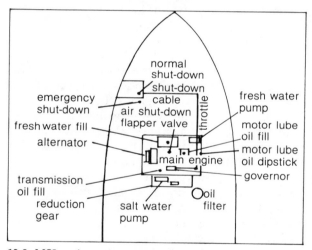

normal shut-down
shut-down
emergency shut-down
cable
air shut-down
flapper valve
fresh water fill
alternator
throttle
fresh water pump
motor lube oil fill
motor lube oil dipstick
main engine
governor
transmission oil fill
reduction gear
salt water pump
oil filter

13-2. MSL main engine components.

Standard safety equipment includes life jackets, two life rings, and a 15-pound CO_2 fire extinguisher. The boats do not have flotation installed and thus are suitable only for day training in the immediate vicinity of the Naval Academy.

After midshipmen have completed basic sail training, they use the MSL for basic training in handling single-screw powerboats, and in learning the rules of the road, basic chart reading and piloting, deck seamanship, and safe engineering practices. Each of these areas is a necessary prerequisite for midshipmen before they continue their training in the 80-foot Yard Patrol (YP) Craft.

The two powerboats illustrated in figure 13-3 are used at the Naval Academy to assist larger vessels in patrolling sailing areas, ferrying people, and for general utility work. One is a 20-foot line-handling boat, the other, a 22-foot utility boat. Both are diesel powered and of fiberglass construction. These two boats have a type of helm that is a bit awkward to use, at first. It is an upright lever connected to the rudder by a bar and yoke. The rudder is put to the left by pulling the lever aft, and to the right by pushing it forward. It is wise to spend some time practicing with this type of helm before maneuvering in restricted waters.

Both these boats steer somewhat sluggishly at slow speeds due to their small rudders. This is particularly true of the 20-foot line handler, because she has a cylindrical rudder that encloses the propeller. This rudder, designed to keep lines out of the propeller, is rather inefficient at slow speeds and makes the boat somewhat hard to handle.

The capacity of the 20-foot line handler is 6 men, including the crew; the 22-foot utility boat will carry 16, including crew. These boats, of course, should never be loaded beyond their capacity. Life jackets for each passenger are carried under the seats or in the *forepeak* (the space beneath the foredeck). Each carries a 15-pound, CO_2 fire extinguisher, and has running lights

13-3. A 20-foot line handler and a 22-foot utility boat. The line handler is shown at full speed. Note the vertical steering lever on both boats.

and a horn. All of the 22-foot utility boats are equipped with high-capacity bilge pumps for pumping out knockabouts and other craft.

Illustrated in figure 13-4 is a 33-foot utility boat. These craft are used at the Naval Academy primarily as tenders for the yawls and for ferrying people. They may be used to carry cargo. They are diesel powered, built of fiberglass and are capable of carrying up to 45 men, including crew. The crew usually consists of three men: a *coxswain* (man in charge who steers the boat and runs the engine), and a *bow hook* and *stern hook* (men in the bow and stern to handle lines). These boats are equipped with a horizontal steering wheel and hydraulic clutch-and-throttle control. This arrangement gives the coxswain good visibility and adds to the boat's maneuverability. Life jackets are located under the

seats and in the forepeak. A 15-pound CO_2 fire extinguisher is mounted near the engine box.

Shown in figure 13-5 are two 50-foot motorboats: the motor launch and the utility boat. The 50-foot motor launch is diesel powered and of carvel-planked, round-bottom construction. She normally carries a crew of four and has a maximum capacity of 150 men. Life jackets are located beneath the after seats and in the forepeak. She is equipped with two 15-pound CO_2 fire extinguishers.

The motor launch is steered with a tiller. The coxswain handling the motor launch stands on the afterdeck. The engine is controlled by an engineer at the engine, amidships. The boat's bell is used by the coxswain to relay orders to the engineer. This signal system will be described in detail later in the chapter. Wooden motor launches with this type of control are being phased out of service in the Navy and replaced by the newer utility boats, all of which give the coxswain direct engine control.

The 50-foot utility boat is also diesel powered and of round-bottom, wooden construction. She has a maximum capacity of 150 men, including the crew of 4: coxswain, engineer, bow hook,

13-4. A 33-foot utility boat. This boat is shown running at full speed.

13-5. A 50-foot motor launch and a 50-foot utility boat. Note the horizontal steering wheel on the utility boat and the tiller on the motor launch.

and stern hook. There are two 15-pound CO_2 fire extinguishers on board. This utility boat, like the 33-foot utility boat, is steered by a horizontal wheel on the port side, amidships. The clutch is a foot-operated mechanical model, and the throttle control is on the steering column.

Both these boats have very large propellers, turning at a relatively low speed, which adds to their maneuverability at slow speeds. The utility boat has a great deal more power than the motor launch: 165 horsepower, compared to 60 horsepower. She also has a faster hull. For these reasons she is capable of a top speed of 11 knots fully loaded, while the motor launch will make only 8 knots. Both these boats carry life jackets for the crew and passengers beneath the seats

and in the forepeak. They are equipped with electric horns and navigational lights. Each boat has at least two bilge pumps, and two 15-pound CO_2 fire extinguishers installed. For additional equipment, they should normally carry magnetic compasses, harbor charts, oars, boat hooks, dock lines, and an anchor and rode.

Another type of small boat used at the Naval Academy by sailing coaches is the gasoline outboard-motor powered Boston Whaler. She is illustrated in figure 13-6. These boats have a planing hull and are capable of speeds up to 30 knots. All are equipped with a compass, navigational lights, fire extinguisher, and floatable cushions. They are steered with a wheel and have a single-lever clutch and throttle control. The maximum capacity of these boats is eight. They are of double-hull, fiberglass construction and have flotation foam between the hulls, which makes them unsinkable. They are extremely maneuverable, but because the outboard shaft and propeller extend well below the bottom of the hull, they are very vulnerable to damage caused by running over floating objects. Great care must be taken to keep the propeller clear of debris and mooring lines, especially when running at high speeds.

Engine order bells. It was mentioned that on the 50-foot motor launch, engine orders are given on the boat's bell. This is done because the engineer is unable to hear verbal commands when the engine is running. Four signals are used to control the engine. One bell means put the engine *ahead slow*. Two bells means idle the engine in *neutral*. Three bells means *back slow,* and four bells means to use full throttle in whichever direction the engine is running when the signal is given. For example, the sequence, 2 bells, 1 bell, 4 bells,

13-6. A Boston Whaler. The Whaler's nearly flat bottom gives her a high degree of initial stability and allows her to plane very easily. There should be a fire extinguisher on the port side of the steering console.

means idle, go ahead slow, increase to full speed ahead. Remember that when the bells are used to give engine orders there will always be some time lag. The engine orders must always be anticipated.

Boat crew duties. The number of men in a boat crew will differ with the size of the boat. The normal crew size of the larger personnel boats is four. Each crew consists of a coxswain, an engineer, a bow hook, and a stern hook. The safety of the passengers embarked and the smartness of the boat depend to a great extent on how well these crewmen do their jobs.

The coxswain is in charge of the boat and is the helmsman, subject to supervision and possible relief by the Boat Officer or the senior line officer aboard the boat. It should be noted here that although the boat coxswain and assigned Boat Officer share in the responsibility for any mishap, Navy Regulations make it very clear that the final responsibility rests with the senior line officer aboard, even if he is only a passenger. *United States Navy Regulations* states: "When embarked in a boat the senior line officer (including commissioned warrant and warrant officers), eligible for command at sea, has authority over all persons embarked therein, and is responsible under all circumstances for the safety and management of the boat."

The coxswain is responsible for making certain that all necessary gear is aboard the boat and that it is in proper working order. It is also his responsibility to enforce safety precautions and supervise the loading and unloading of the boat. He must ensure that the boat is never loaded beyond capacity. The posted capacity prescribes the maximum number of persons allowed aboard during good weather in a protected anchorage. When the weather is questionable and sea conditions become hazardous, this capacity must be reduced. In addition to these duties, the coxswain is responsible for the proper helmsmanship and safe navigation of his boat. He must obey the rules of the road, pilot carefully, and use common sense in handling his boat near piers, anchored vessels, and crowded channels.

The engineer is responsible for the operation and maintenance of the engine. On the motor launches, he controls the clutch and throttle in response to the bell orders given by the coxswain. In all cases, he is responsible for fueling the boat.

The bow hook is the forward line handler and, as such, handles the bow line, sea painter, forward fenders and the bow boat hook, from which he derives his title. He also acts as forward lookout while underway and should always be stationed in the forward part of the boat.

The stern hook handles stern lines, stern fenders, the stern boat hook, and acts as an after lookout.

The boat crew should always be in the uniform of the day, wear boat sneakers and, when conditions warrant them, life jackets.

Boat officer responsibilities. The Boat Officer has a very delicate job, for he must supervise the coxswain and his crew and make certain that safety precautions are followed and the boat safely navigated without interfering needlessly with the coxswain's control of the boat, passengers, and crew. The Boat Officer is a safety observer and should only take charge of the boat personally when absolutely necessary. In such a case, he should formally relieve the coxswain.

Navy small-boat safety precautions result from years of experience. They should be obeyed by the passengers and crew and enforced by the coxswain. The Boat Officer is responsible for seeing that safety precautions are carried out.

A summary of small-boat safety precautions.
• All safety equipment, including life jackets, lights, and bilge pump, should be inspected regularly.
• The smoking lamp is always out.
• Passengers must always remain seated on thwarts and seats, with hands and fingers inside the gunwales.
• Boat crews must keep their stations, especially when weather conditions are unpleasant, for it is usually during these times that vigilance is most needed.
• Boats must always be properly loaded for the sea state. In heavy weather, the boat should be loaded slightly down by the stern and the passengers and crew kept in life jackets.

• Bilges should be kept free of oil.
• Shafts and engine equipment should be kept covered.
• All passengers should be kept clear of the boat while refueling.
• Boats should be loaded and unloaded in a safe, orderly fashion.

Yard patrol craft. The Naval Academy has 15 yard patrol craft. All are of the 654 Class, and while some of the newer vessels have slightly different equipment, they all have identical characteristics and tactical data. Table 13-1 lists their important characteristics. Many of these facts are required only occasionally, and this table can be referred to when necessary. Some, however, must be remembered, for they are essential to proper shiphandling. Length, draft, "masthead" height, and rudder angles should be memorized.

Also important to the shiphandler are the YP's performance characteristics, which include turning circle (see figure 12-5 for explanation of turning circle), acceleration and deceleration figures, and the relationship between engine rpm and hull speed. Table 13-2 indicates the hull speed in knots compared to engine rpm. The speeds of 5 knots and 5.6 knots are achieved by turning only one shaft. For all other speeds, both shafts are required. The EOT (engine order telegraph) settings are also indicated. The EOT will be explained later in the section on ship's control equipment.

Also included in table 13-2 is data essential to shiphandling in a formation. This "tactical data" standardizes speeds and distances used in formation maneuvering.

Turning and deceleration data for the 654-Class YP are found in table 13-3. Of all the statis-

length over-all	80'5"
extreme beam	18'9"
draft (light load)	5'4"
displacement	69.5 tons
main propulsion	(4) GM-6-71 diesels, 165 horsepower each
generator	(1) 120-volt, 30-kilowatt, A.C. generator
propellers	(2) 3-bladed, 36"-diameter screws
fuel oil capacity	2,070 gallons
lubricating oil capacity	35 gallons
fresh water	420 gallons
maximum speed	13.5 knots
cruising speed	10 knots
maximum safe capacity	60 people
rudder angles (twin rudders)	
standard	13½°
full	25°
hard	35°
heights	
top of mast to boot top	37'10"
yard arm to boot top	34'10" (double for use with stadimeter)
radar antenna to boot top	28'
vertical distance between sidelights and masthead light	13'1"
height of eye (6-foot man)	
main deck (forward)	12.8'
main deck (aft)	11.6'
signal bridge	19.6'

Table 13-1. YP 654-class characteristics.

EOT setting	Speed in knots		RPM
starboard (or Port) engine ahead ⅓	5	(one shaft)	680
starboard (or Port) engine ahead ⅓	5.6	(one shaft)	810
all engines ahead ⅓	6		680
all engines ahead ⅓	7		810
all engines ahead ⅔	8		940
all engines ahead standard	9		1,070
all engines ahead full	10		1,200
all engines ahead flank	11		1,400
(speeds above flank must be ordered on	12		1,700
the 1JV sound-powered telephone)	13.5		1,800
all engines back ⅓			600
all engines back ⅔			1,000
all engines back full			1,500

TACTICAL DATA

Tactical
normal speed	7	knots
stationing speed	11	knots
operational speed	13	knots

Tactical Diameters
standard diameter	200	yards. Standard rudder (13½ degrees)
reduced diameter	125	yards. Full rudder (25 degrees)

Distances
standard distance	200	yards
circle spacing	200	yards

Table 13-2. Speed and RPM.

tics in this table, the most important to remember are the tactical diameters for standard and full rudder at 8 and 10 knots (200 yards and 125 yards), and the deceleration time and distance covered when going from full ahead to stop by backing full (8 seconds and 57 feet). The YP will accelerate from 7 to 10 knots in 22 seconds. The surge rate when changing speed is 9 yards for each knot of speed differential. This factor is very important when station-keeping in formation. For example, in order for a YP making 10 knots to maintain station alongside one making 7 knots, she must slow to 7 knots when 27 yards from station (3 × 9 = 27).

Ship control equipment. The main propulsion engines aboard the 654-Class YPs are four 165-horsepower General Motors 6-71 diesels. These are nonreversible, fuel-injected, two-cycle engines. They are installed two to a shaft with a hydraulic clutch and 2:1 reduction gear. Their maximum forward speed is 1,800 rpm and the maximum reverse speed is 1,500 rpm. The throttle control and clutch are in a control booth in the engine room, and are controlled manually from this station by an engineer. Engine orders are transmitted to him by the Engine Order Telegraph (EOT) system. This is a mechanical system which links a signal device in the pilot house to one in the engine room (see figure 13-9). EOT is to port of the helm in the pilot house. It has one handle for each bank of en-

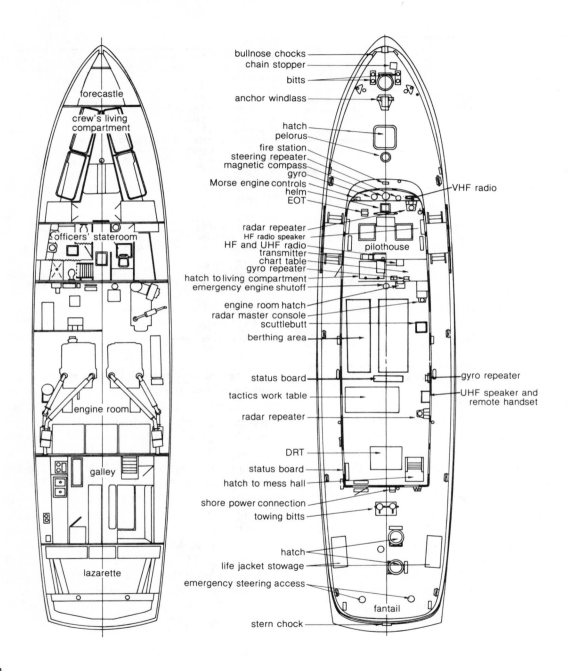

forecastle

crew's living compartment

officers' stateroom

engine room

galley

lazarette

bullnose chocks
chain stopper
bitts
anchor windlass

hatch
pelorus
fire station
steering repeater
magnetic compass
gyro
Morse engine controls
helm
EOT

VHF radio

radar repeater
HF radio speaker
HF and UHF radio transmitter
chart table
gyro repeater
hatch to living compartment
emergency engine shutoff

pilothouse

engine room hatch
radar master console
scuttlebutt

berthing area

status board

gyro repeater

tactics work table

UHF speaker and remote handset

radar repeater

DRT

status board
hatch to mess hall

shore power connection
towing bits

hatch
life jacket stowage

emergency steering access

fantail

stern chock

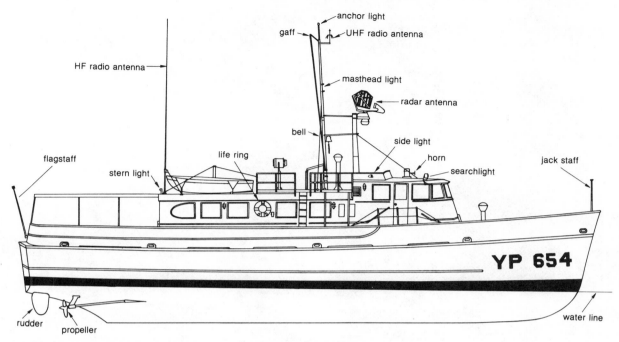

13-7. Yard patrol craft 654; outboard profile, anterior arrangement, and deck plan.

gines. The port and starboard shafts are controlled by the port and starboard handles. Beneath each handle the telegraph face is divided into the following positions: Ahead Flank, Ahead Full, Ahead Standard, Ahead ⅔, Ahead ⅓, Stop, Back ⅓, Back ⅔, Back Full.

As engine speeds are ordered, they are answered manually by the engineer in the control booth. When they have been answered, a follow-up pointer under the handle will so indicate. It should be noted that to shift from forward to reverse or vice versa, the engine must be slowed to idling speed in order to shift into and out of reverse gear. This takes several seconds. For this reason, unless an emergency exists, Stop

should always be ordered before changing the direction of shaft rotation. Engine speeds other than normal (those indicated in table 13-2) may be ordered by calling the engineer on the 1JV sound-powered telephone, located next to the EOT.

The YPs have now been modified with the installation of Morse engine controls. Figure 13-9 shows the clutch, throttle, and all gauges which monitor engine operating parameters. This console is installed to port of the helm and provides direct control of the engines from the pilot house.

The 654-Class YPs have two rudders, one astern of each propeller, for added maneu-

13-8. The YP 660 running in a smooth sea.

verability. The rudders are linked together and controlled mechanically by the helm in the pilot house. A rudder angle indicator is located forward of the steering wheel on the steering stand. The full throw of the rudders is 70 degrees, from 35 degrees port to 35 degrees starboard. Hard rudder, 35 degrees, should be avoided except in an emergency, because the mechanical linkage is likely to jam in this position. The maximum rudder angle used under normal circumstances should be 30 degrees. When backing at speeds greater than 2/3, never use more than 10 degrees rudder. Care must be taken when backing to hold the steering wheel firmly. If it is let go, it will spin hard over and the rudders will jam in the stops.

Emergency steering on the YP is effected by connecting tiller extensions through deck fittings on the *fantail* (afterdeck) to the starboard rudder post, which is located in the lazarette. The rudder posts are linked so that both rudders respond to tiller movements from the fantail.

For ground tackle the YP-654 Class carries two Danforth anchors, one of 75 pounds and one of

Speed (Knots)	Rudder Angle (Standard 13½° Full 25°)	Time to Turn (Min.–Sec.)						Advance and Transfer (Yards)						Diameter (Feet)		Deceleration to Dead in Water		
		30°	60°	90°	180°	270°	360°	30° Adv.	30° Tr.	60° Adv.	60° Tr.	90° Adv.	90° Tr.	Tactical	Final	Backing Speed	Reach Ahead (Feet)	Time (min.–sec.)
6	Standard	0–27	0–41	0–57	1–40	2–24	3–10									Full	24	0–6
																⅔	31	0–11
	Full	0–13	0–23	0–34	1–04	1–33	2–02									⅓	69	0–27
																0	160	2–11
7	Standard	0–22	0–36	0–50	1–27	2–04	2–40									Full	31	0–8
																⅔	41	0–12
	Full	0–12	0–21	0–30	0–56	1–20	1–45									⅓	74	0–28
																0	194	2–36
8	Standard	0–20	0–32	0–43	1–14	1–45	2–16	Standard Rudder—75 Full Rudder—51	Standard Rudder—15 Full Rudder—6	Standard Rudder—112 Full Rudder—70	Standard Rudder—57 Full Rudder—32	Standard Rudder—130 Full Rudder—80	Standard Rudder—112 Full Rudder—66	Standard Rudder—200 Full Rudder—125	Standard Rudder—190 Full Rudder—120	Full	39	0–8
	Full	0–12	0–18	0–26	0–49	1–09	1–31									⅔	49	0–13
																⅓	81	0–28
9	Standard	0–18	0–28	0–37	1–04	1–31	1–57									Full	47	0–8
	Full	0–11	0–17	0–23	0–44	1–01	1–20									⅔	57	0–14
																⅓	87	0–29
10	Standard	0–17	0–25	0–33	0–56	1–20	1–43									Full	49	0–8
	Full	0–10	0–16	0–20	0–39	0–54	1–12									⅔	66	0–16
																⅓	97	0–30
11	Standard	0–15	0–23	0–30	0–51	1–12	1–32									Full	54	0–8
	Full	0–10	0–15	0–19	0–34	0–50	1–05									⅔	72	0–17
																⅓	99	0–31
12	Standard	0–15	0–22	0–27	0–47	1–06	1–23									Full	57	0–8
	Full	0–10	0–14	0–18	0–31	0–46	1–00									⅔	77	0–18
																⅓	103	0–31

Table 13-3. Turning and deceleration data—YP 654 class.

150 pounds, and 70 *fathoms* (six feet to a fathom) of one-half-inch chain. The anchor windlass pictured in figure 13-10 is a power-driven, nonreversible, single-speed (20 feet per minute) model which can only be used to heave in. It can, in an emergency, be operated manually. The windlass is activated by a button on its after side. The *wildcat* (a concave drum) over which the chain is heaved in, is engaged by a handwheel friction clutch on the starboard side of the windlass (see figure 13-10). This wheel is turned clockwise to engage the wildcat. In addition to the clutch there is a handbrake. The *gypsy head,* a horizontally mounted drum, operates continuously and can be used independently from the wildcat by disengaging the wildcat and setting the brake. The anchoring procedure will be discussed in a later section of this chapter.

The navigation equipment aboard the 654-Class YP is extensive. Each YP has one standard

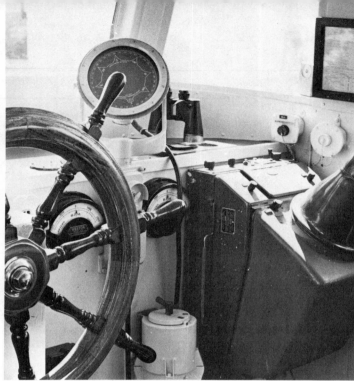

13-9A. YP pilot house. Notice the Engine Order Telegraph to port of the steering wheel. A fire extinguisher is against the bulkhead. A sound-powered telephone is above the EOT. Forward and to port of the helm is the Sperry gyrocompass. Directly forward of the helm is the magnetic compass. To starboard of the wheel is the radar. Morse controls are now installed on most YPs. This unit is mounted directly forward of the EOT.

13-9B. YP Morse control.

The two control levers provide for remote operation of the main engines. Moving the lever forward engages the transmission and also controls engine speed for moving the YP ahead. Before backing down, the engine should be returned to idle speed and the transmission disengaged by returning the clutches to the neutral or stop position shown in the photograph. Astern speed is controlled by pulling the levers back and adjusting the throttles for the desired engine rpm. A complete set of gauges provides a remote display of important engine-operating parameters. The YPs also have automatic alarms which sound in the event an engine overheats or loses oil pressure.

13-10. YP anchor windlass. The wildcat is shown with the chain around it. The handwheel on the wildcat is the wildcat clutch. The after handwheel is the brake. Note the winch drum, also called a gypsy head, on the far side of the windlass. The bitts atop the windlass are used for belaying a line while the large horned bit serves as a fairlead when leading a line to the gypsy head.

6½-inch magnetic compass installed immediately forward of the helm. To port of the helm, a Sperry gyrocompass Mark 22, Model O is mounted. This master gyro provides an input for six gyro repeaters located in the pilot house (2), the combat information center (CIC), forecastle, and the bridge (2). In addition the Mark 22 gyro supplies true ship's head to the master radar console, both radar repeaters, the dead reckoning tracer (DRT), and the dead reckoning analyzer (DRA). The control panel that connects these stations with the master gyro is located in the pilot house beneath the gyro.

The YP-654 Class carry as navigational lights one white 20-point masthead light, one white 12-point stern light, one white 32-point anchor light, one 10-point green starboard sidelight and one 10-point red port sidelight.

There are three 20-point white lights arranged vertically on the mast as towing lights and two 32-point red lights for breakdown lights. The control panel for the navigational lights is in the pilot house over the chart table. The ship's horn is electric and is atop the pilot house. It is operated by a push button located to the right of the helm. The ship's bell is on the mast. A 7-inch, sealed-beam navigational searchlight is installed atop the pilot house and is controlled from within the pilot house.

The YP has three *peloruses* (rotatable circles marked in degrees with sights for taking visual bearings) mounted on the gyrocompass repeaters on the bridge wings and on the forecastle. Each YP carries at least one *stadimeter*, an optical ranging device with which to obtain visual distance using known masthead heights. Each vessel also carries a depth recorder and radar. These navigational devices will be discussed in the section on electronic equipment.

Communications equipment. The communications equipment on the YP-654 Class falls into two basic categories, internal and external. Internal communication aboard the YP is accomplished by voice tubes and *sound-powered telephone* circuits. (This is a telephone that generates its own power by the sound vibrations of the voice.) The voice tubes connect the bridge with the pilot house and CIC, the pilot house with the captain's stateroom, the pilot house chart table with the forward pelorus, and the pilot house with the signal bridge. Of these, the voice tubes most commonly used are those located on each wing of the bridge, connecting the bridge with the helmsman in the pilot house.

There are five sound-powered telephone circuits installed aboard the YP. These circuits and

Circuit		Stations				
		Pilot House	Forecastle	Engine Room	Bridge	CIC
JA	Captain's Battle Circuit	1			2	JX4
JW	Navigation Circuit	1	1		2	JX5
1JV	Engineering Circuit	1 (handset)		1 (handset)		
21JS	Radar Information Circuit No. 1					1 JX1, JX2, JX6
22JS	Radar Information Circuit No. 2	1				

Note: As mentioned in the text the seven outlets JXI–JX7 may be used with any of the circuits except the 1JV. They are usually used as listed above.

Table 13-4. Sound-powered phone circuits.

their stations are listed in table 13-4. The sound-powered telephone jack boxes for the bridge, engine room, forecastle, and pilot house stations (with one exception) are clearly labeled by circuit designators. The jack boxes for the CIC stations (with one exception) can be patched into any of the five circuits. These jack boxes, labeled JX1 through JX6, are controlled by a master control panel on the starboard bulkhead in CIC. Outlet JX7, in the pilot house, is also controlled by this panel.

For external communication, the 654-Class YP is equipped with three radios, one 12-inch signal searchlight, and two sets of standard Navy signal flags. The ultra high frequency (UHF) radio is installed in the pilot house. This transmitter-receiver combination gives line-of-sight radio communication in the frequency range of 225-400 megahertz. The UHF is the primary ship-to-ship tactical communications system. There are three speakers for the UHF radio, one in CIC, one on the bridge, and one in the pilot house. There are remote transmitting stations on the bridge and in CIC.

There is also one high frequency (HF) radio installed in the pilot house. This radio has a longer range than the UHF. The frequency range is between 1,500 and 12,000 kilohertz. There are speakers for the HF radio in the pilot house and in CIC. A remote transmitter is also located in CIC.

Each YP is also equipped with a VHF radio which is installed in the pilot house to starboard of the helm. Operating in the marine VHF-FM band, this unit provides very reliable communications with lower power. The VHF radio may be controlled locally in the pilot house or from a remote unit located on the flying bridge. Table 13-5 lists the channels found on the VHF installed in the YP.

Electronic equipment. The 654-Class YP, in addition to the radios, carries a radar and a fathometer. YPs 654-659, 662 and 663 are equipped with AN/SPS-35 radar, YPs 660, 661, 664, 665, 666, 667, and 668 with AN/SPS-53 radar. Although differing in model number, these radars are all similar, and all are excellent at relatively short range. The master console in all installations is located in the forward starboard corner of CIC. In addition there are two repeaters, one located aft in CIC and the other in the pilot house.

The YP has two fathometers, an AN/UQN-1 and a Raytheon DE 725. The AN/UQN-1 is located in CIC and is capable of recording depths up to 36,000 feet. The depth indicated is measured from the transducer, which is approximately 3'6" below the waterline. The Raytheon model is located in the pilot house and provides a digital display of depth. This unit records depth up to 295 feet. This fathometer also has an alarm setting which provides an audible alarm when the depth beneath the keel reaches the depth set into the unit by the operator. The depth indicated is measured from a separate transducer located 4'6" below the waterline. For both models the difference between the location of the transducer and the waterline must be added to the displayed sounding to get the actual depth of water.

The dead reckoning tracer (DRT) is an electro-mechanical device used primarily for tracking surface contacts and secondarily for navigation. The DRT and its associated equipment, the dead reckoning analyzer (DRA), are located in the after part of CIC, the DRA on the after bulkhead and the DRT just forward of the bulkhead. The DRA, using inputs of ship's course and speed fed to it by the gyro and a dummy log, breaks down the ship's movement into north-south and east-west components. North-south and east-west signals move a *bug* (small, moving light) in the DRT which simulates the ship's track by continuously displaying the ship's position from beneath a tracing paper. The scale of the DRT is adjustable between 500 and 32,000 yards per inch, and there is a 200-yard-per-inch scale for use in man-overboard plotting. A parallel motion protractor is positioned atop the DRT for use in plotting surface contacts.

Table 13-5. VHF-FM channels.

VHF-FM CHANNELS	USE
Channel 6	Intership safety. Mandatory worldwide on all marine VHF-FM-equipped vessels. This channel should only be used for safety.
Channel 12	Port operations. Intership and ship to shore.
Channel 13	Navigational channel. Used for bridge-to-bridge communications.
Channel 16	Distress, safety, calling. Intership and ship to shore. Common to all VHF equipped ships, U.S. Coast Guard, and marine operators.
Channel 26 28	Ship to Shore. The local marine operator monitors these channels and will connect the ship to a commercial telephone for a fee.
Channel 68	Working channel.
Channel 82A	U.S. Government use only. Monitored by Small Craft Harbor Control at the U.S. Naval Station, Annapolis.
Channel WX1	Weather broadcast. Frequency 162.400 MHz.
Channel WX2	Weather broadcast. Frequency 162.550 MHz.

Safety equipment. For lifesaving, the 654-Class YP carries 30 life preservers, 25 inflatable and 5 kapok, two 18-man life rafts, and one 12-foot *wherry* (small rowboat). All of the life preservers are stowed in a deck box on the fantail. The life rafts are mounted on the house above CIC, as is the wherry. The procedure for lowering the wherry will be discussed in a later section. Two 24-inch life rings with attached float lights are positioned on deck amidships, one on each side. Six aircraft *smoke floats* (floating markers that emit smoke) are stowed in racks on the bulkhead abaft the pilot house, three to port and three to starboard. A first aid kit is located on the mess deck.

The fire fighting and damage control equipment carried aboard the 654-Class YP is listed in table 13-6. The use of this equipment will be covered in a later section.

Conning. The basics of handling alongside were discussed in chapter 12. Quite often the *conning officer* (the officer doing the handling) will actually be steering and controlling the engines. When this is the case, conning is analagous to driving a car—the person conning has the "feel" of the boat in his own hands and decisions can be translated directly into actions. The YPs can be conned in this manner from the pilot house. On large ships, however, the conning officer does not handle the helm or engine order telegraph, for he must be free to move about on the open bridge to have the visibility necessary to do the job. When this is the case, a new dimen-

EQUIPMENT	LOCATION	QUANTITY
15 pound portable	crew's living compartment	1
CO_2 extinguishers	officers' stateroom	1
	engine room	2
	galley	1
	pilot house	1
	CIC	2
	lazarette	1
PKP dry chemical extinguisher	engine room	1
	CIC	1
	galley	1
5 gallon cans of liquid foam/AFFF	lazarette	5
1½ inch mechanical foam nozzle with pick-up tube	lazarette	1
fire stations (firemain outlet, 4-ft. fog applicator, 1½ inch fire hose, all purpose nozzle, spanner wrench)	forecastle (50 feet of hose)	1
	fantail (50 feet of hose)	1
	engine room (25 feet of hose)	1
fire axes	lazarette	2
damage control plugs and wedges	lazarette	1 bag
pipe patching kit	lazarette	1 bag
battle lanterns	all compartments except head and officer's stateroom	13

Note: The CO_2 extinguisher is a general purpose fire extinguisher and specifically intended for electrical (Class C) fires.

Table 13-6. Damage control equipment.

sion is added to the conning problem, because the conning officer must translate his decisions into commands to the helmsman or *lee helmsman* (man operating the engine order telegraph and standing by to assist the helmsman) rather than carry them out himself. A different sense of timing is needed by the conning officer when he is controlling the ship through others, rather than by his own action. This is a skill that requires a great deal of practice. It is also a skill that is essential for all officers who go to sea in surface ships or submarines. It is for this reason that the YP, while on drills, is always conned from the open bridge.

With regard to steering, there are two distinctly different methods for conning a vessel from the bridge. The first, which can be called positive control, is recommended in all maneuvering situations when the conning officer wants direct control over rudder angle. For this method of conning, all steering commands relate to the positioning of the rudder. There is no reference to the compass or ship's head and, in fact, the compass is not required. This method of conning comes as close as possible to actually steering oneself. The standard commands for this method are listed with their meanings in table 13-7a.

In the second method, a certain amount of helm control is relinquished by the conning officer to the helmsman, and commands relate to ship's head and compass courses. Once given a course—and courses must always be given when using this method—the helmsman will use the rudder required to keep the vessel on the ordered course. This second method is recommended for normal conning in channels and in formation. The standard commands for this method are listed in table 13-7b.

There are some general rules that apply to all standard conning commands. The most important is that *only* standard commands may be used. For this reason, the prospective conning officer must learn the commands and their meanings verbatim. Orders to the lee helmsman are always given in the following format: engine, direction, speed. The word "engine" or "engines" is always used, and the words "port" and "starboard," not "left" and "right," are used to indicate to which engine the order applies. The engine speeds that are available on standard Navy engine order telegraphs were discussed in a preceding section. Emergency orders are indicated on the EOT by ordering Ahead Flank or Back Full several times in rapid succession.

All commands given by the conning officer to either the helmsman or lee helmsman should be repeated verbatim by the helmsman or lee helmsman. If the order has been heard and repeated correctly the conning officer should answer with a "Very well." Once the engine order has been answered by the engine room or the helm order accomplished by the helmsman, the lee helmsman should so inform the conning officer with a "Port engine answers Back ⅓," or "All engines answer Ahead Full," and the helmsman with "My rudder is Right Standard," or "steady, zero six zero," etc. The proper response from the conning officer is again, "Very well." The helmsman and lee helmsman should continue to repeat the information until answered by the conning officer.

Engine direction should never be changed except in an emergency without first ordering Stop. This allows the engine to idle before clutching. When conning by compass heading, a course order should always follow a rudder order. This ensures that the vessel will not swing

Commands	Meaning
"Left (Right) _____ Degrees Rudder."	Put on the left (right) rudder ordered.
"Left (Right) Standard Rudder."	Put on the previously specified amount of left (right) rudder required to turn the ship in her "standard tactical diameter."
"Left (Right) Full Rudder."	Put on the previously specified amount of left (right) rudder to turn the ship in her "reduced tactical diameter."
"Hard Left (Right) Rudder."	Use maximum left (right) rudder.
"Ease the Rudder to _____ Degrees."	Decrease the rudder angle to _____ degrees.
"Shift the Rudder."	Change from left to right rudder (or vice versa) an equal amount.
"Rudder amidships."	Put the rudder amidships (to decrease the rate of swing).
"How is your rudder?"	Report the rudder's position.

Table 13-7A. Standard commands for positive control conning.

Commands	Meaning
"Steady on course _____."	Steady on course _____, using the amount of rudder previously ordered.
"Come left (right) to _____."	Put the rudder left (right), and steady on new course _____.
"Come left (right) handsomely to _____."	Use a small amount of rudder and come to course _____ (used when a very small course change is desired).
"Nothing to the left (right) of _____."	Do not steer to the left (right) of ordered heading.
"Steady," or "Steady as she goes."	Steer the course on which the ship is heading when the command is received. The helmsman's reply is "Steady as she goes; course _____, Sir."
"Meet her."	Use rudder as necessary to check the swing.
"Mind your rudder."	Steer more carefully.
"How does she head?" or	
"Mark your head."	What is the ship's heading?
"Keep her so."	Steer the course that has just been reported as ship's heading.

Table 13-7B. Standard commands for conning by compass heading.

past the desired course. Course changes up to 15 degrees should be ordered by giving the direction of turn followed by the new course. For example, when steadied on 050 degrees, the proper order of a change to 055 degrees would be, "Come right to zero five five." For course changes greater than 15 degrees, a rudder order may be given, followed by the new course. For example, to change course from 050 degrees to 090 degrees, the conning officer might say, "Right Standard Rudder. Come to course zero nine zero." Rudder orders may be given in degrees or by the commands, standard, full and hard. As mentioned before, hard rudder should be used only in an emergency, because in this position the rudder is apt to jam in the stops.

Remember that the helmsman always goes by the last order given, and a change in rudder order will supersede a previous course given. Finally, the terms "belay my last," "negate my last," and "disregard" are never used. When an incorrect order has been given, simply correct it with a proper one.

Typical maneuvers. *Anchoring*—In addition to receiving instruction in handling alongside (as discussed in chapter 12), the midshipmen get training in: station keeping, lowering the wherry, maneuvering alongside while underway, and precision anchoring.

Anchoring is often required on the YPs. The anchors are stowed on deck on the forecastle and are *not* connected to the anchor chain. To ready the anchor for use, first the handbrake and the clutch on the windlass must be released. Then enough chain to reach through the starboard hawse hole, over the bulwarks, and back to the anchor on deck must be hauled by hand from the chain locker. When the anchor chain and an-

chor buoy line have been bent onto the anchor, the *anchor davit fall* (tackle on a small crane for handling the anchor) is hooked onto the anchor (see figure 13-11). The anchor is then hoisted, swung out over the bulwarks, and lowered to the rub rail. The wildcat is then engaged and the slack taken out of the chain. The anchor should remain just outboard of the starboard hawse hole until dropped. After the anchor is in position, the handbrake is set up, the wildcat disen-

13-11. YP anchor davit and fall. The Danforth anchor is secured to the bulwark abaft the davit, where it is stowed when not in use.

gaged, and the anchor davit fall slacked and unhooked. The anchor is then ready for letting go.

The forecastle crew should be informed when within 1,000 yards and 500 yards from the anchorage. When the YP is head to wind or current, as the case may be, with all way off, the anchor is let go by releasing the windlass handbrake. When the anchor is on the bottom, sternway should be made to pay the chain out of the chain locker and finally to set the anchor. During this process, the forecastle crew should be reporting to the bridge the amount of chain at the water's edge, the direction it is tending, and the amount of strain (slack, light, moderate, or heavy strain). When the chain is snubbed, the report that the anchor is holding or dragging should be made.

When weighing anchor, it is usually "heaved around" to a short stay first; that is, the scope is shortened as much as possible without breaking out the anchor. Once the command to "heave on in" is given, the forecastle crew weighs anchor, reporting when it is "up and down" (the chain is vertical), "aweigh" (the anchor is broken out and lifted clear of the bottom), "in sight," "clear," or "foul," "clear of the water," and "to the hawse hole." While anchored, the proper signals under the appropriate Rules of the Road must be observed; a black anchor ball hoisted at the yardarm by day, and a white, 32-point light shown by night.

Lowering the wherry—When stowed for sea, the wherry is *griped* (strapped down) to the chocks on deck above CIC abaft the signal bridge on the port side. The wherry davit is rigged inboard. Before launching, the cover and gripes are removed, the chain bridle, attached fore and aft in the wherry, is connected to the davit fall, and a *sea painter* (long, heavy, tending line attached to the bow of a small boat that is to be launched at sea) is made fast to the wherry. The sea painter must be led outboard and well forward, especially if the wherry is to be launched while the YP is underway, as it is this line which controls the wherry once she is in the water.

When the preparations are complete, a strain is taken on the fall, and the wherry is lifted clear of the boat chocks. The davit and wherry are then swung aft and out over the side. The davit has fore-and-aft guys with which to swing and control it. The guys should be belayed to hold the davit in place once the wherry has been swung outboard. The wherry can then be lowered into the water. The crew should board the wherry by the *Jacob's ladder* (a rope or chain ladder with wooden or iron rungs, which is secured over the bulwarks).

Usually the wherry will be launched while the YP is at anchor or dead in the water. Because of the maneuverability of the YP, there is seldom a need to launch the wherry in the open sea. If she did have to be launched in a seaway, the YP should be turned so that the wherry is on the lee side. When launching in a seaway, it is usually best to keep a little headway on.

When the wherry is picked up, the launching sequence is reversed. In a seaway, the wherry should always be picked up to leeward.

Formation shiphandling—Operating with other ships in a formation presents the Officer of the Deck (OOD) with many problems not encountered when conning a ship which is maneuvering independently. In addition to a knowledge of basic shiphandling, a familiarity with formation shiphandling is required, particularly as described in Allied Tactical Publication, ATP 1

(B), Volumes I and II. Also essential to the OOD maneuvering in formation is a thorough understanding of relative motion and the ability to work a maneuvering board. It is beyond the scope of this book to present a detailed explanation of Navy tactical publications or to attempt to teach the *maneuvering board* (a printed polar coordinate plotting sheet with convenient scales and a nomogram and logarithmic scale used to solve relative motion problems). It is possible and pertinent, however, to point out some of the problems encountered in formation shiphandling and their solutions.

When ships are operating in a formation, they are all assigned specific positions relative to each other. One ship, usually the largest and when possible the one in the center, is designated the "Guide." This ship is always assumed to be *on station* (in the correct position) and to be making precisely the signaled course and speed. All other ships keep their stations with reference to the Guide. It is therefore essential that the OOD keep track of base course and speed and the range and bearing to the Guide when maintaining station.

It is up to the OOD to keep his ship on station. Staying within 3 degrees in bearing and 50 yards in range is usually acceptable on the YP. The standard maneuvering board scale used on the YPs is 100 yards per circle.

Station keeping is quite simple, as figure 13-12 indicates, but takes *constant* attention, requiring continued alteration of course and speed.

When stationed ahead of the Guide, as in Situation A in figure 13-12, changes of speed affect range, and course changes alter bearing. When stationed on the beam, as in Situation B of figure 13-12, the effect is the opposite, with course alterations changing range, and speed

changes affecting bearing. Usually, as in Situation C of figure 13-12, the station is neither directly ahead nor abeam of the Guide, in which case station keeping is a function of combined course and speed changes. For example, if, in Situation C, the OOD wanted to keep the bearing to the Guide constant, but decrease the range, he would have to alter course to the left to close the Guide and thereby decrease the range, and at the same time increase speed in order not to fall behind while closing, and thereby change the bearing.

The best advice for station keeping is to work out a solution and then take action, using common sense backed up by a maneuvering board solution to choose a course and speed to produce the desired relative motion to move the ship from her actual to her desired position with respect to the Guide. Course and speed changes should be gradual and a constant check kept on the resulting change in position relative to the Guide. An attempt to regain station should never be made by radical course and speed changes, for when wrong, this type of solution is *very* wrong, and when right, before base course and speed can be resumed, the ship often will be as far from station as before, but in the opposite direction.

When station keeping, a constant check may be kept on the range to the Guide by using the *stadimeter* (an optical range-finding device that computes distance to an object of known height once the angle between the bottom and top of the object is measured). The masthead height of the Guide must be set on the stadimeter before accurate ranges can be determined. It should be remembered that the masthead height of the 654-Class YP is 34 feet 10 inches. Since the masthead height scale on the stadimeter cannot be set

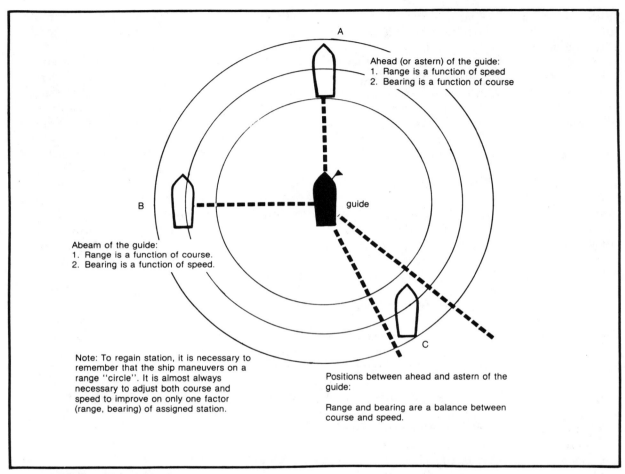

A

Ahead (or astern) of the guide:
1. Range is a function of speed
2. Bearing is a function of course

B

guide

Abeam of the guide:
1. Range is a function of course.
2. Bearing is a function of speed.

C

Note: To regain station, it is necessary to remember that the ship maneuvers on a range "circle". It is almost always necessary to adjust both course and speed to improve on only one factor (range, bearing) of assigned station.

Positions between ahead and astern of the guide:

Range and bearing are a balance between course and speed.

13-12. Station keeping (course versus speed).

this low, a setting of 70 feet (twice the height) is therefore used, and all ranges read from the stadimeter must be halved to get true ranges.

To stay on station, all movements of the Guide must be followed precisely. All turns, unless otherwise indicated, should be executed when the Guide turns and with standard rudder. The use of standard rudder ensures that all ships turn with the same tactical diameter, in this case 200 yards, and thus the range to the Guide from each ship remains the same. When full rudder is prescribed, the result is the same, except that all ships turn with reduced tactical diameter, 125 yards for the YP. (See table 13-3.)

The safety of the ship is the paramount responsibility of the OOD. The OOD should never assume that all ships will act on a given signal correctly. For this reason, a constant check should always be kept on other ships in the formation, especially those toward which the ship is turning, to ensure that they are turning in the same direction.

When ordered to move from one station in a formation to another, the OOD at the earliest possible moment should acquaint himself with the new station number, the range and bearing to the Guide from the new station, and the initial direction of turn if it has been prescribed. From this information, the OOD should be able to work out a rough course and speed solution to get to the new station. As soon as the maneuvering board solution for the problem is available, it should be checked against this initial rough calculation.

It must be remembered that the maneuvering board will often show solutions on paper that in reality are not practical. For instance, a speed increase from 7 knots to a stationing speed of 10 knots is not a practical solution for moving ahead 150 yards. In this case, the *three-minute rule* (speed, or relative speed, in knots times 100 equals distance traveled, or relative distance if relative speed was used, in yards in three minutes) would indicate that at 3 knots relative speed, it would only take 1½ minutes to travel the required relative distance of 150 yards. When it is remembered that it will take 22 seconds to accelerate from 7 knots to 10 knots, and that the 7-knot formation speed should be resumed when 27 yards from station, it will be realized that the 10-knot speed could only be kept on for about one minute. Although this solution may at first be indicated on the maneuvering board, common sense suggests a more moderate one.

If a signal is executed before the precise course and speed solution to station is known, the best action is to turn in the correct direction and use the estimated rough course and speed. Course and speed can always be refined on the way to station.

The straight maneuvering board solution does not allow for other ships that may be obstructing the direct route from one station to another. A YP should not be passed by another closer than 100 yards, and an attempt should be made to pass under the stern whenever possible. This is especially true when maneuvering close to the Guide. While proceeding to station, a constant check must be kept on range and bearing to the guide. If the range and bearing are not changing as they should be, a return to base course and speed will at least maintain the status quo until the proper solution can be determined.

When proceeding to a new station, the number of the station should be indicated by an information signal flown from the yardarm. The proper signal is the Designation pennant followed by the numeral flag (never pennant unless out of flags) of the new station. This signal is flown *at the dip* (two or three feet below the yardarm) as soon as the new station is assigned. It is *closed up* (hoisted to the yardarm) while proceeding to station, and hauled down when on the new station. Station indicators are used to determine where other ships are going. If another YP is flying the same station number you are flying, assignments should be rechecked.

When maneuvering in formation:

• Always know the base course and speed of the formation.

- Know your ship's course and speed.
- Know the proper range and bearing of the Guide.
- Know the actual range and bearing to the Guide and check them continually.
- Always look before maneuvering and don't count on correct action from other vessels.
- Using all available information and a good deal of common sense, make decisions promptly and then take action.
- Most important, keep in mind that at all times the OOD's primary responsibility is the safety of the ship, and only a constant vigil will keep the ship out of danger. This is particularly important when operating in close company.

Maneuvering alongside: replenishment—The YP OOD will occasionally be required to maneuver alongside another YP while underway, either in a replenishment drill or to transfer a piece of equipment. In most cases, the delivering ship will act as control ship and Guide. A replenishment course should be chosen that is into both wind and sea. When wind and sea are not from the same direction, the course should be into whichever element is the more significant. Replenishment speed should be the minimum speed required for responsive shiphandling. For the YPs, 8 knots is a good replenishment speed. Once signaled, the control ship should maintain replenishment course and speed. The ship designated to go alongside should, prior to her approach, steady on replenishment course and speed astern of the control ship. This gives the OOD an opportunity to check for gyro error and speed difference. On the YP, these differences, especially in gyro error, can be significant.

Flag hoist procedures used in Navy replenishment operations are found in ATP 1 (B), Volume II, pages 2-5, and are used during YP drills. Before an approach, fenders should be rigged along the appropriate sides of the delivering and receiving ships. On each ship, the most experienced helmsman and lee helmsman should be on watch. A helm error on either ship while alongside can cause a collision.

In making the approach, the OOD of the receiving ship should use a speed differential of from 3 to 5 knots. Three knots is recommended for the YPs. It should be kept in mind that surge for the 654-Class YP is 9 yards per knot. This dictates that with a 3-knot speed advantage, the OOD should reduce speed when 27 yards from station alongside. A much higher speed advantage combined with an appropriate backing bell is often used in the Fleet, but is not required or recommended for the YP.

The approach should be made from astern on the appropriate quarter. By the time the receiving ship begins to overlap the delivering ship, the approach course should be within two or three degrees of, or the same as, the course during replenishment. The separation between the two vessels at this point should never be less than the eventual desired separation. For the YPs this is not less than 20 feet. For the separation to be greater is merely to err on the safe side. It is during the approach and breakaway phases of the replenishment operation that the greatest danger of collision exists. The bow shape of the two ships as they come together acts to form a funnel. The water forced into this funnel increases in velocity as it passes between the two ships. As the velocity of the water between the ships increases, the pressure on their inboard sides is reduced relative to the pressure on their outboard sides. In effect, there is a force tending to pull them together (see illustration of Bernoulli's Principle, figure 3-11). During the approach and breakaway phases of the operation, any rudder action that tends to swing the stern of the receiving ship towards the delivering ship causes an increase in this force which can result in the vessels being drawn together. This is why a near-parallel approach course is recommended. The same is true for breaking away. Speed should be increased to clear the side of the delivering ship, but course should not be altered significantly until the receiving ship is clear ahead. If, while alongside, the replenishment course must be changed, it should be changed very gradually, in 5-degree increments, and with great caution.

Emergency procedures. Emergencies can occur on any vessel at any time, but the watch officer who makes a habit of thinking ahead can visualize many emergencies and prevent them, or at least be prepared to meet them. The only way to prepare for emergencies is to be alert at all times and to know in advance exactly what action must be taken in a given situation. It is good practice for the watch officer, when conditions permit, to discuss emergency procedures with other members of the watch and with all hands whenever possible.

While not the only emergencies possible, man overboard, breakdown, collision, fire, and grounding are the most likely and pose the greatest threat to the YP or any other vessel. The proper procedures to cope with these emergencies must be known by the OOD. It is also his responsibility to keep the Officer-in-Charge of the YP informed of emergency situations and casualties, but action should precede reporting. It is obvious that this discussion is as pertinent to the skipper of a small auxiliary as it is to the OOD of a YP or the captain of a destroyer. All must know how to deal immediately with an emergency situation when it occurs.

Man overboard. There are a number of man overboard recovery methods. (Recovery methods for sailboats were discussed in chapter 11.) The three most common are: (1) Williamson turn for night or low visibility, (2) race-track turn for fastest recovery when proceeding at high speed in clear weather, and (3) Y-backing, for ships with large turning circles and great backing power proceeding at slow speeds. These three methods are illustrated in figure 13-13. Very large ships often use a small boat to recover a man from the water. Smaller vessels will use the small-boat recovery method as well when the sea is very rough, and the possibility of getting the man close alongside the ship is small. The principles mentioned earlier about launching a small boat in a seaway would apply if this method were used on the YP.

Regardless of which recovery method is used, the same basic principles and required action apply. Initially a life ring, life jacket, floating light, or smoke float is thrown overboard to provide flotation for the man and to mark his position. At the same time, the report is made to the OOD, "Man overboard, starboard (port) side." The OOD swings the stern away from the man with full rudder. If it is possible to stop the shaft on the side toward the man before he reaches the screws, this should be done. If it is not, which is likely, continue the recovery without attempting to stop the screw. CIC must be informed immediately, in order that the man on the DRT can mark the ship's position when the man went overboard, shift the DRT scale to 200 yards to the inch, and provide continual ranges and bearings to the man. The word must be

METHOD AND PRIMARY USE	DIAGRAM (SHIP ON COURSE 090; NUMBERS REFER TO THE EXPLANATION)	EXPLANATION	ANALYSIS	
			ADVANTAGES	DISADVANTAGES
WILLIAMSON TURN 1. USED IN REDUCED VISIBILITY BECAUSE IT MAKES GOOD THE ORIGINAL TRACK. 2. USED WHEN IT IS BELIEVED THAT A MAN FELL OVERBOARD SOME TIME PREVIOUSLY AND HE IS NOT IN SIGHT.	⊗ = MAN	1. PUT THE RUDDER OVER FULL IN THE DIRECTION CORRESPONDING TO THE SIDE OVER WHICH THE MAN FELL. STOP THE INBOARD ENGINE. 2. WHEN CLEAR OF THE MAN, GO AHEAD FULL ON ALL ENGINES, CONTINUE USING FULL RUDDER. 3. WHEN HEADING IS 60° BEYOND THE ORIGINAL COURSE, SHIFT THE RUDDER WITHOUT HAVING STEADIED ON A COURSE. 60° IS PROPER FOR MANY SHIPS, HOWEVER, THE EXACT AMOUNT MUST BE DETERMINED THROUGH TRIAL AND ERROR (50° FOR YPs). 4. COME TO THE RECIPROCAL OF THE ORIGINAL COURSE, USING FULL RUDDER. 5. USE THE ENGINES AND RUDDER TO ATTAIN THE PROPER FINAL POSITION (SHIP UPWIND OF THE MAN AND DEAD IN THE WATER WITH THE MAN ALONGSIDE, WELL FORWARD OF THE PROPELLERS).	1. SIMPLICITY, THE REASON WHY IT IS TAUGHT ON YP DRILLS. 2. MAKES GOOD THE ORIGINAL TRACK IN THE OPPOSITE DIRECTION, EXCEPT FOR THE EFFECTS OF WIND AND CURRENT.	1. SLOW 2. TAKES THE SHIP A RELATIVELY GREAT DISTANCE FROM THE MAN, WHEN SIGHT MAY BE LOST.
ONE TURN ("ANDERSON") USED BY DESTROYERS, SHIPS WHICH HAVE CONSIDERABLE POWER AVAILABLE AND RELATIVELY TIGHT TURNING CHARACTERISTICS.		1. PUT THE RUDDER OVER FULL IN THE DIRECTION CORRESPONDING TO THE SIDE OVER WHICH THE MAN FELL. STOP THE INBOARD ENGINE. 2. WHEN CLEAR OF THE MAN, GO AHEAD FULL ON THE OUTBOARD ENGINE ONLY. CONTINUE USING FULL RUDDER. 3. WHEN ABOUT TWO-THIRDS OF THE WAY AROUND, BACK THE INBOARD ENGINE 2/3 OR FULL. ORDER ALL ENGINES STOPPED WHEN THE MAN IS WITHIN ABOUT 15 DEGREES OF THE BOW, THEN EASE THE RUDDER AND BACK THE ENGINES AS REQUIRED TO ATTAIN THE PROPER FINAL POSITION (AS FOR THE OTHER METHODS). 4. MANY VARIATIONS OF THIS METHOD ARE USED, DIFFERING PRIMARILY IN RESPECT TO THE USE OF ONE OR BOTH ENGINES, AND THE TIME WHEN THEY ARE STOPPED AND BACKED TO RETURN TO THE MAN AND TIGHTEN THE TURN. THE VARIATION USED SHOULD REFLECT INDIVIDUAL SHIP'S CHARACTERISTICS, SEA CONDITIONS, PERSONAL PREFERENCES, ETC.	THE FASTEST RECOVERY METHOD.	1. REQUIRES A RELATIVELY HIGH DEGREE OF PROFICIENCY IN SHIPHANDLING BECAUSE OF THE LACK OF A STRAIGHT-A-WAY APPROACH TO THE MAN. 2. OFTEN IMPOSSIBLE FOR A SINGLE PROPELLER SHIP.
RACETRACK TURN (TWO 180° TURNS) USED IN GOOD VISIBILITY WHEN A STRAIGHT FINAL APPROACH LEG IS DESIRED.		1. A VARIATION OF THE ONE TURN METHOD WHICH PROVIDES A DESIRABLE STRAIGHT FINAL APPROACH TO THE MAN. 2. PUT THE RUDDER OVER FULL IN THE DIRECTION CORRESPONDING TO THE SIDE OVER WHICH THE MAN FELL. STOP THE INBOARD ENGINE. 3. WHEN CLEAR OF THE MAN, GO AHEAD FULL ON ALL ENGINES, CONTINUE USING FULL RUDDER TO TURN TO THE RECIPROCAL OF THE ORIGINAL COURSE. 4. STEADY FOR A DISTANCE WHICH WILL GIVE THE DESIRED RUN FOR A FINAL STRAIGHT APPROACH. 5. USE FULL RUDDER TO TURN TO THE MAN. 6. USE THE ENGINES AND RUDDER TO ATTAIN THE PROPER FINAL POSITION (SHIP UPWIND OF THE MAN AND DEAD IN THE WATER WITH THE MAN ALONGSIDE WELL FORWARD OF THE PROPELLERS).	1. THE STRAIGHT FINAL APPROACH LEG FACILITATES A MORE CALCULABLE APPROACH. 2. THE SHIP WILL BE RETURNED TO THE MAN IF HE IS LOST FROM SIGHT. 3. REASONABLY FAST. 4. EFFECTIVE WHEN THE WIND WAS FROM ABEAM ON THE ORIGINAL COURSE.	SLOWER THAN THE ONE TURN METHOD.
DELAYED TURN USED WHEN WORD IS RECEIVED THAT A MAN FELL OVERBOARD, MAN IN SIGHT AND CLEAR ASTERN OF THE SHIP.		1. A VARIATION OF THE ONE TURN METHOD. 2. PUT THE RUDDER OVER FULL IN THE DIRECTION CORRESPONDING TO THE SIDE OVER WHICH THE MAN FELL. GO AHEAD FULL ON ALL ENGINES. 3. HEAD TOWARDS THE MAN. 4. USE THE ENGINES AND RUDDER TO ATTAIN THE PROPER FINAL POSITION (SHIP UPWIND OF THE MAN AND DEAD IN THE WATER WITH THE MAN ALONGSIDE, WELL FORWARD OF THE PROPELLERS).	1. THE FASTEST METHOD WHEN THE MAN IS IN SIGHT AND ALREADY CLEAR ASTERN OF THE SHIP. 2. PROVIDES A STRAIGHT RUN IN THE CRITICAL FINAL PHASE. 3. EFFECTIVE WHEN THE WIND IS FROM AHEAD OR ASTERN OF THE SHIP ON THE ORIGINAL COURSE.	1. DOES NOT ENSURE RETURN TO THE MAN. 2. REQUIRES GOOD VISIBILITY. 3. TAKES THE SHIP FARTHER FROM THE MAN THAN THE OTHER METHODS.
Y BACKING USED BY SUBMARINES BECAUSE THE SHIP (LOW HEIGHT OF EYE) REMAINS COMPARATIVELY CLOSE TO THE MAN.		1. PUT THE RUDDER OVER FULL IN THE DIRECTION CORRESPONDING TO THE SIDE OVER WHICH THE MAN FELL. STOP THE INBOARD ENGINE. 2. WHEN CLEAR OF THE MAN, BACK THE ENGINES WITH FULL POWER, USING OPPOSITE RUDDER. 3. GO AHEAD. USE THE ENGINES AND RUDDER TO ATTAIN THE PROPER FINAL POSITION (SHIP UPWIND OF THE MAN AND DEAD IN THE WATER WITH THE MAN ALONGSIDE, WELL FORWARD OF THE PROPELLERS).	THE SHIP REMAINS COMPARATIVELY CLOSE TO THE MAN.	MOST SHIPS BACK INTO THE WIND/SEA, RESULTING IN POOR CONTROL OF THE SHIP WHILE BACKING.
BOAT RECOVERY 1. USED BY SHIPS LACKING SUFFICIENT MANEUVERABILITY TO MAKE A GOOD APPROACH FOR A BOAT RECOVERY. 2. USED WHEN THE SHIP IS DEAD IN THE WATER WITH THE MAN CLOSE ABOARD BUT NOT ALONGSIDE. 3. CAN BE USED IN CONJUNCTION WITH ANY OF THE METHODS SHOWN ABOVE.	BASIC BOAT RECOVERY METHOD:	BASIC BOAT RECOVERY METHOD: 1. PUT THE RUDDER OVER FULL IN THE DIRECTION CORRESPONDING TO THE SIDE OVER WHICH THE MAN FELL. STOP THE INBOARD ENGINE. 2. WHEN THE MAN IS CLEAR, BACK ALL ENGINES FULL TO NEARLY STOP THE SHIP. USE RUDDER TO THE SIDE OF THE READY LIFEBOAT TO PROVIDE A SLICK IN WHICH THE BOAT CAN BE LOWERED. STOP THE ENGINES WHILE THE SHIP STILL HAS VERY SLIGHT HEADWAY TO PERMIT BETTER CONTROL OF THE BOAT AND TO KEEP IT OUT OF THE PROPELLER WASH.	BASIC BOAT RECOVERY METHOD: 1. SIMPLE 2. FOR ANY GIVEN TYPE OF SHIP, THE SHIP WILL REMAIN CLOSER TO THE MAN THAN BY ANY OF THE OTHER METHODS. 3. DOES NOT REQUIRE THAT A PARTICULAR FINAL POSITION BE ATTAINED.	BASIC BOAT RECOVERY METHOD: 1. THE MAN MUST BE IN SIGHT. 2. SEA AND WEATHER CONDITIONS MUST BE SATISFACTORY FOR LOWERING AND RECOVERING THE LIFEBOAT AND FOR SMALL BOAT OPERATIONS.

13-13. Methods of man-overboard recovery.

passed throughout the ship, so that all man overboard stations can be manned. These stations should be manned by one or more strong swimmers, line tenders, and a man with a first aid kit. On the bridge, as many men as can be spared should be detailed to *keep the man overboard in sight*. Visual bearings and approximate ranges should be sent to CIC for cross-checking with the DRT plot.

Other ships in company must be informed of the emergency and be kept informed of recovery progress. Voice radio is the best method. In addition, six short blasts should be sounded at frequent intervals. As time permits, the Oscar flag should be hoisted during daylight, or the two, vertical, red, 32-point lights turned on and pulsated at night.

The man should be recovered in the shortest possible time. For the YPs, in good weather this means the race-track method; at night or in low visibility, the Williamson turn—though not the fastest recovery method—must be used to bring the ship back along her track. With any method, the desired final position is beam to the wind slightly to windward of the man with all way off. When in this position a lee is provided for the man, and since the ship will make more leeway than the man, she will drift toward, rather than away from him. As has been mentioned, swimmers with life jackets and tending lines donned should be ready to go into the water.

Man overboard maneuvering instructions for naval vessels involved in tactical evolutions can be found in ATP 1 (B), Volume I. Of specific importance to the YP OOD are the instructions for man overboard recovery from a column formation. In this situation, the ship that loses the man takes action to avoid him, and others do as well, with odd-numbered ships in the column clearing to starboard, and even-numbered ships clearing to port. The ship in the best position to recover the man does so, keeping the other vessels informed of her actions. All ships resume stations when clear.

In summary, when a man falls overboard, the following actions should be taken as rapidly as possible:

• Drop a life ring or jacket, light, or smoke float.

• Swing stern away from man.

• Inform CIC and ship's company.

• Keep man in sight.

• Inform other ships by radio, sound, and visual signals.

• Maneuver to recover man using race-track, Y-backing, or Williamson-turn method.

• Put your ship to windward of the man.

• Assist the recovery with swimmers.

Breakdown. Breakdowns that prevent the YP from maneuvering do not occur very frequently, because there are two engines to each shaft and a direct mechanical linkage for rudder control. When a breakdown occurs, the immediate reaction must always be to try to maintain control of the vessel. If there is a rudder casualty, the ship may be steered with the engines.

All ships in company should be notified of the casualty by voice radio. Six short blasts should be sounded and during daylight the Five flag should be hoisted. At night, the six blasts should be sounded, the breakdown lights turned on, and the running lights turned off. The vessel should be anchored, if necessary.

When the nature of the breakdown has been determined, the senior officer present should be notified and given an estimate of repair time. If the casualty cannot be repaired and the YP is without power, preparations for towing should be made.

It will occasionally be necessary for the YP to tow another vessel, and infrequently one may have to accept a tow. There are no hard and fast rules for towing or being towed, because wind and sea conditions and the size of the vessels involved are variable. Each situation must be evaluated before decisions are made. (See chapter 12.) In every towing situation, a heaving line with a towline attached must be passed to the disabled vessel. The YPs each have a 2¾-inch, nylon, 300-foot towline. The towline is made up to the anchor chain of a large vessel being towed, and this chain is veered to provide a shock absorbing catenary in the towline. For smaller vessels, the chain is not required.

The critical point in the towing operation, regardless of the size of the towed vessel, is taking the strain. The towing ship must increase speed very gradually and overcome the inertia of the other vessel slowly in order to keep the towline from parting. Once underway, speed may be increased gradually to the hull speed of the vessel under tow, conditions permitting. Being towed at greater than hull speed can do considerable damage to a vessel.

When towing at night, the YP should carry on her mast, in addition to her masthead light, her two, white, 20-point, towing lights. (If towing in international waters, and the length of the tow is less than 600 feet, measured from the YP's stern to the stern of the tow, then only one of the towing lights should be carried in addition to the masthead light.)

Collision. Collisions do not "just happen." They can usually be prevented by prudent, timely ac-

tion on the part of the OOD. Even when timely action is not taken, a collision involving a YP should never occur because of the vessel's great backing power and maneuverability. If the OOD of a YP does find himself *in extremis* with another vessel (in a situation where action by both vessels is required to avoid collision), then both are burdened to take action, and emergency shiphandling procedures must be used in order to avoid collision. There are three important factors that must be considered by the OOD when choosing an emergency course of action. What action will best avoid a collision? What action will the other vessel probably take? Where will the collision occur if it cannot be avoided? There are no set rules, especially for the YP with her maneuverability and power. The decision must be rapid and action immediate. If a collision occurs, an inspection of damage should be made at once, the bilge pumps started, and, if possible, the YP returned to the Small Craft Facility.

Fire. As has been mentioned, fires at sea must be fought quickly, because limited fire fighting equipment is available, and escape is difficult. All crew members must know the location of the fire fighting equipment and its use.

In the Navy, fires are classified according to the type of combustible material involved. There are three classes of fire: Alpha, solid combustibles, such as wood, rags, or canvas: Bravo, petroleum products; and Charlie, electrical. There is equipment aboard the YP for combating each of these types of fires (See table 13-6). The proper equipment must be used for each type of fire. A solid stream of water often is the most effective means of combating a class Alpha fire, but may enlarge a class Bravo fire, because the burning oil may be spread by the water. If a stream of water is used against a class Charlie fire, the fire fighter could be electrocuted, because water will conduct electricity.

Special equipment available for fighting class Bravo and Charlie fires consists of fog spray nozzles, foam extinguishers, and PKP chemical for Bravo fires, and CO_2 extinguishers for Charlie fires. PKP is an excellent extinguisher, but bear in mind that it can cause damage to equipment. The water spray can be used on an oil fire because it cools a large area without disturbing the burning surface. The foam and CO_2 smother, rather than cool, a fire.

If a fire occurs in a YP, the Officer-in-Charge should be notified immediately. The O-in-C is responsible for notifying the engineers so that the fire pump and bilge pump can be started, and electrical power to the applicable section of the vessel turned off. Leading a fire party at the scene, the O-in-C can promptly fight the fire with the proper equipment. In order to ensure that the YP fire fighting gear is properly maintained and in working order, it should be checked frequently.

Grounding. With the array of navigational gear aboard the YP, it should certainly be possible to keep her in deep water. If a YP should run aground, the reaction should be exactly the same as it would be on any power vessel. (See the sections on grounding in chapters 2 and 12.)

An immediate attempt should be made to back the grounded YP off, but the engines should not be run full astern for long. The YP should take advantage of being a twin-screw vessel. A twist can often be used alternatively with full astern to break the YP free of the bottom. If the initial attempts are not successful the crew will have time to plan a new course of ac-

tion. The YP should be carefully inspected for leaks or other damage. The salt-water strainers for the engines should be checked to ensure that the engines are receiving a proper supply of cooling water.

If the hull is intact and there is no engine damage the wherry should be lowered and the anchor put out for a kedge. With the anchor windlass taking a strain on the kedge anchor forward and the engines twisting at full power, the YP should be able to free herself. If these efforts are unsuccessful, remember that a little higher tide will help the vessel off. If, however, it is already high tide, or if the vessel is being damaged, towing assistance should be requested.

Basic communications procedures. *Internal communications: sound-powered telephone.* Internal communications between the many stations in a YP are essential to the smooth running and safe handling of the ship. These internal communications are conducted for the most part over sound-powered telephones that connect the various stations. (See table 13-4 for the YP sound-powered telephone circuits.) On sound-powered telephones, the button on the mouthpiece must be depressed before speaking.

There will often be many stations on the circuit, and for this reason precise phone talking procedure and specific message format must be used by the telephone talkers in order to eliminate confusion and ensure efficient communications. Messages should never be transmitted while the circuit is busy. When the line is clear, the station originating the message does so using the following format: station called, station calling, message. For example, if the CIC officer wants the OOD on the bridge to know the range and bearing to the Guide, the transmission on the JA circuit (see table 13-4) would be "Bridge, Combat, Guide bears 030, 620 yards." The bridge talker would then answer if he received the message, "Bridge aye." If he had not received the message, he would say, "Combat, Bridge, say again," and the CIC talker would send the message again. The primary advantage of this type of format is brevity and a degree of familiarity that can come about only through the repetitive use of a format that never varies.

This brief format used on the sound-powered telephone always takes concentrated attention on the part of the talkers and, initially, considerable practice. Familiarity with the general subject matter usually transmitted on a particular circuit is also a help to the talker. Telephone talkers should be briefed on the standard format and expected subject matter and nomenclature before being assigned to a circuit. Sound-powered telephone talkers must not interpret messages they are given to send, or that they receive. Rather, these messages should be sent and relayed verbatim. When vital messages between stations are so transmitted, there is little chance of misinterpretation.

External communications. External communications, or ship-to-ship and ship-to-shore communications, are accomplished in the YP by the use of the radiotelephone, flashing light, and signal flag hoists. Of these three, the radiotelephone and signal flag hoists are used to send the majority of messages.

To send tactical signals, the code in ATP 1(B), Volume II, is used. This code, which breaks messages into two-letter groups and associated numbers, is intended primarily for brevity and only secondarily for secrecy. It also allows Allied, non-English speaking navies to use the code, as the alphabet is always spoken phonetically. (See table 13-8 for phonetic alphabet.) Signals encoded from ATP 1(B), Volume II, may be sent by radio, flashing light, or flag hoist.

Non-naval vessels use the *International Code of Signals* (U.S. Naval Oceanographic Publication No. 102) to encode and decode messages. This publication contains one-, two-, and three-letter groups with standard meanings to simplify the sending of messages. The single-letter groups are the most frequently used, for they have either very urgent or very common meanings. The meanings of the single-letter signals are set forth in table 13-9. When these signals are flown by a naval vessel, they are always preceded by the special pennant, Code. Flags and flag hoist procedures will be explained in a later section.

Radiotelephone communications. The radiotelephone is used for rapid, short-range, tactical communications between ships, as well as for long-range, ship-to-shore communication. Specific procedures are prescribed for each type of communication in the *Fleet Communications NTP 4*. These procedures will merely be sum-

A	Alfa	J	Juliet	S	Sierra
B	Bravo	K	Kilo	T	Tango
C	Charlie	L	Lima	U	Uniform
D	Delta	M	Mike	V	Victor
E	Echo	N	November	W	Whiskey
F	Foxtrot	O	Oscar	X	X-Ray
G	Golf	P	Papa	Y	Yankee
H	Hotel	Q	Quebec	Z	Zulu
I	India	R	Romeo		

Table 13-8. Allied phonetic alphabet.

A	I am undergoing a speed trial.
B	I am taking in or discharging explosives.
C	Yes (Affirmative).
D	Keep clear of me—I am maneuvering with difficulty.
E	I am directing my course to starboard.
*F	I am disabled. Communicate with me.
G	I require a pilot.
H	I have a pilot on board.
I	I am directing my course to port.
J	I am going to send a message by semaphore.
*K	You should stop your vessel instantly.
*L	You should stop. I have something important to communicate.
M	I have a doctor on board.
N	No (Negative).
*O	Man overboard.
*P	IN HARBOR ("Blue Peter")—All persons are to repair on board as the vessel is about to proceed to sea. (Note—To be hoisted at the foremast head.) AT SEA—Your lights are out, or burning badly.
Q	My vessel is healthy and I request free pratique.
*R	The way is off my ship; you may feel your way past me.
S	My engines are going full speed astern.
T	Do not pass ahead of me.
*U	You are standing into danger.
*V	I require assistance.
*W	I require medical assistance.
X	Stop carrying out your intentions and watch for my signals.
Y	I am carrying mails.
*Z	To be used to address or call shore stations.

*These signals only may be sent by flashing light.

Table 13-9. Single letter signals from the international code of signals.

Proper radiotelephone format and procedure is as important to the proper functioning of a group of naval ships as is proper internal communication procedure to the individual ship. Specific message headings are used on the radiotelephone. On tactical circuits, "call signs" are used. Call signs are words of two or more syllables used for identifying ships, groups of ships, and ship-group commanders. On nontactical circuits and ship-to-shore circuits, call signs are replaced by YP hull numbers. Hull numbers and call signs are never used on the same circuit. Table 13-10 lists international call signs for the individual YPs.

As has been mentioned, the phonetic alphabet is always used to identify any letter of the alphabet. Numbers are spoken digit by digit, ex-

YP Hull Number	International Call Sign
654	NOSE
655	NHVC
656	NRCE
657	NJOE
658	NNAZ
659	NOTA
660	NRBC
661	NNCJ
662	NJQO
663	NOTN
664	NYTG
665	NPSS
666	NSGH
667	NSVV

Table 13-10. International call signs for the 654-class YPs.

marized here. Frequent reference should be made to NTP 4 to ensure correctness of format, phraseology, and procedure. *Communication Instructions Radiotelephone Procedure* (ACP 125 series) prescribes specific details with regard to radiotelephone voice procedures.

cept for multiples of hundreds and thousands, which may be spoken normally. For example, 10 is spoken "one zero," while 100 is spoken "one hundred." Procedure words, or prowords, are used to simplify radiotelephone format. These prowords have standard meanings that cannot

Table 13-11. Common Navy prowords.

PROWORD	EXPLANATION
MESSAGE FOLLOWS	A message which requires recording is about to follow. Transmitted immediately after the call.
SIGNALS FOLLOW	The groups which follow are taken from a signal book. Not used on nets primarily employed for conveying signals. Intended for use when signals are passed on non-tactical nets such as the CI Net.
BREAK	I hereby indicate the separation of the text from other portions of the message.
CORRECTION	An error has been made in this transmission. Transmission will continue with the last word correctly transmitted.
DISREGARD THIS TRANSMISSION	This transmission is in error; disregard it, not used to cancel any message that has been completely transmitted and for which receipt or acknowledgement has been received.
NEGATIVE	Not received. No.
AFFIRMATIVE	Yes. Permission granted.
SAY AGAIN	Repeat all (or portion indicated) of your last transmission.
I SAY AGAIN	I am repeating transmission or portion indicated.
VERIFY	Verify entire message (or portion indicated) with the originator and send correct version.
I VERIFY	That which follows has been verified at your *request* and is repeated.
I SPELL	I shall spell the next word phonetically.
EXECUTE TO FOLLOW	Action on the message or signal which follows is to be carried out upon receipt of the proword "EXECUTE."
EXECUTE	Carry out the purport of the message or signal to which this applies.
ROGER	I have *received* your last transmission *satisfactorily*.
ACKNOWLEDGE	Let me know that you have received and understand this message.
WILCO	Reply to "ACKNOWLEDGE," meaning "I have received your message, understand it, and will comply." Must be authorized by the Commanding Officer (Officer-in-Charge).
OVER	This is the end of my transmission to you and a response is necessary. Go ahead; transmit. (Note: All transmissions must end with OVER or OUT.)
OUT	This is the end of my transmission to you and no answer is required or expected.
WORD AFTER	The word of the message to which I have reference is that which follows _____.
WORD BEFORE	The word of the message to which I have reference is that which precedes _____.

be varied. Table 13-11 lists some common prowords and their meanings. Note in this table the use and meaning of the proword "say again." A very common error on the radiotelephone is to use the word "repeat," instead of "say again." Also note that all transmissions must be ended with either "over" or "out."

There are two methods for executing tactical signals over the radiotelephone. One, called the nonexecutive method, is used for information signals over the radiotelephone. One, called the the signal is executed as soon as it is understood. If a signal is an emergency signal, the word "emergency" is included in the text of the message, and the text is repeated. (See table 13-12 for the precise format used in transmitting nonexecutive signals.)

The second method, called the executive method, prescribes a precise moment for the execution of each signal. There are two formats that can be used with this method, the delayed executive and the immediate executive. Examples of each will be found in table 13-12. The delayed executive format is used for signals that must be executed simultaneously by all ships, but need not be executed immediately. The initial signal is sent and acknowledged, and then another signal is sent at the time of execution. This is the preferred format, because it allows time to decode the signal between receipt and execution. The immediate executive format is used for readily understood signals that require simultaneous, immediate execution, as the name implies. Note that with the immediate executive format, the text must be repeated before it is executed. Signals sent by the immediate executive method should be in plain language or limited to commonly used signals, because there is no opportunity for verification, repetition, or acknowledgment between receipt and execution.

It should be noted in table 13-12 that for both methods of execution, the same message format is used. This format consists of a heading, the call sign of the ship or unit signaled, and that of the ship or unit signaling. The heading indicates precisely whom the signal is to and whom it is from. The heading is separated from the text by the proword, "break." The proword, "break," is used again to separate the text from the ending. The call signs in the ending indicate which ships should acknowledge the signal. This assignment of responsibility for acknowledgment must not be confused with the heading that indicates which ships are to take action on the signal. The

Methods of Execution
As Spoken on Tactical Nets

Nonexecutive Method
Peso, this is Antagonize, break, (signal), break, Beerfoam, over.
This is Beerfoam, roger, out.

Emergency Situation
Peso, this is Antagonize, break, *emergency* turn niner, I say again, *emergency* turn niner, break, Aimwell, Beerfoam, over.
This is Aimwell, roger, out.
This is Beerfoam, roger, out.

Executive Method

Delayed Executive
Peso, this Antagonize, *execute to follow*, break, turn niner, break, Drexel, over.
This is Drexel, roger, out.
Peso, this is Antagonize, turn niner, standby, *execute*, break, Enjoyment, over.
This is Enjoyment, roger, out.

Immediate Executive
Peso, this is Antagonize, *immediate execute*, break, turn niner, *I say again*, turn niner, standby, *execute*, break, Geraldine, over.
This is Geraldine, roger, out.

Note: Commas as used above signify pauses.

Table 13-12. Tactical signal execution.

ending is used by the originator to ensure that the transmission has been received. If no specific call sign is used in the ending, all units called in the heading answer by call sign in alphabetical order.

Visual signaling. There are three methods of visual communication: flag hoist, flashing light, and semaphore. The YPs use the flag hoist method extensively and flashing light only occasionally, usually in conjunction with a flag hoist to attract attention to it, or to relay the signal to a ship from which the flags cannot be seen. Semaphore is seldom used. Midshipmen are required to learn signal flags, flag hoist procedures, and the Morse code for use in flashing light, but they are not required to learn semaphore.

Flag hoist signaling is a rapid, accurate, and secure system for handling tactical and informational signals during daylight. The signals must be as brief as possible, and ships must be within easy visual range. For flag hoist signaling, the Navy uses standard international alphabet flags (square-shaped) and numeral pennants (triangular), and also numeral flags and special flags and pennants. (See appendix J.)

In addition to the flags and pennants, *tack lines* are used in visual signaling. A tack line is a length of halyard about three feet long and it is used between signals or groups of numerals to avoid ambiguity and to indicate a break. It is also used when specified by the signal book. When a signal to be flown is so long that it cannot be bent onto one hoist, it should be broken where a tack line would normally occur and flown from more than one halyard.

Multiple hoists must be hoisted in the order in which they are to be read. Signals on the YP are flown from either the port or starboard yardarm and are read from top to bottom, and from outboard to inboard on each side.

Flag hoist procedure. The ship originating a flag hoist will hoist signals *close up* (with the top of the hoist touching the block on the yardarm). All ships respond by hoisting the identical signal, flag for flag, and fly it *at the dip* (three-fourths of the way up). Small vessels or vessels without a required flag may hoist the answering pennant at the dip instead of the entire hoist. The hoist should remain at the dip until the signal is understood. When understood, the signal is closed up. The signal is executed when the originator hauls down his signal. Normally, this will not be done until all vessels have the signal closed up. When the signal is executed, all vessels haul down the signal. Some signals may prescribe a certain time for execution. Signals preceded by the emergency pennant are executed as soon as understood.

Flag hoists originated by the *OTC* (Officer in Tactical Command) are considered to be addressed to all ships unless a specific ship or ships are indicated in the heading. Ships are indicated by their visual call, a one-letter, type-of-ship designator and a numeral pennant. The numeral pennant will be the last digit of the ship's hull number. For example, the usual call for YP-658 would be: Y8. Numeral pennants, not numeral flags, are used in these visual calls.

When ships are positioned so that the originator cannot be seen by all of them, such as in a column, a signal relay system is used. Ships nearest the originator have "visual responsibility" for those farther away in the same direction. The signal closed up on the originator is hoisted at the dip on the nearest ships. It is not closed up by them until the signal is both understood on board and the correct signal has been closed up on the next ship in line away from the originator. In this manner the originator knows that when the adjacent ship or ships close up the signal, it is ready for execution on all ships. If the originator should execute the signal before all ships have acknowledged, those ships which have answered should close up and execute the signal and then relay the signal by other means to the ships for which they are responsible.

Acknowledging ships may question a signal by hoisting Interrogative while leaving the questioned signal at the dip. Flag hoists are canceled by the originator by hoisting Negative on an adjacent halyard. If only one of many signals is to be canceled it must be repeated and preceded by Negative. When all ships have acknowledged the cancellation, the hoists are cleared.

When proceeding independently in or out of port, naval ships are obliged to fly speed information signals indicating the speed that they are making through the water. Speed is always indicated by two numeral flags (never pennants)

flown at the dip. The special pennant, Speed, is never flown in conjunction with these speed indicator flags.

All ships that are designated as radio transmitting and receiving stations are assigned international radio call signs by the federal government. These call signs are flown by Navy ships from the outboard port signal halyard while underway in Inland waters. YPs hoist these international call signs smartly as soon as all lines are cast off when getting underway, and lower them leaving Annapolis Roads when red flashing bell buoy No. 8 on the port hand comes in line and forms a range with the fixed light of Greenbury Point. When entering Annapolis Roads, they will be hoisted at this same point and lowered when the first mooring line is put ashore. The international call signs for the 654-Class YPs are listed in table 13-10.

The flashing light is used aboard the YP primarily as a back-up communication system. Nonetheless, international Morse code symbols and elementary flashing light procedures must be learned. For ease of learning, the Morse code

Table 13-13. International Morse Code symbols.

Group 1	Group 2	Group 3	Group 4	Group 5
• E	• — A	— • N	— T	• — — — — 1
• • I	• — — W	— • • D	— — M	• • — — — 2
• • • S	• — — — J	— • • • B	— — — O	• • • — — 3
• • • • H	• — • R	— • — K	— — • G	• • • • — 4
• • — U	• — • • L	— • — • C	— — • • Z	• • • • • 5
• • — • F	• — — • • P	— • — — Y	— — • — Q	— • • • • 6
• • • — V		— • • — • X		— — • • • 7
				— — — • • 8
				— — — — • 9
				— — — — — 0

has been broken down into five separate groups in table 13-13.

Honors and ceremonies. The national ensign is flown from the gaff of the YP at all times while underway. When not underway, the national ensign and union jack are flown between 0800 and sunset from the flagstaff aft and jack staff forward, respectively. A ship changes status from underway to not underway when the first mooring line is put over or the anchor let go. At this moment colors are shifted with ceremony. Men are stationed at the flagstaff, jack staff, and the signal bridge. One blast on a hand whistle is sounded when the status is shifted, for example from underway to not underway, and the command, "shift colors," is given. At this command, the national ensign is lowered from the gaff and the international call sign from the yardarm. At the same time, the national ensign is run up on the flagstaff and the union jack raised on the jack staff. If the ship moors before 0800 or after sunset, the national ensign and the union jack are not raised, of course.

The ceremonial raising and lowering of the national ensign and union jack in port at 0800 and sunset is referred to as morning and evening colors. The procedure for carrying out morning and evening colors aboard the YP and other naval vessels is standard. All ships follow the timing of the Senior Officer Present. Five minutes before the ceremony, Prep is hoisted by all vessels. Prep is hauled down and attention sounded (one long blast on the hand whistle) precisely at 0800 and at sunset. All hands face the national ensign and salute. When men are formed in ranks, only the officer or petty officer in charge salutes, while the rest remain at attention. The ensign and jack are hoisted smartly and lowered slowly. They are never hoisted and then broken out. After the colors ceremony, "carry on" is sounded by three short blasts on a hand whistle.

When boarding a naval vessel between the hours of 0800 and sunset, naval officers face and salute the national ensign and then turn and salute the OOD. Civilians should face the national ensign before facing the OOD to ask permission

Table 13-14. Passing honor procedures.

OOD OF JUNIOR SHIP	OOD OF SENIOR SHIP	HAND WHISTLE SIGNAL
1. Sound "attention to (port/starboard)"		1 whistle for attention to starboard 2 whistles for attention to port
	2. Sound "attention to (port/starboard)"	
3. Sound "hand salute"	4. Sound "hand salute" 5. (after approximately 3 seconds) sound "two"	1 short whistle
6. Sound "two"		2 short whistles
8. Sound "carry on"	7. Sound "carry on"	3 short whistles

to board. The reverse order is used when disembarking. The OOD returns the salute to both the national ensign and himself.

Salutes are rendered to naval vessels by private vessels underway by *dipping* (lowering halfway) the national ensign. When these salutes are received from vessels under the registry of nations formally recognized by the United States, naval vessels will return the salute, dip for dip. To return a dip, the ensign is lowered halfway, held momentarily, and then rehoisted. When the dip has been answered, the saluting ship rehoists her colors. Naval vessels never initiate dips; they only return them.

Appropriate honors are rendered to other naval vessels, both United States and foreign, and to embarked high-ranking naval officers and civilians when they are passed close aboard. These *passing honors,* as they are called, are accomplished by calling the crew to attention on the appropriate side and having them render a hand salute. This salute is then answered by the honored ship, and then both ships carry on. The precise steps in this procedure, together with the proper hand whistle signals, are found in table 13-14. Passing honors are not rendered before 0800 or after sunset, and they are not exchanged by YPs engaged in drills. Procedures for dressing ship, half-masting colors, entering a harbor, anchoring or using a guest mooring, and other points of etiquette afloat will be covered in the next chapter.

14. Etiquette Afloat

To most seamen, a love of boats and the sea is accompanied by a profound respect and admiration for those age-old traditions long associated with the sea. These often unwritten customs and traditions provide the basis of etiquette afloat.

When entering and leaving port, particular attention should be paid to the appearance of the vessel. Lines should never be left trailing over the side. This is true at any time, of course, but such sloppiness is particularly noticeable in harbor. When a boat enters port, fenders and fender boards should be left on deck until nearing the dock. They should be taken aboard immediately after clearing the dock when leaving. There are few things that spoil the sight of a beautiful boat more than three or four fenders hanging over the side.

When entering harbor in a sailboat under power, sails should be furled neatly, sheets and halyards belayed and coiled properly, and loose gear, including clothes and towels, should be put below. Leave no *Irish pennants* (dangling rope ends). The importance of presenting a seamanlike appearance when entering and leaving harbor cannot be overemphasized.

Once in the harbor, don't anchor too close to other boats already moored. Always allow for shifts in the wind and current, leaving room to swing a full 360 degrees around the anchor. Also keep in mind that deep-draft sailboats will often swing to the current while shallow-draft boats swing to the wind. This means extra care and foresight when anchoring a sailboat in a harbor with many powerboats, and vice versa.

Often in a crowded anchorage there will be guest moorings provided by the community or local yacht club for visiting vessels. Do not pick up these moorings without first checking with the yacht club or harbor master. This is not only a courtesy, but also a precaution, since the mooring may be in disrepair or not heavy enough for your vessel.

When anchored or moored in a crowded anchorage, keep in mind that sound travels easily over the water. Late gatherings in the cockpit should be kept reasonably quiet. Boisterousness lasting until the early hours of the morning is not appreciated by others in the anchorage. Tying halyards away from aluminum masts will eliminate an objectionable source of noise on a windy evening. Keep radios turned low.

Never throw trash overboard in harbors or inland waters. The rule definitely applies to the Chesapeake Bay, since a Maryland law prohibits such pollution of its waters. All trash and garbage should be disposed of ashore or saved until well clear of the land when going offshore.

When under power, always respect the rights of boats under sail, and remember the effect that a large wake will have on a sailboat, slowing whenever possible when passing her and giving her a wide berth. Sometimes an ignorant or rude sailboat skipper will needlessly interfere with a powerboat navigating in a channel. This discourteous conduct must be taken in stride by the powerboat man and the sailboat allowed to proceed without interference. Sailboats racing should be given an especially wide berth, because wakes and wind interference left by powerboats or other sailboats can seriously affect the outcome of the race. This is especially true in light weather. When maneuvering around racing sailboats, reduce speed to minimize wake and always pass astern and to leeward of them, so their wind is not disturbed. Don't anchor near racing marks or starting or finish lines.

Channels, like roads, have two sides. Don't be a channel hog, keep to the right, and remember the proper whistle signals.

When in harbor, always proceed at a very slow speed, leaving little or no wake. In many areas, a maximum speed of five knots is allowed by law and will be posted. Whether posted or not, this rule of courtesy should be observed. This is especially important for heavy-displacement boats that make large waves.

When proceeding under sail, never interfere with a power vessel just to emphasize a sailboat's right of way. Try not to harass powerboats negotiating a crowded channel, and do not interfere with large steam vessels in restricted waters. Such prudent respect for size is common sense and also law under both International and Inland Rules of the Road.

Regatta protocol. There are many rules of etiquette afloat that are peculiar to regattas and sailboat racing in general. Entry forms required for most regattas must be filled in accurately. They often provide the basis for handicapping the entrants, and all information contained on them is assumed to be correct. These entry forms often stipulate conditions of the race or regatta (for example, rules governing the shifting of ballast, required safety equipment, etc.). These stipulations are honored without question. By the same unwritten rule of conduct, the skipper of the yacht racing under a handicap system is honor bound to race his boat loaded as nearly as possible as she was when measured. Particularly important in this regard is ballast of any type or heavy deck gear, such as the dinghy.

If, after entering a race, the skipper finds he will not be able to race his boat, he should try to notify the race committee of his change in plans before the date of the race.

Before starting a race, it is required by the racing rules (and it is also common courtesy) to keep clear of the starting area while other classes start. The same principle applies after finishing. It is also expected that boats that have not started or are not racing will keep clear of boats that are racing, regardless of who may have the right of way.

When racing, keep clear of other racing classes whenever possible. It is considered poor sportsmanship to use racing tactics such as covering and blanketing, against boats of other classes that are not actual competitors. Luffing might be considered a reasonable tactic to discourage a larger boat in another class from passing you to windward.

All boats in a possible collision situation should of course seek to avoid collision. The boat with the right of way must hold course until in extremis, but must then maneuver to avoid collision, just as the other boat must. If the skipper of a racing yacht feels that another skipper is in danger of violating the racing rules, he should so inform him. If the rules are violated and a protest results, the protesting skipper should try to inform the protested skipper immediately. The racing rules require that the red protest flag be flown and the race committee be informed of the protest when finishing, or as soon as possible.

Whenever a skipper of a boat being protested realizes that he is in fact guilty of an infraction of the rules, he should immediately withdraw from the race unless penalties are provided for the particular infraction. If, after withdrawal, he elects to continue to sail in the vicinity of the course, he must keep well clear of all racing yachts. The skipper that misses a mark or rounds a buoy the wrong way and cannot correct his mistake should immediately withdraw, regardless of whether or not any other boats are aware of his error.

It is not ethical to drop a protest just because the protested boat is eventually beaten in the race. If an infraction of the rules occurred, the case should be protested and decided. Information given to the members of the protest committee should be as accurate as possible.

In summarizing these sections, it may be sufficient to note that, interestingly enough, most rules of etiquette afloat are also good rules of safety afloat.

Flag etiquette. The flying of flags or *colors* (the term may include all of the flags flown by a vessel or it may refer only to the national or yacht ensign) on sailing and power vessels is a subject governed primarily by custom and tradition. The right of private vessels to fly national colors stems indirectly from the Navy's long traditional use of the stars and stripes. When the Continental Congress established a national flag in June, 1777, it was immediately thereafter flown from naval vessels. As the Navy then and for some time thereafter was supplemented by large numbers of privateersmen, it became customary for these privately owned naval vessels to fly the national standard as well.

The yacht ensign, a Betsy Ross flag with a fouled anchor inside the circle of thirteen white stars, is usually flown from yachts instead of the national flag (see Appendix J). It was designed by the New York Yacht Club and adopted in 1849 by the Secretary of the Navy as a signal to be flown by certain merchantmen, exempting them from entering and clearing at customs houses. Because of its similarity to the national flag, it has become the yacht ensign and is today the customary ensign for yachts to fly. All U.S. Naval Academy vessels fly the national ensign, as they are naval vessels.

Colors are flown aboard yachts, as they are in naval vessels, from 0800 until sunset while in port. Underway, entering or leaving port, they may be flown whenever there is enough light to distinguish them, but before 0800 or after sunset, they should be hauled down immediately after anchoring. When underway offshore, colors may be flown whenever required, such as when meeting other vessels. They may also be flown as needed when approaching lightships or nearing foreign shores.

14-1. The former Naval Academy 60-foot sloop *Guerriere*. Notice that it is now accepted practice to fly the national ensign (or yacht ensign) from a stern staff while under sail. The boat would give a more shipshape appearance if there were no lines hanging overboard.

a. U.S. Navy FLAG BAG: *(starting from bow)*
3, 4, p1, S, 1st, A, Prep, C, M, Speed, J, p5, R, p9, Z, Corpen, 8, U, 6, X, Negat, 2, Port, N, p2, T, 2nd, B, D, Turn, 5, Station, K, p6, W, p0, 1, 0, 3rd, H, E, Emerg, L, p7, 0, Int, Div, p4, 9, 4th, P, Form, V, G, Stbd, I, F, Q, p8, Y, Desig, 7, p3, Squad, Ans.

b. Standard FLAG BAG: *(starting from bow)*
AB 2, UJ 1, KE 3, GH 6, IV 5, FL 4, DM 7, PO 3rd, RN 1st, ST 0, CX 9, WQ 8, ZY 2nd

Table 14-1. Sequence of bunting for full-dress ship.

When making colors in the morning, if short-handed, the ensign is raised first, then the *yacht club burgee* (flag, usually triangular, designating a specific yacht club). At sunset, colors are executed in the reverse order, if shorthanded. Whenever possible, however, all colors should be raised and lowered simultaneously. The Senior Officer Present should initiate morning and evening colors, all others following his timing and example.

If the ensign is to be flown at half-mast, it must first be mastheaded and then lowered to half-mast (actually about two-thirds of staff height). Before lowering from half-mast, colors should first be mastheaded and then lowered.

At anchor, all yachts should fly the yacht ensign from a staff aft. It should be noted that members of the *U.S. Power Squadrons* (an educational organization dedicated to safety afloat and good seamanship) are entitled to fly the U.S. Power Squadron ensign in place of the yacht ensign. The Power Squadron ensign is pictured in Appendix J. Underway, the ensign is flown from a staff aft on a powerboat or a sailboat under power.

14-2. The *Fearless* in full dress.
Notice that the signal flags extend below the rail at the bow and stern. The Union Jack is shown at the bow, the Naval Academy Sailing Squadron burgee at the masthead and the Tango signal flag (launch requested) below the starboard lower spreader.

Traditionally, U.S. yachts have always flown the ensign from the leech of the after sail, but now it is permissible and proper to fly it from a staff at the stern when under sail.

The yacht club *burgee* is flown both at anchor and underway from a bow staff on powerboats, from the foremast truck of schooners, and from the mainmast truck of all other rigs.

On the Luders yawls, the U.S. Naval Academy Sailing Squadron burgee (Appendix J) is flown from the mainmast head while underway (except when racing outside Chesapeake Bay) or at anchor.

Sailing Squadron members holding the ranks of commodore, vice commodore, and rear commodore should display the flag of their rank at the mizzen masthead in the Luders yawls, except when racing. These flags should be flown day and night.

On national holidays, at regattas, and when ordered or on other special occasions, a vessel may "dress ship" with signal flags and pennants of the International Code of Signals. In order to achieve the most colorful sequence of flags and pennants, the Navy method of two signal flags to one pennant is recommended. Table 14-1 gives the order of flags for dressing ship. The ship should be dressed at 0800 and should remain dressed until sunset. The signal flags should reach from the waterline forward to the heads of all masts, and down to the waterline aft (see figure 14-2).

When visiting in foreign waters, the national ensign of the host country should be displayed from the starboard, lower mainmast spreader between 0800 and sunset.

It should go without saying that exemplary behavior and proper protocol are especially important in foreign countries, for you and your crew are in effect emissaries, or at least conspicuous representatives, of your country.

Appendix A. Inland Rules of the Road

Navigation Rules for Harbors, Rivers, and Inland Waters Generally

Inland Rules

The statutory rules for the navigation of rivers, harbors, and inland waters of the United States presently in effect are presented here (Sec. 1, 30 Stat. 96, as amended, 49 Stat. 669, as amended, 77 Stat. 281; 33 U.S.C. 154, et seq., 232, 157a). The Inland Rules do not apply to the Great Lakes and their connecting and tributary waters as far east as Montreal and the waters of the Mississippi River between its source and the Huey P. Long Bridge and all of its tributaries emptying thereinto and their tributaries, and that part of the Atchafalaya River above its junction with the Plaquemine-Morgan City alternate waterway, and the Red River of the North.

Preliminary

Demarcation of High Seas Lines (33 U.S.C. 151)

The Commandant of the Coast Guard is authorized, empowered, and directed from time to time to designate and define by suitable bearings or ranges with lighthouses, light vessels, buoys, or coast objects, the lines dividing the high seas from rivers, harbors, and inland waters.

(See Title 33, Code of Federal Regulations, Part 82.)

Adoption of Rules for Navigation of Harbors, Rivers, and Inland Waters (33 U.S.C. 154)

The following regulations for preventing collisions shall be followed by all vessels upon the harbors, rivers, and other inland waters of the United States, except the Great Lakes and their connecting and tributary waters as far east as Montreal, and the waters of the Mississippi River between its source and the Huey P. Long Bridge, and all of its tributaries emptying thereinto and their tributaries and that part of the Atchafalaya River above its junction with the Plaquemine-Morgan City alternate waterway, and the Red River of the North; and are declared special rules duly made by local authority.

Authority for Pilot Rules (33 U.S.C. 157)

(a) The Secretary of the Department in which the Coast Guard is operating shall establish such rules to be observed, on the waters described in section 154 of this title, by steam vessels in passing each other and as to the lights and day signals to be carried on such waters by ferryboats, by vessels and craft of all types when in tow of steam vessels or operating by hand power or horsepower or drifting with the current, and by any other vessels not otherwise provided for, not inconsistent with the provisions of this Act, as he from time to time may deem necessary for safety, which rules are declared special rules duly made by local authority. A pamphlet containing such Act and regulations shall be furnished to all vessels and craft subject to this Act. On vessels and craft over sixty-five feet in length the pamphlet shall, where practicable, be kept on board and available for ready reference.

(b) Except in an emergency, before any rules or any alteration, amendment, or repeal thereof, are established by the Secretary under the provisions of this section, the said Secretary shall publish the proposed rules, alterations, amendments, or repeals, and public hearings shall be held with respect thereto on such notice as the Secretary deems reasonable under the circumstances.

[Also see Article 9(d) on page 338.]

Navy and Coast Guard Vessel Exceptions (Sec. 1, 59 Stat. 590; 33 U.S.C. 360)

Any requirement as to the number, position, range of visibility, or arc of visibility of lights required to be displayed by vessels under * * * sections 154 to 231 of this title * * * and all laws amendatory thereto, shall not apply to any vessel of the Navy or of the Coast Guard, where the Secretary of the Navy, or the Secretary of Transportation in the case of Coast Guard vessels operating under the Department of Transportation, or such official or officials as either may designate, shall find or certify that, by reason of special construction, it is not possible with respect to such vessel or class of vessels to comply with the statutory provisions as to the number, position, range of visibility, or arc of visibility of lights. The lights of any such exempted vessel or class of vessels shall, however, comply as closely to the requirements of the applicable sections as the Secretary shall find to be feasible.

(See Title 33, Code of Federal Regulations, Part 135, and Title 32, Code of Federal Regulations, Parts 706 and 707.)

Publication of Navy and Coast Guard Vessel Exceptions (Sec. 2, 59 Stat. 591; 33 U.S.C. 360a)

When the Secretary of the Navy or the Secretary of Transportation, or such official or officials as either may designate, shall make any finding or certification as prescribed in section 360 of this title, notice of such finding or certification and the character and position

of the lights to be displayed on such vessel shall be published in "Notice to Mariners".

Penalty for Violations by Pilot, Engineer, Mate or Master (33 U.S.C. 158)

Every licensed and unlicensed pilot, engineer, mate, or master of any vessel who violates the provisions of this Act or the regulations established pursuant hereto shall be liable to a penalty of not exceeding $500, and for all damages sustained by any passenger, in his person or baggage, as a result of such violation: *Provided,* That nothing herein shall relieve any vessel, owner, or corporation from any liability incurred by reason of such violation.

Penalty for Violations by Vessel (33 U.S.C. 159)

Every vessel which is navigated in violation of any of the provisions of this Act or the regulations established pursuant hereto shall be liable to a penalty of $500, one-half to go to the informer, for which sum such vessel may be seized and proceeded against by action in any district court of the United States having jurisdiction of the offense.

Definitions

"Sailing Vessel," "Steam Vessel," and "Under Way" Defined (33 U.S.C. 155)

In the following rules every steam vessel which is under sail and not under steam is to be considered a sailing vessel, and every vessel under steam, whether under sail or not, is to be considered a steam vessel.

The words "steam vessel" shall include any vessel propelled by machinery.

A vessel is "under way" within the meaning of these rules, when she is not at anchor, or made fast to the shore, or aground.

"Visible" as Applied to Lights Defined (33 U.S.C. 156)

The word "visible" in these rules, when applied to lights, shall mean visible on a dark night with a clear atmosphere.

Lights

Time for Lights

Article 1. The rules concerning lights shall be complied with in all weathers from sunset to sunrise, and during such time no other lights which may be mistaken for the prescribed lights shall be exhibited.

Steam Vessels Under Way

Art. 2. A steam vessel when under way shall carry—

(a) On or in front of the foremast, or if a vessel without a foremast then in the fore part of the vessel, a bright white light so constructed as to show an unbroken light over an arc of the horizon of twenty points of the compass, so fixed as to throw the light ten points on each side of the vessel, namely, from right ahead to two points abaft the beam on either side, and of such a character as to be visible at a distance of at least five miles.

(b) On the starboard side a green light so constructed as to show an unbroken light over an arc of the horizon of ten points of the compass, so fixed as to throw the light from right ahead to two points abaft the beam on the starboard side, and of such a character as to be visible at a distance of at least two miles.

(c) On the port side a red light so constructed as to show an unbroken light over an arc of the horizon of ten points of the compass, so fixed as to throw the light from right ahead to two points abaft the beam on the port side, and of such a character as to be visible at a distance of at least two miles.

(d) The said green and red side lights shall be fitted with inboard screens projecting at least three feet forward from the light, so as to prevent these lights from being seen across the bow.

(e) A seagoing steam vessel when under way may carry an additional white light similar in construction to the light mentioned in paragraph (a) of this article. These two lights shall be so placed in line with the keel that one shall be at least fifteen feet higher than the other, and in such a position with reference to each other that the lower light shall be forward of the upper one. The vertical distance between these lights shall be less than the horizontal distance.

(f) All steam vessels (except seagoing vessels and ferryboats), shall carry in addition to green and red lights required by article 2(b) and (c), and screens as required by article 2(d), a central range of two white lights; the after light being carried at an elevation at least fifteen feet above the light at the head of the vessel. The headlight shall be so constructed as to show an unbroken light through twenty points of the compass, namely, from right ahead to two points abaft the beam on either side of the vessel, and the after light so as to show all around the horizon.

Steam Vessels—When Towing or Pushing

Art. 3. (a) A steam vessel when towing another vessel or vessels alongside or by pushing ahead shall, in addition to her side lights, carry two bright white lights in a vertical line, one over the other, not less than three feet apart, and when towing one or more vessels astern, regardless of the length of the tow, shall carry an additional bright white light three feet above or below such lights. Each of these lights shall be of the same construction and character, and shall be carried in the same position as the white light mentioned in article 2(a) or the after range light mentioned in article 2(f).

(b) A steam vessel carrying towing lights the same as the white light mentioned in article 2(a), when pushing another vessel or vessels ahead, shall also carry at or near the stern two bright amber lights in a vertical line, one over the other, not less than three feet apart; each of these lights shall be so constructed as to show an unbroken light over an arc of the horizon of twelve points of the compass, so fixed as to show the light six points from right aft on each side of the vessel, and of such a character as to be visible at a distance of at least two miles. A steam vessel carrying towing lights the same as the white light mentioned in article 2(a) may also carry, irrespective of the position of the tow, the after range light mentioned in article 2(f); however, if the after range light is carried by such a vessel when pushing another vessel or vessels ahead, the amber lights shall be carried in a vertical line with and at least three feet lower than the after range light. A steam vessel carrying towing lights the same as the white light mentioned in article 2(a), when towing one or more vessels astern, may also carry, in lieu of the stern light specified in article 10, a small white light abaft the funnel or aftermast for the tow to steer by, but such light shall not be visible forward of the beam.

Sailing Vessels and Vessels in Tow

Art. 5. A sailing vessel under way and any vessel being towed, except barges, canal boats, scows, and other vessels of nondescript type, when in tow of steam vessels, shall carry the same lights as are prescribed by article 2 for a steam vessel under way, with the exception of the white lights mentioned therein, which they shall never carry.

Small Vessels in Bad Weather

Art. 6. Whenever, as in the case of vessels of less than ten gross tons under way during bad weather, the green and red side lights cannot be fixed, these lights shall be kept at hand, lighted and ready for use; and shall, on the approach of or to other vessels, be exhibited on their respective sides in sufficient time to prevent collision, in such manner as to make them most visible, and so that the green light shall not be seen on the port side nor the red light on the starboard side, nor, if practicable, more than two points abaft the beam on their respective sides. To make the use of these portable lights more certain and easy the lanterns containing them shall each be painted outside with the color of the light they respectively contain, and shall be provided with proper screens.

Small Rowing Boats, Rafts, and Other Craft not Provided For

Art. 7. Rowing boats, whether under oars or sail, shall have ready at hand a lantern showing a white light which shall be temporarily exhibited in sufficient time to prevent collision.

Art. 9(d). Rafts, or other water craft not herein provided for, navigating by hand power, horse power, or by the current of the river, shall carry one or more good white lights, which shall be placed in such manner as shall be prescribed by the Commandant of the Coast Guard.

Pilot Vessels

Art. 8. Pilot vessels when engaged on their stations on pilotage duty shall not show the lights required for other vessels, but shall carry a white light at the masthead, visible all around the horizon, and shall also exhibit a flare-up light or flare-up lights at short intervals, which shall never exceed fifteen minutes.

On the near approach of or to other vessels, they shall have their side lights lighted, ready for use, and shall flash or show them at short intervals, to indicate the direction in which they are heading, but the green light shall not be shown on the port side nor the red light on the starboard side.

A pilot vessel of such a class as to be obliged to go alongside of a vessel to put a pilot on board may show the white light instead of carrying it at the masthead, and may, instead of the colored lights above mentioned, have at hand ready for use, a lantern, with a green glass on the one side and a red glass on the other, to be used as prescribed above.

Pilot vessels, when not engaged on their station on pilotage duty, shall carry lights similar to those of other vessels of their tonnage.

A steam pilot vessel, when engaged on her station on pilotage duty and in waters of the United States, and not at anchor, shall in addition to the lights required for all pilot boats, carry at a distance of eight feet below her white masthead light a red light, visible all around the horizon and of such a character as to be visible on a dark night with a clear atmosphere at a distance of at least two miles, and also the colored side lights required to be carried by vessels when under way.

When engaged on her station on pilotage duty and in waters of the United States, and at anchor, she shall carry in addition to the lights required for all pilot boats the red light above mentioned, but not the colored side lights.

When not engaged on her station on pilotage duty, she shall carry the same lights as other steam vessels.

Fishing Vessels

Art. 9(a). Fishing vessels of less than ten gross tons, when under way and when not having their nets, trawls, dredges, or lines in the water, shall not be required to carry the colored side lights; but every such vessel shall, in lieu thereof, have ready at hand a lantern with a green glass on one side and a red glass on the other side, and on approaching to or being approached by another vessel such lantern shall be exhibited in sufficient time to prevent collision, so that the green light shall not be seen on the port side nor the red light on the starboard side.

(b) All fishing vessels and fishing boats of ten gross tons or upward, when under way and when not having their nets, trawls, dredges, or lines in the water, shall carry and show the same lights as other vessels under way.

(c) All vessels, when trawling, dredging, or fishing with any kind of drag nets or lines, shall exhibit, from some part of the vessel where they can be best seen, two lights. One of these lights shall be red and the other shall be white. The red light shall be above the white light, and shall be at a vertical distance from it of not less than six feet and not more than twelve feet; and the horizontal distance between them, if any, shall not be more than ten feet. These two lights shall be of such a character and contained in lanterns of such construction as to be visible all around the horizon, the white light a distance of not less than three miles and the red light of not less than two miles.

Stern Lights

Art. 10(a). A vessel when underway, if not otherwise required by these rules to carry one or more lights visible from aft, shall carry at her stern a white light, so constructed that it shall show an unbroken light over an arc of the horizon of twelve points of the compass, so fixed as to show the light six points from right aft on each side of the vessel, and of such a character as to be visible at a distance of at least two miles. Such light shall be carried as nearly as practicable on the same level as the side lights.

(b) In a small vessel, if it is not possible on account of bad weather or other sufficient cause for this light to be fixed, an electric torch or a lighted lantern shall be kept at hand ready for use and shall, on the approach of an overtaking vessel, be shown in sufficient time to prevent collision.

Anchor Lights

Art. 11(a). Except as provided in paragraph (c) of this article, a vessel under one hundred and fifty feet in length when at anchor shall carry forward, where it can best be seen, a white light in a lantern so constructed as to show a clear, uniform, and unbroken light visible all around the horizon at a distance of at least two miles.

(b) Except as provided in paragraph (c) of this article, a vessel of one hundred and fifty feet or upward in length, when at anchor, shall carry in the forward part of the vessel, at a height of not less than twenty feet above the hull, one such light, and at or near the stern of the vessel, and at such a height that it shall be not less than fifteen feet lower than the forward light, another such light.

(c) The Secretary of Transportation may, after investigation, by rule, regulation, or order, designate such areas as he may deem proper as 'special anchorage areas'; such special anchorage areas may from time to time be changed, or abolished, if after investigation the Secretary of Transportation shall deem such change or abolition in the interest of navigation. When anchored within such an area—

(1) a vessel of not more than sixty-five feet in length shall not be required to carry or exhibit the white light required by this article;

(2) a barge, canal boat, scow, or other nondescript craft of one hundred and fifty feet or upward in length may carry and exhibit the single white light prescribed by paragraph (a) of this article in lieu of the two white lights prescribed by paragraph (b) of this article; and

(3) where two or more barges, canal boats, scows, or other nondescript craft are tied together and anchored as a unit, the anchor light prescribed by this article need be displayed only on the vessel having its anchor down.

Signals to Attract Attention

Art. 12. Every vessel may, if necessary, in order to attract attention, in addition to the lights which she is by these rules required to carry, show a flare-up light or use any detonating signal that cannot be mistaken for a distress signal.

Naval Lights and Recognition Signals

Art. 13. Nothing in these rules shall interfere with the operation of any special rules made by the Government of any nation with respect to additional station and signal lights for two or more ships of war or for vessels sailing under convoy, or with the exhibition of recognition signals adopted by shipowners, which have been authorized by their respective Governments, and duly registered and published.

Steam Vessel Under Sail by Day

Art. 14. A steam vessel proceeding under sail only, but having her funnel up, may carry in daytime, forward, where it can best be seen, one black ball or shape two feet in diameter.

Sound Signals and Conduct in Restricted Visibility

Preliminary

Art. 15. All signals prescribed by this article for vessels under way shall be given: 1. By "steam vessels" on the whistle or siren. 2. By "sailing vessels" and "vessels towed" on the foghorn.

The words "prolonged blast" used in this article shall mean a blast of from four to six seconds duration.

A steam vessel shall be provided with an efficient whistle or siren, sounded by steam or by some substitute for steam, so placed that the sound may not be intercepted by any obstruction, and with an efficient foghorn; also with an efficient bell.

A sailing vessel of twenty tons gross tonnage, or upward shall be provided with a similar foghorn and bell.

If fog, mist, falling snow, or heavy rainstorms, whether by day or night, the signals described in this article shall be used as follows, namely:

Steam Vessel Under Way

(a) A steam vessel under way shall sound, at intervals of not more than one minute, a prolonged blast.

Sailing Vessel Under Way

(c) A sailing vessel under way shall sound, at intervals of not more than one minute, when on the starboard tack, one blast; when on the port tack, two blasts in succession, and when with the wind abaft the beam, three blasts in succession.

Vessel at Anchor

(d) A vessel when at anchor shall, at intervals of not more than one minute, ring the bell rapidly for about five seconds, except that the following vessels shall not be required to sound this signal when anchored in a special anchorage area established pursuant to paragraph (c) of article 11: (1) a vessel of not more than sixty-five feet in length; and (2) a barge, canal boat, scow, or other nondescript craft.

Vessels Towing or Towed

(e) A steam vessel when towing, shall, instead of the signals prescribed in paragraph (a) of this article, at intervals of not more than one minute, sound three blasts in succession, namely, one prolonged blast followed by two short blasts. A vessel towed may give this signal and she shall not give any other.

Rafts or Other Craft Not Provided For

(f) All rafts or other water craft, not herein provided for, navigating by hand power, horse power, or by the current of the river, shall sound a blast of the foghorn, or equivalent signal, at intervals of not more than one minute.

Speed in Fog

Art. 16. Every vessel shall, in a fog, mist, falling snow, or heavy rainstorms, go at a moderate speed, having careful regard to the existing circumstances and conditions.

A steam vessel hearing, apparently forward of her beam, the fog signal of a vessel the position of which is not ascertained shall, so far as the circumstances of the case admit, stop her engines, and then navigate with caution until danger of collision is over.

Steering and Sailing Rules

Preliminary

Risk of collision can, when circumstances permit, be ascertained by carefully watching the compass bearing of an approaching vessel. If the bearing does not appreciably change, such risk should be deemed to exist.

Sailing Vessels

Art. 17. When two sailing vessels are approaching one another, so as to involve risk of collision, one of them shall keep out of the way of the other as follows, namely:

(a) A vessel which is running free shall keep out of the way of a vessel which is close-hauled.

(b) A vessel which is close-hauled on the port tack shall keep out of the way of a vessel which is close-hauled on the starboard tack.

(c) When both are running free, with the wind on different sides, the vessel which has the wind on the port side shall keep out of the way of the other.

(d) When both are running free, with the wind on the same side, the vessel which is to the windward shall keep out of the way of the vessel which is to the leeward.

(e) A vessel which has the wind aft shall keep out of the way of the other vessel.

Vessels Meeting, Nearing Bends, Leaving Berths and Overtaking

Art. 18. Rule I. When steam vessels are approaching each other head and head, that is, end on, or nearly so, it shall be the duty of each to pass on the port side of the other; and either vessel shall give, as a signal of her intention, one short and distinct blast of her whistle, which the other vessel shall answer promptly by a similar blast of her whistle, and thereupon such vessels shall pass on the port side of each other.

But if the courses of such vessels are so far on the starboard of each other as not to be considered as meeting head and head, either vessel shall immediately give two short and distinct blasts of her whistle, which the other vessel shall answer promptly by two similar blasts of her whistle, and they shall pass on the starboard side of each other.

The foregoing only applies to cases where vessels are meeting end on, or nearly end on, in such a manner as to involve risk of collision; in other words, to cases in which, by day, each vessel sees the masts of the other in a line, or nearly in a line, with her own, and by night to cases in which each vessel is in such a position as to see both the sidelights of the other.

It does not apply by day to cases in which a vessel sees another ahead crossing her own course, or by night to cases where the red light of one vessel is opposed to the red light of the other, or where the green light of one vessel is opposed to the green light of the other, or where a red light without a green light or a green light without a red light, is seen ahead, or where both green and red lights are seen anywhere but ahead.

Rule III. If, when steam vessels are approaching each other, either vessel fails to understand the course or intention of the other, from any cause, the vessel so in doubt shall immediately signify the same by giving several short and rapid blasts, not less than four, of the steam whistle.

Rule V. Whenever a steam vessel is nearing a short bend or curve in the channel, where, from the height of the banks or other cause, a steam vessel approaching from the opposite direction cannot be seen for a distance of half a mile, such steam vessel, when she shall have arrived within half a mile of such curve or bend, shall give a signal by one long blast of the steam whistle, which signal shall be answered by a similar blast given by any approaching steam vessel that may be within hearing. Should such signal be so answered by a steam vessel upon the farther side of such bend, then the usual signals for meeting and passing shall immediately be given and answered; but, if the first alarm signal of such vessel be not answered, she is to consider the channel clear and govern herself accordingly.

When steam vessels are moved from their docks, or berths, and other boats are liable to pass from any direction toward them, they shall give the same signal as in the case of vessels meeting at a bend, but immediately after clearing the berths so as to be fully in sight they shall be governed by the steering and sailing rules.

Rule VIII. When steam vessels are running in the same direction, and the vessel which is astern shall desire to pass on the right or starboard hand of the vessel ahead, she shall give one short blast of the steam whistle, as a signal of such desire, and if the vessel ahead answers with one blast, she shall direct her course to starboard; or if she shall desire to pass on the left or port side of the vessel ahead, she shall give two short blasts of the steam whistle as a signal of such desire, and if the vessel ahead answers with two blasts, shall direct her course to port; or if the vessel ahead does not think it safe for the vessel astern to attempt to pass at that point, she shall immediately signify the same by giving several short and rapid blasts of the steam whistle, not less than four, and under no circumstances shall the vessel astern attempt to pass the vessel ahead until such time as they have reached a point where it can be safely done, when said vessel ahead shall signify her willingness by blowing the proper signals. The vessel ahead shall in no case attempt to cross the bow or crowd upon the course of the passing vessel.

Rule IX. The whistle signals provided in the rules under this article, for steam vessels meeting, passing, or overtaking, are never to be used except when steamers are in sight of each other, and the course and position of each can be determined in the day time by a sight of the vessel itself, or by night by seeing its signal lights.

In fog, mist, falling snow, or heavy rainstorms, when vessels can not see each other, fog signals only must be given.

Two Steam Vessels Crossing

Art. 19. When two steam vessels are crossing, so as to involve risk of collision, the vessel which has the other on her own starboard side shall keep out of the way of the other.

Sailing Vessel Right-Of-Way

Art. 20. When a steam vessel and a sailing vessel are proceeding in such directions as to involve risk of collision, the steam vessel shall keep out of the way of the sailing vessel. This rule shall not give to a sailing vessel the right to hamper, in a narrow channel, the safe passage of a steam vessel which can navigate only inside that channel.

Stand-on Vessel Duty

Art. 21. Where, by any of these rules, one of the two vessels is to keep out of the way, the other shall keep her course and speed.
[See Articles 27 and 29, pp. 342–343.]

Give-Way Vessel Duty

Art. 22. Every vessel which is directed by these rules to keep out of the way of another vessel shall, if the circumstances of the case admit, avoid crossing ahead of the other.

Art. 23. Every steam vessel which is directed by these rules to keep out of the way of another vessel shall, on approaching her, if necessary, slacken her speed or stop or reverse.

Overtaking

Art. 24. Notwithstanding anything contained in these rules every vessel, overtaking any other, shall keep out of the way of the overtaken vessel.

Every vessel coming up with another vessel from any direction more than two points abaft her beam, that is, in such a position, with reference to the vessel which she is overtaking that at night she would be unable to see either of the vessel's side lights, shall be deemed to be an overtaking vessel; and no subse-quent alteration of the bearing between the two vessels shall make the overtaking vessel a crossing vessel within the meaning of these rules, or relieve her of the duty of keeping clear of the overtaken vessel until she is finally past and clear.

As by day the overtaking vessel cannot always know with certainty whether she is forward of or abaft this direction from the other vessel she should, if in doubt, assume that she is an overtaking vessel and keep out of the way.

Narrow Channels

Art. 25. In narrow channels every steam vessel shall, when it is safe and practicable, keep to that side of the fairway or midchannel which lies on the starboard side of such vessel.

In narrow channels a steam vessel of less than sixty-five feet in length shall not hamper the safe passage of a vessel which can navigate only inside that channel.
[See Article 18, Rule V, pp. 341.]

Fishing Vessel Right-of-Way

Art. 26. Sailing vessels under way shall keep out of the way of sailing vessels or boats fishing with nets, lines, or trawls. This rule shall not give any vessel or boat engaged in fishing the right of obstructing a fairway used by vessels other than fishing vessels or boats.

General Prudential Rule

Art. 27. In obeying and construing these rules due regard shall be had to all dangers of navigation and collision, and to any special circumstances which may render a departure from the above rules necessary in order to avoid immediate danger.

Sound Signals for Vessels in Sight of One Another

Backing Signal

Art. 28. When vessels are in sight of one another a steam vessel under way whose engines are going at full speed astern shall indicate that fact by three short blasts on the whistle.
[See Article 18, page 341.]

Miscellaneous

Rule of Good Seamanship

Art. 29. Nothing in these rules shall exonerate any vessel, or the owner or master or crew thereof, from the consequences of any neglect to carry lights or signals, or of any neglect to keep a proper lookout, or of the neglect of any precaution which may be required by the ordinary practice of seamen, or by the special circumstances of the case.

Lights on United States Naval Vessels and Coast Guard Cutters

Art. 30. The exhibition of any light on board of a vessel of war of the United States or a Coast Guard cutter may be suspended whenever, in the opinion of the Secretary of the Navy, the commander in chief of a squadron, or the commander of a vessel acting singly, the special character of the service may require it.

Distress Signals

Art. 31. When a vessel is in distress and requires assistance from other vessels or from the shore the following shall be the signal to be used or displayed by her, either together or separately, namely:

In the daytime—

A continuous sounding with any fog-signal apparatus, or firing a gun.

At night—

First. Flames on the vessel as from a burning tar barrel, oil barrel, and so forth.

Second. A continuous sounding with any fog-signal apparatus, or firing a gun.

Orders to Helmsmen

Art. 32. All orders to helmsmen shall be given as follows:

"Right Rudder" to mean "Direct the vessel's head to starboard."

"Left Rudder" to mean "Direct the vessel's head to port."

Appendix B. International Regulations for Preventing Collisions at Sea, 1972

Part A. General

Application

Rule 1. (a) These Rules shall apply to all vessels upon the high seas and in all waters connected therewith navigable by seagoing vessels.

(b) Nothing in these Rules shall interfere with the operation of special rules made by an appropriate authority for roadsteads, harbours, rivers, lakes or inland waterways connected with the high seas and navigable by seagoing vessels. Such special rules shall conform as closely as possible to these Rules.

(c) Nothing in these Rules shall interfere with the operation of any special rules made by the Government of any State with respect to additional station or signal lights or whistle signals for ships of war and vessels proceeding under convoy, or with respect to additional station or signal lights for fishing vessels engaged in fishing as fleet. These additional station or signal lights or whistle signals shall, so far as possible, be such that they cannot be mistaken for any light or signal authorized elsewhere under these Rules.

(d) Traffic separation schemes may be adopted by the Organization for the purpose of these Rules.

(e) Whenever the Government concerned shall have determined that a vessel of special construction or purpose cannot comply fully with the provisions of any of these Rules with respect to the number, position, range or arc of visibility of lights or shapes, as well as to the disposition and characteristics of sound-signalling appliances, without interfering with the special function of the vessel, such vessel shall comply with such other provisions in regard to the number, position, range or arc of visibility of lights or shapes, as well as to the disposition and characteristics of sound-signalling appliances, as her Government shall have determined to be the closest possible compliance with these Rules in respect to that vessel.

Responsibility

Rule 2. (a) Nothing in these Rules shall exonerate any vessel, or the owner, master or crew thereof, from the consequences of any neglect to comply with these Rules or of the neglect of any precaution which may be required by the ordinary practice of seamen, or by the special circumstances of the case.

(b) In construing and complying with these Rules due regard shall be had to all dangers of navigation and collision and to any special circumstances, including the limitations of the vessels involved, which may make a departure from these Rules necessary to avoid immediate danger.

General Definitions

Rule 3. For the purpose of these Rules, except where the context otherwise requires:

(a) The word "vessel" includes every description of water craft, including non-displacement craft and seaplanes, used or capable of being used as a means of transportation on water.

(b) The term "power-driven vessel" means any vessel propelled by machinery.

(c) The term "sailing vessel" means any vessel under sail provided that propelling machinery, if fitted, is not being used.

(d) The term "vessel engaged in fishing" means any vessel fishing with nets, lines, trawls or other fishing apparatus which restrict manoeuvrability, but does not include a vessel fishing with trolling lines or other fishing apparatus which do not restrict manoeuvrability.

(e) The word "seaplane" includes any aircraft designed to manoeuvre on the water.

(f) The term "vessel not under command" means a vessel which through some exceptional circumstance is unable to manoeuvre as required by these Rules and is therefore unable to keep out of the way of another vessel.

(g) The term "vessel restricted in her ability to manoeuvre" means a vessel which from the nature of her work is restricted in her ability to manoeuvre as required by these Rules and is therefore unable to keep out of the way of another vessel.

The following vessels shall be regarded as vessels restricted in their ability to manoeuvre: (i) a vessel engaged in laying, servicing or picking up a navigation mark, submarine cable or pipeline; (ii) a vessel engaged in dredging, surveying or underwater operations; (iii) a vessel engaged in replenishment or transferring persons, provisions or cargo while underway; (iv) a vessel engaged in the launching or recovery of aircraft; (v) a vessel engaged in minesweeping operations; (vi) a vessel engaged in a towing operation such as severely restricts the towing vessel and her tow in their ability to deviate from their course.

(h) The term "vessel constrained by her draught" means a power-driven vessel which because of her draught in relation to the available depth of water is severely restricted in her ability to deviate from the course she is following.

(i) The word "underway" means that a vessel is not at anchor, or made fast to the shore, or aground.

(j) The words "length" and "breadth" of a vessel mean her length overall and greatest breadth.

(k) Vessels shall be deemed to be in sight of one another only when one can be observed visually from the other.

(l) The term "restricted visibility" means any condition in which visibility is restricted by fog, mist, falling snow, heavy rainstorms, sandstorms or any other similar causes.

Part B. Steering and Sailing Rules

Section I. Conduct of Vessels in Any Condition of Visibility

Application

Rule 4. Rules in this Section apply in any condition of visibility.

Look-out

Rule 5. Every vessel shall at all times maintain a proper look-out by sight and hearing as well as by all available means appropriate in the prevailing circumstances and conditions so as to make a full appraisal of the situation and of the risk of collision.

Safe Speed

Rule 6. Every vessel shall at all times proceed at a safe speed so that she can take proper and effective action to avoid collision and be stopped within a distance appropriate to the prevailing circumstances and conditions.

In determining a safe speed the following factors shall be among those taken into account:

(a) By all vessels: (i) the state of visibility; (ii) the traffic density including concentrations of fishing vessels or any other vessels; (iii) the manoeuvrability of the vessel with special reference to stopping distance and turning ability in the prevailing conditions; (iv) at night the presence of background light such as from shore lights or from back scatter of her own lights; (v) the state of wind, sea and current, and the proximity of navigational hazards; (vi) the draught in relation to the available depth of water.

(b) Additionally, by vessels with operational radar: (i) the characteristics, efficiency and limitations of the radar equipment; (ii) any constraints imposed by the radar range scale in use; (iii) the effect on radar detection of the sea state, weather and other sources of interference; (iv) the possibility that small vessels, ice and other floating objects may not be detected by radar at an adequate range; (v) the number, location and movement of vessels detected by radar; (vi) the more exact assessment of the visibility that may be possible when radar is used to determine the range of vessels or other objects in the vicinity.

Risk of Collision

Rule 7. (a) Every vessel shall use all available means appropriate to the prevailing circumstances and conditions to determine if risk of collision exists. If there is any doubt such risk shall be deemed to exist.

(b) Proper use shall be made of radar equipment if fitted and operational, including long-range scanning to obtain early warning of risk of collision and radar plotting or equivalent systematic observation of detected objects.

(c) Assumptions shall not be made on the basis of scanty information, especially scanty radar information.

(d) In determining if risk of collision exists the following considerations shall be among those taken into account: (i) such risk shall be deemed to exist if the compass bearing of an approaching vessel does not appreciably change; (ii) such risk may sometimes exist even when an appreciable bearing change is evident, particularly when approaching a very large vessel or a tow or when approaching a vessel at close range.

Action to Avoid Collision

Rule 8. (a) Any action taken to avoid collision shall, if the circumstances of the case admit, be positive, made in ample time and with due regard to the observance of good seamanship.

(b) Any alteration of course and/or speed to avoid collision shall, if the circumstances of the case admit, be large enough to be readily apparent to another vessel observing visually or by radar; a succession of small alterations of course and/or speed should be avoided.

(c) If there is sufficient sea room, alteration of course alone may be the most effective action to avoid a close-quarters situation provided that it is made in good time, is substantial and does not result in another close-quarters situation.

(d) Action taken to avoid collision with another vessel shall be such as to result in passing at a safe distance. The effectiveness of the action shall be carefully checked until the other vessel is finally past and clear.

(e) If necessary to avoid collision or allow more time to assess the situation, a vessel shall slacken her speed or take all way off by stopping or reversing her means of propulsion.

Narrow Channels

Rule 9. (a) A vessel proceeding along the course of a narrow channel or fairway shall keep as near to the outer limit of the channel or fairway which lies on her starboard side as is safe and practicable.

(b) A vessel of less than 20 metres in length or a sailing vessel shall not impede the passage of a vessel which can safely navigate only within a narrow channel or fairway.

(c) A vessel engaged in fishing shall not impede the passage of any other vessel navigating within a narrow channel or fairway.

(d) A vessel shall not cross a narrow channel or fairway if such crossing impedes the passage of a vessel which can safely navigate only within such channel or fairway. The latter vessel may use the sound signal prescribed in Rule 34(d) if in doubt as to the intention of the crossing vessel.

(e) (i) In a narrow channel or fairway when overtaking can take place only if the vessel to be overtaken has to take action to permit safe passing, the vessel intending to overtake shall indicate her intention by sounding the appropriate signal prescribed in Rule 34(c) (i). The vessel to be overtaken shall, if in agreement, sound the appropriate signal prescribed in Rule 34(c) (ii) and take steps to permit safe passing. If in doubt she may sound the signals prescribed in Rule 34(d). (ii) This Rule does not relieve the overtaking vessel of her obligation under Rule 13.

(f) A vessel nearing a bend or an area of narrow channel or fairway where other vessels may be obscured by an intervening obstruction shall navigate with particular alertness and caution and shall sound the appropriate signal prescribed in Rule 34(e).

(g) Any vessel shall, if the circumstances of the case admit, avoid anchoring in a narrow channel.

Traffic Separation Schemes

Rule 10. (a) This Rule applies to traffic separation schemes adopted by the Organization.

(b) A vessel using a traffic separation scheme shall: (i) proceed in the appropriate traffic lane in the general direction of traffic flow for that lane; (ii) so far as practicable keep clear of a traffic separation line or separation zone; (iii) normally join or leave a traffic lane at the termination of the lane, but when joining or leaving from the side shall do so at as small an angle to the general direction of traffic flow as practicable.

(c) A vessel shall so far as practicable avoid crossing traffic lanes, but if obliged to do so shall cross as nearly as practicable at right angles to the general direction of traffic flow.

(d) Inshore traffic zones shall not normally be used by through traffic which can safely use the appropriate traffic lane within the adjacent traffic separation scheme.

(e) A vessel, other than a crossing vessel, shall not normally enter a separation zone or cross a separation line except: (i) in cases of emergency to avoid immediate danger; (ii) to engage in fishing within a separation zone.

(f) A vessel navigating in areas near the terminations of traffic separation schemes shall do so with particular caution.

(g) A vessel shall so far as practicable avoid anchoring in a traffic separation scheme or in areas near its terminations.

(h) A vessel not using a traffic separation scheme shall avoid it by as wide a margin as is practicable.

(i) A vessel engaged in fishing shall not impede the passage of any vessel following a traffic lane.

(j) A vessel of less than 20 metres in length or a sailing vessel shall not impede the safe passage of a power-driven vessel following a traffic lane.

Section II. Conduct of Vessels in Sight of One Another

Application

Rule 11. Rules in this Section apply to vessels in sight of one another.

Sailing Vessels

Rule 12. (a) When two sailing vessels are approaching one another, so as to involve risk of collision, one of them shall keep out of the way of the other as follows: (i) when each has the wind on a different side, the vessel which has the wind on the port side shall keep out of the way of the other; (ii) when both have the wind on the same side, the vessel which is to windward shall keep out of the way of the vessel which is too leeward; (iii) if a vessel with the wind on the port side sees a vessel to windward and cannot determine with certainty whether the other vessel has the wind on the port or on the starboard side, she shall keep out of the way of the other.

(b) For the purposes of this Rule the windward side shall be deemed to be the side opposite to that on which the mainsail is carried or, in the case of a square-rigged vessel, the side opposite to that on which the largest fore-and-aft sail is carried.

Overtaking

Rule 13. (a) Notwithstanding anything contained in the Rules of this Section any vessel overtaking any other shall keep out of the way of the vessel being overtaken.

(b) A vessel shall be deemed to be overtaking when coming up with another vessel from a direction more than 22.5 degrees abaft her beam; that is, in such a position with reference to the vessel she is overtaking, that at night she would be able to see only the sternlight of that vessel but neither of her sidelights.

(c) When a vessel is in any doubt as to whether she is overtaking another, she shall assume that this is the case and act accordingly.

(d) Any subsequent alteration of the bearing between the two vessels shall not make the overtaking vessel a crossing vessel within the meaning of these Rules or relieve her of the duty of keeping clear of the overtaken vessel until she is finally past and clear.

Head-on Situation

Rule 14. (a) When two power-driven vessels are meeting on reciprocal or nearly reciprocal courses so as to involve risk of collision each shall alter her course to starboard so that each shall pass on the port side of the other.

(b) Such a situation shall be deemed to exist when a vessel sees the other ahead or nearly ahead and by night she could see the masthead lights of the other in a line or nearly in a line and/or both sidelights and by day she observes the corresponding aspect of the other vessel.

(c) When a vessel is in any doubt as to whether such a situation exists she shall assume that it does exist and act accordingly.

Crossing Situation

Rule 15. When two power-driven vessels are crossing so as to involve risk of collision, the vessel which has the other on her own starboard side shall keep out of the way and shall, if the circumstances of the case admit, avoid crossing ahead of the other vessel.

Action by Give-way Vessel

Rule 16. Every vessel which is directed to keep out of the way of another vessel shall, so far as possible, take early and substantial action to keep well clear.

Action by Stand-on Vessel

Rule 17. (a) (i) Where one of two vessels is to keep out of the way the other shall keep her course and speed. (ii) The latter vessel may however take action to avoid collision by her manoeuvre alone, as soon as it becomes apparent to her that the vessel required to keep out of the way is not taking appropriate action in compliance with these Rules.

(b) When, from any cause, the vessel required to keep her course and speed finds herself so close that collision cannot be avoided by the action of the give-way vessel alone, she shall take such action as will best aid to avoid collision.

(c) A power-driven vessel which takes action in a crossing situation in accordance with sub-paragraph (a) (ii) of this Rule to avoid collision with another power-driven vessel shall, if the circumstances of the case admit, not alter course to port for a vessel on her own port side.

(d) This Rule does not relieve the give-way vessel of her obligation to keep out of the way.

Responsibilities between Vessels

Rule 18. Except where Rules 9, 10 and 13 otherwise require:

(a) A power-driven vessel underway shall keep out of the way of: (i) a vessel not under command; (ii) a vessel restricted in her ability to manoeuvre; (iii) a vessel engaged in fishing; (iv) a sailing vessel.

(b) A sailing vessel underway shall keep out of the way of: (i) a vessel not under command; (ii) a vessel restricted in her ability to manoeuvre; (iii) a vessel engaged in fishing.

(c) A vessel engaged in fishing when underway shall, so far as possible, keep out of the way of: (i) a vessel not under command; (ii) a vessel restricted in her ability to manoeuvre.

(d) (i) Any vessel other than a vessel not under command or a vessel restricted in her ability to manoeuvre shall, if the circumstances of the case admit, avoid impeding the safe passage of a vessel constrained by her draught, exhibiting the signals in Rule 28. (ii) A vessel constrained by her draught shall navigate with particular caution having full regard to her special condition.

(e) A seaplane on the water shall, in general, keep well clear of all vessels and avoid impeding their navigation. In circumstances, however, where risk of collision exists, she shall comply with the Rules of this Part.

Section III. Conduct of Vessels in Restricted Visibility

Conduct of Vessels in Restricted Visibility

Rule 19. (a) This Rule applies to vessels not in sight of one another when navigating in or near an area of restricted visibility.

(b) Every vessel shall proceed at a safe speed adapted to the prevailing circumstances and conditions of restricted visibility. A power-driven vessel shall have her engines ready for immediate manoeuvre.

(c) Every vessel shall have due regard to the prevailing circumstances and conditions of restricted visibility when complying with the Rules of Section I of this Part.

(d) A vessel which detects by radar alone the presence of another vessel shall determine if a close-quarters situation is developing and/or risk of collision exists. If so, she shall take avoiding action in ample time, provided that when such action consists of an alteration of course, so far as possible the following shall be avoided: (i) an alteration of course to port for a vessel forward of the beam, other than for a vessel being overtaken; (ii) an alteration of course towards a vessel abeam or abaft the beam.

(e) Except where it has been determined that a risk of collision does not exist, every vessel which hears apparently forward of her beam the fog signal of another vessel, or which cannot avoid a close-quarters situation with another vessel forward of her beam, shall reduce her speed to the minimum at which she can be kept on her course. She shall if necessary take all her way off and in any event navigate with extreme caution until danger of collision is over.

Part C. Lights and Shapes

Application

Rule 20. (a) Rules in this Part shall be complied with in all weathers.

(b) The Rules concerning lights shall be complied with from sunset to sunrise, and during such times no other lights shall be exhibited, except such lights as cannot be mistaken for the lights specified in these Rules or do not impair their visibility or distinctive character, or interfere with the keeping of a proper look-out.

(c) The lights prescribed by these Rules shall, if carried, also be exhibited from sunrise to sunset in restricted visibility and may be exhibited in all other circumstances when it is deemed necessary.

(d) The Rules concerning shapes shall be complied with by day.

(e) The lights and shapes specified in these Rules shall comply with the provisions of Annex I to these Regulations.

Definitions

Rule 21. (a) "Masthead light" means a white light placed over the fore and aft centerline of the vessel showing an unbroken light over an arc of the horizon of 225 degrees and so fixed as to show the light from right ahead to 22.5 degrees abaft the beam on either side of the vessel.

(b) "Sidelights" means a green light on the starboard side and a red light on the port side each showing an unbroken light over an arc of the horizon of 112.5 degrees and so fixed as to show the light from right ahead to 22.5 degrees abaft the beam on its respective side. In a vessel of less than 20 metres in length the sidelights may be combined in one lantern carried on the fore and aft centerline of the vessel.

(c) "Sternlight" means a white light placed as nearly as practicable at the stern showing an unbroken light over an arc of the horizon of 135 degrees and so fixed as to show the light 67.5 degrees from right aft on each side of the vessel.

(d) "Towing light" means a yellow light having the same characteristics as the "sternlight" defined in paragraph (c) of this Rule.

(e) "All-round light" means a light showing an unbroken light over an arc of the horizon of 360 degrees.

(f) "Flashing light" means a light flashing at regular intervals at a frequency of 120 flashes or more per minute.

Visibility of Lights

Rule 22. The lights prescribed in these Rules shall have an intensity as specified in Section 8 of Annex I to these Regulations so as to be visible at the following minimum ranges:

(a) In vessels of 50 metres or more in length:
a masthead light, 6 miles;
a sidelight, 3 miles;
a sternlight, 3 miles;
a towing light, 3 miles;
a white, red, green or yellow all-round light, 3 miles.

(b) In vessels of 12 metres or more in length but less than 50 metres in length:
a masthead light, 5 miles; except that where the length of the vessel is less than 20 metres, 3 miles;
a sidelight, 2 miles;
a sternlight, 2 miles;
a towing light, 2 miles;
a white, red, green or yellow all-round light, 2 miles.

(c) In vessels of less than 12 metres in length:
a masthead light, 2 miles;
a sidelight, 1 mile;
a sternlight, 2 miles;

a towing light, 2 miles;
a white, red, green or yellow all-round light, 2 miles.

Power-driven Vessels Underway

Rule 23. (a) A power-driven vessel underway shall exhibit: (i) a masthead light forward; (ii) a second masthead light abaft of and higher than the forward one; except that a vessel of less than 50 metres in length shall not be obliged to exhibit such light but may do so; (iii) sidelights; (iv) a sternlight.

(b) An air-cushion vessel when operating in the nondisplacement mode shall, in addition to the lights prescribed in paragraph (a) of this Rule, exhibit an all-round flashing yellow light.

(c) A power-driven vessel of less than 7 metres in length and whose maximum speed does not exceed 7 knots may, in lieu of the lights prescribed in paragraph (a) of this Rule, exhibit an all-round white light. Such vessel shall, if practicable, also exhibit sidelights.

Towing and Pushing

Rule 24. (a) A power-driven vessel when towing shall exhibit: (i) instead of the light prescribed in Rule 23(a)(i), two masthead lights forward in a vertical line. When the length of the tow, measuring from the stern of the towing vessel to the after end of the tow exceeds 200 metres, three such lights in a vertical line; (ii) sidelights; (iii) a sternlight; (iv) a towing light in a vertical line above the sternlight; (v) when the length of the tow exceeds 200 metres, a diamond shape where it can best be seen.

(b) When a pushing vessel and a vessel being pushed ahead are rigidly connected in a composite unit they shall be regarded as a power-driven vessel and exhibit the lights prescribed in Rule 23.

(c) A power-driven vessel when pushing ahead or towing alongside, except in the case of a composite unit, shall exhibit: (i) instead of the light prescribed in Rule 23(a)(i), two masthead lights forward in a vertical line; (ii) sidelights; (iii) a sternlight.

(d) A power-driven vessel to which paragraphs (a) and (c) of this Rule apply shall also comply with Rule 23(a)(ii).

(e) A vessel or object being towed shall exhibit: (i) sidelights; (ii) a sternlight; (iii) when the length of the tow exceeds 200 metres, a diamond shape where it can best be seen.

(f) Provided that any number of vessels being towed alongside or pushed in a group shall be lighted as one vessel, (i) a vessel being pushed ahead, not being part of a composite unit, shall exhibit at the forward end, sidelights; (ii) a vessel being towed alongside shall exhibit a sternlight and at the forward end, sidelights.

(g) Where from any sufficient cause it is impracticable for a vessel or object being towed to exhibit the lights prescribed in paragraph (e) of this Rule, all possible measures shall be taken to light the vessel or object towed or at least to indicate the presence of the unlighted vessel or object.

Sailing Vessels Underway and Vessels under Oars

Rule 25. (a) A sailing vessel underway shall exhibit: (i) sidelights; (ii) a sternlight.

(b) In a sailing vessel of less than 12 metres in length the lights prescribed in paragraph (a) of this Rule may be combined in one lantern carried at or near the top of the mast where it can best be seen.

(c) A sailing vessel underway may, in addition to the lights prescribed in paragraph (a) of this Rule, exhibit at or near the top of the mast, where they can best be seen, two all-round lights in a vertical line, the upper being red and the lower green, but these lights shall not be exhibited in conjunction with the combined lantern permitted by paragraph (b) of this Rule.

(d)(i) A sailing vessel of less than 7 metres in length shall, if practicable, exhibit the lights prescribed in paragraph (a) or (b) of this Rule, but if she does not, she shall have ready at hand an electric torch or lighted lantern showing a white light which shall be exhibited in sufficient time to prevent collision. (ii) A vessel under oars may exhibit the lights prescribed in this Rule for sailing vessels, but if she does not, she shall have ready at hand an electric torch or lighted lantern showing a white light which shall be exhibited in sufficient time to prevent collision.

(e) A vessel proceeding under sail when also being propelled by machinery shall exhibit forward where it can best be seen a conical shape, apex downwards.

Fishing Vessels

Rule 26. (a) A vessel engaged in fishing, whether underway or at anchor, shall exhibit only the lights and shapes prescribed in this Rule.

(b) A vessel when engaged in trawling, by which is meant the dragging through the water of a dredge net or other apparatus used as a fishing appliance, shall exhibit: (i) two all-round lights in a vertical line, the upper being green and the lower white, or a shape consisting of two cones with their apexes together in a vertical line one above the other; a vessel of less than 20 metres in length may instead of this shape exhibit a basket; (ii) a masthead light abaft of and higher than the all-round green light; a vessel of less than 50 metres in length shall not be obliged to exhibit such a light but may do so; (iii) when making way through the water, in addition to the lights prescribed in this paragraph, sidelights and a sternlight.

(c) A vessel engaged in fishing, other than trawling, shall exhibit: (i) two all-round lights in a vertical line, the upper being red and the lower white, or a shape consisting of two cones with apexes together in a vertical line one above the other; a vessel of less than 20 metres in length may instead of this shape exhibit a basket; (ii) when there is outlying gear extending more than 150 metres horizontally from the vessel, an all-round white light or a cone apex upwards in the direction of the gear; (iii) when making way through the water, in addition to the lights prescribed in this paragraph, sidelights and a sternlight.

(d) A vessel engaged in fishing in close proximity to other vessels engaged in fishing may exhibit the additional signals described in Annex II to these Regulations.

(e) A vessel when not engaged in fishing shall not exhibit the lights or shapes prescribed in this Rule, but only those prescribed for a vessel of her length.

Vessels Not under Command or Restricted in Their Ability to Manoeuvre

Rule 27. (a) A vessel not under command shall exhibit: (i) two all-round red lights in a vertical line where they can best be seen; (ii) two balls or similar shapes in a vertical line where they can best be seen; (iii) when making way through the water, in addition to the lights prescribed in this paragraph, sidelights and a sternlight.

(b) A vessel restricted in her ability to manoeuvre, except a vessel engaged in minesweeping operations, shall exhibit: (i) three all-round lights in a vertical line where they can best be seen. The highest and lowest of these lights shall be red and the middle light shall be white; (ii) three shapes in a vertical line where they can best be seen. The highest and lowest of these shapes shall be balls and the middle one a diamond; (iii) when making way through the water, masthead lights, sidelights and a sternlight, in addition to the lights prescribed in subparagraph (i); (iv) when at anchor, in addition to the lights or shapes prescribed in subparagraphs (i) and (ii), the light, lights or shape prescribed in Rule 30.

(c) A vessel engaged in a towing operation such as renders her unable to deviate from her course shall, in addition to the lights or shapes prescribed in subparagraph (b) (i) and (ii) of this Rule, exhibit the lights or shape prescribed in Rule 24(a).

(d) A vessel engaged in dredging or underwater operations, when restricted in her ability to manoeuvre, shall exhibit the lights and shapes prescribed in paragraph (b) of this Rule and shall in addition, when an obstruction exists, exhibit: (i) two all-round red lights or two balls in a vertical line to indicate the side on which the obstruction exists; (ii) two all-round green lights or two diamonds in a vertical line to indicate the side on which another vessel may pass; (iii) when making way through the water, in addition to the lights prescribed in this paragraph, masthead lights, sidelights and a sternlight; (iv) a vessel to which this paragraph applies when at anchor shall exhibit the lights or shapes prescribed in subparagraphs (i) and (ii) instead of the lights or shape prescribed in Rule 30.

(e) Whenever the size of a vessel engaged in diving operations makes it impracticable to exhibit the shapes prescribed in paragraph (d) of this Rule, a rigid replica of the International Code flag "A" not less than 1 metre in height shall be exhibited. Measures shall be taken to ensure all-round visibility.

(f) A vessel engaged in minesweeping operations shall, in addition to the lights prescribed for a power-driven vessel in Rule 23, exhibit three all-round green lights or three balls. One of these lights or shapes shall be exhibited at or near the foremast head and one at each end of the fore yard. These lights or shapes indicate that it is dangerous for another vessel to approach closer than 1,000 metres astern or 500 metres on either side of the minesweeper.

(g) Vessels of less than 7 metres in length shall not be required to exhibit the lights prescribed in this Rule.

(h) The signals prescribed in this Rule are not signals of vessels in distress and requiring assistance. Such signals are contained in Annex IV to these Regulations.

Vessels Constrained by Their Draught

Rule 28. A vessel constrained by her draught may, in addition to the lights prescribed for power-driven vessels in Rule 23, exhibit where they can best be seen three all-round red lights in a vertical line, or a cylinder.

Pilot Vessels

Rule 29. (a) A vessel engaged on pilotage duty shall exhibit: (i) at or near the masthead, two all-round lights in a vertical line, the upper being white and the lower red; (ii) when underway, in addition, sidelights and a sternlight; (iii) when at anchor, in addition to the lights prescribed in sub-paragraph (i), the anchor light, lights or shape.

(b) A pilot vessel when not engaged on pilotage duty shall exhibit the lights or shapes prescribed for a similar vessel of her length.

Anchored Vessels and Vessels Aground

Rule 30. (a) A vessel at anchor shall exhibit where it can best be seen: (i) in the fore part, an all-round white light or one ball; (ii) at or near the stern and at a lower level than the light prescribed in sub-paragraph (i), an all-round white light.

(b) A vessel of less than 50 metres in length may exhibit an all-round white light where it can best be seen instead of the lights prescribed in paragraph (a) of this Rule.

(c) A vessel at anchor may, and a vessel of 100 metres and more in length shall, also use the available working or equivalent lights to illuminate her decks.

(d) A vessel aground shall exhibit the lights prescribed in paragraph (a) or (b) of this Rule and in ad-

dition, where they can best be seen: (i) two all-round red lights in a vertical line; (ii) three balls in a vertical line.

(e) A vessel of less than 7 metres in length, when at anchor or aground, not in or near a narrow channel, fairway or anchorage, or where other vessels normally navigate, shall not be required to exhibit the lights or shapes prescribed in paragraphs (a), (b) or (d) of this Rule.

Seaplanes

Rule 31. Where it is impracticable for a seaplane to exhibit lights and shapes of the characteristics or in the positions prescribed in the Rules of this Part she shall exhibit lights and shapes as closely similar in characteristics and position as is possible.

Part D. Sound and Light Signals

Definitions

Rule 32. (a) The word "whistle" means any sound signalling appliance capable of producing the prescribed blasts and which complies with the specifications in Annex III to these Regulations.

(b) The term "short blast" means a blast of about one second's duration.

(c) The term "prolonged blast" means a blast of from four to six seconds' duration.

Equipment for Sound Signals

Rule 33. (a) A vessel of 12 metres or more in length shall be provided with a whistle and a bell and a vessel of 100 metres or more in length shall, in addition, be provided with a gong, the tone and sound of which cannot be confused with that of the bell. The whistle, bell and gong shall comply with the specifications in Annex III to these Regulations. The bell or gong or both may be replaced by other equipment having the same respective sound characteristics, provided that manual sounding of the required signals shall always be possible.

(b) A vessel of less than 12 metres in length shall not be obliged to carry the sound signalling appliances prescribed in paragraph (a) of this Rule but if she does not, she shall be provided with some other means of making an efficient sound signal.

Manoeuvring and Warning Signals

Rule 34. (a) When vessels are in sight of one another, a power-drive vessel underway, when manoeuvring as authorized or required by these Rules, shall indicate that manoeuvre by the following signals on her whistle:

one short blast to mean "I am altering my course to starboard";

two short blasts to mean "I am altering my course to port";

three short blasts to mean "I am operating astern propulsion."

(b) Any vessel may supplement the whistle signals prescribed in paragraph (a) of this Rule by light signals, repeated as appropriate, whilst the manoeuvre is being carried out: (i) these light signals shall have the following significance:

one flash to mean "I am altering my course to starboard";

two flashes to mean "I am altering my course to port";

three flashes to mean "I am operating astern propulsion";

(ii) the duration of each flash shall be about one second, the interval between flashes shall be about one second, and the interval between successive signals shall be not less than ten seconds; (iii) the light used for this signal shall, if fitted, be an all-round white light, visible at a minimum range of 5 miles, and shall comply with the provisions of Annex I.

(c) When in sight of one another in a narrow channel or fairway: (i) a vessel intending to overtake another shall in compliance with Rule 9(e)(i) indicate her intention by the following signals on her whistle:

two prolonged blasts followed by one short blast to mean "I intend to overtake you on your starboard side";

two prolonged blasts followed by two short blasts to mean "I intend to overtake you on your port side".

(ii) the vessel about to be overtaken when acting in accordance with Rule 9(e)(i) shall indicate her agreement by the following signal on her whistle: one prolonged, one short, one prolonged and one short blast, in that order.

(d) When vessels in sight of one another are approaching each other and from any cause either vessel fails to understand the intentions or actions of the other, or is in doubt whether sufficient action is being taken by the other to avoid collision, the vessel in doubt shall immediately indicate such doubt by giving at least five short and rapid blasts on the whistle. Such signal may be supplemented by a light signal of at least five short and rapid flashes.

(e) A vessel nearing a bend or an area of a channel or fairway where other vessels may be obscured by an intervening obstruction shall sound one prolonged blast. Such signal shall be answered with a prolonged blast by any approaching vessel that may be within hearing around the bend or behind the intervening obstruction.

(f) If whistles are fitted on a vessel at a distance apart of more than 100 metres, one whistle only shall be used for giving manoeuvring and warning signals.

Sound Signals in Restricted Visibility

Rule 35. In or near an area of restricted visibility, whether by day or night, the signals prescribed in this Rule shall be used as follows:

(a) A power-driven vessel making way through the water shall sound at intervals of not more than 2 minutes one prolonged blast.

(b) A power-driven vessel underway but stopped and making no way through the water shall sound at intervals of not more than 2 minutes two prolonged blasts in succession with an interval of about 2 seconds between them.

(c) A vessel not under command, a vessel restricted in her ability to manoeuvre, a vessel constrained by her draught, a sailing vessel, a vessel engaged in fishing and a vessel engaged in towing or pushing another vessel shall, instead of the signals prescribed in paragraphs (a) or (b) of this Rule, sound at intervals of not more than 2 minutes three blasts in succession, namely one prolonged followed by two short blasts.

(d) A vessel towed or if more than one vessel is towed the last vessel of the tow, if manned, shall at intervals of not more than 2 minutes sound four blasts in succession, namely one prolonged followed by three short blasts. When practicable, this signal shall be made immediately after the signal made by the towing vessel.

(e) When a pushing vessel and a vessel being pushed ahead are rigidly connected in a composite unit they shall be regarded as a power-driven vessel and shall give the signals prescribed in paragraphs (a) or (b) of this Rule.

(f) A vessel at anchor shall at intervals of not more than one minute ring the bell rapidly for about 5 seconds. In a vessel of 100 metres or more in length the bell shall be sounded in the forepart of the vessel and immediately after the ringing of the bell the gong shall be sounded rapidly for about 5 seconds in the after part of the vessel. A vessel at anchor may in addition sound three blasts in succession, namely one short, one prolonged and one short blast, to give warning of her position and of the possibility of collision to an approaching vessel.

(g) A vessel aground shall give the bell signal and if required the gong signal prescribed in paragraph (f) of this Rule and shall, in addition, give three separate and distinct strokes on the bell immediately before and after the rapid ringing of the bell. A vessel aground may in addition sound an appropriate whistle signal.

(h) A vessel of less than 12 metres in length shall not be obliged to give the above-mentioned signals but, if she does not, shall make some other efficient sound signal at intervals of not more than 2 minutes.

(i) A pilot vessel when engaged on pilotage duty may in addition to the signals prescribed in paragraphs (a), (b) or (f) of this Rule sound an identity signal consisting of four short blasts.

Signals to Attract Attention

Rule 36. If necessary to attract the attention of another vessel any vessel may make light or sound signals that cannot be mistaken for any signal authorized elsewhere in these rules, or may direct the beam of her searchlight in the direction of the danger, in such a way as not to embarrass any vessel.

Distress Signals

Rule 37. When a vessel is in distress and requires assistance she shall use or exhibit the signals prescribed in Annex IV to these Regulations.

Part E. Exemptions

Exemptions

Rule 38. Any vessel (or class of vessels) provided that she complies with the requirements of the International Regulations for Preventing Collisions at Sea, 1960, the keel of which is laid or which is at a corresponding stage of construction before the entry into force of these Regulations may be exempted from compliance therewith as follows:

(a) The installation of lights with ranges prescribed in Rule 22, until four years after the date of entry into force of these Regulations.

(b) The installation of lights with colour specifications as prescribed in Section 7 of Annex I to these Regulations, until four years after the date of entry into force of these Regulations.

(c) The repositioning of lights as a result of conversion from Imperial to metric units and rounding off measurement figures, permanent exemption.

(d) (i) The repositioning of masthead lights on vessels of less than 150 metres in length, resulting from the prescriptions of Section 3(a) of Annex I, permanent exemption. (ii) The repositioning of masthead lights on vessels of 150 metres or more in length, resulting from the prescriptions of Section 3(a) of Annex I to these Regulations, until nine years after the date of entry into force of these Regulations.

(e) The repositioning of masthead lights resulting from the prescriptions of Section 2(b) of Annex I, until nine years after the date of entry into force of these Regulations.

(f) The repositioning of sidelights resulting from the prescriptions of Sections 2(g) and 3(b) of Annex I, until nine years after the date of entry into force of these Regulations.

(g) The requirements for sound signal appliances prescribed in Annex III, until nine years after the date of entry into force of these Regulations.

Annex I

Positioning and Technical Details of Lights and Shapes

1. Definition

The term "height above the hull" means height above the uppermost continuous deck.

2. Vertical Positioning and Spacing of Lights

(a) On a power-driven vessel of 20 metres or more

in length the masthead lights shall be placed as follows: (i) the forward masthead light, or if only one masthead light is carried, then that light, at a height above the hull of not less than 6 metres, and, if the breadth of the vessel exceeds 6 metres, then at a height above the hull not less than such breadth, so however that the light need not be placed at a greater height above the hull than 12 metres; (ii) when two masthead lights are carried the after one shall be at least 4.5 metres vertically higher than the forward one.

(b) The vertical separation of masthead lights of power-driven vessels shall be such that in all normal conditions of trim the after light will be seen over and separate from the forward light at a distance of 1000 metres from the stem when viewed from sea level.

(c) The masthead light of a power-driven vessel of 12 metres but less than 20 metres in length shall be placed at a height above the gunwale of not less than 2.5 metres.

(d) A power-driven vessel of less than 12 metres in length may carry the uppermost light at a height of less than 2.5 metres above the gunwale. When however a masthead light is carried in addition to sidelights and a sternlight, then such masthead light shall be carried at least 1 metre higher than the sidelights.

(e) One of the two or three masthead lights prescribed for a power-driven vessel when engaged in towing or pushing another vessel shall be placed in the same position as the forward masthead light of a power-driven vessel.

(f) In all circumstances the masthead light or lights shall be so placed as to be above and clear of all other lights and obstructions.

(g) The sidelights of a power-driven vessel shall be placed at a height above the hull not greater than three quarters of that of the forward masthead light. They shall not be so low as to be interfered with by deck lights.

(h) The sidelights, if in a combined lantern and carried on a power-driven vessel of less than 20 metres in length, shall be placed not less than 1 metre below the masthead light.

(i) When the Rules prescribe two or three lights to be carried in a vertical line, they shall be spaced as follows: (i) on a vessel of 20 metres in length or more

such lights shall be spaced not less than 2 metres apart, and the lowest of these lights shall, except where a towing light is required, not be less than 4 metres above the hull; (ii) on a vessel of less than 20 metres in length such lights shall be spaced not less than 1 metre apart and the lowest of these lights shall, except where a towing light is required, not be less than 2 metres above the gunwale; (iii) when three lights are carried they shall be equally spaced.

(j) The lower of the two all-round lights prescribed for a fishing vessel when engaged in fishing shall be at a height above the sidelights not less than twice the distance between the two vertical lights.

(k) The forward anchor light, when two are carried, shall not be less than 4.5 metres above the after one. On a vessel of 50 metres or more in length this forward anchor light shall not be less than 6 metres above the hull.

3. Horizontal Positioning and Spacing of Lights

(a) When two masthead lights are prescribed for a power-driven vessel, the horizontal distance between them shall not be less than one half of the length of the vessel but need not be more than 100 metres. The forward light shall be placed not more than one quarter of the length of the vessel from the stem.

(b) On a vessel of 20 metres or more in length the sidelights shall not be placed in front of the forward masthead lights. They shall be placed at or near the side of the vessel.

4. Details of Location of Direction-Indicating Lights for Fishing Vessels, Dredgers and Vessels Engaged in Underwater Operations

(a) The light indicating the direction of the outlying gear from a vessel engaged in fishing as prescribed in Rule 26(c) (ii) shall be placed at a horizontal distance of not less than 2 metres and not more than 6 metres away from the two all-round red and white lights. This light shall be placed not higher than the all-round white light prescribed in Rule 26(c) (i) and not lower than the sidelights.

(b) The lights and shapes on a vessel engaged in dredging or underwater operations to indicate the obstructed side and/or the side on which it is safe to pass, as prescribed in Rule 27(d) (i) and (ii), shall be placed at the maximum practical horizontal distance, but in no case less than 2 metres, from the lights or shapes prescribed in Rule 27(b) (i) and (ii). In no case shall the upper of these lights or shapes be at a greater height than the lower of the three lights or shapes prescribed in Rule 27 (b) (i) and (ii).

5. Screens for Sidelights

The sidelights shall be fitted with inboard screens painted matt black, and meeting the requirements of Section 9 of this Annex. With a combined lantern, using a single vertical filament and a very narrow division between the green and red sections, external screens need not be fitted.

6. Shapes

(a) Shapes shall be black and of the following sizes: (i) a ball shall have a diameter of not less than 0.6 metre; (ii) a cone shall have a base diameter of not less than 0.6 metre and a height equal to its diameter; (iii) a cylinder shall have a diameter of at least 0.6 metre and a height of twice its diameter; (iv) a diamond shape shall consist of two cones as defined in (ii) above having a common base.

(b) The vertical distance between shapes shall be at least 1.5 metre.

(c) In a vessel of less than 20 metres in length shapes of lesser dimensions but commensurate with the size of the vessel may be used and the distance apart may be correspondingly reduced.

7. Colour Specification of Lights

The chromaticity of all navigation lights shall conform to the following standards, which lie within the boundaries of the area of the diagram specified for each colour by the International Commission on Illumination (CIE).

The boundaries of the area for each colour are given by indicating the corner co-ordinates, which are as follows:

(i) *White*

| x | 0.525 | 0.525 | 0.452 | 0.310 | 0.310 | 0.443 |
| y | 0.382 | 0.440 | 0.440 | 0.348 | 0.283 | 0.382 |

(ii) *Green*

| x | 0.028 | 0.009 | 0.300 | 0.203 |
| y | 0.385 | 0.723 | 0.511 | 0.356 |

(iii) *Red*

| x | 0.680 | 0.660 | 0.735 | 0.721 |
| y | 0.320 | 0.320 | 0.264 | 0.259 |

(iv) *Yellow*

| x | 0.612 | 0.618 | 0.575 | 0.575 |
| y | 0.382 | 0.382 | 0.425 | 0.406 |

8. Intensity of Lights

(a) the minimum luminous intensity of lights shall be calculated by using the formula:

$$I = 3.43 \times 10^6 \times T \times D^2 \times K^{-D}$$

where I is luminous intensity in candelas under service conditions.

T is threshold factor 2×10^{-7} lux,

D is range of visibility (luminous range) of light in nautical miles,

K is atmospheric transmissivity. For prescribed lights the value of K shall be 0.8, corresponding to a meteorological visibility of approximately 13 nautical miles.

(b) A selection of figures derived from the formula is given in the following table:

Range of visibility (luminous range) of light in nautical miles	Luminous intensity of light in candelas for K = 0.8
D	I
1	0.9
2	4.3
3	12.0
4	27.0
5	52.0
6	94.0

Note. The maximum luminous intensity of navigation lights should be limited to avoid undue glare.

9. Horizontal Sectors

(a) (i) In the forward direction, sidelights as fitted on the vessel must show the minimum required intensities. The intensities must decrease to reach practical cut-off between 1 degree and 3 degrees outside the prescribed sectors. (ii) For sternlights and masthead lights and at 22.5 degrees abaft the beam for sidelights, the minimum required intensities shall be maintained over the arc of the horizon up to 5 degrees within the limits of the sectors prescribed in Rule 21. From 5 degrees within the prescribed sectors the intensity may decrease by 50 per cent up to the prescribed limits; it shall decrease steadily to reach practical cut-off at not more than 5 degrees outside the prescribed limits.

(b) All-round lights shall be so located as not to be obscured by masts, topmasts or structures within angular sectors of more than 6 degrees, except anchor lights, which need not be placed at an impracticable height above the hull.

10. Vertical Sectors

(a) The vertical sectors of electric lights, with the exception of lights on sailing vessels shall ensure that: (i) at least the required minimum intensity is maintained at all angles from 5 degrees above to 5 degrees below the horizontal; (ii) at least 60 per cent of the required minimum intensity is maintained from 7.5 degrees above to 7.5 degrees below the horizontal.

(b) In the case of sailing vessels the vertical sectors of electric lights shall ensure that: (i) at least the required minimum intensity is maintained at all angles from 5 degrees above to 5 degrees below the horizontal; (ii) at least 50 per cent of the required minimum intensity is maintained from 25 degrees above to 25 degrees below the horizontal.

(c) In the case of lights other than electric these specifications shall be met as closely as possible.

11. Intensity of Non-Electric Lights

Non-electric lights shall so far as practicable comply with the minimum intensities, as specified in the Table given in Section 8 of this Annex.

12. Manoeuvring Light

Notwithstanding the provisions of paragraph 2(f) of this Annex the manoeuvring light described in Rule 34(b) shall be placed in the same fore and aft vertical plane as the masthead light or lights and, where practicable, at a minimum height of 2 metres vertically above the forward masthead light, provided that it shall be carried not less than 2 metres vertically above or below the after masthead light. On a vessel where only one masthead light is carried the manoeuvring light, if fitted, shall be carried where it can best be seen, not less than 2 metres vertically apart from the masthead light.

13. Approval

The construction of lanterns and shapes and the installation of lanterns on board the vessel shall be to the satisfaction of the appropriate authority of the State where the vessel is registered.

Annex II

Additional Signals for Fishing Vessels Fishing in Close Proximity

1. General

The lights mentioned herein shall, if exhibited in pursuance of Rule 26(d), be placed where they can best be seen. They shall be at least 0.9 metre apart but at a lower level than lights prescribed in Rule 26(b) (i) and (c) (i). The lights shall be visible all round the horizon at a distance of at least 1 mile but at a lesser distance than the lights prescribed by these Rules for fishing vessels.

2. Signals for Trawlers

(a) Vessels when engaged in trawling, whether using demersal or pelagic gear, may exhibit: (i) when shooting their nets: two white lights in a vertical line; (ii) when hauling their nets: one white light over one red light in a vertical line; (iii) when the net has come fast upon an obstruction: two red lights in a vertical line.

(b) Each vessel engaged in pair trawling may exhibit: (i) by night, a searchlight directed forward and in the direction of the other vessel of the pair; (ii) when shooting or hauling their nets or when their nets have come fast upon an obstruction, the lights prescribed in 2(a) above.

3. Signals for purse seiners

Vessels engaged in fishing with purse seine gear may exhibit two yellow lights in a vertical line. These lights shall flash alternately every second and with equal light and occultation duration. These lights may be exhibited only when the vessel is hampered by its fishing gear.

Annex III

Technical Details of Sound Signal Appliances

1. *Whistles*

(a) *Frequencies and range of audibility.* The fundamental frequency of the signal shall lie within the range 70–700 Hz.

The range of audibility of the signal from a whistle shall be determined by those frequencies, which may include the fundamental and/or one or more higher frequencies, which lie within the range 180–700 Hz (±1 percent) and which provide the sound pressure levels specified in paragraph 1(c) below.

(b) *Limits of fundamental frequencies.* To ensure a wide variety of whistle characteristics, the fundamental frequency of a whistle shall be between the following limits: (i) 70–200 Hz, for a vessel 200 metres or more in length; (ii) 130–350 Hz, for a vessel 75 metres but less than 200 metres in length; (iii) 250–700 Hz, for a vessel less than 75 metres in length.

(c) *Sound signal intensity and range of audibility.* A whistle fitted in a vessel shall provide, in the direction of maximum intensity of the whistle and at a distance of 1 metre from it, a sound pressure level in at least one ⅓-octave band within the range of frequencies 180–700 Hz (±1 percent) of not less than the appropriate figure given in the table below.

Length of vessel in metres	⅓d-octave band level at 1 metre in dB referred to 2×10^{-5} N/m²	Audibility range in nautical miles
200 or more	153	2.0
75 but less than 200	138	1.5
20 but less than 75	130	1.0
Less than 20	120	.5

The range of audibility in the table above is for information and is approximately the range at which a whistle may be heard on its forward axis with 90 percent probability in conditions of still air on board a vessel having average background noise level at the listening posts (taken to be 68 dB in the octave band centred on 250 Hz and 63 dB in the octave band centred on 500 Hz).

In practice the range at which a whistle may be heard is extremely variable and depends critically on weather conditions; the values given can be regarded as typical but under conditions of strong wind or high ambient noise level at the listening post the range may be much reduced.

(d) *Directional properties.* The sound pressure level of a directional whistle shall not be more than 4 dB below the sound pressure level on the axis at any direction in the horizontal plane within ±45 degrees of the axis. The sound pressure level at any other direction in the horizontal plane shall be not more than 10 dB below the ground pressure level on the axis, so that the range in any direction will be at least half the range of the forward axis. The sound pressure level shall be measured in that ⅓-rd-octave band which determines the audibility range.

(e) *Positioning of whistles.* When a directional whistle is to be used as the only whistle on a vessel, it shall be installed with its maximum intensity directed straight ahead.

A whistle shall be placed as high as practicable on a vessel, in order to reduce interception of the emitted sound by obstructions and also to minimize hearing damage risk to personnel. The sound pressure level of the vessel's own signal at listening posts shall not exceed 110 dB (A) and so far as practicable should not exceed 100 dB (A).

(f) *Fitting of more than one whistle.* If whistles are fitted at a distance apart of more than 100 metres, it shall be so arranged that they are not sounded simultaneously.

(g) *Combined whistle systems.* If due to the presence of obstructions the sound field of a single whistle or of one of the whistles referred to in paragraph 1(f) above is likely to have a zone of greatly reduced signal level, it is recommended that a combined whistle system be fitted so as to overcome this reduction. For the purposes of the Rules a combined whistle system is to be regarded as a single whistle. The whistles of a combined system shall be located at a distance apart of not more than 100 metres and arranged to be sounded simultaneously. The frequency of any one whistle shall differ from those of the others by at least 10 Hz.

2. Bell or Gong

(a) *Intensity of signal.* A bell or gong, or other device having similar sound characteristics shall produce a sound pressure level of not less than 110 dB at 1 metre.

(b) *Construction.* Bells and gongs shall be made of corrosion-resistant material and designed to give a clear tone. The diameter of the mouth of the bell shall be not less than 300 mm for vessels of more than 20 metres in length, and shall be not less than 200 mm for vessels of 12 to 20 metres in length. Where practicable, a power-driven bell striker is recommended to ensure constant force but manual operation shall be possible. The mass of the striker shall be not less than 3 percent of the mass of the bell.

3. Approval

The construction of sound signal appliances, their performance and their installation on board the vessel shall be to the satisfaction of the appropriate authority of the State where the vessel is registered.

Annex IV

Distress Signals

1. The following signals, used or exhibited either together or separately, indicate distress and need of assistance:

(a) a gun or other explosive signal fired at intervals of about a minute;

(b) a continuous sounding with any fog-signalling apparatus;

(c) rockets or shells, throwing red stars fired one at a time at short intervals;

(d) a signal made by radiotelegraphy or by any other signalling method consisting of the group . . . − − − . . . (SOS) in the Morse Code;

(e) a signal sent by radiotelephony consisting of the spoken word "Mayday";

(f) the International Code Signal of distress indicated by N.C.;

(g) a signal consisting of a square flag having above or below it a ball or anything resembling a ball;

(h) flames on the vessel (as from a burning tar barrel, oil barrel, etc.);

(i) a rocket parachute flare or a hand flare showing a red light;

(j) a smoke signal giving off orange-coloured smoke;

(k) slowly and repeatedly raising and lowering arms outstretched to each side;

(l) the radiotelegraph alarm signal;

(m) the radiotelephone alarm signal;

(n) signals transmitted by emergency position–indicating radio beacons.

2. The use or exhibition of any of the foregoing signals except for the purpose of indicating distress and need of assistance and the use of other signals which may be confused with any of the above signals is prohibited.

3. Attention is drawn to the relevant sections of the International Code of Signals, the Merchant Ship Search and Rescue Manual and the following signals:

(a) a piece of orange-coloured canvas with either a black square and circle or other appropriate symbol (for identification from the air);

(b) a dye marker.

Appendix C. Racing Rules

*Parts I and IV of the 1977 Yacht Racing Rules of the
International Yacht Racing Union as adopted by the
United States Yacht Racing Union.*

Part I. Definitions

When a term defined in Part I is used in its defined
sense it is printed in *italic* type. All preambles and
definitions rank as rules.

Racing. A yacht is *racing* from her preparatory signal until she has either *finished* and cleared the finishing line and finishing *marks* or retired, or until the
race has been *postponed, abandoned* or *cancelled,* except
that in match or team races, the sailing instructions
may prescribe that a yacht is *racing* from any specified
time before the preparatory signal.

Starting. A yacht *starts* when, after fulfilling her
penalty obligations, if any, under rule 51.1(c), (Sailing
the Course), and after her starting signal, any part of
her hull, crew or equipment first crosses the starting
line in the direction of the course to the first *mark.*

Finishing. A yacht *finishes* when any part of her hull,
or of her crew or equipment in normal position,
crosses the finishing line from the direction of the
course from the last *mark,* after fulfilling her penalty
obligations, if any, under rule 52.2, (Touching a Mark).

Luffing. Altering course towards the wind until head
to wind.

Tacking. A yacht is *tacking* from the moment she is
beyond head to wind until she has *borne away,* when
beating to windward, to a *close-hauled* course; if not
beating to windward, to the course on which her
mainsail has filled.

Bearing Away. Altering course away from the wind
until a yacht begins to *gybe.*

Gybing. A yacht begins to *gybe* at the moment
when, with the wind aft, the foot of her mainsail
crosses her centre line, and completes the *gybe* when
the mainsail has filled on the other *tack.*

On a Tack. A yacht is *on a tack* except when she is
tacking or *gybing.* A yacht is on the *tack* (starboard or
port) corresponding to her *windward* side.

Close-hauled. A yacht is *close-hauled* when sailing by
the wind as close as she can lie with advantage in
working to windward.

Clear Astern and *Clear Ahead; Overlap.* A yacht is
clear astern of another when her hull and equipment
in normal position are abaft an imaginary line projected abeam from the aftermost point of the other's
hull and equipment in normal position. The other
yacht is *clear ahead.* The yachts *overlap* when neither
is *clear astern;* or if, although one is *clear astern,* an intervening yacht *overlaps* both of them. The terms *clear
astern, clear ahead* and *overlap* apply to yachts on opposite *tacks* only when they are subject to rule 42,
(Rounding or Passing Marks and Obstructions).

Leeward and *Windward.* The *leeward* side of a yacht is that on which she is, or, if *luffing* head to wind, was, carrying her mainsail. The opposite side is the *windward* side.

When neither of two yachts on the same *tack* is *clear astern,* the one on the *leeward* side of the other is the *leeward yacht.* The other is the *windward yacht.*

Proper Course. A *proper course* is any course which a yacht might sail after the starting signal, in the absence of the other yacht or yachts affected, to *finish* as quickly as possible. The course sailed before *luffing* or *bearing away* is presumably, but not necessarily, that yacht's *proper course.* There is no *proper course* before the starting signal.

Mark. A *mark* is any object specified in the sailing instructions which a yacht must round or pass on a required side.

Every ordinary part of a *mark* ranks as part of it, including a flag, flagpole, boom or hoisted boat, but excluding ground tackle and any object either accidentally or temporarily attached to the *mark.*

Obstruction. An *obstruction* is any object, including a vessel under way, large enough to require a yacht, when not less than one overall length away from it, to make a substantial alteration of course to pass on one side or the other, or any object which can be passed on one side only, including a buoy when the yacht in question cannot safely pass between it and the shoal or object which it marks.

Postponement. A *postponed* race is one which is not started at its scheduled time and which can be sailed at any time the race committee may decide.

Abandonment. An *abandoned* race is one which the race committee declares void at any time after the starting signal, and which can be re-sailed at its discretion.

Cancellation. A *cancelled* race is one which the race committee decides will not be sailed thereafter.

Part IV. Right of Way Rules

Rights and Obligations when Yachts Meet

The rules of Part IV do not apply in any way to a vessel which is neither intending to *race* nor *racing;* such vessel shall be treated in accordance with the International Regulations for Preventing Collisions at Sea or Government Right of Way Rules applicable in the area concerned.

The rules of Part IV apply only between yachts which either are intending to *race* or are *racing* in the same or different races, and, except when rule 3.2(b)(ii), (Race Continues After Sunset), applies, replace the International Regulations for Preventing Collisions at Sea or Government Right of Way Rules applicable to the area concerned, from the time a yacht intending to *race* begins to sail about in the vicinity of the starting line until she has either *finished* or retired and has left the vicinity of the course.

Section A. Obligations and Penalties

31. Disqualification

31.1 A yacht may be disqualified or otherwise penalized for infringing a rule of Part IV only when the infringement occurs while she is *racing,* whether or not a collision results.

31.2 A yacht may be disqualified before or after she is *racing* for seriously hindering a yacht which is *racing,* or for infringing the sailing instructions.

32. Avoiding Collisions

A right-of-way yacht which fails to make a reasonable attempt to avoid a collision resulting in serious damage may be disqualified as well as the other yacht.

33. Rule Infringement

33.1 Accepting Penalty. A yacht which realises she has infringed a racing rule or a sailing instruction is under an obligation either to retire promptly or to exonerate herself by accepting an alternative penalty when so prescribed in the sailing instructions, but when she does not retire or exonerate herself and persists in *racing,* other yachts shall continue to accord her such rights as she may have under the rules of Part IV.

33.2 Contact Between Yachts Racing. When there is contact between the hull, equipment or crew of two yachts, both shall be disqualified or otherwise penalized unless: either (a) one of the yachts retires in acknowledgement of the infringement, or exonerates herself by accepting an alternative penalty when so prescribed in the sailing instructions, *or* (b) one or both of these yachts acts in accordance with rule 68.3, (Protests).

33.3 When an incident is the subject of action by the race committee under rule 33.2 but under no other rule of Part IV, it may waive the requirements of rule 33.2 when it is satisfied that the contact was minor and unavoidable.

34. Hailing

34.1 Except when *luffing* under rule 38.1, (Luffing and Sailing above a Proper Course after Starting), a right-of-way yacht which does not hail before or when making an alteration of course which may not be foreseen by the other yacht may be disqualified as well as the yacht required to keep clear when a collision resulting in serious damage occurs.

34.2 A yacht which hails when claiming the establishment or termination of an *overlap* or insufficiency of room at a *mark* or *obstruction* thereby helps to support her claim for the purposes of rule 42, (Rounding or Passing Marks and Obstructions).

Section B. Principal Right of Way Rules and their Limitations

These rules apply except when over-ridden by a rule in Section C.

35. Limitations on Altering Course

When one yacht is required to keep clear of another, the right-of-way yacht shall not so alter course as to prevent the other yacht from keeping clear; or so as to obstruct her while she is keeping clear, except:

(a) to the extent permitted by rule 38.1, (Same Tack, Luffing and Sailing above a Proper Course after Starting), and

(b) when assuming a *proper* course: either (i) to *start*, unless subject to rule 40, (Same Tack, Luffing before Starting), or to the second part of rule 44.1(b), (Returning to Start), *or* (ii) when rounding a *mark*.

36. Opposite Tacks—Basic Rule

A *port-tack* yacht shall keep clear of a *starboard-tack* yacht.

37. Same Tack—Basic Rules

37.1 *When Overlapped.* A *windward yacht* shall keep clear of a *leeward yacht*.

37.2 *When Not Overlapped.* A yacht *clear astern* shall keep clear of a yacht *clear ahead*.

37.3 *Transitional.* A yacht which establishes an *overlap* to *leeward* from *clear astern* shall allow the *windward yacht* ample room and opportunity to keep clear.

38. Same Tack—Luffing and Sailing above a Proper Course after Starting

38.1 *Luffing Rights.* After she has *started* and cleared the starting line, a yacht *clear ahead* or a *leeward yacht* may *luff* as she pleases, subject to the *proper course* limitations of this rule.

38.2 *Proper Course Limitations.* A *leeward yacht* shall not sail above her *proper course* while an *overlap* exists, if when the *overlap* began or, at any time during its existence, the helmsman of the *windward yacht* (when sighting abeam from his normal station and sailing no higher than the *leeward yacht*) has been abreast or forward of the mainmast of the *leeward yacht*.

38.3 *Overlap Limitations.* For the purpose of this rule: An *overlap* does not exist unless the yachts are clearly within two overall lengths of the longer yacht; and an *overlap* which exists between two yachts when the leading yacht *starts*, or when one or both of them completes a *tack* or *gybe*, shall be regarded as a new *overlap* beginning at that time.

38.4 *Hailing to Stop or Prevent a Luff.* When there is doubt, the *leeward yacht* may assume that she has the right to *luff* unless the helmsman of the *windward yacht* has hailed "Mast Abeam", or words to that effect. The *leeward yacht* shall be governed by such hail, and, when she deems it improper, her only remedy is to protest.

38.5 *Curtailing a Luff.* The *windward yacht* shall not cause a *luff* to be curtailed because of her proximity to the *leeward yacht* unless an *obstruction*, a third yacht or other object restricts her ability to respond.

38.6 *Luffing Two or More Yachts.* A yacht shall not *luff* unless she has the right to *luff* all yachts which would be affected by her *luff*, in which case they shall all respond even when an intervening yacht or yachts would not otherwise have the right to *luff*.

39. Same Tack—Sailing Below a Proper Course after Starting

A yacht which is on a free leg of the course shall not

sail below her *proper course* when she is clearly within three of her overall lengths of either a *leeward yacht* or a yacht *clear astern* which is steering a course to pass to *leeward*.

40. Same Tack—Luffing before Starting

Before a right-of-way yacht has *started* and cleared the starting line, any *luff* on her part which causes another yacht to have to alter course to avoid a collision shall be carried out slowly and in such a way as to give a *windward yacht* room and opportunity to keep clear, but the *leeward yacht* shall not so *luff* above a *close-hauled* course, unless the helmsman of the *windward yacht* (sighting abeam from his normal station) is abaft the mainmast of the *leeward yacht*. Rules 38.4, (Hailing to Stop or Prevent a Luff); 38.5, (Curtailing a Luff); and 38.6, (Luffing Two or more Yachts), also apply.

41. Changing Tacks—Tacking and Gybing

41.1 Basic Rule. A yacht which is either *tacking* or *gybing* shall keep clear of a yacht *on a tack*.

41.2 Transitional. A yacht shall neither *tack* nor *gybe* into a position which will give her right of way unless she does so far enough from a yacht *on a tack* to enable this yacht to keep clear without having to begin to alter her course until after the *tack* or *gybe* has been completed.

41.3 Onus. A yacht which *tacks* or *gybes* has the onus of satisfying the race committee that she completed her *tack* or *gybe* in accordance with rule 41.2

41.4 When Simultaneous. When two yachts are both *tacking* or both *gybing* at the same time, the one on the other's *port* side shall keep clear.

Section C—Rules which Apply at Marks and Obstructions and other Exceptions to the Rules of Section B

When a rule of this section applies, to the extent to which it explicitly provides rights and obligations, it over-rides any conflicting rule of Section B, Principal Right of Way Rules and their Limitations except rule 35, (Limitations on Altering Course).

42. Rounding or Passing Marks and Obstructions

42.1 Room at Marks and Obstructions When Overlapped.

When yachts are about to round or pass a *mark*, other than a starting *mark* surrounded by navigable water, on the same required side or an *obstruction* on the same side:

(a) An outside yacht shall give each yacht *overlapping* her on the inside, room to round or pass the *mark* or *obstruction*, except as provided in rules 42.1(c), 42.1(d) and 42.4, (At a Starting Mark Surrounded by Navigable Water).

Room includes room for an *overlapping* yacht to *tack* or *gybe* when either is an integral part of the rounding or passing manoeuvre.

(b) When an inside yacht of two or more *overlapped* yachts either on opposite *tacks*, or on the same *tack* without *luffing* rights, will have to *gybe* in order most directly to assume a *proper course* to the next *mark*, she shall *gybe* at the first reasonable opportunity.

(c) When two yachts on opposite *tacks* are on a beat or when one of them will have to *tack* either to round the *mark* or to avoid the *obstruction*, as between each other rule 42.1 shall not apply and they are subject to rules 36, (Opposite Tacks—Basic Rule), and 41, (Changing Tacks—Tacking and Gybing).

(d) An outside *leeward yacht* with luffing rights may take an inside yacht to windward of a *mark* provided that she hails to that effect and begins to *luff* before she is within two of her overall lengths of the *mark* and provided that she also passes to windward of it.

42.2 Clear Astern and Clear Ahead in the Vicinity of Marks and Obstructions

When yachts are about to round or pass a *mark*, other than a starting *mark* surrounded by navigable water, on the same required side or an *obstruction* on the same side:

(a) A yacht *clear astern* shall keep clear in anticipation of and during the rounding or passing manoeuvre when the yacht *clear ahead* remains on the same *tack* or *gybes*.

(b) A yacht *clear ahead* which *tacks* to round a *mark* is subject to rule 41, (Changing Tacks—Tacking and Gybing), but a yacht *clear astern* shall not *luff* above *close-hauled* so as to prevent the yacht *clear ahead* from *tacking*.

42.3 Limitations on Establishing and Maintaining an Overlap in the Vicinity of Marks and Obstructions.

(a) A yacht *clear astern* may establish an inside *overlap* and be entitled to room under rule 42.1(a), (Room at Marks and Obstructions when Overlapped), only when the yacht *clear ahead*:

(i) is able to give the required room and

(ii) is outside two of her overall lengths of the *mark* or *obstruction*, except when either yacht has completed a *tack* within two overall lengths of the *mark* or *obstruction*, or when the *obstruction* is a continuing one as provided in rule 42.3(f).

(b) A yacht *clear ahead* shall be under no obligation to give room to a yacht *clear astern* before an *overlap* is established.

(c) When an outside yacht is *overlapped* at the time she comes within two of her overall lengths of a *mark* or an *obstruction*, she shall continue to be bound by rule 42.1(a), (Room at Marks and Obstructions when Overlapped), to give room as required even though the *overlap* may thereafter be broken.

(d) A yacht which claims an inside *overlap* has the onus of satisfying the race committee that the overlap was established in proper time.

(e) An outside yacht which claims to have broken an *overlap* has the onus of satisfying the race committee that she became *clear ahead* when she was more than two of her overall lengths from the *mark* or *obstruction*.

(f) A yacht *clear astern* may establish an *overlap* between the yacht *clear ahead* and a continuing *obstruction* such as a shoal or the shore or another vessel, only when at that time there is room for her to pass between them in safety.

42.4 At a Starting Mark Surrounded by Navigable Water

When approaching the starting line to *start*, a leeward yacht shall be under no obligation to give any *windward yacht* room to pass to leeward of a starting *mark* surrounded by navigable water; but, after the starting signal, a *leeward yacht* shall not deprive a *windward yacht* of room at such a *mark* by sailing either above the course to the first *mark* or above *close-hauled*.

43. Close-Hauled, Hailing for Room to Tack at Obstructions

43.1 Hailing. When two *close-hauled* yachts are on the same *tack* and safe pilotage requires the yacht *clear ahead* or the *leeward yacht* to make a substantial alteration of course to clear an *obstruction*, and when she intends to *tack*, but cannot *tack* without colliding with the other yacht, she shall hail the other yacht for room to *tack* and clear the other yacht, but she shall not hail and *tack* simultaneously.

43.2 Responding

The hailed yacht at the earliest possible moment after the hail shall:—either

(a) *tack*, in which case the hailing yacht shall begin to *tack* either:—

(i) before the hailed yacht has completed her *tack*, or

(ii) when she cannot then *tack* without colliding with the hailed yacht, immediately she is able to *tack* and clear her;

or

(b) reply "You *tack*", or words to that effect, when in her opinion she can keep clear without *tacking* or after postponing her *tack*.

In this case:—

(i) the hailing yacht shall immediately *tack* and

(ii) the hailed yacht shall keep clear.

(iii) The onus of satisfying the race committee that she kept clear shall lie on the hailed yacht which replied "You *tack*".

43.3 Limitation on Right to Room When the Obstruction is a Mark.

(a) When the hailed yacht can fetch an *obstruction* which is also a *mark*, the hailing yacht shall not be entitled to room to *tack* and clear the hailed yacht and the hailed yacht shall immediately so inform the hailing yacht.

(b) If, thereafter, the hailing yacht again hails for room to *tack* and clear the hailed yacht she shall, after receiving room, retire immediately or exonerate herself by accepting an alternative penalty when so prescribed in the sailing instructions.

(c) When, after having refused to respond to a hail under rule 43.3(a), the hailed yacht fails to fetch, she shall retire immediately, or exonerate herself by accepting an alternative penalty when so prescribed in the sailing instructions.

44. Returning to Start

44.1

(a) After the starting signal is made, a premature starter returning to *start,* or a yacht working into position from the course side of the starting line or its extensions, shall keep clear of all yachts which are *starting* or have *started* correctly, until she is wholly on the pre-start side of the starting line or its extensions.

(b) Thereafter, she shall be accorded the rights under the rules of Part IV of a yacht which is *starting* correctly; but when she thereby acquires right of way over another yacht which is *starting* correctly, she shall allow that yacht ample room and opportunity to keep clear.

44.2 A premature starter while continuing to sail the course and until it is obvious that she is returning to *start,* shall be accorded the rights under the rules of Part IV of a yacht which has *started.*

45. Re-rounding after Touching a Mark

45.1 A yacht which has touched a *mark,* and is about to exonerate herself in accordance with rule 52.2, (Touching a Mark), shall keep clear of all other yachts which are about to round or pass it or have rounded or passed it correctly, until she has rounded it completely and has cleared it and is on a *proper course* to the next *mark.*

45.2 A yacht which has touched a *mark* while continuing to sail the course and until it is obvious that she is returning to round it completely in accordance with rule 52.2, (Touching a Mark), shall be accorded rights under the rules of Part IV.

46. Anchored, Aground or Capsized

46.1 A yacht under way shall keep clear of another yacht *racing* which is anchored, aground or capsized. Of two anchored yachts, the one which anchored later shall keep clear, except that a yacht which is dragging shall keep clear of one which is not.

46.2 A yacht anchored or aground shall indicate the fact to any yacht which may be in danger of fouling her. Unless the size of the yachts or the weather conditions make some other signal necessary, a hail is sufficient indication.

46.3 A yacht shall not be penalized for fouling a yacht in distress which she is attempting to assist or a yacht which goes aground or capsizes immediately ahead of her.

(Numbers 47, 48 and 49 are spare numbers)

Appendix D. U.S.N.A. Training Cruise

Circumnavigation of Delmarva
26-30 May 1978

Sailing Instructions

1. *Purpose.* The objectives of this event are to provide offshore sailing experience for the midshipmen crews in preparation for the Summer Sail Training Program, and to enhance their professional development as Naval Officers in the areas of leadership, navigation, and seamanship.

2. *Organization.* The Sail Group shall consist of:

Insurgente	(US 14571)
Mistral	(NA–63)
Patriot	(US 7777)
Fair American	(US 17711)
Intrepid	(NA–1)
Alert	(NA–2)
Frolic	(NA–5)
Restless	(NA–6)
Fearless	(NA–8)
Flirt	(NA–9)
Lively	(NA–10)
Swift	(NA–11)
Vigilant	(NA–12)

3. *Presail Conference.* There will be a presail conference in Robert Crown Center at 1300 Friday, 26 May for all Coaches and Sailing Masters. All yachts shall be underway and proceed individually at 1600 Friday, 26 May.

4. *Course.* The course will be down Chesapeake Bay, exiting through Chesapeake Channel. Leave the Chesapeake Tower (36° 54.3'N, 75° 42.8'W), R2JS fl. 4 sec. Whistle (38° 05'N, 74° 42.5'W), and Bell "5" fl. 2½ sec. at the mouth of Delaware Bay to port. Reenter Chesapeake Bay and return to Santee Basin. Thomas Point Light, Sharp's Island Light, Smith Point Light, Windmill Point Light, Wolfe Trappe Light, New Point Comfort, Nun 4 off Plum Point and Bell "38" off Worton Point must all be passed on the channel side. If prevailing winds dictate, MISTRAL may sail the course in reverse.

5. *Safety.* All safety equipment required by the Coast Guard must be on board and readily accessible. Fuel and water tanks must be filled to capacity. All yachts must have a full inventory of Category I equipment.

6. *Time Limit.* There is no time limit.

7. *Rules.* The 1977 USYRU Racing Rules shall apply in addition to the official Inland and International Rules of the Road. Yachts approaching a large vessel in a channel shall yield the right of way to that vessel.

8. Special requirements for yachts. All participating yachts are required to perform the below-listed exercises during the Race. Each exercise may be performed at a time selected by the coach as long as the required static conditions are satisfied. Two drills may not be done simultaneously, but two or more could be done consecutively. Performance of each exercise and the time spent will be noted in the log.

Exercise Requirements

Exercise	Minimum static conditions	Mandatory minimum elapsed time
a. simulated man overboard drill (sea rough-day)	TRUE wind at least 12 knots; spinnaker must be set prior to commencing. Continue to practice pick-ups for remainder of drill time.	15 minutes
b. simulated man overboard drill (sea rough-night)	TRUE wind at least 10 knots; light and horseshoe with drogue must be in the water before timing is started. Continue to practice pick-up for remainder of drill time.	15 minutes
c. actual man overboard recovery	Static conditions optional to coach. Subject must be recovered by three different methods with minimal assistance by subject.	30 minutes
	1) Simulating severe injury, use a jib and a halyard to scoop him aboard. Try shackling clew and tack of small genoa into a halyard. Tend head of sail aft in cockpit and lower the bight in the foot of the sail over the side to form a scoop. Attach a forward guy to halyard shackle to control fore and aft position of the sail.	
	2) Use vang at the end of the boom or relead a genoa sheet thru a block at the boom and a grinder to hoist subject aboard. You may need a preventer on the boom to triangulate it with the mainsheet. If you had to put another man in the water to assist (sea conditions permitting), how would you do it?	
	3) Practice putting a second man in the water to assist/rescue another. Always have rescuer attached. A double bowline works well—one bight for rescuer, and the other to be slipped over head of subject.	
d. storm jib/storm trysail	When on normal course, with wind over 20 knots. Tack and jibe a couple of times. Tack and jibe into a heave-to condition.	Experiment for 20 minutes
e. heaving to	True wind greater than 15 knots. Enter with a fully reefed main (or simulated 3 reefs). Experiment with and without storm jib and with helm lashed at various angles.	20 minutes at near dead in the water
f. rig yacht for tow	Fully rig for a tow—include heaving line (messenger), chafing gear; determine fast way to secure line. *Have shroud cutters*, sharp knife, or hatchet handy.	None

g. emergency steering	True wind at least 10 knots. Tack/jibe at least twice. Think about how you would rig an emergency rudder. All boats experiment sailing and maneuvering without a rudder, just sails, or a drogue from the boom.	30 minutes under emergency steering conditions
h. abandon ship drill	Assign specific stations and exercise until all hands know their responsibilities.	None
i. discuss dismasting, broken boom, and rigging emergency spars, damage control and fire	Assign specific stations and plan ahead	None
j. man aloft exercise	As a minimum, once in daylight in the ocean and once at night anywhere. In addition send a man up the headstay. In each case, rig the line to deck. Try securing reaching strut under bosuns chair and rigging two control lines to be tended from the deck.	None

9. *Navigation Requirements.* All yachts will determine their positions by RDF on at least two occasions. All boats are expected to home on the Chesapeake Tower with RDF. Their RDF-plotted positions will be verified by landmark references as soon as practicable. Both the RDF position and the geographic verifications will be entered in the log. Those yachts equipped with operative Loran and/or Omega will determine their position by that means on at least two occasions. At least one evening and one morning position will be determined by celestial navigation, weather permitting. A position will likewise be determined by advancing sunlines at least once. The ship's compass will be checked by celestial azimuth observation at least once on each leg. Coaches are responsible for review and critique of all charts after finishing race. Yachts are free to power as necessary to maintain a 4-knot average. All boats will use radar reflectors at night and in reduced visibility conditions.

10. *Communications.* All yachts will report exiting through Bay Bridge and Tunnel and entering Delaware Bay to the Naval Station Operations Office on SSB and VHF thru a local marine radio-telephone relay. SSB and VHF shall be used. Reverse charges to Naval Station operations (301) 267-3823. A listening watch will be maintained on VHF Channel 16 and SSB 2182 KHz in accordance with the following schedule:

Yacht	Watch commences
Insurgente	0100 and 1300
Patriot	0200 and 1400
Fair American	0300 and 1500
Intrepid	0400 and 1600
Alert	0500 and 1700
Frolic	0600 and 1800
Restless	0700 and 1900
Fearless	0800 and 2000
Flirt	0900 and 2100
Lively	1000 and 2200
Swift	1100 and 2300
Vigilant	1200 and 2400

As each yacht commences the watch, it should transmit an announcement identifying itself and stating that it is commencing radio watch.

Appendix E. U.S. Navy Recreational Sailing Program

(*From* BUPERINST 1710.11, 11 March 1974)

312. Navy Recreation Sailing Program.

Sailing is considered to be an ideal recreation activity for naval personnel. The responsibility for administration and operation of recreational sailing programs rests with the commanding officer administering the Recreation Fund which serves the installation on which appropriate facilities and equipment are maintained. He shall have custody of all such equipment procured with Recreation Funds. The U.S. Naval Sailing Association (USNSA) is recognized as an advisory group to assist in developing and conducting Navy sailing programs. Where established, continued recognition of its various branches as advisory groups is encouraged to assist commanding officers in the development and promotion of boating and sailing programs within their respective commands. When so recognized, the provisions of Chapter Two of this manual will be applicable.

1. Development

a. In determining feasibility of a Recreation Sailing Program, all assets should be considered. Alternatives to the acquisition of sailing craft includes the use of privately owned boats and/or the use of Special Services craft belonging to shore commands with established programs. A vigorous instruction program will broaden the base of personnel qualified to sail and lead to increased utilization of Special Services sailing craft.

b. Standard qualification criteria as outlined in Appendix 3A will facilitate ready use of boats by newly arrived and transient personnel. In granting qualifications, Special Services Directors should require that knowledge and skill of each candidate be examined and qualifications demonstrated to ensure that he is qualified at the level indicated. When qualifications are comparable, each command should honor qualifications granted by another. However, each commanding officer should ensure that new personnel are given adequate familiarization of boats and sailing areas.

c. Instructional material for the Recreation Sailing Program includes the following: the American Red Cross Basic Sailing handbook, the American Red Cross Basic Sailing Instructors Manual, and the American Red Cross Sailing Instructors Visual Aids, developed by the American Red Cross and used at the Naval Academy. Sail and Power, published by the U.S. Naval Institute, is the text used by the Naval Academy in training midshipmen in ocean racing/cruising yachts. It is accepted as the basic instructional material for senior skippers and master skipper level of qualifications.

2. Program

a. Where established, recreational sailing will be included as part of the overall Recreation Program.

3. Funding

The procurement, operation, and maintenance of sailboats; the development of instructional programs in sailing; and the establishment of competitive events at local levels are the responsibility of the commanding officer of the installation on which the sailing facility is located. Appropriated fund support is authorized as specified by reference (d). Such support should be used to the maximum extent authorized. Financial support from nonappropriated recreation funds for recreational sailing is authorized when supported in accordance with Chapter Six of this manual. In general, sailing programs should be self-supporting from fees and charges levied for participation as specified in Chapter Six.

Appendix 3A. Standard Sailing Qualification Criteria

References

(a) American Red Cross Basic Sailing (ARC 2115) Stock No. 321143 (1966)

(b) American Red Cross Basic Sailing Instructors Manual (1967)

(c) American Red Cross Sailing Instructors Visual Aids (1969)

(d) Sail and Power (U.S. Naval Institute)

1. Levels of Sailing Qualification

a. *Mate.* Minimum qualification to crew on small sailing craft.

b. *Skipper.* Qualified to handle small sailing craft in local waters.

c. *Racing Skipper.* Qualified skipper who also has a thorough theoretical and practical knowledge of yacht racing rules and techniques.

d. *Senior Skipper.* Qualified to command a large sailing yacht in local waters.

e. *Master Skipper.* Qualified to command and race a large sailing yacht off shore under all conditions.

2. Details of Qualification Requirements

Each level shall include the requirements of all previous levels.

a. *Mate.* Fulfill present military requirement as swimmer 3rd class. (Enter water feet first from a minimum height of five feet and remain afloat for five minutes. During this time, swim at least 50 yards). Pass an oral examination on nomenclature and demonstrate ability to crew in a sailing craft.

b. *Skipper.* Successfully complete the course for Basic Sailing, reference (a), as taught in accordance with reference (b) by an approved instructor. This course includes classroom work using reference (c), completion of a Basic Sailing written examination and on-the-water instruction leading to a practical examination.

c. *Racing Skipper.* Demonstrate a thorough theoretical and practical knowledge of racing rules. Participate in several races as skipper and serve on a race committee. Demonstrate superior boat handling and sail trimming capability to include use of the spinnaker where available.

d. *Senior Skipper.* Successfully complete a written examination based upon reference (d), including Rules of the Road. Be recommended by two established senior skippers after on-the-water demonstration of skills which should include:

(1) Ability to take charge of a watch at sea;

(2) Sound knowledge of regulations and procedures for preventing a collision at sea;

(3) Working knowledge of pilotage and tidal effects;

(4) Knowledge of when and where to anchor in safety, how to check for anchor drag, and how to clear a fouled anchor;

(5) Measures to be taken in bad weather, including fog, and the use of distress signals;

(6) Understanding simple first aid and lifesaving, to include recovery of man overboard and how to deal with cuts, bleeding, severe bruising, fractures, burns, shock, seasickness, sunstroke, sunburn, exposure and methods of artificial respiration;

(7) Emergency repair of boat and gear;

(8) Simple repairs to sails and maintaining the yacht's gear and standing rigging;

(9) Knowedge of courtesy and customs used at sea, including flag etiquette;

(10) Knowledge of simple meteorology;

(11) Practical knowledge of yacht engines;

(12) Preparing for sea;

(13) Taking charge of all phases of deck work;

(14) Handling a yacht competently under sail and power in confined water, getting underway, coming alongside berth, picking up mooring, and anchoring;

(15) Taking charge at sea; and

(16) Securing a yacht after mooring.

e. *Master Skipper.* Demonstrate ability and personal qualities requisite to taking charge of a yacht offshore including piloting, celestial navigation, visual signaling, and radiotelephone operation. Sail as a member of the afterguard in a major ocean race and be recommended by at least two established master skippers in that afterguard.

3. Availability of Training Material

References(a) through (c) are available from Red Cross field offices world-wide. Reference (d) is available from the U.S. Naval Institute, Annapolis, Maryland 21402.

4. Instructors

Each commanding officer must ascertain to his own satisfaction that the instructor(s)/qualifier(s) in his program are competent. Instructors do not necessarily have to be Navy personnel. It is envisioned that the U.S. Naval Sailing Association branches will assist in creating a nucleus of competent sailing instructors for various ships and stations. Acquisition of Red Cross certification for instructors is encouraged but not required.

5. Waivers

A commanding officer may waive specific requirements at his discretion, based upon past experience of a candidate, provided he is satisfied that the candidate can perform to the level indicated. Deviations from standard criteria should be documented on the certification form.

6. Disqualification

In the event a commanding officer considers that a qualified skipper should be reduced in qualification, he may do so at his discretion after appropriate investigation of circumstances leading to the action.

7. Certification

Certifications should be prepared at the local level and should include the following information:

Section I should be the sailing qualification. It should provide the individual's name and the sailing level for which qualifications have been completed. The qualification should be dated and signed by the instructor/qualifier and the commanding officer. Any deviations from standard criteria should also be noted on the qualification. Section II should be a record of the various sailing levels for which the individual is qualified. It should indicate the date, class boat, qualifier, and pertinent comments concerning each qualification.

Appendix F. Offshore Rating Council

Special Regulations Governing Minimum Equipment and Accommodations Standards

1.0 Purpose and Use

1.1 It is the purpose of these special regulations to establish uniform minimum equipment and accommodations standards for yachts racing under the International Offshore Rule and thereby to aid in promoting uniform offshore racing throughout the world.

1.2 These regulations do not replace, but rather supplement, the requirements of governmental authority, the Racing Rules and the International Offshore Rule. The attention of owners is called to restrictions in the rules on the location and movement of equipment.

1.3 The Offshore Rating Council strongly recommends the use of these special regulations by all organizations sponsoring races under the International Offshore Rule. Race Committees may select the category deemed most suitable for the type of race to be sailed. They are urged to depart from the regulations or modify or make exceptions thereto only when the most compelling circumstances so dictate.

2.0 Owner's Responsibility

2.1 The safety of a yacht and her crew is the sole and inescapable responsibility of the owner, who must do his best to insure that the yacht is fully found, thoroughly seaworthy and manned by an experienced crew who are physically fit to face bad weather. He must be satisfied as to the soundness of hull, spars, rigging, sails and all gear. He must insure that all safety equipment is properly maintained and stowed and that the crew know where it is kept and how it is to be used.

2.2 Neither the establishment of these special regulations, their use by sponsoring organizations, nor the inspection of a yacht under these regulations in any way limits or reduces the complete and unlimited responsibility of the owner.

2.3 It is the sole and exclusive responsibility of each yacht to decide whether or not to start or continue to race.

3.0 Basic Standards

3.1 Hulls of offshore racing yachts shall be self-righting, strongly built, watertight and capable of withstanding solid water and knockdowns. They must be properly rigged and ballasted, be fully seaworthy and must meet the standards set forth herein.

3.2 All equipment must function properly, be readily accessible and be of a type, size and capacity suitable and adequate for the intended use and the size of the yacht, and shall meet standards accepted in the country of registry.

4.0 Inspection

4.1 A yacht may be inspected at any time. If she does not comply with these special regulations her entry may be rejected, or she will be liable to disqualification or such other penalty as may be prescribed by national authority or the sponsoring organization.

5.0 Categories of Offshore Events

5.1 The International Offshore Rating rule is used to rate a wide variety of types and sizes of yachts in many types of races, ranging from long-distance ocean races sailed under adverse conditions to short-course day races sailed in protected waters. To provide for the differences in the standards of safety and accommodation required for such varying circumstances, four categories of races are established, as follows:

5.2 *Category 1 race.* Races of long distance, well offshore, where yachts must be completely self-sufficient for extended periods of time, capable of withstanding heavy storms and prepared to meet serious emergencies without the expectation of outside assistance.

5.3 *Category 2 race.* Races of extended duration, along or not far removed from shorelines or in large unprotected bays or lakes, where a high degree of self-sufficiency is required of the yachts but with the reasonable probability that outside assistance could be called upon for aid in the event of serious emergencies.

5.4 *Category 3 race.* Races across open water, most of which is relatively protected or close to shorelines, including races for small yachts.

5.5 *Category 4 race.* Short races, close to shore in relatively warm or protected waters.

In the following lists the check indicates the item applies to the category in that column.

6.0 Structural Features

6.1 *Hatches, companionways and ports* must be essentially watertight, that is, capable of being strongly and rigidly secured. Cockpit companionways, if extended below main deck level, must be capable of being blocked off to main deck level.

6.2 *Cockpits* must be structurally strong, self-bailing and permanently incorporated as an integral part of the hull. They must be essentially watertight, that is, all openings to the hull below the main deck level must be capable of being strongly and rigidly secured.

√
6.21 The maximum cockpit volume below lowest coamings shall not exceed 6%L times B times FA. The cockpit sole must be at least 2%L above LWL.

√ √ √
6.22 The maximum cockpit volume below lowest coamings shall not exceed 9%L times B times FA. The cockpit sole must be at least 2%L above LWL.

6.31 *Cockpit drains* adequate to drain cockpit quickly but with a combined area (after allowance for screens, if attached) of not less than the equivalent of two 1" (2.5 cm) diameter drains. Yachts built after 1-1-72 must have drains with a combined area (after allowance for screens, if attached) of not less than the equivalent of four ¾" (2.0 cm) drains.

Cat.	
3 4	**6.32** Cockpit drains adequate to drain cockpit quickly but not less in combined area (after allowance for screens, if attached) than the equivalent of two 1" (2.5 cm) diameter drains.
1 2 3	**6.4** *Storm coverings* for all windows more than two square feet in area.
1 2 3	**6.51** *Sea cocks or valves* on all through-hull openings below LWL, except integral deck scuppers, shaft log, speed indicators, depth finders and the like, however a means of closing such openings, when necessary to do so, shall be provided.
1 2 3 4	**6.52** Soft wood plugs, tapered and of various sizes.
	6.6 *Life lines and pulpits:*
1 2 3	**6.61** Fixed bow pulpit (forward of headstay) and stern pulpit (unless lifelines are arranged so as to adequately substitute for a stern pulpit). Pulpits and stanchions must be thru-bolted or welded, and the bases thereof must not be further inboard from the edge of the working deck than 5% of B max. or 6 inches (15 cm), whichever is greater. The head of a stanchion must not be angled from the point of its attachment to the hull at more than 10 degrees from vertical. Taut double life lines, with upper life line of wire at a height of not less than 2 feet (60 cm) above the working deck, to be permanently supported at intervals of not more than 7 feet (2.15 m). A taut lanyard of synthetic rope may be used to secure lifelines, provided that when in position its length does not exceed 4 inches (10 cm). Lower life lines need not extend through the bow pulpit. Life lines need not be affixed to the bow pulpit if they terminate at, or pass through adequately braced stanchions 2 feet (60 cm) above the working deck, set inside of and overlapping the bow pulpit, provided that the gap between the upper life line and the bow pulpit shall not exceed 6 inches (15 cm).
1 2 3	**6.62** Yachts under 21 feet rating in 6.61 above, but with a single taut lifeline not less than 18 inches (45 cm) above the working deck, and a bow pulpit and a stern pulpit (unless life lines are arranged as to adequately substitute for a stern pulpit) to the same height. If the life line is at any point more than 22 inches (56 cm) above the rail cap, a second intermediate life line must be fitted. The bow pulpit may be fitted abaft the forestay with its bases secured at any points on deck, but a point on its upper rail must be within 16 inches (40 cm) of the forestay on which the foremost headsail is hanked.
2	**6.63** As in 6.61 and 6.62 except that a stern pulpit is not required, provided the required height of life line must be carried aft at least to the midpoint of the cockpit.

7.0 Accommodations

Cat.	
1 2	**7.11** *Toilet,* permanently installed
3 4	**7.12** *Toilet,* permanently installed, or fitted bucket.
1 2 3 4	**7.2** *Bunks,* permanently installed.
1 2	**7.31** *Cooking stove,* permanently installed with safe and accessible fuel shutoff control.
3	**7.32** *Cooking stove,* capable of being safely operated in a seaway.
1 2	**7.41** *Galley facilities,* including sink.
3 4	**7.42** *Galley facilities.*
1	**7.51** *Water tanks,* permanently installed and capable of dividing the water supply into at least two separate containers.
2	**7.52** At least one permanently installed water tank, plus at least one additional container capable of holding 2 gallons.
3 4	**7.53** Water in suitable containers.

8.0 General Equipment

Cat.	
1 2 3 4	**8.1** *Fire extinguishers,* readily accessible and of the type and number required by the coun-

try of registry, provided there be at least one in yachts fitted with an engine or stove.

1	2	3	4	Item
✓	✓			8.21 *Bilge pumps,* at least two, manually operated, one of which must be operable with all cockpit seats and all hatches and companionways closed.
		✓		8.22 One manual bilge pump operable with all cockpit seats and hatches and companionways closed.
			✓	8.23 One manual bilge pump.
✓	✓	✓		8.31 *Anchors,* two with cables, except yachts rating under 21 feet, which shall carry at least one such anchor and cable.
			✓	8.32 One anchor and cable.
✓	✓	✓		8.41 *Flashlights,* one of which is suitable for signalling, water resistant, with spare batteries and bulbs.
			✓	8.42 At least one flashlight, water resistant, with spare batteries and bulb.
✓	✓	✓	✓	8.5 *First aid kit* and manual.
✓	✓	✓	✓	8.6 *Foghorn.*
✓	✓	✓	✓	8.7 *Radar reflector.*
✓				8.8 *Set of international code flags* and international code book.
✓	✓	✓	✓	8.9 *Shutoff valves* on all fuel tanks.

9.0 Navigation Equipment

1	2	3	4	Item
✓	✓	✓	✓	9.1 *Compass,* marine type, properly installed and adjusted.
✓	✓	✓		9.2 *Spare compass.*
✓	✓	✓		9.3 *Charts, light list and piloting equipment.*
✓				9.4 *Sextant, tables and accurate timepiece.*
✓	✓			9.5 *Radio direction finder.*
✓	✓	✓	✓	9.6 *Lead line or echo sounder.*
✓	✓	✓		9.7 *Speedometer or distance measuring instrument.*
✓	✓	✓	✓	9.8 *Navigation lights,* to be shown as required by the International Regulations for Preventing Collision at Sea, mounted so that they will not be masked by sails or the heeling of the yacht.

10.0 *Emergency Equipment*

1	2	3	4	Item
✓	✓			10.1 *Spare running lights* and power source.
✓	✓			10.21 *Special storm sail(s)* capable of taking the yacht to windward in heavy weather.
		✓	✓	10.22 *Heavy weather jib and reefing equipment* for mainsail.
✓	✓			10.3 *Emergency steering equipment.*
✓	✓	✓	✓	10.4 *Tools and spare parts,* including a hacksaw.
✓	✓	✓		10.5 *Yacht's name* on miscellaneous buoyant equipment, such as life jackets, oars, cushions, etc. Portable sail number.
✓				10.61 *Marine radio transmitter and receiver* with minimum transmitter power of 25 watts. If the regular antenna depends upon the mast, an emergency antenna must be provided.
	✓	✓	✓	10.62 *Radio receiver* capable of receiving weather bulletins.

11.0 *Safety Equipment*

1	2	3	4	Item
✓	✓	✓	✓	11.1 *Life jackets,* one for each crew member.
✓	✓	✓		11.2 *Whistles* (referee type) attached to life jackets.
✓	✓	✓		11.3 *Safety belt* (harness type) one for each crew member.

√ √ √ √   11.41 *Liferaft(s)* capable of carrying the entire crew and meeting the following requirements:

> Must be carried on deck (not under a dinghy) or in a special stowage opening immediately to the deck, containing life raft(s) only.
>
> Must be designed and used solely for saving life at sea.
>
> Must have at least two separate buoyancy compartments, each of which must be automatically inflatable. Each raft must be capable of carrying its rated capacity with one compartment deflated.
>
> Must have a canopy to cover the occupants.
>
> Must have been inspected, tested and approved within two years by the manufacturer or other competent authority.
>
> Must have the following equipment appropriately secured to each raft:
>> 1 Sea anchor or drogue
>> 1 Bellows, pump or other means for maintaining inflation of air chambers
>> 3 Hand flares
>> 1 Repair kit
>> 1 Signalling light
>> 1 Knife
>> 1 Baler
>> 2 Paddles

√   11.42 Provision for emergency water and rations to accompany raft.

   √   11.51 *Life ring(s)*, at least one horseshoe type life ring equipped with a waterproof light and drogue within reach of the helmsman and ready for instant use.

√ √ √   11.52 At least one horseshoe type life ring equipped with a high-intensity water light and a drogue within reach of the helmsman and ready for instant use.

√ √   11.53 At least one more horseshoe type life ring equipped with a whistle (referee type), dye marker, a high-intensity water light, and a pole and flag. The pole is to be attached to the ring with 25 feet (8 m) of floating line and is to be of a length and so ballasted lhat the flag will fly at least 8 feet (2.45 m) off the water.

√ √ √ √   11.61 *Distress signals* to be stowed in a waterproof container, and meeting the following requirements for each category, as indicated:

√   11.62 Twelve red parachute flares.

   √ √   11.63 Four red parachute flares.

√ √ √ √   11.64 Four red hand flares.

√ √ √ √   11.65 Four white hand flares.

√ √ √ √   11.7 *Heaving line* (50 feet (16 m) minimum length, floating type line) readily accessible to cockpit.

Appendix G. Sea State Codes

Hydrographic Office		International	
Term and height of waves, in feet	Code	Term and height of waves, in feet	Code
calm, 0	0	calm, glassy, 0	0
smooth, less than 1	1		
slight, 1–3	2	rippled, 0–1	1
moderate, 3–5	3	smooth, 1–2	2
rough, 5–8	4	slight, 2–4	3
		moderate, 4–8	4
		rough, 8–13	5

Hydrographic Office		International	
very rough, 8–12	5	very rough, 13–20	6
high, 12–20	6		
very high, 20–40	7	high, 20–30	7
mountainous, 40 and higher	8	very high, 30–45	8
confused	9	phenomenal, over 45	9

Appendix H. Beaufort Scale

Beaufort Force 0.
Wind speed: Less than 1 knot.
Sea: Like a mirror.

Beaufort Force 1.
Wind speed: 1–3 knots.
Sea: Ripples with appearance of scales are formed, but without foam crests.

Beaufort Force 2.
Wind speed: 4–6 knots.
Sea: Small wavelets, still short, but more pronounced; crests have a glassy appearance and do not break.

Beaufort Force 3.
Wind speed: **7—10 knots.**
Sea: **Large wavelets; crests begin to break; foam of a glassy appearance. Perhaps some scattered white horses.**

Beaufort Force 4.
Wind speed: **11—16 knots.**
Sea: **Small waves, becoming longer; fairly frequent white horses.**

Beaufort Force 5.
Wind speed: **17—21 knots.**
Sea: **Moderate waves taking a more pronounced long form; many white horses are formed; chance of some spray.**

Beaufort Force 6.
Wind speed: **22—27 knots.**
Sea: **Large waves begin to form; the white foam crests are more extensive everywhere; probably some spray.**

Beaufort Force 7.
Wind speed: 28–33 knots.
Sea: Sea heaps up and white foam from breaking waves begins to be blown in streaks along the direction of the wind.

Beaufort Force 8.
Wind speed: 34–40 knots.
Sea: Moderately high waves of greater length; edges of crests begin to break into the spindrift. The foam is blown in well-marked streaks along the direction of the wind.

Beaufort Force 9.
Wind speed: 41–47 knots.
Sea: High waves. Dense streaks of foam along the direction of the wind. Crests of waves begin to topple, tumble, and roll over. Spray may affect visibility.

Beaufort Force 10.
Wind speed: 48–55 knots.
Sea: Very high waves with long overhanging crests. The resulting foam, in great patches, is blown in dense white streaks along the direction of the wind. On the whole, the surface of the sea takes on a white appearance. The tumbling of the sea becomes heavy and shocklike. Visibility affected.

Beaufort Force 11.
Wind speed: 53–63 knots, violent storm.
Sea: Exceptionally high waves, sea covered with white foam
patches; visibility still more reduced.

Beauford Force 12.
Wind speed: 64–71 knots, hurricane.
Sea: Air filled with foam; sea completely white with driving
spray; visibility greatly reduced.

Appendix I. Representative Racing Sailboats

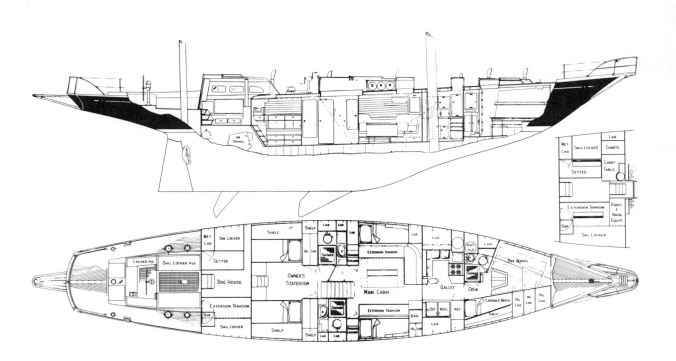

Jubilee III, an aluminum ketch designed for cruising and ocean racing, with a diesel auxiliary. Dimensions, 73'3" L.O.A., 51'9" L.W.L., 16'4" beam, 8'5" draft, 2,535 square feet sail area. Designed by Maclear and Harris, this boat was donated to the Naval Academy in 1968 by Francis D. Wetherill. Two centerboards increase her draft to 14'1" and give the ability to shift the center of lateral resistance forward or aft in order to achieve balance on various points of sailing under various wind conditions. She is at present privately owned.

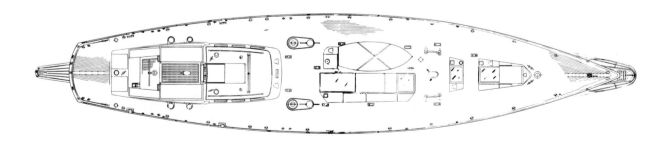

Mistral, a traditional wooden schooner, is shown under genoa jib, forestaysail, gaff foresail, and marconi main. Built in 1938 in Saugus, Massachusetts, this L. Francis Herreshoff design is used for seamanship training at the Naval Academy. Mistral was donated to the Academy in 1976 by Mr. Robert Scarborough. Dimensions: LOA 82 feet; LWL 54 feet; beam 15 feet; draft 7 feet; working sail area 1972 square feet. In 1977 midshipmen and volunteer coaches from the Naval Academy Sailing Squadron sailed *Mistral* across the Atlantic to participate in the Queen of England's Silver Jubilee. After stops in France, Madeira, and Bermuda, *Mistral* returned to Annapolis after a 77-day cruise covering 9,327 miles. In 1978 during an eight-week cruise, midshipmen sailed 4,700 miles, touching port in Nova Scotia, Bermuda, the American Virgin Islands, and the Bahamas.

Rage. Early in his career as a designer, Charles Morgan was noted for his fast keel-centerboard ocean racers, but the *Rage* is one of his first outstandingly successful keel models. Even though she was designed to rate well under the Cruising Club of America handicap rule, the *Rage* is still fairly competitive under the newer International Offshore Rule. Notice her forward-raking transom, which is commonly called a reversed or retroussé transom. Dimensions: 53'5" L.O.A., 37' L.W.L., 12'5" beam, 7'8" draft, 34,000 lbs. displacement, of which 17,000 lbs. is lead ballast. She is now privately owned.

The Valiant 40, a seagoing double-ender that is surprisingly fast. One of these boats is said to have the second fastest time for a boat under 40 feet passaging from the U.S. east coast to Bermuda, and she was sailed singlehanded. Note the cutter rig with double headsails, a yankee jib and staysail.

A twelve meter pursuing a C&C39. Twelve-meter boats are currently used in the America's Cup matches, but this particular boat is racing in the cruising division. The leading 39-footer was designed by Cassian and Cuthbertson, Canadians who are noted for their fast racing-cruisers with spade rudders and swept-back fin keels.

Finisterre, a beamy, 38-foot centerboard design by Sparkman and Stephens that started a trend in American ocean racing craft. *Finisterre* is the only boat to have won the Bermuda Race three times in a row.

The J-24, a very popular racing-cruising one design built by Tillotson-Pearson and designed by Rodney Johnstone. With her light displacement, minimal wetted surface, and bendy five-sixths rig, this 24 footer is a hot performer, and she has done exceedingly well in Midget Ocean Racing Club events.

Cal 40 This famous light displacement 40-footer with fin keel and spade rudder had a tremendous influence on American yacht design. Designed by William Lapworth, boats of this class have won almost every major U.S. ocean race.

PJ 48. A sister to this boat won the 1972 Bermuda Race. She is a Sparkman and Stephens design that has conformed very well to the IOR handicap rule.

Olympic Classes 1980

Finn, a planing, catrigged, centerboard dinghy for singlehanded racing. She has an extremely flexible, unstayed mast. Dimensions: 14'9" L.O.A., 14' L.W.L., 4'10" beam, 2'3" draft, 115 square feet sail area.

Soling a modern fin-keel, spade-rudder sloop. She is fitted with hiking straps but not a trapeze. Her spinnaker is rounder-looking than the typical cruising boat's spinnaker because class rules allow greater girth than most handicap rules. Dimensions: 26'9" L.O.A., 20' L.W.L., 6'3" beam, 4'3" draft, 233 square feet sail area.

The 470, a centerboard dinghy similar to, but smaller than, the Flying Dutchman. She carries a spinnaker and is equipped with hiking straps and a trapeze. Dimensions: 15'6" L.O.A., 5'6" beam, 4'11" draft (board down), 137 sq.ft. sail area.

Tornado. A catamaran which is extremely fast reaching even though she carries no spinnaker. Her wide beam and trapeze provide high initial stability, but her range of stability is low when compared with a keel boat. Dimensions: 20' L.O.A., 19'2" L.W.L., 10' beam, 2'6" draft (board down), and 272 sq.ft. sail area.

Flying Dutchman, a very sophisticated, light displacement, planing centerboard dinghy. She carries a Genoa jib and spinnaker and has a trapeze for maximum advantage in hiking. Dimensions: 19'10" L.O.A., 18' L.W.L., 5'7" beam, 3'7" draft, 200 square feet sail area.

Star, an ancient class boat (nearly 70 years old) with a hard chine, fin keel, and separated rudder hinged on a skeg. She has a tall, flexible rig and is somewhat tender, but she does not carry a spinnaker. No special hiking devices are used. Dimensions: 22'7½" L.O.A., 15' L.W.L., 5'8" beam, 3'4" draft, 285 square feet sail area.

Index

This comprehensive index also serves as a glossary of terms and a list of illustrations. Defined terms are indicated by an italicized entry and page number; illustrations are indicated by a boldfaced page number.

Credits

B. Devereux Barker III: 223.
Peter Barlow: 386.
William E. Brooks III: 118, 119, 120, 121, 144, 163, 166, 184, 190, 197, 200, 235, 240, 260, 261, 270, 271, 273, 282, 283, 284, 285, 286, 288, 292.
Sam Chambliss: 189.
Rex Combs: 252.
Robert de Gast: 149, 155, 186, 188, 219, 229, 328.
Bob Dollard: 91, 196, 222.
Environment Canada: 376–78.
Joe Fuller: 44, 45, 99, 100, 195, 385, 386.
Graham Hall: 388.
Her Britannic Majesty's Stationery Office: 379.
Ed Holm: 54, 226.
Pat Healy: 15, 115, 125.
Dr. Norris D. Hoyt: 249.
Jensen Marine: 384.
Bob Johnstone: 384.
Frank B. Lawson, Jr.: 193, 381.
Medalist Universal Motors: 274–75, 278–80.
National Archives: 294.
R. K. Pilsbury: 30–33.

Performance Sailcraft: 116.
David Q. Scott: 184, 293, 303, 309, 333.
R. A. Simerl: 237.
Mrs. Fred Thomas: 383.
U.S. Yacht Racing Union, Inc.: 360–63.
Valiant Corporation: 382.
Volvo Penta: 282.
Westerbeke: 160–62.

Miscellaneous uncredited photographs are either official U.S. Navy or from the collection of Richard Henderson.

The text and drawing on pages 262–63 are from *Hand, Reef and Steer* by Richard Henderson, copyright 1965, and reprinted by permission of Contemporary Books, Inc, Chicago.

The paragraphs on kerosene and LP stoves on pages 232–33 are from *Sea Sense* by Richard Henderson and reprinted by permission of International Marine Publishing Company, Camden, Maine.

Line illustrations by Richard Henderson.

Other books by Richard Henderson

First Sail for Skipper
Hand, Reef, and Steer
Dangerous Voyages of Captain William Andrews (*Ed.*)
The Racing-Cruiser
Sea Sense
The Cruiser's Compendium
Singlehanded Sailing
Better Sailing
East to the Azores
Choice Yacht Designs